ANCIENT CHURCHES REVEALED

ANCIENT
CHURCHES
REVEALED

EDITED BY YORAM TSAFRIR

ISRAEL EXPLORATION SOCIETY

JERUSALEM 1993

BIBLICAL ARCHAEOLOGY SOCIETY

WASHINGTON D.C.

Editor: Yoram Tsafrir
Assistant Editor: Janet Amitai
Copy Editor: Robert Amoils
Layout and Graphics: Abraham Pladot

This volume contains articles adapted from

QADMONIOT

Quarterly for the Antiquities of Eretz-Israel and Bible Lands
Published in Hebrew by the Israel Exploration Society

Edited by Yigael Yadin from 1968 to 1978

Editor: E. Stern; *Editorial Board:* M. Broshi, A. Eitan, Y. Tsafrir,
D. Ussishkin; *Hebrew Style:* R. Eshel; *Layout:* A. Pladot; *Adminstrative
Editor:* J. Aviram

ISBN 965–221–016–1

Plates by Old City Press Ltd., Jerusalem
Typeset and printed in Israel by Ben-Zvi Printing Enterprises, Jerusalem

Contents

MAP: Sites in the Holy Land where archaeological remains of churches have been found — *Prepared by Y. Tsafrir and L. Di Segni* • *Following page 6*

FRONT COVER PHOTO:
The basilican church of Kursi on the eastern shore of the Sea of Galilee (photo by Duby Tal–Moni Haramati, Albatross Aerial Photography)

BACK COVER PHOTO:
The Church of the Nativity, Bethlehem: angel on north wall (photo by G. Kühnel)

List of Plates

Abbreviations

AASOR	*Annual of the American Schools of Oriental Research*
CAHL	G.C. Bottini, L. Di Segni and E. Alliata (eds.), *Christian Archaeology in the Holy Land. New Discoveries (V. Corbo Volume)* (Jerusalem, 1990)
Ch. Coüasnon	Ch. Coüasnon, *The Church of the Holy Sepulchre* (Jerusalem/London, 1974)
Corbo, *Sepolchro*	V. Corbo, *Il Sancto Sepolcro de Gerusalemne, Aspetti arceologici delle origini al periodo crociato*, I–III (Jerusalem, 1981–1982)
Crowfoot	J.W. Crowfoot, *Early Churches in Palestine* (London, 1941)
DOP	*Dumbarton Oaks Papers*
EI	*Eretz-Israel. Archaeological, Historical and Geographical Studies*
Fitzgerald	G.M. Fitzgerald, *Beth-Shan Excavations 1921–1923. The Arab and Byzantine Levels* (Philadelphia, 1931)
Forsyth and Weitzmann	G.H. Forsyth and K. Weitzmann with I. Ševčenco and F. Anderegg, *The Monastery of Sainte Catherine at Mount Sinai, The Church and Fortress of Justinian.* I. *Plates* (Ann Arbor, 1970)
Gerasa	C.H. Kraeling (ed.), *Gerasa, City of the Decapolis* (New Haven, 1938)
Hamilton	R.W. Hamilton, *The Church of the Nativity, Bethlehem. A Guide* (Jerusalem, 1947)
IEJ	*Israel Exploration Journal*
Jérusalem nouvelle	L.H. Vincent and F.M. Abel, *Jérusalem nouvelle* (Paris, 1914–1924)
Krautheimer, *Architecture*	R. Krautheimer, *Early Christian and Byzantine Architecture* (Harmondsworth, 1965; 3rd ed., 1979)
LA	*Liber Annuus. Studium Biblicum Franciscanum*
Meehan, *Adamnan's De Locis Sanctis*	D. Meehan (ed.), *Adamnan's De Locis Sanctis* (Dublin, 1958)
PEQ	*Palestine Exploration Quarterly*
QDAP	*Quarterly of the Department of Antiquities of Palestine*
RB	*Revue biblique*
Richmond	E.T. Richmond, *QDAP* 6 (1936)
ZVPV	*Zeitschrift des deutschen Palästina-Vereins*

Foreword

In the fourth century C.E. Christianity throughout the Roman world underwent a dramatic change. The rather few modest and private houses that had served the Christian congregations were replaced by numerous larger basilicas. This process was accelerated in the Holy Land, the cradle of Christianity. Indeed, the survey of churches of the Byzantine and Crusader periods in Israel has noted several hundred foundations, either of simple congregational churches in cities or villages, or of lavish edifices commemorating the *loca sancta.* Many of these ruins were discovered and studied in recent years, and are presented here in English for the first time. Others have previously been published in detail.

It is not the aim of this volume to present a complete corpus of excavated churches, but merely to provide an insight into the vast new material in a semipopular, amply illustrated, but professional manner. Most of the reports were written by the archaeologists who carried out the excavations. Thus, we are provided with a firsthand summary of current activity in the field of Christian archaeology in Israel.

Like the previously-published volumes of "The Holy Land Revealed" series of the Israel Exploration Society, *Jerusalem Revealed* and *Ancient Synagogues Revealed*, this book, primarily, is based on articles which appeared in the Hebrew quarterly, *Qadmoniot* (1968–1990). To these were added papers from other Hebrew publications; however, several articles were written especially for this volume.

Ancient Churches Revealed is divided into sections according to geographical units of the country from the Galilee, through Jerusalem, Judah and the Negev, to Sinai, now in Egypt. The first section comprises introductory material on ecclesiastical architecture from the Byzantine to Crusader periods, as well as ancient Christian liturgy. Articles in other sections also discuss general aspects, but are more limited in their chronological or geographical framework, such as monasticism in the Judean Desert and Sinai. Together, the papers represent the wide spectrum of the field of Christian archaeology: liturgy, tradition, history, architecture, art and epigraphy.

The process of writing, translating, and editing this book has been long and tiresome. First to be thanked are the authors who contributed new articles or updated old ones, and the editors of *Qadmoniot* and other Hebrew publications who did the initial editorial work. Their labors were continued by Rafi Grafman and Roberta Maltese who began the editing of the first English articles submitted. The book, as a whole, was prepared for publication by Janet Amitai and the copy editor, Robert Amoils, while the graphics and layout are the work of Abraham Pladot. Joseph Aviram, assisted by Nehama Litani, directed the project from its initiation to completion.

YORAM TSAFRIR

CHURCHES IN PALESTINE —
FROM CONSTANTINE TO THE CRUSADERS

The Development of Ecclesiastical Architecture in Palestine

Yoram Tsafrir

Palestine underwent one of the greatest cultural changes in its history during the Byzantine period when Christianity triumphed over paganism and came to power.[1] The process by which Christianity established itself in the Holy Land was long and difficult. It began in the time of Jesus and the Apostles who struggled with both the monarchy and the pagan, Jewish, and Samaritan inhabitants of the land, and culminated in 324 C.E., when a new era began under Constantine, the first Christian emperor. Once the country was in his hands, Christianity spread at an accelerated pace, uninterrupted until the Arab conquest in 630–640.

Byzantine culture was an amalgam of Roman tradition, Hellenistic-Greek civilization, and Christianity. The former two elements represented a continuity deriving from Rome, the West, and from the Hellenistic East. Christianity was the revolutionary innovation. The rise of Constantine secured the preeminence of the Christian religion. Its particular hierarchy of values changed Roman society beyond recognition. In Palestine, where the Christian Messiah was born and died, the spread of Christianity and its subsequent dominance with the foundation of the Christian empire, was more accelerated than in the other Roman provinces. By 326 the Empress Helena had already traveled to the Holy Land. Her visit — to which many legends were later attached, such as the discovery of the True Cross and the building of the church on Mt. Sinai — played an important part in

expediting the construction of the first churches. The imperial court accorded high priority to Christianizing the Holy Land.

Indeed, the primary artistic and architectural effort placed emphasis on the construction of churches. Byzantine architects ceased competing with their Roman predecessors in the field of secular architecture, both public and private. They devoted their energies and powers of invention to designing impressive, ornate churches.

The Christian church building, whether a basilica or with a central focus, is the creation of the early fourth century C.E. From the time of the establishment of Christianity until the fourth and fifth centuries, Christian communities assembled for worship in private, rather than public, buildings. That kind of a community building was called *domus ecclesia*, or "church house." It comprised a large room for prayer, rituals, and communal meals (*agape*), and others for storage and services. Sometimes there was a separate *baptisterium*, as well as a room where candidates for baptism (*catechumeni*) assembled. (As they were as yet unbaptized, they were prohibited from taking part in the Eucharist ceremony — the *liturgia*, or mass.) Buildings of this kind have been found in Rome, and there is also a particularly famous example at Dura Europos, on the Euphrates.

A similar *domus ecclesia* has been discovered, according to its excavator, V.C. Corbo, at Capernaum, beneath an octagonal church, in the place thought to have been Peter's house.[2]

---

[1] This introductory article is based on Y. Tsafrir, *Eretz Israel from the Destruction of the Second Temple to the Muslim Conquest*. II. *Archaeology and Art* (Jerusalem, 1984), pp. 223–264 (Hebrew; the expanded English edition is in press).

[2] V.C. Corbo, *Cafarnao*, I (Jerusalem, 1975), pp. 59–111; also idem, *The House of Saint Peter at Capharnaum* (Jerusalem, 1972); and in this volume, "The Church of the House of St. Peter at Capernaum", pp. 71–76.

1

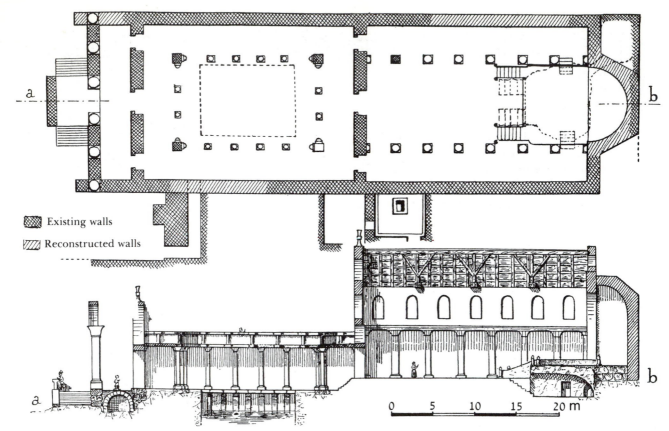

The Eleona on the Mt. of Olives, Jerusalem: ground plan and reconstructed elevation (*Jérusalem nouvelle*, Fig. 154)

Corbo believes that the Jewish-Christian community of Capernaum used the house from the first through the fourth centuries. A large, nearly square (21 × 21 m) structure was subsequently built on top of it, and the entire building then served as a *domus ecclesia*. That structure — traditionally known as the House of St. Peter — was not replaced by the octagonal church until the mid-fifth century.

The first basilica in the region was built in Tyre in Phoenicia, and not in Palestine. It was erected by Bishop Paulinus in ca. 314 C.E.,[3] about the same time that the first congregational basilica was being built in Rome on the Lateran Hill (San Giovani in Laterano). However, the decisive step in the design of Christian churches was taken later, under Constantine's rule, in the third and fourth

decades of the fourth century C.E. In Palestine, the emperor endowed and encouraged the construction of the first four churches: the Church of the Holy Sepulchre, the Church on the Mt. of Olives (Eleona), the Church of the Nativity in Bethlehem, and the Mamre Church near Hebron. In addition to these, others were built to commemorate the many holy places (*loca sancta*) in the country, and the long-range influence of edifices at these sites on Christian architecture can hardly be exaggerated.[4]

Generally, churches can be divided into two categories on the basis of their function and plan. The large majority, both early and late, contain a long central hall of the type scholars call "basilica." The basilica had a rectangular central hall that was divided by longitudinal

---

[3] Eusebius, *Ecclesiastical History*, X, 4.

[4] See A. Grabar, *Martyrium* (Paris, 1946); idem, "Christian Architecture, East and West," *Archaeology* 2 (1949): 95–104.

rows of columns into three (or five) spaces. The roof of the basilica was gabled and generally constructed with wooden beams and surfaced with tiles. It was supported by both the outer walls and the columns in the hall, so that the part over the central section was considerably higher than that over the sides. The central space, called the nave, was wider than those on the sides, or aisles. A wide, high doorway opened onto the nave, whereas the entries to the aisles were generally smaller.

At one end of the church building, in most cases on the east (where the sun rises), was the chancel, or *bema*, also called the *presbyterium*, "the priests' place." The eastern wall terminated in an apse bearing a half dome that usually was decorated with frescos or mosaics featuring the figure of Jesus. That part of the church — the sanctuary — was restricted to the priests. From the chancel a narrow flight of stairs led up to the *ambo*, or pulpit for delivering sermons, which was situated within the nave, usually near one of the columns.

The architectural source of the Christian basilica was the multipurpose Roman civic building of the same name, found in public places, within sacred compounds, and in private palaces. The most common type of Roman basilica was the basilica of the forum, after the temple the major public building in Roman cities. The Christian basilica was reminiscent of the forum in design: it was a spacious, rectangular building, within which four double rows of columns formed aisles parallel to the four walls. The central area was higher than the aisles and the roof was generally gabled, supported by wooden beams, and surfaced with tiles. Some basilicas, however, had vaulted ceilings and domed roofs. The main entrance was usually in one of the long walls, emphasizing the building's width. On one side of the basilica a raised apse held a statue of a god or of the emperor. It was also the place from which speeches were delivered and magistrates adjudicated business disputes.

It was quite natural that the Christian architects at the time of Constantine adopted the Roman basilica as their religious building. The Christian church, like its predecessor, the

Jewish synagogue, was intended for public use within its walls, in contrast to the pagan temple, where the worshippers were restricted to the temenos outside. The spacious basilica thus offered a practical solution to the physical needs of the congregation. By choosing the basilica and not the temple form, the Christians also emphasized the distinction between their religious practices and those of paganism. The architectural changes in the basilica necessary for Christian worship were few, but they had a powerful effect on the final character of the building. The Christians left only the colonnades that ran parallel to the long walls of the building; they placed the chancel and apse deeper within one of the short side walls (usually the eastern one), and the entrance was located opposite it. Thus, the colonnaded, static interior of the Roman basilica was transformed into an elongated space drawing the visitor inwards. From the moment the believer entered the church, his eyes and heart were directed toward the apse and the altar.

Churches reflected the tendencies and spiritual struggles of the Christian leaders, in detail as well as overall design. When Constantine became the patron of the Christian faith and elevated it to an official, honored status, the heads of the Church were obliged to adopt an elaboration befitting the imperial religion. The emperor encouraged the bishops to decorate the religious edifices to the same extent as the pagans had embellished theirs. It was a significant step in the struggle for the soul of the masses, who hesitated between the new religion and the traditional cult. Although the early Christians had been comfortable with the modest *domus ecclesia* and its atmosphere of intimate fraternity and humility, values in the time of Constantine changed in that there was a desire to absorb the masses into the Christian community, and to impress them by royal splendor no less than by spirituality. The interior of the church (see Pl. Ia–b) was decorated lavishly with carved columns, mosaics and wall paintings, expensive building materials, and gold chandeliers. The priests wore elaborate litur-

3

Church of St. Catherine, Mt. Sinai: sixth-century C.E. roof trusses above nave and sanctuary (Forsyth and Weitzmann, Pl. LXXXII)

gical vestments. The shadowy interior of the building, with burning candles and incense, gave the finishing touches to an atmosphere of mystery characteristic of Christian worship.

In contrast, the exterior of the church, although elegant, was relatively modest. It suited the traditional Christian value of shunning wealth and ostentatious display. This marked contrast between the exterior and the interior of the structure is representative of the introspection emphasized in Christianity, which its architects sought to present. In time basilicas became numerous and could be found in every city and village. Very few of them rivaled the first churches in size and wealth, but even they maintained the primary basic principles of design and interior decoration.

Most of the churches in Palestine were basilicas. A considerable number of them, as we shall detail here, were built at holy places. The majority, however, were simply congregational churches in which mass was held, and were found in every city, village and monastery. The Eucharist, the main part of the

Church of St. Catherine, Mt. Sinai: the roof, view from the northeast (Forsyth and Weitzmann, Pl. XXXV)

Christian liturgy, was celebrated by the priests before the altar, in the apse. The hall was divided from the chancel by a screen, and in the hall the male and female congregants were separated, the men being placed on one of its sides and the women on the other. The basilica was complemented by auxiliary rooms and wings, some of which were part of the original building and others added later: the *prothesis*, the chamber in which the bread and wine were prepared for the Eucharist; various chapels; the *baptisterium*; the *diaconicon*, the storage room for ritual objects and donations from the congregation; the narthex, a broad corridor built in front of the church at the facade of the main hall; and the atrium, a front courtyard usually completely or partially surrounded by porticos.[5]

Many basilicas were resplendent with such holy relics as tombs or the remains of early Christian martyrs. Occasionally these were actual objects, such as a piece of the True Cross, or a stone from Golgotha or from the stoning of St. Stephan the martyr, and the like. The tombs, actual or not, were often located in underground chapels (crypts) beneath one of the wings of the church or at its center under the chancel and altar. Smaller relics were placed in special reliquary boxes, which were also deposited in the apse, beneath the altar, or in one of the side rooms. Palestine, which was remarkable for the number of holy places connected to biblical traditions or to the life and death of Jesus and his Apostles, was particularly rich in commemorative churches (*martyria, memoria*). The evolution of church architecture in the Holy Land, therefore, is particularly important in the study of church architecture in general.

From the beginning, a special form of church evolved that was architecturally more

Church of Sts. Peter and Paul, Gerasa (540 C.E.): reconstruction of the basilica (Crowfoot)

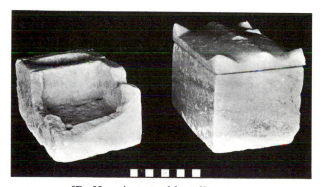

ᶜEn Ḥanniya: marble reliquary

Church of St. Basilius, Riḥab, Jordan (594 C.E.): reliquary embedded in apse's floor below altar. Note the depressions in which the legs of the altar were placed [Piccirillo, *LA* 30 (1980), Photo ll]

---

[5] A very important source of information about the structure of the church and the names of its parts in the fourth century is the Syrian document known as *Testamentum Domini Nostri Iesu Christi*, I, 19, ed. I. Rahmani (Mainz, 1899). It was translated into English by D.J. Chitty and published with commentary in C.H. Kraeling (ed.), *Gerasa, City of the Decapolis* (New Haven, 1938), pp. 175–184.

Church of the Jacob's Well, Shechem-Neapolis (a commemorative church): Arculf's depiction of the plan. The well, covered by a high roof, is located at the point of transection of the arms of the cross (Meehan, *Adamnan's De Locis Sanctis*, figure opposite title page)

suitable for commemorative purposes than the basilica. It emphasized its center, which was circular, octagonal, square or cruciform. In contrast to the basilica, this plan was not based on the apse at the end of the building (although it existed and was used for prayers and the Eucharist), but rather on the geometrical center of the church, which was further accentuated by the height of its dome (as in the rotunda of the Holy Sepulchre (see Pl. Ic) and the Ascension churches), by the apex of its conical roof (the Church of the Nativity in Bethlehem in the time of Constantine), or by its cross intersection and dome (as we know from the description of the pilgrim Arculf in the Church of Jacob's Well near Shechem-Neapolis). Thus, a kind of elaborate, raised

canopy was created, epitomizing the holy place on or under the floor below it.

These centric churches also varied in their architectural features. They recall monumental Roman buildings, both secular structures (such as round chambers, roofed garden pavilions of palaces, or bathhouses), and religious (round temples like the Pantheon in Rome). In the main, however, they were inspired by monumental tombs (*mausolea*) of emperors and patricians of Rome.[6]

The development of the Christian liturgy also significantly influenced the function and design of parts of the church, although we are as yet unable to distinguish between buildings belonging to different traditions and sects, for example between the Arian, Nestorian, or Monophysite churches on one hand, and those of the Orthodox on the other. The service itself, its principles and formal sources, is not germane to our discussion here, but it is evident that its immediate allusions, and those of church terminology, are to be found in Scripture and in the architecture and liturgy of the Temple of the Jews in Jerusalem. The church is also termed a temple (ναός) or house (ὸἶκος); the Eucharist table is called an altar; the preparation of holy bread is called *prothesis* (Πρόθεσις), the term used in the Septuagint for the shewbread; and the religious functionaries are known as priests.

Highly important among the churches in Palestine were the four constructed during the lifetime of the Emperor Constantine and mentioned above. They were definitely commemorative, and their design reflects that intent (the exception is the Mamre Church, whose plan cannot be reconstructed with certainty).[7]

[6] See the discussion by Grabar in *Martyrium* (note 4), and J.B. Ward-Perkins, "Memoria, Martyr's Tomb and Martyr's Church," *Atti del Congresso Internazionale di Archeologia Christiana* 7 (1965): 3–25; R. Krautheimer, "Constantine's Church Foundations," ibid.: 237–256; A. Grabar, "Martyrium ou 'Vingt ans après,'" *Cahiers Archéologique* 18 (1968): 239–244. On church ritual, see in this volume, J. Wilkinson, "Christian Worship in the Byzantine Period," pp. 17–22.

[7] A.E. Mader, *Memre, Die Ergebnisse der Ausgrabungen im heiligen Bezirk, Ramat el-Halil in Sud-Palästina* (Freiburg-im-Breisgan, 1957).

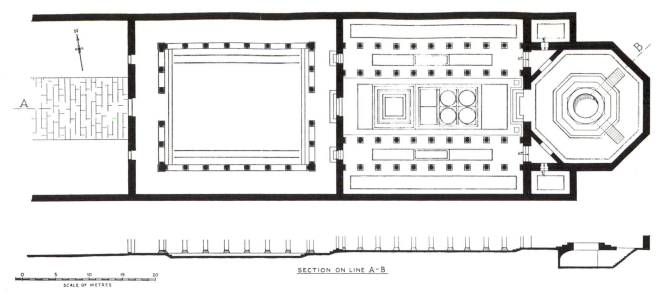

Church of the Nativity, Bethlehem in the time of Constantine: plan based on excavations, and a cross-section showing floor levels (Richmond, p. 66, Fig. 1)

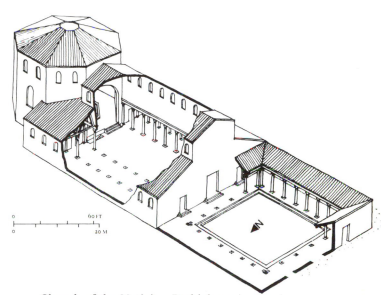

Church of the Nativity, Bethlehem: isometric reconstruction (Krautheimer, *Architecture*, p. 61, Fig. 26)

Church of the Nativity, Bethlehem: reconstruction of the Constantinian enclosure looking southwest (Hamilton, Fig. 3)

The Eleona Church (see illustration, p. 2) was built close to the summit of the Mt. of Olives, on its western slope, facing the Temple Mount. It was situated above a cave in which, according to tradition, Jesus sat with his disciples. Although only the foundations remain, H. Vincent has succeeded in reconstructing the design.[8] The atrium was in the

[8] H. Vincent, "L'église de L'Eleona," *RB* 19 (1910): 573–574; 20 (1911): 219–265; H. Vincent and F.M. Abel, *Jérusalem nouvelle*, II (Paris, 1914), pp. 337–360, 374–412; H. Vincent, "L'Eleona, Sanctuaire primitif de l'ascension," *RB* 64 (1957): 48–71.

western part of the church complex. It was entered through a peristyle court surrounded by porticoes (the internal dimensions were about 25 × 19 m). From the atrium three entrances led to the basilica itself, which was divided by two rows of columns into a nave and two aisles. Its interior length, including the apse, was about 30 m, and its width equalled that of the atrium, 19 m. Due to the topography of the site, steps were built to offer access from the outside to the atrium, and from it to the interior of the church. The raised chancel was above the venerated cave to which two flights of stairs were built, one for descent and one for ascent to facilitate the uninterrupted procession of worshippers and pilgrims. The apse of the Eleona Church (9 m wide and 4.5 m deep) is external, that is, it extends outward to the east, beyond the main, rectangular structure of the church. The Eleona Church represents an incorporation of a holy place, which attracted masses of pilgrims, into a basilica church.

The Church of the Nativity in Bethlehem is also a basilica whose function is primarily commemorative. The excavations carried out there in the 1930s as part of the renovations at the site, showed that it had been built in two major stages: the first under the Emperor Constantine, and the second under the Emperor Justinian.[9] The present church represents the later stage dating to the sixth century C.E., after renovations and restorations. The earlier, Constantinian church had an unusual design. Above its most sanctified focus, the Cave of the Nativity, a large octa-

gon was built (the length of each side of which was 7.90 m). It was covered by a conical wooden roof. In the center of the floor, which was octagonal, was an opening surrounded by a balustrade that in turn was surrounded by a walkway, the *ambulatorium*. As they walked, the faithful could look down at the place of the nativity. An *oculus* ("eye"), an opening in the ceiling, was set in the apex of the octagonal roof in perfect alignment with the birthplace. The main church included a hall of typical basilica plan, which was nearly square (26.80 × 27.70 m) and was divided by four rows of nine columns into a central hall and two aisles on either side. The raised octagonal

Church of the Nativity, Bethlehem: the bema during excavation in the 1930s, looking east. In the background, to the left, are the northern stairs leading to the cave of the Nativity. Under the new pavements, foundations of the ring wall surrounding the opening to the cave can be discerned (Israel Antiquities Authority)

[9] W. Harvey, *Structural Survey of the Church of the Nativity, Bethlehem* (Oxford, 1935); idem, "Recent Discoveries at the Church of the Nativity, Bethlehem," *Archaeologia* 87 (1937): 7–18; E.T. Richmond, "Basilica of the Nativity, Discovery of the Remains of an Earlier Church," *QDAP* 5 (1936): 75–81; idem, "The Church of the Nativity. The Plan of the Constantinian Building," *QDAP* 6 (1938): 63–66; idem, "Alterations Carried out by Justinian," ibid.: 67–72; H. Vincent, "Bethléem sanctuaire de la nativité, d'après les fouilles récentes," *RB* 45 (1936): 551–574; 46 (1937): 93–121; and B. Bagatti, *Gli antichi edifici sacri di Betlemme* (Jerusalem, 1951). See also Grabar, *Martyrium* (note 4), vol. I, pp. 245–251, and the comparison there between the octagon in Bethlehem and the mausoleum of Diocletian in Spalato.

Interior of the Church of St. Catherine, Mt. Sinai (Z. Radovan)

Exterior of the Church of the Nativity, Bethlehem (Z. Radovan)

area was reached by stairs from the aisles — probably one side for ascending and the other for descending. In front of the church four porticoes surrounded a square atrium measuring 27 sq m. The level of the porticoes was two steps above that of the court. Access to the church was gained from the atrium through three entrances, and another three openings linked the atrium to a paved area to its west which served the caravans of the pilgrims.

The church's plan served to facilitate the viewing of the Nativity place by large groups of pilgrims. The form of the octagonal structure above the cave recalls the mausoleum ordered by Emperor Diocletian for himself in Spalato in Dalmatia (today Split, Yugoslavia). Perhaps this is a prime example of the direct influence of imperial commemorative architecture on that of the Christians.

The mausoleum of Split, Yugoslavia

Attaching a large basilica to an octagon with a pointed top was well suited to the particular needs of the site, but it also had a serious drawback in that it did not allow for space for regular Christian service, for the altar, and for the priests. If Communion was held in the church, which is quite likely, it must have taken place under particularly uncomfortable conditions. This shortcoming was corrected by renovations undertaken by the architects of Emperor Justinian in the sixth century C.E.

The most important church in Palestine was the Church of the Holy Sepulchre in Jeru-salem.[10] It was built during the reign of Constantine, but subsequently underwent numerous changes including renewed construction in the Crusader period which fundamentally altered the building. Our knowledge of the plan of the church during the fourth century C.E. is mainly based on historical sources, especially on Eusebius' contemporary description in *The Life of Constantine*. Since the 1960s various excavations have been carried out at the church as part of its renovation. They permit us to reconstruct the Constantinian edifice with a large degree of certainty (see in this volume, J. Patrich, "The Early Church of the Holy Sepulchre in the Light of Excavations and Restoration," pp. 101–117; and M. Broshi, "Excavations in the Holy Sepulchre in the Chapel of St. Vartan...," pp. 118–122).

In the first construction phase the natural slopes of Golgotha were leveled (in the opinion of Coüasnon, the French architect who explored the Church of the Holy Sepulchre, the area was originally an abandoned quarry), so that Golgotha itself, the site of the crucifixion and of the nearby sepulchre, would stand above its surroundings, a monument in stone. From the main road (Cardo Maximus) of Aelia Capitolina, running from east to west, the church compound was entered through a gatehouse (*propyleum*). Steps led to the first atrium, a trapezoidal courtyard measuring, according to Coüasnon's reconstruction, 22–28 × 36 m. Three openings led from that atrium to the basilica itself, which was then called the "martyrium." Four rows of columns divided the basilica into a central room with four aisles. The estimated dimensions of the basilica were 36 × 42 m, and 22 m in height.

In Coüasnon's opinion, the civic basilica of Roman Jerusalem was located in that very place, as the city's forum stood not very far

[10] The major contributions to recent investigations of the Constantinian Church of the Holy Sepulchre have been made by C. Coüasnon, o.p., *The Church of the Holy Sepulchre in Jerusalem. The Schweich Lectures 1972* (London, 1974), and by the excavator V. Corbo, *Il Santo Sepolcro de Gerusalemme*, I–III (Jerusalem, 1981). For a description of the existing remains and a comprehensive analysis of literary sources, see Vincent and Abel, *Jérusalem nouvelle* (note 8), pp. 40–300.

away, to the south. According to the sources, the temple of Aphrodite had also been located nearby, above the tomb itself. Coüasnon claimed that part of the foundations of the Roman basilica was used for the Christian building, for, unlike a pagan temple, the Roman civic basilica was not considered impure. Some of those foundations were unearthed in excavations of sections of the Church of the Holy Sepulchre. The apse of the basilica was found beneath the floor of today's Greek Catholikon. Originally, unlike its present orientation and in contrast to the practice in most churches, it faced westward toward the tomb.

To the west of the basilica was a courtyard in front of the tomb, a kind of interior atrium. Its southeast side was raised above the rock of Golgotha (upon which a symbolic cross was later erected). The Golgotha chapel was built on that spot, close to the rock. The main part of the church — the Holy Sepulchre itself — rose beyond the inner atrium, to the west. At first the tomb stood like a monument carved in the rock within an open courtyard, about 15 × 15 m in size, but in the latter part of Constantine's reign, construction was begun on a rotunda, a round building with a wooden domed roof, which served to ornament the tomb like a gigantic canopy. The rotunda was completed in the mid-fourth century; it was quite large, about 35 m in diameter. Parts of the original wall stand to this day, rising to a height of about 11 m, and serve as the foundation for the walls of the present rotunda. This part of the church was called *Anastasis*, "the Resurrection." It was entered through a splendid entrance the gable of which was borne by pillars. Inside, columns and piers supported a dome over its central portion, doubling the building's height.

Most probably there was a baptistery to the south of the rotunda. Rooms and chapels surrounded the entrance to the tomb, creating an architectural compound more than 130 m long, with an average width of over 60 m. The difference between the rotunda, with its single focus, built for commemorative purposes over the holy tomb, and the basilica, which was used for worship, is clear both in the plan of the building and in its use. This disparity emphasizes the relations between the form and arrangement of the building and the functional content and spiritual meaning it is intended to represent.

Most of the churches from the Byzantine period discovered in Israel are, as noted, of the basilica type. They are mainly small, modest structures compared to the Constantinian churches, and they served rural or urban congregations or monasteries. Even the smallest villages possessed churches, and middle-sized towns had a number of them. In the town of Madaba, in Transjordan, fourteen have been found, and in Jerusalem there were several dozen churches and chapels.

In Palestine, basilicas commonly had only two rows of columns dividing their interior into a nave and two aisles. The principal variation in the church plan was usually to be found in the eastern part of the building. Sometimes a single apse extended beyond the general contours of a rectangular structure (as we have seen, for example, in the Eleona Church), but more frequently, apses lay within the church, creating a room at the end of each aisle on the east. Sometimes these chambers were included in the area of the chancel, entry to which was restricted to priests. The functions of the side rooms are not clear. In later centuries the northern room was generally a *prothesis*, where the bread and wine were prepared for mass. It is not known if such use was common already in the early Byzantine period, although it is not impossible. The southern one was sometimes used to store donations and ritual objects, although the former were usually kept in the *diaconicon* located near the entrance to the church. In some instances the room to the south of the apse was used as a chapel where holy relics and bones were kept. It was not fenced off with bars so that the members of the congregation as well as the priests had access to it.[11]

[11] J. Lassus, *Sanctuaires chrétiens de Syrie* (Paris, 1957), pp. 161–183; A. Negev, "The Churches of the Central Negev. An Architectural Survey," *RB* 81 (1974): 416–421.

Shivta: The triapsidal Northern Church (Z. Radovan)

From the mid-fifth century C.E. onward, a new type of basilica became common in Palestine. Instead of a square room on either side of the central apse, two small apses were built. Such a "triapsidal" basilica is found at Emmaus, at the Monastery of Euthymius (Ḥan el-Aḥmar) in the Judean Desert, at Gerasa, in cities of the central Negev, and elsewhere.[12] Apparently, from the fifth century onward, a long room, the *narthex*, served to create a corridor as an additional transitional zone between the profane world outside and the sanctified interior. It was added at the western end of the church, between the atrium and the nave. The *catechumeni*, gathered in the narthex during the Eucharist mass of the believers. In this way they could hear the mysterious ceremony without actually being present.

[12] Regarding the triapsidal church and its date, see J.W. Crowfoot's discussion in *Gerasa* (above, note 5), pp. 323–333; J.W. Crowfoot, *Early Churches in Palestine* (London, 1941), pp. 67–72; and in particular R. Rosenthal-Hogenbottom, *Die Kirchen von Sobota und die Dreiapsiderkirchen des nähen Ostens* (Wiesbaden, 1982), especially pp. 203–222. And see also in this volume, J. Wilkinson, "Constantinian Churches in Palestine," pp. 23–27; A. Negev, "The Cathedral at Ḥaluẓa (Elusa)," pp. 286–293, and Y. Tsafrir, "The Early Byzantine Town of Reḥovot-in-the-Negev and Its Churches," pp. 294–302.

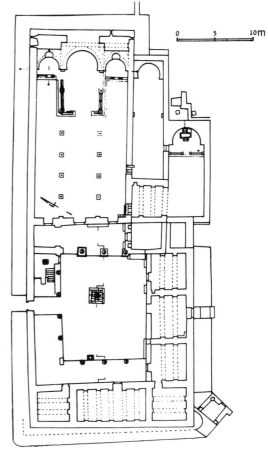

Shivta: plan of The Northern Church [R. Rosenthal, *Das heilige Land* (1976), p. 12]

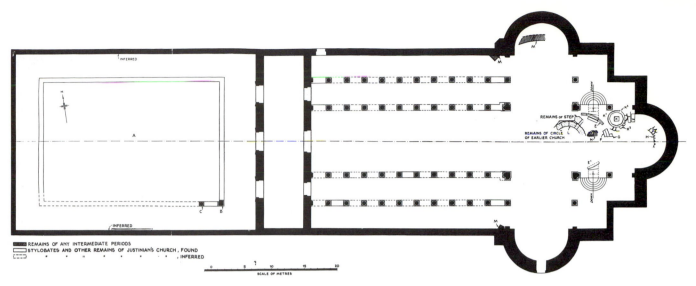

The Church of the Nativity, Bethlehem in the time of Justinian (Richmond, p. 72, Fig. 1)

Certain scholars have tried to date the various stages in the evolution of ecclesiastic architecture. Although it cannot be denied that there were developments when new elements such as those mentioned above were introduced, a chronological framework has not yet been convincingly elaborated. Not infrequently we find churches built in the sixth and seventh centuries C.E. according to the simple and apparently earlier design.

A distinction can be drawn between centric churches designed for commemorative purposes, and basilicas, which were mainly congregational churches, but many basilicas also served to commemorate holy sites (such as the Eleona). There were primary and secondary holy places, some of which were "discovered" during the Byzantine period or whose sanctity derived from objects purchased and stored within them. A few were authentic, such as the tombs of sainted monks, but in others the "holy" objects or relics had been recently fabricated or "miraculously" discovered. Those relics, mainly fragments of a saint's bones, were kept in metal or marble reliquary boxes that were, as mentioned above, interred beneath the main altar of the church or in one of the side rooms. Occasionally the relics were placed in a special chapel or a crypt.

The best-known church with a crypt arrangement is the one in Bethlehem built dur-ing the reign of Justinian. The earlier, Constantinian church there was renovated several times. The most important addition was a splendid mosaic floor, probably laid during the fifth century C.E. In the sixth century, under Justinian, an entirely new building was erected, perhaps following the destruction caused by the Samaritan revolt of 529. The nave was not greatly changed, but a narthex was added at its western end (cutting off part of the atrium), that exists to this day. The main substantive change was made on the eastern side of the church. The octagon was removed and in its place three apses in a cloverleaf array were erected. At that stage the difficulties that had stood in the way of celebrating the mass were eliminated, and it was possible to install a chancel and altar in the church and to hold regular prayer services and ceremonies. The pilgrims, who were mainly interested, as they are today, in visiting the Cave of the Nativity, and not in the daily prayers of the church, entered the cave by a flight of stairs on one side and left it by a second flight on the other. Thus it was possible to maintain without interference the daily services while large numbers of pilgrims were visiting the cave below the chancel. Similar crypts with separate flights of stairs for descent and ascent have been found in the Eleona Church, as detailed above, in the

13

Monastery of St. Catherine, Mt. Sinai: Chapel of the Burning Bush (Forsyth and Weitzmann, Pl. C)

North Church, Reḥovot-in-the-Negev: the southern entrance of the crypt viewed from the north

Church at Ḥorvat Berachot in the Hebron Hills, in the northern church at Reḥovot-in-the-Negev, at the Elianos Church in Madaba, and, apparently, in the Church of Jacob's Well near Shechem.

The church at the Monastery of St. Catherine on Mt. Sinai has the same processional feature. There, however, the holy place is not in a crypt below the apse but outside, in a small garden. This is the venerated site of the "Burning Bush." The Chapel of the Bush was added in the Middle Ages. It was obviously planned to allow pilgrims to walk down the side aisles and through the chapels to the sacred site without interrupting the daily liturgy in the main church.[13]

Churches with a concentric plan were, as mentioned above, particularly well suited to

commemorate holy places. An example is the Church of the Ascension, which was built ca. 380 C.E. on the summit of the Mt. of Olives. Originally its plan was circular, about 26.5 m in diameter. The rock from which Jesus ascended to heaven was featured in its center.[14] Another commemorative edifice, the Church of Jacob's Well, was, according to the drawing by Arculf, cruciform, with the ancient well at the center of the cross. The roof above it was undoubtedly raised higher than the other sections to emphasize the well. At Capernaum, in the fifth century C.E., by way of comparison, an octagonal church was built above the House of St. Peter.

However, not all the churches built around a single center were commemorative. Any such classification or generalization must also take into account the significant number of buildings expressing individual talent, crea-

[13] G.H. Forsyth, "The Monastery of St. Catherine at Mount Sinai: The Church and Fortress of Justinian," *DOP* 22 (1968): 1–19. See also the description and additional bibliography in this volume in Y. Tsafrir, "Monks and Monasteries in Southern Sinai," pp. 315–333.

[14] Vincent and Abel, *Jérusalem nouvelle* (see note 8), pp. 360–419; V. Corbo, "Scavo archeologico a ridosso della basilica dell'Ascensione," *LA* 10 (1959–1960): 205–248.

14

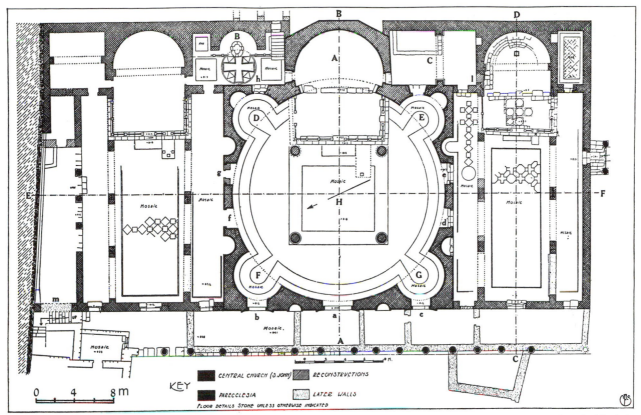

Church complex of John the Baptist, St. George (left) and Sts. Cosmas and Damianus (right), Gerasa (first half of the sixth century C.E.): the circular church with an inner square structure is flanked by basilican chapels which share its auxiliary rooms. The circular wall with four niches supports a dome (*Gerasa*, Pl. XXXVII)

tive urge and originality of the architect. The circular church unearthed on the summit of Tel Beth-shean is an example,[15] as are the following: the Church of Mary on Mt. Gerizim, built in 484, which was an octagon surrounded by chapels;[16] the Church of the Prophets, Apostles, and Martyrs in Gerasa, dating from the second half of the fifth century, which was square with an inner cruciform division;[17] and the square Church of John the Baptist in Gerasa which had an interior circular niched structure flanked on either side by basilican chapels.[18] The cathedral of Bosra[19] in the early sixth century was also square (its external dimensions were about 38 × 38 m) with an inner niched circular plan. An apse and elongated chapels with stone vaults were added to its eastern side. In the center of the nave there were four piers, in the form of a square (about 14 × 14 m), that once bore arches and a dome, apparently made of wood. Some view this church as a precursor of the innovative Byzantine style that reached its apex in the Hagia Sophia Cathedral in Constantinople, and is typical of Orthodox churches all over Greece, the Balkans and the East even today.

[15] G.M. Fitzgerald, *Beth Shan. Excavations 1921–1923*. III: *The Arab and Byzantine Levels* (Philadelphia, 1931), pp. 18–30.

[16] A.M. Schneider, "Römische und byzantinische Bauten auf dem Garizem," *ZVPV* 68 (1951), 210–234; J. Wilkinson, "Architectural Procedures in Byzantine Palestine," *Levant* 13 (1981): 156–172; and in this volume, Y. Magen, "The Church of Mary Theotokos on Mt. Gerizim," pp. 170–196.

[17] Crowfoot on *Gerasa* (see note 5), pp. 256–159, Pl. XLI.

[18] Ibid., pp. 241–248, Pl. XXXVII.

[19] H.C. Butler, *Princeton Expedition to Syria* II, A (Leiden, 1906–1919), Part 4, pp. 281–286; J.W. Crowfoot, *Churches at Bosra and Samaria-Sebasta* (London, 1937), pp. 1–23, Pls. 1–10.

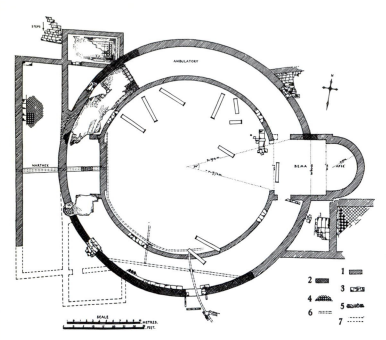

Round church, Tel Beth-shean: concentric plan (probably sixth century C.E.) comprises an inner stylobate. The arcades above its columns supported the roof of the *ambulatorium*. Legend — 1) foundation walls; 2) walls standing to pavement level; 3) stone pavement slabs, steps and thresholds; 4) red and white square pavement; 5) mosaic fragments; 6) underground channels; 7) reconstruction (Fitzgerald, Fig. 20)

As described above, the churches were very lavishly decorated.[20] Thus, they incorporated the essentials of Byzantine artistic creativity. Their exterior, although more modestly decorated than the interior, revealed beautifully-carved jambs and lintels bearing Christian symbols as well as geometric, floral or figural patterns. Wooden doors were often carved on both their inner and outer faces. Inside the church, an impressive and elaborate exposition of arts was displayed. The columns had molded bases and capitals, and the wooden ceiling beams were carved and painted. The pavements were usually laid with mosaics, although these were inferior to marble-colored stone plaques (*opus sectile*). The walls were, in many cases, coated with frescos or wall mosaics. Both were the most important expressions of Christian monumental art. Among the very few which have survived is the magnificent sixth-century apse mosaic of St. Catherine Monastery in Sinai. The chancel screen panel, either made of limestone or marble, was delicately carved in low relief or in lacework fashion. The artistic complex was completed by various smaller objects of art: glass and metal candelabra, gold and silver liturgical implements, and icons mostly made of wood. Undoubtedly, the early icons of Sinai are the best preserved collection in the world.

The relationships between Christian faith and cult and ecclesiastical art and architecture are explicit. The themes of the the wall frescos, wall mosaics, many of the minor objects, chancel screen panels, and icons were based on the Old and New Testament and incorporated Christian symbols. Nonetheless, numerous decorations, mostly hewn stone and floor mosaics, bear no religious symbolism. These are very similar to contemporary non-religious designs in Jewish and probably Samaritan synagogues. If no contradictions in principles of faith and liturgical functions existed, both religions shared the same means of expressions.[21] It was, however, the Christian culture that was the leading force in the Byzantine times and the most dominant factor in the art and architecture of the period.

[20] See in general, Tsafrir, *Archaeology and Art* (note 1), pp. 389–449.

[21] Y. Tsafrir, "The Byzantine Setting and Its Influence on Ancient Synagogues," in L.I. Levine (ed.), *The Synagogue in Late Antiquity* (Philadelphia, 1987), pp. 147–157.

Christian Worship in the Byzantine Period

John Wilkinson

A description of the services held in Palestinian churches during the Byzantine period suggests that the church structures were designed not only to meet the purely functional requirements of the liturgy, but also to embody older, familiar symbols. The buildings reflect the conjunction of function and symbol, the merging of two very different processes.

Baptism

Two main services will be described here. The first is baptism, a rite in which candidates were admitted to Christianity, which has no obvious parallel in Jewish liturgy. The second is the Christian assembly (or *synaxis*) on Sunday, the first part of which has a great many parallels in the Jewish synagogue service. It should also be noted at the start that the Christian calendar in use in the late fourth century in Jerusalem had many similarities to the Jewish calendar. Two of the feasts were the same (Easter and Tabernacles, which the Christians in Jerusalem kept as their dedication festival), and a third, Christmas, may well be a Christian form of Hannukkah. The early Christian calendar grew out of the Jewish one, and the differences were of detail.

Christian initiation is described for us in a wealth of detail by Egeria, who made a pilgrimage to Jerusalem in the late fourth century.[1] In her day initiation was still for adults; only in the mid-fifth century did the practice of baptizing infants imply that few, if any, adults came to be made Christians. In Egeria's time, when an adult decided to become a Christian, he went with his friends and relations to the basilica of the Holy Sepulchre, where they met the bishop in the middle of the nave. When the people supporting the candidate had testified to his good behavior, he was enrolled as a catechumen (καφεχούμενος). A catechumen was obliged to attend daily sessions in the church. First individual meetings were held with a member of the clergy, who exorcised him or her with prayers for deliverance from sin. Then there was a daily three-hour lecture by the bishop, at first in regard to the interpretation of the Bible and then the Christian creed. The catechumens was baptized before the assembly on Easter Day and received Holy Communion with the other members of the congregation. Until this time, the meaning of baptism and the Eucharist could not be revealed to them, and they had to attend more discourses in the week following Easter to learn about those two services. The oldest complete set of lessons to catechumens that is known comes from the pen of St. Cyril of Jerusalem, who was bishop of Jerusalem in the middle of the fourth century C.E.[2]

Baptism was sometimes carried out in a baptistery that was separate from the church. In his lectures St. Cyril described one that had at least two rooms. Normally, however, the baptistery was attached to the church; there was no traditional place for baptism except perhaps in the Negev, where several fonts (Mamshit East and Shivta South) were located outside the west door of the church.

The Christian Assembly

The main Christian assembly on Sundays will be described here in two parts. When the members of the congregation arrived, they

[1] J. Wilkinson, *Egeria's Travels* (London, 1971).

[2] F.T. Cross (ed.), *St. Cyril of Jerusalem's Lectures on the Christian Saclaments* (London, 1980).

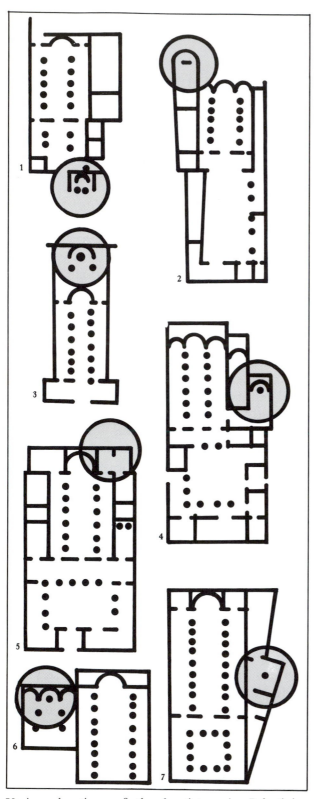

Various locations of the baptistery in Palestinian churches: the font is circled. Legend — 1) Avdat North; 2) Beth Yeraḥ; 3) Imwas North; 4) Shivta North; 5) Kursi; 6) Susita Cathedral; 7) Mamshit East

made their offerings (see below). The first part of the service began in many places (both in synagogues and churches) with a procession, which may have been introduced in the Christian rite of Palestine some time after the fourth century. In the synagogue a processional hymn was provided (*Avodah Zarah* 24b). Both forms of liturgy then continued with readings from Scriptures (which in the case of Christians included the New Testament), a sermon, and a blessing. The likeness between the Jewish synagogue service and the first part of the Christian assembly is illustrated by the following table:

	Jewish Synagogue Service	First Part of the Christian Sunday Assembly
Entry	Sometimes there was a procession to place the Scriptures in position.	Entry of the bishop to the sanctuary, and of the book of Gospels.
Prayer	Call to prayer. The Shema: eighteen benedictions and petitions.	Greeting. Prayer of preparation.
Readings	The Law [Psalm?] The Prophets	The Law Psalm The Prophets
		Psalm Reading from the New Testament Hymn Gospel
	Sermon	Sermon
Blessings	Blessing (if a priest was present).	Blessings for those about to be dismissed.

The first part of the Christian service, like the Jewish one, could take place in any kind of hall suitable for readings, but the architecture of the church, like that of the synagogue, had symbolic meaning. In both, the part of the buildings corresponding to the nave meant earth and the part corresponding to the sanctuary meant heaven. The same symbolism also applied to the nave and sanctuary (the Holy of Holies and holy place of the Tabernacle) in

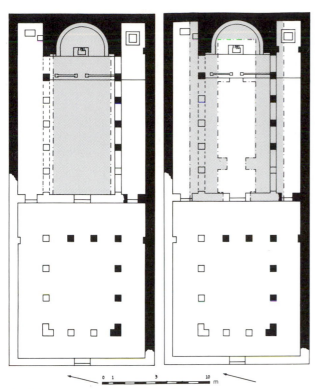

ᶜEn Ḥanniya: the church is divided into the Holy of Holies and the holy place by the sanctuary step. Left, compared to the Tabernacle; right, compared to Ezekiel's temple

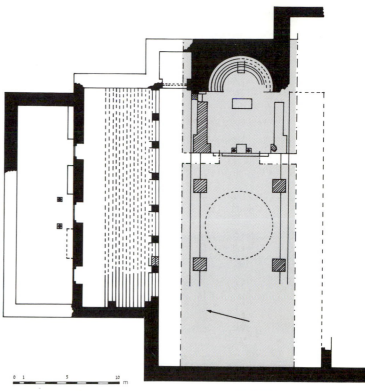

Siloam: the church is divided into nave and sanctuary by the superimposition on the plan of rooms of Ezekiel's temple

the Temple at Jerusalem. In fact, in most churches, the central space is divided horizontally, like the Tabernacle and the Temple, by either the steps of the sanctuary or the chancel rail. At the church at ᶜEn Ḥanniya near Jerusalem we have an example of a sanctuary step separating the sanctuary from the nave. On the left, the church's sanctuary followed the layout of the Tabernacle, which fits inside it, while in the drawing on the right, the plan of the Holy of Holies of Ezekiel's temple is superimposed on the En Ḥanniya sanctuary, and does not have the same proportions. Another example is given below, where the overlay of the two inner rooms of Ezekiel's temple creates the same nave-sanctuary division for the church at Siloam.

The plans for the position of the pulpit in churches in Palestine depend on the same proportional scheme. The three churches in the Negev all lend themselves to the same

division as the rooms of Ezekiel's temple. Avdat North is divided by the sanctuary step and the other two churches by the chancel rail. The plan of the North Church at Shivta follows that of Ezekiel's Temple superimposed on it, paralleling the division of the sanctuary and nave; they correspond with the Holy of Holies and the holy place of the Tabernacle. In all the churches represented in the illustrations above, the pulpit stood at the end of the nave and was joined by a bridge to the sanctuary from where it was entered. Thus, the divinely inspired Scriptures are drawn from the sanctuary into the nave, or, symbolically speaking, out of heaven unto earth.

The beginning of the Christian assembly had a preliminary feature that was really linked to the second part of the service. Each individual was free to bring the church a gift, and in the second part of the service those who had brought such offerings were specially

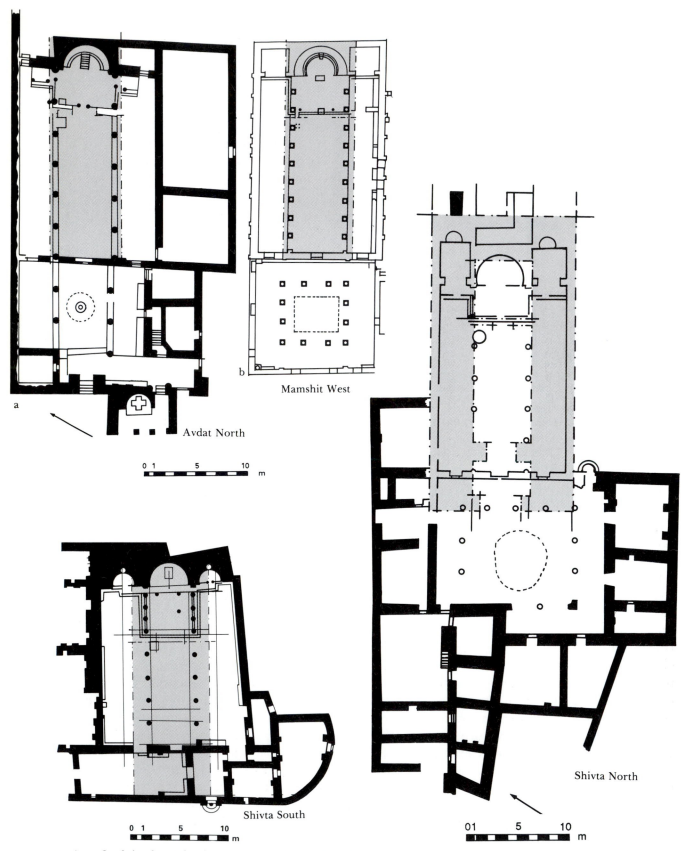

a

Avdat North

b

Mamshit West

Shivta South

Shivta North

0 1   5   10   m

0 1   5   10   m

01   5   10   m

Location of pulpits shown by the superimposition of Ezekiel's temple in the fifth century (Avdat North, Mamshit West and Shivta South) and in the sixth century (Shivta North)

20

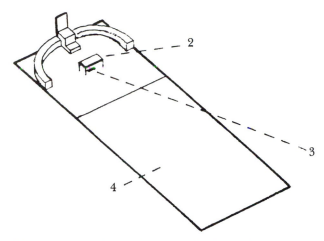

The heavenly tabernacle as seen by John, the author of Revelation, to which the chapter and verse numbers refer: 1) "A throne stood in heaven.... round the throne were twenty-four thrones" (4:2, 4); 2) "The golden altar before the throne" (8:3); 3) "Under the altar the souls of those who had been slain for the word of God" (6:9); 4) "The outer hall of the tent of witness in heaven" (15:5)

mentioned in prayer. The deacon who received them was responsible for registering the names of their donors. The contributions might be money or gifts in kind — some for the poor, like honey, and some for the general purposes of the church, like lamp oil. These especially included bread and wine for that particular service, and a loaf and supply of wine would be selected to be taken to the sanctuary to be blessed.

These gifts were presented in a room that bore the name of the minister who received them. He was a deacon, and his room was called a *diaconicon*. In the Syriac document known as the *Testamentum Domini*,[3] which is the basis of Eusebius' description of the church type in Palestine, the *diaconicon* is said to be "to the right of the right-hand entry" at the west of the church. Indeed, there are some churches in Jordan that have *diaconica* in this position. In later Byzantine usage this room was called the *prothesis*, and its position was in the north beside the main apse. In early churches in Palestine, however, the *diaconicon* may have been situated anywhere, and it is a mistake to use the late Byzantine term *prothe-*

sis, especially as the latter chamber was used for other purposes, such as the veneration of a martyr.

As the second part of the Christian assembly began, the arrangements in the church underwent a change. When all who could not take part had been blessed and dismissed, the doors of the church were shut and one of the deacons sat to guard them. This change in the number of participants may well have been expressed in the plan. At ʿEn Ḥanniya (see illustrations above) the plan of the Ezekiel temple does not correspond to the proportions of the church's sanctuary and would suit the needs of the first part of the assembly; the Tabernacle's exact superimposition would conform to the needs of the second group. Furthermore, curtains were drawn around the sanctuary, above the chancel rail. Chancel curtains were used in Palestine, but the archaeological evidence for them has largely been overlooked. Egeria (*Itinerary* 25.8), for example, comments on the beauty of such hangings.

The church, therefore, symbolized both the Tabernacle and heaven. It was an incarnation of the Tabernacle (as at En Ḥanniya), as the Holy of Holies was hidden by a veil, and the altar, or *ciborium*, stood for the Ark of the Covenant. In a late document from Constantinople, the *ciborium* is likened to the ark and called as such in the Ethiopian liturgy. Although no Palestinian document gives it this name, the deacons on either side holding fans should be seen as representing the cherubim on either side of the ark.

The fact that the church also became a symbol of heaven is explicitly stated by St. Maximus Confessor from Constantinople in the seventh century.[4] This was certainly so in Palestine, and fourteen fifth- and sixth-century churches have sanctuary remains that lend support to this hypothesis. In Jewish and Christian literature, one of the most common pictures of heaven was as a tabernacle or temple. The details of this building are de-

[3] See in this volume, Y. Tsafrir, "The Development of Ecclesiastical Architecture in Palestine," pp. 1–16, n. 5.

[4] *St. Maximus Confessor*, G.C. Berthold, ed. (New York, 1985).

scribed by John, the author of the Book of Revelation. (The picture of the heavenly Tabernacle as described by John appears in the drawing.)

In the Septuagint version of 1 Kings 6:17, the holy place of Solomon's Temple is called *naos*, so when the Book of Revelation speaks of "the *naos* of the tent of witness in heaven," it can only mean the holy place, or the large room inside the main entry. Thus, the Tabernacle in heaven has the same plan as the earthly Tabernacle. In the Holy of Holies there is the throne of God, an idea familiar to those who had read Isaiah 6:1 or 1 Kings 22:19. This throne forms the center of the curve of a circle that contains twenty-four other thrones for the presbyters. Before the throne of God was a golden altar, and beneath it were "the souls of those who had been slain for the word of God" (Revelations 6:9). This picture of the heavenly Tabernacle remarkably recalls the plan of many sanctuaries in Palestine. Many sanctuaries have all three characteristics, which can hardly be a coincidence. Indeed the central nave of nine out of ten churches in Palestine has the same proportions, either divided according to the Tabernacle or the Temple rooms.

The second part of the Christian assembly started with the deacons bringing the selected bread and wine to the altar. Then the main officiant (with the deacons bearing fans on either side of him, representing the cherubim) said a long prayer of thanksgiving and blessing over the bread and wine, and the curtains were drawn back from the sanctuary. He then invited the people to receive the bread and wine, saying, "Holy things to holy people," and the heavenly banquet began. The last part of the second section of the service ended with short prayers of thanksgiving, a blessing, and a dismissal.

Our brief study of the two main services in the early Byzantine period ends here. We have seen that church architecture should not be interpreted entirely in functional terms, but symbolically as well. The symbols are well documented in the New Testament, and were much beloved by the early Christians and for many centuries thereafter.

Constantinian Churches in Palestine

John Wilkinson

The Emperor Constantine is regarded as a saint by Christians in the Eastern Church, and rightly so, for he set it at liberty after a long persecution, and to him must be credited, at least financially, the very large number of churches that were built or rebuilt during his reign. In Palestine he founded four, three of which were visited and "dedicated" by his mother, Empress Helena, on her tour in 329. The act of dedication, at this time, took place when, or close to the date that, the construction was begun, for the buildings were completed much later. The fourth church was built after Helena's death, at Mamre. As it has hardly any Constantinian remains, apart from the apse, it will not be treated here.

Constantine, as Eusebius tells us in Chapter 25 of the *Life of Constantine*, began his work in Palestine by ordering the construction of a church on the site of Christ's Resurrection. In Chapters 26 and 27, Eusebius gives a fuller account of the place: it was the rock tomb in which Jesus was buried and at which the Temple of Aphrodite was subsequently built by Hadrian. This part of his narrative relates to the site's history, but because the rock tomb had not yet been located, he could not describe it. Constantine gave special orders that the building material from the pagan temple should be removed.

The site of the Resurrection was well known in antiquity. Melito of Sardis, who visited Jerusalem, mentions three times in his sermon "On the Pascha" that it was located inside the city walls. He preached the sermon in about 160. In Chapter 28 of the *Life of Constantine*, Eusebius describes the demolition of the Temple of Aphrodite and says that, when the earth beneath the pavements was

removed, unexpectedly, the tomb was revealed. When the miracle was reported to Constantine, he wrote — in a letter that is quoted by Eusebius — that a "basilica" should be built on the site.[1] His wish was that "the basilica itself ... surpass all others in beauty." Constantine gave no plan for the church (he did not even mention it), but he went into considerable detail about the materials that should be used.

From the variety of churches built in other parts of the Roman Empire during Constantine's reign, as seen in the drawing below, it is clear that there must have been some local tradition of church planning current before the official destruction in the persecution of 303. Eusebius also described a structure built at Tyre before Constantine came to power in the eastern part of the Empire. There is another church in Phoenicia — at Heliopolis (Baalbek) in the Lebanon — one with three apses, that may well be Constantinian (see drawing below). Other triapsidal edifices were certainly known in the fourth century (at Gethsemane in Jerusalem, St. Epiphanius at Salamis in Cyprus, the Basilica Martyrium in Milan, and St. Pudenziana in Rome), but the main clue to the antiquity of the church at Baalbek lies in the fact that it had a sanctuary not at its eastern but at its western end. In the Eastern Empire, four churches are known to have this orientation; the other three are Constantinian.

Since 1959 restorations have been carried out at the Church of the Holy Sepulchre in

---

[1] The word *basilica* is used here to mean "church." It is rarely employed in this sense in Greek and is limited to this passage in Eusebius and to one other work, which may also be a translation from Latin.

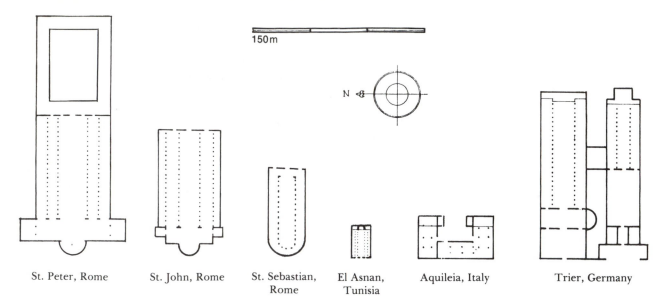

St. Peter, Rome · St. John, Rome · St. Sebastian, Rome · El Asnan, Tunisia · Aquileia, Italy · Trier, Germany

Churches built during the reign of Emperor Constantine

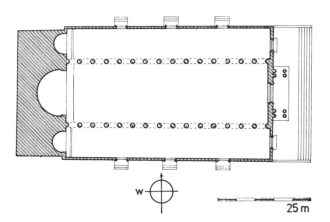

Heliopolis (Baalbek): Th. Wiegand's reconstruction of the earlier church. Wiegand's arches are replaced by columns

Jerusalem. A good picture of the archaeological discoveries there is given by Father V. Corbo in his report on the excavation.[2] My own reconstruction, largely based on Corbo's, appears here. One of the features Corbo reports is that the three small northeastern doors of the round church (the Rotunda or Anastasis) can be reconstructed with certainty. But such doors in a facade can only have

---

[2] V. Corbo, *Il Santo Sepolcro di Gerusalemme*, I–III (Jerusalem, 1982); see also in this volume, J. Patrich, "The Early Church of the Holy Sepulchre in the Light of Excavations and Restorations," pp. 101–117.

been designed to match columns that formed a colonnade in front of the building. The court outside in front of the Anastasis would thus have had small porticoes on three of its sides, with a fourth and much more impressive one at the Anastasis facade. Because, in his description of the church, Eusebius only mentions the three small porticoes, it is possible that the rotunda of the Anastasis and its portico had not yet been built in 337, the year in which he was writing. According to a chronicle, the architect Zenobius was dispatched only in 338. This court thus was larger and contained the rock-cut monument of the Holy Sepulchre in the middle, at its western end, and the rock Calvary in the southeastern corner, both still open to the sky. Beyond it, to the east, was a large basilican church called the Martyrium, of which only the foundations remain. We know that it was crudely built, because its eastern wall was not at right angles to those adjacent to it. Beyond the Martyrium, to the east, was a court leading onto the main street.

Corbo has also noticed that the half-columns that are at present built into the circle around the Holy Sepulchre may have been taken from Hadrian's Temple of Aphrodite. If these columns in fact belong to the first church surrounding the Anastasis, they pro-

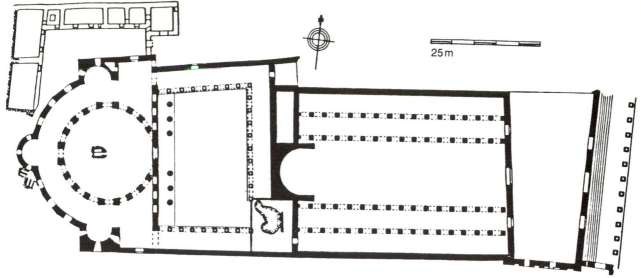

Church of the Holy Sepulchre, Jerusalem: reconstruction of the Constantinian Anastasis and Martyrium based on V. Corbo's excavations

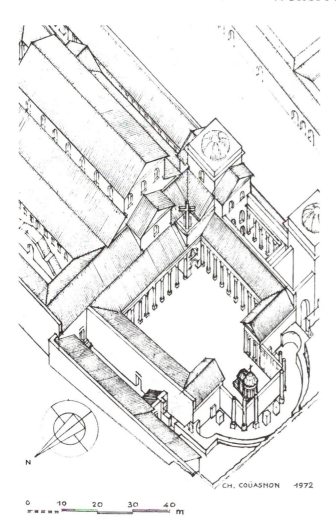

CH. COÜASNON 1972

Church of the Holy Sepulchre, Jerusalem: reconstruction of the early stage prior to the construction of the Anastasis (Ch. Coüasnon, Pl. VII).

vide additional reason to believe that the Anastasis had not yet been built when Eusebius wrote his description, as this author emphasizes the emperor's order to remove all the temple's building materials from the site.

In fact, for Constantine's churches, a long time elapsed between the laying of the foundation and the completion of the building. The church on the site of the Resurrection and the church at Bethlehem (see illustration on p. 27) were both planned before 330, but one was dedicated in 335 and the other in 339. The rotunda of the Anastasis must have been finished after Eusebius wrote his description, in the year of Constantine's death. The completed building is described for the first time in a work written in about 347.

The construction of eastern sanctuaries was introduced in Syria, as far as we know, in the churches at Bethlehem and on the Mt. of Olives (also called the "Eleona") (see ground plan below).[3] From their time on (if the

[3] Père L.H. Vincent o.p. was present at the excavations of the Eleona, and wrote a report on it; see H. Vincent, "L'eglise de l'Eleona," *RB* 19 (1910): 573–574. Although scanty evidence was found, its reconstruction is possible. The only point of doubt, as far as the proportions are concerned, is that the inside of the apse is missing, and the extent of the chancel conjectural. This church was also described by Eusebius as a "Temple." Plan a reproduces the Temple proportionally. The whole complex of the Eleona (Plan b) had a ground plan that fitted the Temple rooms. In other words the Eleona is another example of a church plan similar to that of a synagogue.

25

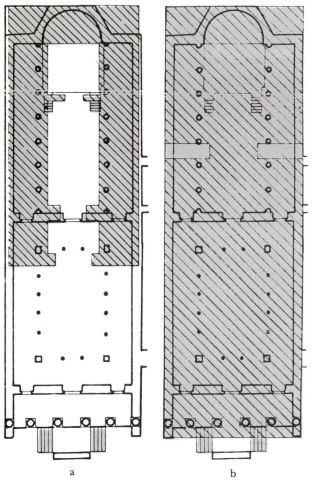

a   b

Church of Eleona on the Mt. of Olives, Jerusalem:
two proportions of the temple superimposed on the
church plan (see n. 3)

many synagogues (such as the ones at Gerasa and Caesarea). A specially interesting feature connecting it to the Jerusalem Temple is that the two inside pillars on the facade (not shown in the plan) were, according to Eusebius, raised on cushioned plinths exactly like the ones outside the synagogue at Kh. Susiya. These pairs of columns must represent Jachin and Boaz, the two columns outside the Jerusalem Temple (1 Kings 7:21).

Eusebius also describes the church at Bethlehem as a temple. It had an octagonal sanctuary (see Plan a), for the octagon was a sign of perfection to Christians. Bethlehem, too, was carelessly built: the axis of the octagon is not the same as that of the nave. No pillars were found, but there were four colonnades whose position is reasonably easy to conjecture. The proportions of the Temple rooms are easy to see, for the chancel step divides one from the other, and the Holy of Holies of the Jerusalem Temple, according to the Bible, fits the octagon, or the Christian sanctuary, very well.

The proportion of the plan presented in Plan b is, however, surprising. It shows that the Jerusalem Temple and the church were aligned in opposite directions. Fortunately a check exists in the design of the mosaic pavement: a square geometric design in the nave fits exactly into the Temple's Holy of Holies. In addition, the eastern end of the Temple is marked by a line in the mosaic in the octagon. The line comes between a part of the octagon (dotted in the illustration) and the end of the Temple. It is clear that it does not depend on the octagonal pattern, because it misses the corner. Clearly it is aligned with the inside of the eastern wall of the aisles. At Bethlehem the plan of the Temple used by the church architect was a reversal of that employed in other churches: the Holy of Holies of the Temple is not directed to the sanctuary but to the entrance in the west. Perhaps this is to be ascribed to the desire to make it correspond with its actual alignment in Jerusalem, which was also from east to west, but this is unlikely. The church at Heliopolis also has a western sanctuary, and as its proportional

church at Heliopolis was Constantinian), all the churches in the Greek-speaking part of the Empire had sanctuaries at the eastern end. It also seems that, from about this period, the Jewish synagogues, which had hitherto been orientated according to the wish of the individual congregation, were converted or rebuilt so that Jerusalem was made the direction of prayer. Assuming, as I do, that churches and synagogues were architecturally the same to begin with, this would have been another way to distinguish a church from a synagogue.

In fact, the church on the site of the Resurrection resembled the Temple; and even the way that the foundations lie proves this point. The church has its doors on the east, like arrangement is like that at Bethlehem, the Temple faces the wrong way.

This reversal of the Temple is certainly not anti-Jewish. Whether in this respect churches imitated synagogues or synagogues imitated churches, it is hard to say. In any case the later synagogue at Jericho has exactly the same square at the main door, which gives us two opposing Temple plans. A discussion reported in the Talmud (Baba Batra 25a), in which two third-century Palestinian rabbis discuss whether God lives in the west or the

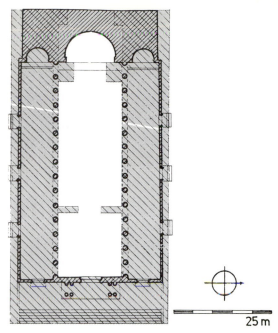

Heliopolis (Baalbek): temple proportions superimposed on the Constantinian church plan

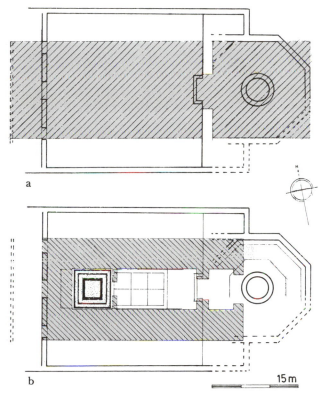

a

b

Church of the Nativity, Bethlehem: the first church. Note the square mosaic in nave b

east, may be indicative of the message of a double proportional scheme, with the Holy of Holies at either end: the belief that God dwells everywhere.

The variety of Constantinian church plans all over the world suggests that local ecclesiastical bodies dictated their architecture. However, the edifices in Palestine and Phoenicia also show differences in alignment and proportion that can hardly be the result of some new development taking place during Constantine's reign. They reflect, rather, a long tradition of church planning, which was, I believe, an effort to differentiate between the architecture of churches and that of synagogues.

27

Churches in the Crusader Kingdom of Jerusalem (1099–1291)

Denys Pringle

After Jerusalem fell to the army of the First Crusade on July 15, 1099, a kingdom of West European type was established in Palestine that was to last for almost two centuries. During the twelfth century, the borders of the Kingdom of Jerusalem stretched from Eilat on the Red Sea to Beirut in the north, and from the Mediterranean coast to the desert of Transjordan in the east. But this territorial floruit was of short duration for, in July 1187, at the Horns of Hattin above Tiberias, the Ayyubid Sultan Salāḥ ad-Dīn, commonly known as Saladin, destroyed the Frankish royal army and captured the king, Guy of Lusignan. From 1192 onward, the Kingdom of Jerusalem was "of Jerusalem" only in name, and except for a brief period from 1229 to 1244, when the city returned temporarily to Christian hands, Frankish settlement was confined to a narrow strip of coastal territory with Acre as its administrative capital.

From 1099 until 1291, when Acre itself finally fell to the Mamluks, Palestine witnessed a spate of building such as it had not known since the fifth and sixth centuries. The physical remains of that activity are still evident in the countryside and in the historic town centers of the land. They include castles, town defenses, houses, farmsteads, harbor works, covered markets, shops, and of course churches.

After the conquest of Crusader Palestine by the Muslims, many churches were converted into mosques, the form in which they have survived. Others were demolished for their building materials, while some were simply allowed to fall into ruin. Buildings belonging to the Eastern Christian communities, however, were usually spared, and several, dating from the twelfth century, are still functioning churches. In addition, a number of buildings that existed in a ruined or semiruined state were acquired by the Franciscans and the French and German governments in the nineteenth century (and in certain instances earlier), and have been restored and reconsecrated for Western liturgical use.

A succession of Christian pilgrims to the Holy Land from the period of the Crusades down to modern times have left us descriptions of the churches and monasteries which they visited on their journeys. A detailed historical, architectural and structural analysis of Crusader church buildings, however, only seriously began in the mid-nineteenth century with the publication of Count Melchior de Vogüé's *Les Églises de la Terre Sainte*. Other major contributions to the study of Crusader churches in Jerusalem were subsequently made by the Dominican Fathers L.H. Vincent and F.M. Abel,[1] and of those in Palestine, Lebanon, and Syria by C. Enlart.[2] Studies of individual buildings have also been carried out by C. Schick, C.N. Johns and the Franciscan Fathers S.J. Saller and B. Bagatti, among others.

As a result of these and other researches, the number of churches built, rebuilt, or simply restored in the Latin Kingdom of Jerusalem in the twelfth and thirteenth centuries, for which there is archaeological evidence,

[1] L.H. Vincent and F.M. Abel, *Jérusalem nouvelle* (Paris, 1914–1926), 4 vols. + album.

[2] C. Enlart, *Les Monuments des Croisés dans le Royaume de Jérusalem: Architecture réligieuse et civile* (Paris, 1925–1928), 2 vols. + album.

can now be reckoned at over 200.[3] When churches attested to by documentary means are added, the total may exceed 400. Amongst these a number of different types of ecclesiastical buildings are represented. Studying them sheds light not only on the art and architecture of the Crusader kingdom, but also on the material culture and the social and political life of its Christian inhabitants.

The Eastern Christian Communities

Among the many and complex forces that helped launch the First Crusade on its ponderous course through Eastern Europe and what are today Turkey and Syria was the desire to free the holy places of Christendom from the Muslims and to bring help to the oppressed Christians of the East. By the end of the eleventh century, these Christians constituted only a minority of the population of Palestine and were, moreover, divided — as they are today — into different communities: Greek and Georgian Orthodox, Syrian Jacobites, Armenians, Copts, Nestorians, and even some Latins. Church buildings were generally small and few in number, and, during the reign of the deranged Fatimid Caliph al-Ḥākim (996–1021), all but a handful were destroyed. In that period of official persecution, not even the Church of the Resurrection in Jerusalem was spared.

The events of al-Ḥākim's reign, however, were exceptional; later Muslim rulers acted more tolerantly toward the minority Christian and Jewish communities. Thus, in 1027 the Byzantine Emperor Constantine VIII obtained permission to rebuild the Church of the Resurrection, and eleven years later work began under Constantine IX (Monomachus). Other Orthodox churches were also rebuilt in this period. Among the surviving examples are the Georgian Monastery of the Cross (ca. 1038–1056) near Jerusalem, the Church of St. John the Baptist at ʿEn Karem, the smaller of the two churches of St. John the Baptist at

Sabastiya (Samaria), the Church of St. Mary (1058) in the village of ʿAbud northwest of Bir Zeit, and probably the smaller basilica (now a mosque) adjoining the Church of St. George in Lydda (Lod). Some of the churches in Jerusalem were also rebuilt, including that of St. Mary Latin (today the Church of the Redeemer). However, it appears that the neglect of five centuries and the destruction in the early eleventh century had created a larger gap than could be filled within the space of only a few decades. Thus, when Jerusalem returned once more to Christian control in 1099, the momentum of building continued through the twelfth century.

This opportunity was seized not only by the newcomers from the West, but also by the

The Armenian Cathedral of St. James, Jerusalem

[3] Cf. D. Pringle, "Les édifices ecclésiastiques du Royaume latin de Jérusalem: Une liste provisoire," *RB* 89 (1982): 92–98.

native Christian communities. Indeed, the Franks seem at times to have actively encouraged the local Christians to build churches. The earliest reference to the rebuilt Armenian Cathedral of St. James, for example, comes only shortly after the visit made to Jerusalem by King Thoros II in ca. 1163. Although the general planning of this church was evidently dictated by the particular requirements of the Armenian liturgy, much of the workmanship, including the capitals and doorways, is Frankish in character; furthermore, the masonry marks visible on the southern narthex suggest that the construction work itself was also organized along Western lines. Western features can also be seen in the Church of St. Mark, rebuilt in the twelfth century as the church of the Syrian Jacobite community.

It was also in the 1160s, during a time of relative friendliness between the kings of Jerusalem, Baldwin III and Amalric, and Emperor Manuel I (Comnenus), that a number of Orthodox churches and monasteries were reconstructed: the Monastery of St. Joachim (today St. George) at Choziba in Wadi Kelt, St. Elias (between Jerusalem and Bethlehem), St. John the Baptist, St. Gerasimus (unidentified) and St. Mary of Kalamon (which is now called St. Gerasimus) in the Jordan Valley, east of Jericho. In Jerusalem the churches of St. Nicholas, St. Thecla, and the Deir al-cAdas (Convent of Lentils, or St. Nicodemus) were also probably rebuilt in the twelfth century. At this time too the paintings and mosaics in the sixth-century church at Bethlehem were renewed with imperial assistance, even though the church was under the authority of a Latin bishop.

The Latin Cathedrals

Most of the churches built in Palestine during the twelfth century were Latin. But whereas the Greek and Latin Churches in Jerusalem today depend on different patriarchs and have separate priesthoods and church buildings, in the twelfth century this distinction was less obvious. In the Kingdom of Jerusalem, church unity was accomplished by appointing Latin bishops to Orthodox sees as they fell vacant, thereby ensuring the authority of Rome over a Church previously dependent on Constantinople. At a lower level, however, Latin and Greek priests, both theoretically dependent on the (Latin) Patriarch of Jerusalem, were free to conduct the worship in their churches according to their own particular rite. Certain changes nevertheless had to be made to the ancient Byzantine ecclesiastical divisions of the country, to take into account new political and geographical realities.[4]

The Church of the Holy Sepulchre (known to Eastern Christians as the Church of the Resurrection) represented not only the patriarchal cathedral of Jerusalem and the principal parish church for Latin and Orthodox Christians in the city, but also the holiest of all the holy places, the site of the death, burial, and resurrection of Christ. Between 1036 and 1048, the rotunda covering the Tomb of Christ had been rebuilt by the Greeks with the addition of a gallery and an eastern apse to serve as a congregational church. During the first half of the twelfth century, the Latins enlarged the building by constructing a new choir and a transept to the east, thereby bringing all the traditional sites associated with the Passion, such as the Prison of Christ, Calvary, Golgotha, and the Place of Annointing, under one roof. To the east of this, on the site of the vast basilica constructed by Constantine I and destroyed by al-Ḥākim, they erected a cloister surrounded by a conventual building for the regular canons who served the church. The cloister also covered an underground chapel of St. Helena, built to commemorate the discovery of the relic of the True Cross.

Below the Patriarch of Jerusalem were the archbishops of Tyre, Caesarea, Nazareth, and Karak in Transjordan. The cathedral church of Karak was converted into a mosque in 1196, and traces of it could still be seen until the mosque was demolished and rebuilt in 1897. At Caesarea the ruins of the cathedral were excavated in 1960–1961. Like the

[4] See B. Hamilton, *The Latin Church in the Crusader States. The Secular Church* (London, 1980), pp. 52–85.

Crusader cathedral, Caesarea: the east end. Note temporary apse built in front of the thirteenth century sanctuary and, in foreground, an antique column-drum reused as reinforcement in one of the nave piers

church at Karak, this was a relatively modest structure, measuring overall some 55 × 22 m. The nave was divided into three aisles that terminated in the east in three semicircular apses. In common with a number of other twelfth-century Crusader churches, the vaulting was supported on rectangular piers and pilasters, with an engaged column on each face; traces of a floor composed of mosaic tesserae and fragments of reused marble are also visible. The eastern end of the building seems to have been rebuilt in the thirteenth century, probably after damage sustained in 1187 or 1220. The new pilasters flanking the central apse are different from the old ones and do not fit precisely onto their bases. While this rebuilding was in progress, a temporary apse seems to have been constructed in front of the sanctuary to allow cathedral services to continue without interruption.

The cathedrals of Nazareth and Tyre, although architecturally similar to the one in Caesarea, have very different proportions. Some idea of the size of the twelfth-century Church of the Annunciation in Nazareth may be gained from that of the present church, built in 1959–1969, which occupies precisely the same ground plan. Overall, this building measures some 70 × 30 m. The cathedral in Tyre had almost identical dimensions, but with the addition of projecting transepts. Little now remains of either building, but the lavishness of the decoration of the former can be detected in some of the surviving sculptural fragments such as the five capitals preserved in the lower church. They date from just before Saladin's conquest (1187) and represent one of the high points of Frankish artistic achievement in the East.

Below the four archbishops were nine suf-

Cathedral Church of St. George, Lydda: the apse, with its elaborate cornice frieze survives incorporated into the Greek parish church built in 1870

decoration of the church was completely reworked.

In Beirut a new cathedral church was built in the first half of the twelfth century. It survives today as the Jami al-Umari. Overall the building measured a modest 37 × 23 m. The style is purely Romanesque, although, in common with other Crusader church buildings, the arches and vaults are all pointed. The central nave is barrel vaulted and the aisles groin vaulted; as at Caesarea, Tyre, and Nazareth, the vaults are supported on rectangular piers and pilasters with engaged columns. At the western end of the church, there was originally a two-storied porch flanked by twin bell towers.

In Hebron the Crusader Cathedral Church of St. Abraham was constructed within the eastern part of the Herodian precinct above the Cave of Machpelah. Some form of church building already existed there by 1120, when the entrance to the cave was accidentally discovered by one of the Augustinian canons, and relics — supposedly those of Abraham, Isaac, and Jacob — were recovered and placed in the church. The Crusaders' building survives today as the Mosque of Abraham.

The cathedral church of the bishop of Ramla and Lydda was the Basilica of St. George at Lydda. A church had existed on the site of the martyr's tomb since the sixth century, and possibly earlier, but when the Crusaders reached Lydda in June 1099 they found it in ruins. The church they built around the middle of the twelfth century to replace the Byzantine structure seems to have conformed to the same overall ground plan, some 50 × 26 m. It was constructed with three aisles and five bays and was groin vaulted throughout. It differed from the other buildings so far described in its having a transept that was the same height as the nave that takes up the second bay, probably with a dome over the crossing. To the south of this church was a smaller one that may have formed part of the original Byzantine episcopal complex; it seems to have been restored in the eleventh century and survived to be converted into a mosque in the fifteenth century. The mosque is still

fragan bishops, not counting those of Jubail and Sinai which lay outside the secular control of the kingdom. We have no archaeological evidence of three of the nine cathedral churches: Sidon, Banias, and Tiberias. The Cathedral of the Holy Cross in Acre was located where the Jazar Pasha Mosque now stands. In Bethlehem little reconstruction was required, because the sixth-century basilica had miraculously escaped destruction by al-Ḥākim. Frankish work can be detected, however, in the cloister and conventual buildings erected on the north side of the church and intended for the canons who served it. The entrances to the Cave of the Nativity were also decorated with finely carved portals and, as has been mentioned, the mosaic and painted

Crusader parish church, Gaza, today the Umariya Mosque, looking west

Crusader parish church, Ramla, today the Great Mosque, looking east

standing but the main church was destroyed by Saladin in 1191, and only the main apse and one arch in the southern nave arcade survive (incorporated into the present Greek church which was built in 1870).

Finally, at Sabastiya the outer walls of the twelfth-century cathedral church form today the precinct wall of the village mosque, the vaulting having long since collapsed. The architectural style of this building is somewhat more advanced than that of any of the other cathedrals described, suggesting a date in the third quarter of the twelfth century. The building was rectangular in plan, some 54 × 26 m, with a projecting central apse, the curved outer face of which was decorated with round pilasters. The central nave had four

bays: two on the west and one on the east appear to have been covered by sexpartite rib vaulting; the remaining bay on the east formed an inscribed transept, as at Lydda, covered by a lantern tower — or more likely a dome. The nave piers that supported the vaulting alternated with free-standing pairs of columns; these originally would have supported the clerestory walls and the rib-vaulted bays of the aisles.

The Latin Parish Churches
The size and distribution of the Latin parish churches constructed by the Crusaders conformed closely with what we know of the size and distribution of the Frankish population itself. In general, Westerners appear to have

been concentrated in the major towns, with only occasional groups settled in the countryside. Some of the parish churches in the larger towns were of a size comparable to that of the cathedrals. At Gaza and Ramla, for example, the twelfth-century churches that survive today as the main mosques of these towns are high buildings with vaulted naves and aisles. In Nablus the central mosque was also built on the site of the main Crusader church, but its reconstruction and enlargement had already disguised its original character before remaining traces, including an elaborately carved portal, were destroyed by an earthquake in 1927.

One form of Crusader colonization was the "new town" (*nova villa*), where, as in the West, a landowner sponsored the establishment of a settlement on his land by offering tenants building plots and agricultural lands on attractive terms. Remains of the churches at two foundations of this kind, *Magna* and *Parva Mahumeria*, established by the canons of the Holy Sepulchre at al-Bira and al-Qubaiba, respectively, in the first four decades of the

twelfth century, have been found to be so strikingly similar as to suggest that the same architect or planning committee was responsible for both. Each was a three-aisled basilica of four bays, about 34 × 20 m in size, with three semicircular eastern apses, the central one enclosed by a rectangular projection. An aisled parish church of comparable proportions survived in a fragmented condition as the village mosque of Yibna (Yavne) until 1948, and others have been recorded or excavated at Beit Nuba, Saffuriya, Tiberias, and Tel Yoqnᶜeam (medieval Qaimun, or Caymont). Village churches, however, were often more modest buildings, with simple boxlike naves covered by groin vaults or a single barrel vault and with a semicircular projecting apse. Such, for instance, are the surviving village mosques in Faḥma, near Jenin, and Sinjil north of Ramallah, and the present Franciscan Church of St. Peter, in Tiberias. Ruined examples include churches at Baitin, Dabburiya, Zirᶜin, and ᶜAmwas.

Another type of church building connected with parish functions was the cemetery chapel. In Jerusalem a chapel belonging to the canons of the Holy Sepulchre, and known, somewhat curiously, as St. Mamilla, existed in the Mamilla cemetery west of the city on a site now occupied by the Customs Department building. South of the city, the Order of St. John also maintained a free burial service for poor pilgrims in Aceldama (the burial place for strangers, bought with the money from Judas' betrayal), where the vaults that enclosed the vast charnel pit beneath their chapel can still be seen.

Monastic Churches and Holy Places
Beside the parochial and diocesan organization of the Crusader kingdom, another important part of the Latin religious establishment was represented by the monastic orders. There had been a few Latin monasteries in Palestine before the Crusades; those existing in the early ninth century are listed in a document known as *Commemoratorium de Casis Dei Vel Monasteriis*. In 1099, however, the only Latin houses in Jerusalem were the Italian

Village mosque, Sinjil (Casale Sancti Egidii): formerly a church built in the twelfth century by the monks of Mt. Tabor, looking east. Note that the apse has been suppressed and the vaulting rebuilt. Crusader features include a pointed-arched door, now a window, in the south wall, and the capitals and bases of the columns flanking the mihrab (at the right)

Vaulted charnel pit in Aceldama, Jerusalem: formerly the foundation of a cemetery-chapel constructed by the Order of St. John in the twelfth century

Benedictine Monastery of St. Mary Latin and its sister foundation for nuns, St. Mary Magdalene (later called St. Mary Parva, or Majora); these had both been rebuilt between ca. 1036 and 1070, and both continued to exist until 1187.

On the Mt. of Olives, the ruined circular Byzantine Church of Christ's Ascension was replaced in the twelfth century by an octagonal building, in the center of which there was an octagonal aedicule decorated with finely carved capitals that survived although it was covered later by a dome. This monastery was fortified and was served by Augustinian canons. In the Valley of Jehoshaphat, a new church was constructed over the Byzantine crypt that enclosed the Tomb of the Virgin Mary, and a large monastic complex was laid out to the west of it for a community of Benedictine monks. Just inside the eastern, or Jehoshaphat, gate of the city stands the Church of St. Anne, one of the best preserved Crusader churches in existence. In the twelfth century, this served a convent of Benedictine nuns. The largest church in Jerusalem was that of St. Mary on Mt. Zion, built by Augustinian canons outside the city wall on the supposed site of the death of the Virgin Mary. All that is left of it today is a southern gallery chapel that would formerly have overlooked the sanctuary of the main church in much the same way that the chapel of Calvary overlooks the choir of the Holy Sepulchre. This chapel was associated with the room in which Christ took the Last Supper with His disciples, where He appeared to them after His crucifixion, and where the Holy Spirit descended on them at the time of Pentecost. To architectural

35

Cloister of the Benedictine Abbey Church of St. Mary
Latin (today the Church of the Redeemer), Jerusalem

St. Mary of Mt. Sion, the Chapel of the Holy Spirit,
Jerusalem, looking northwest

historians it is one of the most controversial Crusader buildings in Jerusalem. Although the style of its early Gothic vaulting finds its nearest parallels in Cyprus and in the West in the early thirteenth century, it is hard to understand how such an architectural feature could have been employed after the Crusaders had lost Jerusalem in 1187. Scholarly opinion is therefore divided between those who think that the chapel was built in more or less its present form before 1187, and those who regard it as more likely that it was built between 1229 and 1244. By this later period, however, the great Church of St. Mary, of which the chapel formed a part, had already been destroyed.

Outside Jerusalem, the Benedictines possessed a large monastery on Mt. Tabor that enclosed the Church of the Transfiguration; and Benedictine nuns with royal patronage constructed a fortified convent around the churches of St. Lazarus and Sts. Mary (often identified at this period with Mary Magdalen and Martha in Bethany). The Cistercians owned a small isolated monastery, called St. John in the Woods, at ᶜEn Karem, known today as the Church of the Visitation; and a second Cistercian house, called Salvation, may be identified with the ruins of a chapel and other buildings at ᶜAllar as-Sufla (Ḥ. Tannūr) near Matta. The Premonstratensian order built the Church of St. Samuel over the tomb of the prophet on Mt. Joy, within sight of the Holy City. They also possessed the monastery of St. George de Lebeyne, the remains of which can still be seen in the Christian village of Deir al-ᶜAsad in Galilee. Almost nothing survives of their monasteries of St. Habakkuk (just east of Ben-Gurion Airport) and St. Joseph of Arimathea (in the village of Rantis). Finally, between ca. 1220 and 1283, the Carmelites, an order of hermits established in the Crusader kingdom itself, built a monastery and a church to St. Mary in Wadi ᶜEn as-Siyah on the western edge of Mt. Carmel, where, according to Carmelite tradition, Elijah and Elisha had likewise once sought solitude with God.

It will by now be apparent that many of the monastic churches, and some of the cathe-

Premonstratensian Abbey Church of St. Samuel (Nebi Samwil): view of the crossing from the south transept (choir suppressed)

Rural monastic house, Allar as-Sufla (Ḥ. Tannur), possibly to be identified with the Cistercian monastery of "Salvation," looking east across the cloister with the north wall of the chapel visible behind

Premonstratensian Abbey Church of St. George of Lebeyne, Deir al-ᶜAsad: west facade seen through an arch of the cloister

drals, built by the Latins in Palestine in the twelfth and thirteenth centuries were associated with holy places referred to in either the Old or the New Testament, such as the "Spring of Emmaus" at Abu Ghosh. Some of the orders mentioned above also appropriated other holy places and constructed churches there. Thus, the monastery on the Mt. of Olives also took responsibility for the Chapel of the Lord's Prayer on the site of the Byzantine church originally built by Empress Helena in the early fourth century. The Monastery of St. Mary in the Valley of Jehoshaphat cared for the cave church of Gethsemane and the nearby Church of the Saviour's Agony, today marked by the Church of All Nations. To the Monastery of St. Mary Latin belonged the chapel marking the site of the martyrdom of St. Stephen outside the north gate of the city. The Abbey of Mt. Zion constructed the Chapel of the Saviour's Condemnation (then House of Caiaphas) between the Church of St. Mary and the present Zion Gate. In the third quarter of the twelfth century, the nuns of Bethany built a new church at Jacob's Well, near Nablus, where Jesus talked to the woman from Samaria.

The Military Orders and Castle Chapels

In addition to the Western monastic communities that established houses in Palestine in the twelfth and thirteenth centuries, the Crusades

Church of the Resurrection, Abu Ghosh (Qaryat al-ʿInab): the "Spring of Emmaus" in the crypt beneath the church, built probably by the Order of St. John in the mid-twelfth century, looking south

also gave rise to the development of an entirely new kind of religious group. This was the military order, made up of knights organized as a religious community. In the early twelfth century, the brothers serving in the hospital just south of the Holy Sepulchre, founded by Benedictines from Amalfi in the eleventh century, extended their charitable activities from assisting the ailing poor to protecting pilgrims on their way to Jerusalem. In 1113, the community was recognized by Pope Paschal II as the Order of St. John of Jerusalem, taking its name from the dedication of the small Orthodox church that had become the hospital's chapel. The Templar Order was founded soon after as a purely military order, with its headquarters in the al-ʿAqsa Mosque in the southern part of the Temple precinct (Ḥarām esh-Sharīf). These two orders were later emulated by others, including the Teutonic Order (a German equivalent of the Hospitallers), the Order of Our Lady of Mt. Joy (an order of leper knights under the patronage of St. Lazarus), and the English Order of St. Thomas of Canterbury.

The castles of the military orders were in effect religious houses, so that a chapel was an essential feature in them. Unfortunately, few castle chapels survive from the Kingdom of Jerusalem itself. In Transjordan the chapels of the secular castles of Karak, Shaubak (Montreal), and al-Wuʿaira (li Vaux Moysi) are all rectangular barrel-vaulted rooms with a semicircular apse at the eastern end. At Shaubak a second, somewhat larger aisled building may represent the church of the civilian settlement that developed around the castle in the twelfth century. Pilgrims' Castle (ʿAtlit), built by the Templars from 1218 onwards, had a large twelve-sided chapel whose internal measurements were 26 m across, its Gothic vaulting supported on a slender central column. The Templars' chapel in their castle at Safed (1240–1266) may have been similar.

Although in the West a number of surviving Templar and Hospitaller chapels have circular or polygonal plans, apparently imitating the rotunda of the Holy Sepulchre (or in the Templars' case the Dome of the Rock, identified as the "Temple of the Lord"), in the Crusader kingdom, their castle chapels were more often rectangular. Such, for example, are the chapels of the Hospitallers in Syria at Crac des Chevaliers (Qalat al-Ḥisn) and Marqab, and the *église donjon* of the Templars at Safita. At Belvoir Castle in Galilee the Hospitaller chapel was also apparently rectangular and placed above the main gate to the inner ward. At Beit Jibrin a large aisled church was constructed in the twelfth century against the outside face of the Hospitaller castle's inner ward, thereby seriously impairing its defensibility. As at Shaubak, it seems quite possible that this church was intended to serve the needs of the community of civilian settlers, which developed there under Hospitaller patronage after 1153. In both cases the church may have been located inside the castle partly for reasons of security; but this may also have been a legal maneuver, designed to protect the parishoners against interference by the bishop, under whose jurisdiction they would otherwise have fallen.

Conclusion

The building programs undertaken by the Crusaders in Palestine in the twelfth and thirteenth centuries provided opportunities for architects, artists, and artisans from both East and West. In the architectural sculpture of twelfth-century Crusader churches, for instance, stylistic borrowings from contemporary Romanesque schools in Provence, Burgundy, Aquitaine, and Tuscany are apparent, while the evidence of inscriptions and masonry marks also reveals the presence of Greeks, Armenians, and native Syrian Arabs among the masons. The south facade of the Church of the Holy Sepulchre in Jerusalem, built around the middle of the twelfth century, represents a perfect blending of Eastern and Western styles and motifs of architectural decoration in a single elevation. However, in spite of the Eastern influences that are often evident in the decoration of twelfth-century Crusader churches — whether in their sculpture, paintings, or mosaics — very few of the buildings themselves would look at all out of place if transported to the south of France. Among the very few architectural features that might serve to distinguish Crusader churches of the twelfth century from contemporary Romanesque churches in the West are the invariable use of pointed arches and vaults and the common employment of a dome on pendentives to roof the intersection of nave and transepts.

It is hard to assess the legacy that the massive building program of the Crusaders may have passed on to later builders in the East or West. Recent research in southern Italy has identified certain groups of architectural sculpture which may very probably have been produced, or at least inspired, by artists fleeing the Holy Land after the disaster of 1187.

One might expect to find closer parallels in Cyprus, which fell to Richard I of England in 1191 and remained in Western hands for three and a half centuries. Unfortunately, since so few thirteenth-century churches survive in the Kingdom of Jerusalem itself, it is hard to draw comparisons with the surviving thirteenth- and fourteenth-century Cypriot examples.

One sphere in which Crusader architecture did have a discernible influence on later building was the architecture of the Ayyubids and early Mamluks in Palestine itself. In some cases, such as the southern facade of the al-ᶜAqsa Mosque in Jerusalem, this may simply be the result of the wholesale reuse of architectural elements derived from disassembled Crusader buildings. It seems very probable, however, that many of the Christian and Muslim masons of Eastern origin who had worked for the Franks in the twelfth or thirteenth century would have continued working for Muslim patrons as Palestine was gradually brought back under their control. In Nablus, the Mosque of al-Khidr, or the Daughters of Jacob, for instance, has often been identified as a Crusader church on account of its rib vaulting, even though it is dated by an inscription to the reign of Sultan Qalawun; and the resemblance of the minaret of the White Mosque in Ramla (built by Sultan Baybars in 1268) to an early Gothic bell tower has led some Western travelers from the seventeenth century onward to think that it too had once been a church.

Such examples serve to illustrate the dangers of viewing Crusader — and in this case Mamluk — architecture from a too narrowly Western perspective. A great deal more painstaking documentation of Christian and Muslim buildings, dating to before, during and after the Crusader occupation, is needed before it will be possible to speak confidently about the respective architectural contributions of East to West or of West to East in the Crusader kingdom.[5]

---

[5] D. Pringle, *The Churches of the Crusader Kingdom of Jerusalem: A Corpus*, Vol. 1 of 3 (Cambridge University Press, in press).

CHURCHES IN THE GALILEE

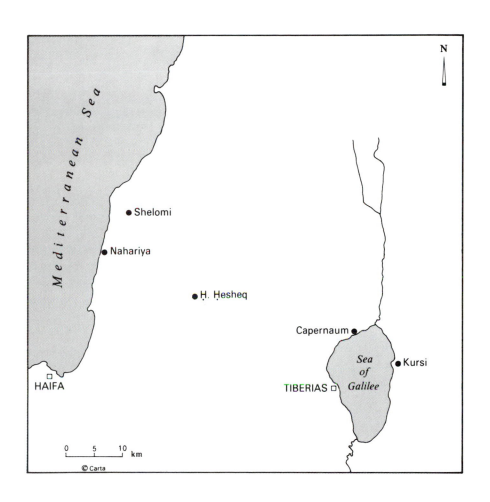

A Byzantine Ecclesiastical Farm at Shelomi

Claudine Dauphin

In the twilight of Byzantine rule in the Levant, not only were churches and monasteries still being erected, but the monasteries themselves were establishing extensive agricultural domains. Such an ecclesiastical estate of a type hitherto known only from literary sources, was uncovered for the first time in archaeological excavations at Shelomi in the Western Galilee.

The Byzantine ruins on a small artificial mound on the northwestern slope of the development town of Shelomi were already known in the early 1960s. Over the years the site was damaged by man and nature, and when it was further endangered by the construction of housing projects nearby, the Israel Department of Antiquites and Museums decided to undertake rescue excavations at the site.[1]

The excavated complex covers an area of 500 sq m and comprises a courtyard (Courty. 1) containing a cistern 5.8 m deep (Cist. 1). To the east of the courtyard is a threshold, 1 m wide, leading to a main room (R. 1). In the northwestern corner of the

courtyard is another chamber (R. 4), perhaps part of a watchtower, whose stratification was observed in an east–west cut. It is associated with a series of arches and channels. To the south of Room no. 1 are two other rooms (R. 2 and R. 3).

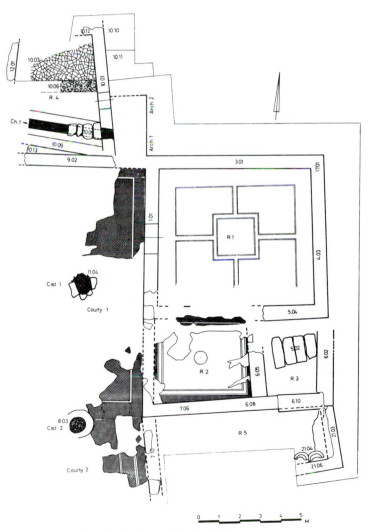

Shelomi: plan of the building

[1] Excavations were carried out in three seasons, in May–June 1976, March–May 1977 and June–July 1978. These were sponsored by the Israel Department of Antiquities and Museums, the Lady Davis Fellowship Trust of The Hebrew University of Jerusalem, the University of Edinburgh in Scotland, the Carnegie Trust for the Universities of Scotland, and the Russell Trust in Scotland, and directed by the author of this article. The Shelomi Local Council provided workers and a bulldozer to cut sondage trenches around the site. Students from the universities of Edinburgh and St. Andrews in Scotland, the Ecole Biblique et Archéologique Française de Jérusalem, the Casa di Santiago in Jerusalem, as well as members and volunteers from the neighboring kibbutzim of Matsuba, Rosh Ha-Niqra, and Beth Ha-Emeq participated in the excavations.

It seems that there were five phases of construction on the site which can be correlated with two archaeological periods. To the first stage, which must be dated to Early Bronze Age I, belong rock-cut basins and cup-marks found in the northern and southern areas of the site. A large quantity of Early Bronze Age I sherds was discovered in the fill made by the Byzantine builders in order to support the structure which they erected on the bedrock.

According to the ceramic evidence, the next four phases (A–D) all belong to the Byzantine period.

Phase A

Courtyard no. 1 was paved with a coarse white mosaic pavement (tesserae 2.3 × 2.9 cm) attached to Cistern no. 1. The lower floor (10.06) of Room no. 4 and its southern wall (10.13) also belong to this stage. Two jambs of a doorway are visible in the eastern section of this area; they are associated with the lower course of stones in the eastern wall of Room no. 4. The floor of the latter, made of large wadi stones, is cut through by a channel (10.09, Channel no. 1) consisting of two courses of stones resting on bedrock. The eastern entrance of the channel is through Arch no. 1. The channel was covered with stone slabs and a capstone was vertically inserted at its western end.

Aligned with Arch no. 1, about 40 cm to the north, remains of another arch were found (Arch no. 2), resting on a rocky ledge. The builders apparently intended to construct a channel parallel to Channel no. 1, but work on it was ceased, perhaps because they realized that the irregular configuration of the rock would not have allowed an easy flow of the water which the channel was intended to drain. In Room no. 1, only two courses of the northern wall remained to an overall height of 90 cm; they were entirely built of dressed stones laid out in headers and stretchers. In the northwestern part of the northern wall, there was a doorway, 85 cm wide, which was subsequently blocked up. Room no. 1 was paved with a plaster floor. Rooms nos. 2 and 3 also had a plaster floor laid on a fill over the

bedrock. These two rooms to the south of Room no. 1, formed a single unit.

On the basis of the discovery of "Late Roman C" sherds with roulette decoration, Phase A may be dated to the fifth–sixth centuries C.E. This date is confirmed by the discovery of a half-follis of Emperor Anastasius (498–518 C.E) found in the bedding of the mosaic of Phase B and above the plaster floor of Phase A in Room no. 1.

Phase B

This stage is merely the continuation of Phase A with a change of plan, and there is no stratigraphic hiatus between the two phases. Their pottery is also identical: ribbed Byzantine sherds, local imitation of "Late Roman Ware" — mainly plates with the imprint of crosses or lambs — and large amphorae. The replanning of the site does not necessarily imply a break in occupation.

In Phase B, Courtyard no. 1 paved with a coarse white mosaic (tesserae 2.5 × 2.5 cm) led to Room no. 1 measuring 6.65 × 7.35 m and paved with a geometric mosaic. The composition is symmetrical: the pattern folds over north to south across a central axis provided by a twisted ribbon. In its western part, the mosaic consists of an intricate network of octagons, triangles, trapezes and rectangles containing grapes, an amphora from which issues a grapevine, and other geometric motifs. In the eastern part, the mosaic solely comprises combinations of circles and ovals. The center of the mosaic is marked by a Hellenic-styled rosette similar to that in the center of the nave of the church in nearby Nahariya. The workmanship is of high quality. The tesserae, the dimensions of which are 0.8 × 1 cm, are of local limestone, and they are black, gray, pink, wine-red, orange, yellow, yellow-ochre, and brown, with a wide range of shades. The background is white.

This mosaic floor is associated with the internally-plastered face of the northern wall, which was built of dressed stones with a packing of stones and earth. The southern unit of Phase A was divided into two rooms (nos. 2 and 3) by a north–south partition wall (6.05).

Shelomi: mosaic floor in Room 1

Shelomi: drawing of mosaic floor in Room 1

Of this wall only two courses of crumbling *nari* stone remain; its overall height is 36–40 cm. It was clearly tagged onto the southern limit of the complex (7.06/6.08).

Room no. 2, the dimensions of which are 4.35–4.65 m (east to west) and 3.8–4 m (north to south), is bounded by walls 7.06/6.08 to the south and by 6.05 to the east. They are both coated internally with a layer of plaster 1 cm thick. There are traces of walls to the north and west. Two stones suggest that a door led from Courtyard no. 1 to Room no. 2. Passage from Room no. 1 to Room no. 2 might have been through a mosaic-paved hall. Only one stone course remains of the walls of Room no. 3; both the walls and floor of that room were plastered. The numerous fragments of storage jars found in parallel rows, in a similar layout to storage jars embedded in the floors of Roman *villae* as at Boscoreale in Italy, may indicate that Room no. 3 was a storeroom.

45

In the northwestern area of the site, a fill of small stones and crumbling *nari* covered floor 10.06 and blocked the entrance. A new floor (10.03) of small wadi pebbles and plaster was laid on the fill in association with the second course of wall 10.01. A new entrance which included a threshold was built over the earlier entrance but about 35 cm further south. The southern edge of Room no. 4 is wall 9.02, built on the remains of wall 10.13. Channel no. 1 projects only 16 cm above floor 10.03.

The white mosaic pavement of Room no. 2, the tesserae of which measure 0.9 × 1 cm, is strewn with alternately pink and gray leaves. In the middle of the mosaic is a medallion with a Greek inscription laid out in gray tesserae; it mentions the year 736 and thus provides a date for Phase B. In the Byzantine Levant, local eras based on the foundation date of major cities in the Hellenistic or Roman periods were frequently used for dating purposes. Shelomi was in the diocese of the Bishop of Tyre and thus one may assume that the date refers to the Era of Tyre which began in 126 B.C.E. Hence the date 736 corresponds to 610 C.E.

Phase B was short-lived. The building was destroyed by a fierce fire as evidenced by the layer of dark ash on the floor containing charred remains of ceiling beams, nails of various sizes, fragments of glass vessels twisted and distorted by the intense heat, chunks of burnt iron, and burnt plaster which was found along the western wall of Room no. 1. The conflagration also left dark strains on the mosaic pavements, particularly in the northwestern and northeastern corners of Room no. 1, along its southern wall, and in the southeastern corner of Room no. 2.

In the layer of ash and in a number of places near the walls of Room no. 1, a great quantity of tesserae was found mixed with chunks of plaster and small pebbles from the bedding of a mosaic pavement. These tesserae, amounting to over 170 kg, represent a far greater quantity than would be needed to complete the missing portions of the mosaic pavement of Room no. 1. This consideration allows for the hypothesis of an upper story paved with a colorful mosaic which fell onto the mosaic pavement of the ground floor in the course of the fire. A number of roof tiles and remnants of windowpanes were discovered, indicating that there were windows. The rooms of the two stories were lit at night with glass vessels suspended from bronze holders with hooks.

The fire which destroyed Phase B may be dated to the Persian Conquest of Palestine between the years 614 and 617 C.E.

Shelomi: bronze lamp chain from which bronze holders and hooks were suspended

Phase C

In this stage, the northern part of the complex of buildings was abandoned, and renewed occupation was concentrated only in the southern zone. A southern wing was constructed contiguous with the southern wall of the original complex. It included a courtyard (Courty. 2) paved with a crude, white mosaic (tesserae 1.5 × 1.4 cm) and containing a cistern 5 m deep (Cistern no. 2), and a trapezoidal room (R. 5), measuring 8 × 2.5 × 8 × 4.52 m, with crudely-made walls of boulders and earth, and a plaster floor. A clear shift in orientation toward the southeast also took place, both in Courtyard no. 2 and in the area to the south of wall 7.06/6.08.

46

The masonry in this phase is cruder, especially in wall 21.03, which is an extension of wall 6.02. The former rests on a layer of packed earth, 20 cm thick, and is built of large stones with a fill of smaller stones and earth. Wall 21.03 turns to the west and is now labeled 21.06. The previous opening (6.10) in wall 6.08 was blocked with stones, protruding in disorderly fashion to the north and south. The joins between walls 21.03 and 6.02 and between 7.10 and 7.06 were made roughly.

The lack of signs of destruction or traces of fire in the southern area is conspicuously in contrast to such evidence in Rooms nos. 1–3. Hence the southern area must postdate the fire which destroyed the rest of the complex. Moreover, a Christo-Palestinian dedicatory inscription at the meeting-point of Courtyards nos. 1 and 2 dates the reoccupation of the site in Phase C to the eighth century C.E. Confirmation of this date was found in twenty-six Late Byzantine Galilean lamps and one Early Arab lamp from a plastered underground chamber, in Room no. 3.

The underground chamber sealed by four stone slabs (5.02) was reused as a burial place. It contained the bones of three adults aged thirty to forty, a sixteen-to eighteen-year-old, children aged sixteen, nine and two years, and fifteen lamps. The northern and southern plaster lining of the chamber had been pierced and *loculi* cut, apparently as part of the transformation of the chamber into a burial place. The southern *loculus* contained the remains of two males, two females, and a four-year-old child, together with five lamps; that to the north included the bones of two adults aged about twenty-five and thirty-five and a child aged about six, as well as the bones of three adults of unknown age and sex, and six lamps. Grave goods in all three burial units included glass vessels, the best preserved of which were found in the central unit: the neck of a green *lacrymatorium* decorated with glass threads, and a green basket-handled perfume bottle. The distribution and state of preservation of the human remains leads one to believe that families were interred over a considerable period of time, earlier remains being displaced to make room for later burials.

Phase D
This phase is merely a technical one, comprising the addition of various features, such as the thickening of walls 21.03 and 21.06 by stacking up two halves of a stone basin (21.04). Crusader and Arab pottery indicate that the area was also inhabited after the Byzantine period.

Conclusion
A clue to the use of the building by monks was provided by the inscription found in Room no. 2: "+ This work was carried out at the time of Father Thomas, the abbot, in the year 736." The site was not a monastery, as there is no cult-place. On the other hand, its remains are both of a domestic nature (door-hinges and parts of door-latches, two latches of boxes and chests) and of agricultural use (a scythe, a sickle, a knife, and a pitchfork).

Moreover, a unique iron rod was found of the type used to measure land for the purpose of taxation. It is 2.59 m long, exactly five Roman cubits. At either end of the rod are triangular prongs for insertion into the earth and between them there is a sliding knob for measuring. Unfortunately the metal was so corroded that even by X-ray it was impossible to distinguish any ruler-like marks on the rod. Instruments of this kind do in fact appear on Roman and Byzantine reliefs, and in the fifth century C.E. the Palestinian monk Epiphanius, who later became Bishop of Salamis on Cyprus, mentions in his *Treatise on Weights and Measures* five Roman cubits as a specifically Levantine and Egyptian unit of measurement. The five-cubit rod found at Shelomi was the first to be discovered.

On this site a large quantity of vegetal remains was collected using the flotation technique applied for the first time to Byzantine material in Israel. All the soil from the site, except for the topsoil, once it had been sifted for small finds, was dumped into a solution of water, paraffin and liquid detergent. Vegetal remains and carbon fragments floated up to the surface in a froth and were scooped out

47

Shelomi: surveyor's rod

using strainers. Wheat, barley, olive kernels and grape pips were found — the staple produce of Roman farms as described in the agricultural treatises of Varro, Columella and Palladius. This evidence supports our interpretation of the site as a farm. The vegetal remains also included a high percentage of weeds, seeds of wild plants, wild grasses and wild legumes — the basic constituents of animal fodder. This indicates that cattle-breeding, the *pastio agrestis* of the Roman texts, was practised on this estate. The fodder was found mixed with the charred beams of the roof which fell onto the mosaic pavement of the hall between Rooms nos. 1 and 2. That burnt layer was, as suggested above, evidence for the existence of an upper story. Thus, the fodder was apparently stored in silos on the upper floor, as was the practice in Roman and Byzantine *villae*.

The mention of an abbot in the Greek inscription of Room no. 2 suggests that this agricultural estate belonged to a monastery. Properties of this kind are known to us from Byzantine sources, and in large Greek monasteries they exist to this day. The Byzantine *praktika*, or cadastral extracts which listed the properties of monasteries, clearly show that the latter derived a great portion of their wealth from rents paid by tenant farmers who lived on extensive agricultural domains in their possession.

The phonetic spelling of the inscription based on local pronunciation indicates that the farmers of this ecclesiastical estate were of Semitic origin and spoke Aramaic and only limited Greek. The cross at the beginning of the inscription signifies that they were Christians.

Located nearby was the Jewish settlement of Betzet mentioned in Talmudic literature as one of the Jewish villages in the Tyre region which were subject to the laws governing tithes and contribution (*ma'aserot* and *trumot*). The existence of a Christian farm alongside a Jewish community might, therefore, indicate that the antagonism between the church and the synagogue, expressed in religious polemical literature, did not always affect daily life.

The Byzantine Church at Nahariya

Claudine Dauphin and Gershon Edelstein

The hill of Givᶜat Katzenelson rises some dozens of meters above the coastal plain in the eastern part of Nahariya. This ancient site was first inhabited in the Persian period and was settled in Roman and Byzantine times, as evidenced by walls, sherds and loose mosaic tesserae; its size, however, is difficult to determine owing to modern building activity. It was one of the many settlements situated between Antioch and Acre-Ptolemais that were connected by a paved road, laid in 56 C.E. during the reign of Emperor Nero. The numerous Byzantine churches discovered along this route indicate that the area was densely populated during that time. They include the excavated churches at Ḥanita, ᶜEvron Ḥosen (Suḥmata), and Shavei-Zion. The church at Nahariya-Givᶜat Katznelson, discovered accidentally in 1964 when foundations were laid for a Youth Center, and excavated in 1972, 1974 and 1976, also falls into this category.[1]

The church at Nahariya is a triapsidal basilica. Measuring 16 × 32 m, it is one of the largest churches in the area. On its south side were traces of rooms belonging to the church complex. The walls of dressed local *kurkar* stone coated with thick plaster rested directly on the rock whereas the pavement lay on a levelled fill containing red earth, pieces of stone, marble, tesserae, pottery and glass as well as plaster from earlier buildings. The pottery from the fill can be dated to the early Byzantine period.

Two rows of six marble columns divided the hall into a nave and two aisles. The capitals of the columns were carved with pomegranates, flowers and leaves. Wooden beams rested on them to support a gallery above each aisle. The timber roof was tiled. The numerous fragments of flat glass windowpanes indicate the existence of windows.

The raised central apse was originally reached by two steps. In the area of the apse a large quantity of marble pieces belonging to the altar were scattered, whilst in the rooms flanking the apse the bases of offertory tables were still *in situ*. An area of about 20 sq m below the main apse was enclosed by a chancel screen. This consisted of twelve chancel screen panels, each either 1.2 m or 1.5 m in length and 60 cm in height, separated by ten square chancel screen posts, some of which were decorated with ivy leaves and had conical tops. The panels were carved on either one or both sides. Two of them bear the motif of a cross flanked by a gazelle. An inscription in Greek on one of the screens indicates that the chancel screen or at least part of it was donated by Leontics, a traveling priest, and his household. Two marble tables, perhaps lecterns, supported by small marble columns, stood inside the chancel. On some of these columns a cross was carved, and the Greek letters IAP appear on three of their capitals. This may be an abbreviation of the donor's name and title, Ἰωάννης ἀρχιεπίσκοπος, "John the Archbishop." This was perhaps John,

[1] The church was excavated in 1972 and 1974 on behalf of the Israel Department of Antiquities and Museums by Gershon Edelstein, assisted by Zahava Demonstein and Fakhri Hason; and in 1976 by Gershon Edelstein and Claudine Dauphin. Yoseph Averbuch has worked since 1972 with admirable patience on the piecing together of the marble fragments. Billefeld Municipality in West Germany has generously supplied the funds for the restoration of the church. For more details, see C. Dauphin, *L'eglise byzantine de Nahariya (Israël)* (Thessaloniki, 1984).

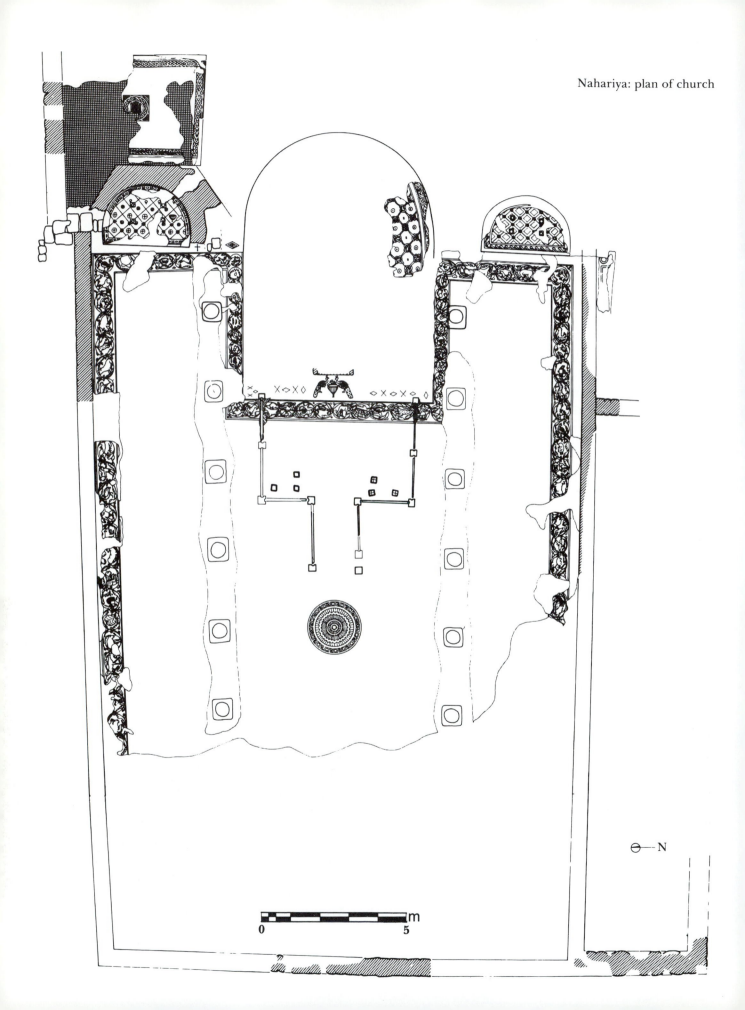

Nahariya: plan of church

Nahariya: carved chancel screen panel

Archbishop of Ptolemais-Acre to which diocese Nahariya belonged, who participated in the Fifth Ecumenical Council of Constantinople in May–June 536 C.E.[2] If our assumption is correct, the church at Nahariya was already in existence in the first third of the sixth century, a dating corroborated by the carved marble capitals which are drilled in a manner characteristic of the reign of Emperor Justinian (527–565 C.E.), by the mosaic pavement, the pottery and the bronze candelabra.

The Mosaics

The most notable feature of this church is a mosaic covering the entire floor. The main field is decorated with a scale pattern in white with a pink and wine-red "heart" for each scale. The central apse and the side rooms are paved with geometric motifs in white, gray, pink and wine-red: rosettes, fleurons and diamonds. In the center of the nave is a large rosette (see Pl. IIa) consisting of white, wine-red, pink and blue-gray stripes, and boxes and swastikas in perspective, treated tridimensionally so that the illusionistic effect is extremely similar to that produced by the Hellenistic mosaics of Antioch.

Below the main apse and in the space enclosed by the chancel, two peacocks are placed symmetrically on either side of a godrooned amphora.

A band about 60 cm wide depicting eighty-seven acanthus scrolls filled with human fig-

ures, mammals and birds, runs along the outer edges of the aisles and the inner edges of the apses over a length of 57 m. Hunters spear lions and cheetahs; a piper sitting on an overturned basket plays on his pipe; a man leads a horse by a rope; a child prods a bird in the next scroll with a stick, with the intention of catching it and putting it in the bird-cage behind him (see Pl. IIb); sheep (see Pl. IIc), a fallow deer, goats and gazelles munch at bunches of grapes; doves fly out of the acanthus whilst cocks, pheasants and francolins are placed at random. Pomegranates, grapes and an apple with a knife beside it exemplify the fruit of the land.

Technically the mosaic is of a high standard for sixth-century Palestine. The tesserae measure 0.8×0.8 cm, with an average of 147 per sq dm. The faces of the human figures, as well as their hands and feet, were executed with smaller tesserae, 0.6×0.5 cm, often cut in the shape of minute triangles, with about 201 tesserae per sq dm. Most tesserae are of local limestone; terracotta was used for yellow, and both translucent and opaque glass for green and blue. The range of colors includes several shades of black, gray, brown, wine-red, pink, yellow, yellow-ochre, red-ochre, green, blue and orange.

Nahariya: detail of mosaic floor — the piper

2   J.D. Mansi, *Sacrorum Conciliorum Nova et Amplissima Collecio* (Graz, 1960), vol. 8, cols. 1073–1081.

The mosaicist appears very classical in his style. Whereas in sixth-century mosaics, as at Madaba in Jordan, the prudish tendency compelled the artist to dress his human figures in the fashion of the time, at Nahariya out of eleven figures, only the bird-catcher is fully dressed. All the others are naked except for a loin-cloth and a triangular kerchief, tied round the neck, their hair being enclosed in a wine-red net; and the piper is completely naked. Together with the child who extracts a thorn from the sole of his left foot — which is a classical theme in sculpture — they all come straight out of a Roman pattern-book.

Although they are depicted like classical *protomai*, their hind parts still in the acanthus leaves, and although they are probably taken from pattern-books, the animals are very lively and in the case of domestic animals well-observed, like the dog curled up on itself to sleep. The artist was not devoid of humor either: a tiger-cub tries desperately to suckle its leaping mother, much too busy growling at a hunter's spear to pay any attention. Most of the figures are represented in motion, an illusion achieved by outlining anatomical features with wine-red tesserae, and by the treatment of light and shade, particularly in the faces.

For the classicizing style and the quality of the workmanship of the mosaics at Nahariya, parallels are to be found not in the mosaics of the region which are predominantly geometric, but in those of the Tyre area: the famous mosaic of the Church of St. Christopher at Qabr Hiram of 575 C.E., which depicts inhabited vine scrolls (its late sixth-century date given by a Greek inscription on the mosaic was originally doubted because of the mosaic's

Nahariya: destruction in northern aisle and apse, from the west

classical treatment), and the mosaics of the Jenah villa.[3]

The Destruction of the Church

The church at Nahariya was destroyed in a great conflagration. The burning wooden roof beams crashed to the floor, together with the bronze candelabra crosses and *chi-rhô* monograms which were suspended from the ceiling: twenty-five of these were discovered on the floor of the nave in six more or less parallel lines revealing their arrangement when they had hung from the roof. The fire must have been very fierce and prolonged, since it cracked even the marble, scattering fragments or reducing them to dust. In many places the fire and the smoke changed the colors of the mosaics and caused black stains. Fragments of glass windows were scattered and fused. The lead spikes that joined the column drums of the southern aisle melted into lumps that were discovered in the debris. In the southern aisle between the first and second columns from the east, several storage jars, jugs and "Late Roman" bowls stood on the floor — an unusual location for such

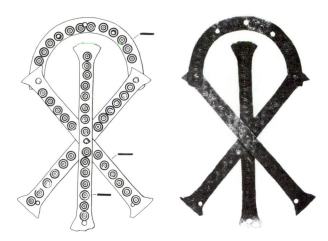

Nahariya: bronze *ch-rho* monogram ornament which hung from the church's ceiling

vessels. It may have been that the population of the settlement fled for protection to the church, bringing with it its supplies of water and food to sustain a siege, as an enemy approached. The church may have been destroyed during the Persian Conquest in 614–617 C.E. A similar fate probably befell the churches at Evron and Shavei-Zion, to the south of Nahariya: they were also destroyed by fire.[4]

---

[3] On the Church of St. Christopher at Qabr Hiram, see E. Renan, *La Mission de Phénicie* (Paris, 1864), pp. 607–626; on mosaic "O" of the Jenah villa which has features in common with Nahariya's acanthus scroll mosaic, see M.H. Chéhab, "Mosaïques du Liban," *Bulletin de Musée de Beyrouth* 14 (1957), p. 64; 15 (1959), Pl. XXX.

[4] On the church at ꜤEvron, see A. Ovadiah, *Corpus of the Byzantine Churches of the Holy Land* (Bonn, 1970), pp. 67–69; on the church at Shavei-Zion, see M.W. Prausnitz, M. Avi-Yonah and D. Barag, *Excavations at Shavei-Zion* (Rome, 1967).

Ḥorvat Ḥesheq: A Church in Upper Galilee

Mordechai Aviam

The site marked on the map as Ḥorvat Ḥesheq/Qaṣr ᶜAsheq (map ref. 1757/2619) comprises a solitary structure located on the spur of a hilly ridge in the Tefen region. It is located approximately 150 m north of Ḥorvat Maḥoz, where the remains of a large settlement dating to the Byzantine and medieval periods were found.

History of Research

The first to observe and mention the structure, although without going into details, was Guérin:

> Higher, on the side of the hill, one may observe the lower courses of a kind of square tower which was built of four blocks and contained within it a cistern and a vaulted magazine. It appeared to me ancient. It was surrounded by evergreens, oaks and terebinths.[1]

The British survey failed to notice Ḥorvat Ḥesheq, devoting most of its efforts to describing Ḥorvat Maḥoz. A renewed investigation of the site was undertaken in the mid-1970s by R. Frankel and the Western Galilee Survey team of the Archaeological Survey of Israel, and for the first time, plans were drawn. Excavations were begun in the summer of 1985[2] and a subsequent season was

held in 1987. The final season was in the summer of 1988.[3]

Description of the Complex

The overall length (west to east) of the building measures 21 m and its width is 16 m. The construction is a combination of ashlars on the facade and part of the interior, and a mixture of mortar and small stones. Today, in the south wall of the structure, two entrances can be observed. The eastern one, measuring 0.7×0.6 m, is constructed of large ashlars. No doubt, this entrance once possessed a stone door since the pivot sockets are still visible in the threshold and lintel, in addition to the bolt socket in the jamb. From the doorway one descends to a small rectangular room measuring 3×2.5 m, with a barrel-vaulted ceiling impressively built of well-dressed ashlars. Directly opposite the entrance is a wall of natural rock which forms the north wall of the room. The floor is missing and only the foundations comprising courses of rubble can be seen today.

The second entrance at the western end of the building led into a well-built water reservoir whose dimensions were $10 \times 3 \times 3$ m. It is constructed from a mixture of stones and mortar. The walls and ceiling are coated with two thick layers of impervious plaster. The undercoat was mixed with sherds dated to the Byzantine period. The reservoir ceiling is built of long stone slabs (average length of 1.3 m) laid above a series of seven stone arches spanning the reservoir walls. Water was drawn

---

[1] M.V. Guérin, *Description de la Palestine, Galilee*, I (Paris, 1880), p. 441.

[2] The excavations were carried out by the writer in preparing his M.A. thesis on the Upper Galilee during the Byzantine period. The research was supervised by Prof. Y. Tsafrir of The Hebrew University of Jerusalem. The excavation was sponsored by the Society for the Protection of Nature. Participating in the excavations were members of the amateur archaeologists' circle of the Har Meron Field School and the Nature Appreciation Circle.

[3] For an extended report, see M. Aviam, "Ḥorvat Ḥesheq — A Unique Church in Upper Galilee: Preliminary Report," in *CAHL*, pp. 351–377.

up through an opening in the ceiling between the second and third arches.

The building abuts a natural terraced rockface (perhaps partly hewn), as seen at the north walls of the vaulted room and the reservoir. Thus, direct access to the upper story of the building was from the north, whereas the south wall stands 4.5 m above ground level.

A small church, with all the characteristic elements, was built as a second floor:

The atrium. This part is located directly above the reservoir and also has an opening for drawing up water. On the east side, two stone columns were discovered *in situ*, and were probably part of the colonnade which encircled the atrium. To the west, three column-bases were discovered which apparently originated from the colonnade.

The narthex. Between the columns and the wall with the two entrances is a narrow corridor, approximately 2 m in width, which apparently served as the building's northern entrance. Here the lintels of all three entrances were found.

The west facade with entrances and lintels. The lintel of the north entrance was found *in situ* on its jambstones. A cross is engraved in its center, with a deep hole in the middle, indicating that at one time a metal cross had been attached there. To the right of the cross were three holes for affixing an object with metal nails; and indeed, in one of the holes were the remains of an iron nail. There were also two holes on its left side. Apparently, the metal Greek letters ΑΩ had been attached on either side of the cross. The lintel of the middle entrance was broken into three pieces. Here, too, was a place in the center for attaching a cross. The southern lintel, also fragmented, was found with an engraved cross and holes on both sides for affixing metal letters. Another entrance leads from the narthex, north of the three entrances, to a long narrow hall connected on the north to the church.

Ḥorvat Ḥesheq: general view of the site

The church. The church is 11 m long × 8.5 m wide; it is divided into a nave and two aisles. The division is effected by two rows of three columns and two pilasters, the latter being located at the beginning and end of each row. *Voussoirs* of the arcades or the columns were also discovered. The columns and arcades supported the galleries above them.

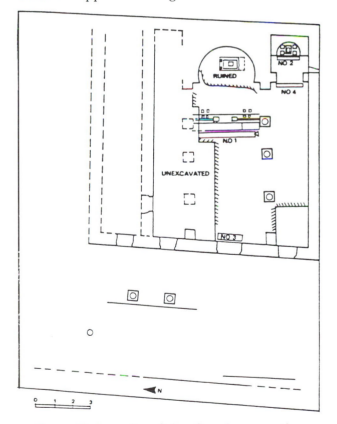

Ḥorvat Ḥesheq: plan of church under excavation

The *bema* and apses. This area was the best preserved element of the church. Even before the excavations began, the eastern facade could be observed rising to a height of 6.5 m above ground level and 3.5 m above the debris inside the church. Both the interior and exterior were constructed of ashlars with a fill of mortar and small stones. The upper segment of the wall of the apses was preserved to the height of one course above the decorated cornice, which in effect marks the division between the main floor and the galleries. To the south of the central apse was a small niche which had been observed by the first surveyors. Because of the obvious symmetry, it is possible to reconstruct a similar small apse to the north, which probably still lies beneath the pile of debris.

The winepress. Alongside the northeast corner of this structure, the remains of a large winepress were exposed. The treading floor measures 5 × 4 m, and was apparently paved with a coarse white mosaic. In the center of the floor is the typical hollow for the screw apparatus used in the pressing of the grapes. In the rock-hewn north wall, a hollow with a radius of 20 cm was noted; it served as the base for an additional pressing-beam. The dimensions of the collecting vat are approximately 3 × 3 m, and it had been blocked by stones from the collapsed church.

The Excavations

In the course of the excavations, five areas were investigated: Area A — the atrium of the church; Area B — the north entrance of the church; Area C — the south aisle, extending to the middle of the nave; Area D — the *bema* and the central apse; Area E — the south apse.

Area A. After excavating a small section of the atrium, we found that it was not paved and was devoid of any mosaic.

Area B. Here the threshold of the north entrance was revealed. Inside, several rows of mosaic tesserae were discovered. Apart from this, the entire area which was excavated,

measuring 2 × 2 m, had been completely destroyed and not even one mosaic panel was found intact. Fragments of banister posts and panels were exposed. The walls are partly plastered and covered with "herringbone pattern" incisions apparently made before the second, thinner top coating of plaster, now missing, was applied.

Area C. This was the largest of the excavated areas (7 × 4.5 m). Here a complete mosaic floor composed of geometric patterns was exposed. On the floor were scattered collapsed architectural elements on top of a layer of earth 10–15 cm thick. Also found in the earth layer above the debris were many terracotta roof tiles. This seems to have been caused by the collapse of the galleries above the two aisles. It now appears that these galleries were paved with a colored mosaic. Four Greek inscriptions were discovered on the floor mosaic of the aisle. The first and largest of them is at the foot of the chancel; the second at the main entrance to the church; the third at the entrance to the south apse; and the fourth at the southern entrance. On the mosaic floor of the nave, several artifacts were discovered — a small reliquary, 30 × 20 cm, and nearby a fragment of sculptured marble, perhaps part of a large flat dish. Also found were a bronze mounting of an overhead lamp, with the glass handles still attached, and a large number of pottery sherds.

Area D. The *bema* is elevated 40 cm above the mosaic floor and has a single dressed-stone step leading up to it. The front of the *bema* is built of dressed ashlars with grooves for the insertion of chancel screen panels and recesses for the chancel screen posts. The screen is made of white marble panels with a wreath decoration whereas the chancel posts are hard limestone. At the back of each chancel screen panel there are four square recesses for inserting the legs of a small table which perhaps had a liturgic function. The two front legs of each table were inserted in the stones of the chancel base while the rear legs stood in the mosaic floor. Only half of the southern table was found, while the northern table was located intact on top of the mosaic floor of the *bema*. The altar was installed above a large rectangular block (0.9 × 0.5 m) made of limestone, which was not placed at the perimeter of the apse, as customary, but within it. In the middle of the block on which the altar is installed, there is a hole, a place for a reliquary (see below). The mosaic floor of the apse was completely missing while the stone itself had sunken somewhat beneath the floor level of the chancel. Discovered in front of the stone was a clay Turkish pipe, which lends support to the assumption that the site was looted in that period. Among the fallen stones lay many *voussoirs* apparently from the dome of the apse.

Area E. Here the entire southern apse was revealed. The floor of this niche is approximately 15 cm higher than that of the south aisle and covered by thin marble panels. At the center of the apse, the four sculptured limestone leg-supports of an altar were discovered. The altar was positioned above a reliquary sunk in the floor. The reliquary measures 35 × 30 cm and has a marble lid with a hole in the middle. Attached to its sides are four bronze clasps with perforations at the edges for latching. On discovery, the clasps were in an open position and the interior of the reliquary was empty. In front of the apse on the mosaic floor, another Greek inscription was exposed. Found also in this area were additional square chancel screen posts and decorated limestone panels. Many roof tiles lay on top of the debris. Preserved in the south wall of the apse is a small aperture, 30 cm high and approximately 10 cm wide.

Architectural Elements

The well-preserved remains at Ḥorvat Ḥesheq permit an almost complete reconstruction of the church. In general the craftsmanship is not of a very high standard but is typical of the rural provincial art of the region. Some of the elements, however, like the banister panels of the galleries and especially the chancel screen panels, are of better quality.

Columns and capitals. The columns of the first floor, three in each row, rose to a height of 3 m, including the capitals, and stood on low bases without pedestals. The only capital found on the first floor is Corinthian sculpted with free-flowing style petals in bas-relief. The middle column had an incision for the affixing of a metal cross. Three column-bases of a smaller size, identical to those of the atrium, were found among the debris of the second floor. The height of the second-floor columns was 2.3 m, including the capitals which are of the flat Corinthian type with only four petals — one in each corner. On two of the three capitals crosses were engraved on all four sides; on one capital, apparently the middle one, crosses were engraved on two opposite sides, whereas the other sides featured floral designs. One face depicted a *fleur de lys*, and the other, a trifolium. During the last season of excavations, additional capitals of this type from the north gallery were observed in the cross-section but left as found.

Found in Area C near the altar were segments of small columns (18 cm in diameter) as well as three corresponding capitals which are also of the flat Corinthian four-petaled type. All the lower column segments bear an engraved cruciform recess for holding a metal cross. In one case, however, a bottom end segment features three incised bands similar to those on the leg-supports of the altar in the south apse. Apparently, the column-bases were inserted into the floor. The number of columns and their dimensions suggest that they belonged to a *ciborium*. The liturgical tables had marble column-like leg-supports, of which four capitals were found; the principal decorative element is the *ovolo* in the center flanked by a simple floral pattern.

Liturgical or offering tables. The liturgical tables were found on either side of the *bema* and attached to the chancel screen. They were made of soft limestone, measured 85 × 24 × 17 cm, and featured sculptured elevated edges. They lack any other decoration. The height of each table is 1 m above the floor of the *bema*. This type of liturgical table in the

Ḥorvat Ḥesheq: limestone liturgy table

chancel area is known from a number of sites in this country.

The *reliquiaria.* Excavations to date have uncovered three reliquaries: in the central apse, in the south apse and a "portable" reliquary discovered in the nave.

The reliquary of the central apse was located within the apse. It is made from worked hard local limestone. Most of the stone was roughly dressed and can be assumed to have been placed beneath the floor level of the apse, so that only the top 15 cm, which had been carefully dressed, protruded above the floor. Two square holes measuring approximately 10 × 10 cm are incised in the north side of the stone, and it may be assumed that another two were located on the south side. The holes were designed to hold the marble leg-supports of the main altar. A shallow recess takes up most of the area of the stone, leaving edges measuring only approximately 15 cm along the narrow sides and 35 cm along the long ones. Around the recess are small perforations made for attaching bronze clasps to fasten the lid. In the middle of the recess, there is a carved square hole measuring 20 × 20 cm, in which the holy object was apparently placed.

The reliquary of the south apse was sunk in the floor. It is 30 cm long, 25 cm wide and 15 cm deep. It was covered with a lid of low-grade yellowish crystalline marble. In the center of the lid is a 5-mm-diameter hole for pouring oil, and small round holes have been bored on all four of its sides with corresponding holes around the top edges of the reliquary. Lead was poured into these holes and pointed bronze pegs were then inserted into the lid to secure it. When the apse was discovered, the clasps of the reliquary were still attached but open. The marble lid was also in place, though broken into two parts, probably in ancient times, and the reliquary was found empty.

The "portable" reliquary box was discovered on top of the mosaic in the center of the nave. It is made of limestone and measures 27 × 17 × 12 cm; it is cracked in a number of places because of fire which changed the color of the stone to gray. There are grooved tracks near the top of the box for sliding in a lid. Near the bottom of the box there is a small bronze spout, 1.2 cm in diameter and 3 cm long. Apparently the lid, which was not found, had a hole into which oil was poured; later the oil was drained through the spout into small

Ḥorvat Ḥesheq: reliquary in the central apse

Ḥorvat Ḥesheq: reliquary's marble lid with bronze pegs
found in southern apse

receptacles held by congregation members. On one side of the reliquary, a carelessly executed cross is engraved within a circle, 6 cm in diamter.

Posts and panels of the gallery banisters. This is a series of medium-hard local limestone panels, measuring 80 × 60 cm and 9 mm in thickness. It is the most impressive discovery from the church's excavation. They were found throughout the debris from the south entrance to the south apse, in the northeast section of the nave and at the north entrance. Since the chancel screen panels are made of marble and a fragment was indeed found *in situ*, it is most probable that the limestone panels were not connected with the chancel screen opposite the *bema*. Their distribution throughout the debris, like that of the square pillars, indicates that these are the banister panels of the galleries. Between each pair of columns which supported the ceiling, there were three square short screen posts, two of which adjoined the round columns and were, therefore, curved on one side. Upright sculptured panels were set between the short posts. It may thus be deduced that in each gallery there were twelve posts and eight decorated panels. On most of the panels there are traces

Ḥorvat Ḥesheq: "portable" reliquary

Ḥorvat Ḥesheq: cross on side of "portable" reliquary

Ḥorvat Ḥesheq: banister pillar and flanking panels

Type 1

Type 2

Type 3

Ḥorvat Ḥesheq: gallery banister panels

of red paint. Six types of panel decoration were recorded based on the arrangement of incised crosses, each of which measures 15 cm, narrow bars in various patterns, floral motifs and animals.

The banister posts. These are small square pillars, 1.1 m in height, made of the same limestone as the panels. Their design is similar to that of regular chancel screen posts found in many churches throughout this region.

The chancel screen posts and panels. As mentioned above a fragment of a marble panel of the chancel screen was discovered *in situ*, fitted into its chiseled groove in the chancel facade. The top of the panel is approximately 5 cm wide and features an engraved cross for inserting a metal counterpart. The other parts of the panel are approximately 3 cm thick. The front side pattern is composed of a circular wreath of three rows of leaves. In the center of the wreath there is a stylized plant-like cross.

The chancel screen posts. These were made of hard limestone and are thicker (23 × 23 cm) than the banister pillars. Their entire front face is decorated and at the top there is

60

Ḥorvat Ḥesheq: engraved marble chancel screen panel

an oval carved knob; just beneath the latter
there is a small 3 × 3 cm cross. Two lead-filled
holes are visible in the post of the north
screen, as well as traces of an iron pivot,
probably belonging to the door providing
access to the *bema*.

The bronze ceiling lamp. A lamp was discovered on the floor of the nave. It has a large
central hook which had been suspended from
a ring in the ceiling; branching from the hook
are three arms, each with a clasp at the end of
a chain. Three glass handles belonging to the
lamp-bowls were found hanging from the
clasps. This lamp type has been found in other
churches in the Galilee.

The Mosaics
The mosaics at Ḥorvat Ḥesheq are reasonably
well preserved in the nave and south side of
the church. In general, they are of simple
design. The size of the tesserae ranges from
10 to 12 mm. In a segment found in the debris
of the collapsed second floor, seventy-five tesserae per sq dm were counted, while there are
ninety-five tesserae per sq dm in the decorated
sections on the floor of the nave. A limited
variety of colors was used, including shades of
white, gray, orange and red. The geometric
patterns are not particularly intricate and are
mainly based on a stylized cross integrated
within other elements. Of interest is the fact
that mixed in the mortar base of the mosaic

Ḥorvat Ḥesheq: bronze ceiling lamp

are many colored stones which are no doubt
chips cast aside by the craftsmen and then
mixed together with the mortar for added
strength. From this it may be deduced that the
craftsmen brought variously colored raw
material to the site and prepared the tesserae
(at least in part) on the spot.

The mosaic of the south aisle. This pavement extends from the opening onto the aisle
in the southeast to the entrance to the south
apse. It is enclosed by a guilloche, each plaited
strand of which comprises four rows of tesserae. The inside row is made of blue-gray
stones, followed by rows of white, orange and
red. The mosaic panel is made up of square
frames and interlaced medallions; inside each
frame there is a diamond pattern, the sides of

Ḥorvat Ḥesheq: mosaic of south aisle

stems and red blossoms. The middle carpet has a design resembling that in the south aisle. The easternmost intercolumniation carpet is set within a frame of four rows of stones: two outer gray rows separated by two red ones. The carpet itself comprises a diamond pattern formed by diagonal lines of gray, red and orange tesserae on either side of a white line. Inside each diamond there is also a small cross. Some crosses are in red, others in gray.

which comprise two rows, one of red and the other of gray stones. In the center of the diamond shapes there are five white stones set in the form of a cross against a red background. The square frames create a sequence of crosses made of red tesserae within a gray frame.

The intercolumniations. There are three intercolumniation carpets, rectangular in shape and measuring 1.5 × 0.5 m each. The westernmost one is framed by a border of two rows of gray-blue tesserae on either side of two rows of red stones. The inner area of the mosaic is dotted with small flowers with gray

Ḥorvat Ḥesheq: mosaic floor of nave

Ḥorvat Ḥesheq: intercolumniation mosaic

The mosaic of the nave. The central pavement has a pattern which is a combination of stylized crosses in red that begin at the points where diamonds touch each other, and a large diamond set in the centre of each cross. The remaining space is filled with a semicircle decoration that creates a floral border. In the center of each semicircle there is a complete circle in red with a small white cross in the middle. The frame is composed of a broad quadriplaited inlay.

The *bema* mosaic. As already noted, the major part of the mosaic of the central apse was severely damaged by intruders in the Turkish period. From the segment that is preserved, we learn that this panel was composed of an outer guilloche in gray, white, orange and red surrounding "Herculean knots" of the same colors. Incorporated into some of the spaces between the "knots" are geometric circle designs and crosses.

The galleries' mosaic. On the basis of the mosaic fragments discovered in the debris from the collapsed second floor, one may assume that the mosaic of the south gallery incorporated the same pattern of crosses as in the south aisle.

Summary

The structure and its function. The church at Ḥorvat Ḥesheq may be regarded as unique in a number of respects. Firstly, it is the best preserved Byzantine church in the northern region of the country. The walls rise to a height of 1 m and more, while the apsidal wall attains a height of over 4.5 m. The mosaic pavements were in the main well preserved, as were nearly all the church's architectural details. We are provided with clear evidence of a church with galleries. Ḥorvat Ḥesheq is the only church known to date in the Galilee, and possibly throughout the Holy Land, that was built in the second story of the building. The technique of building interior and exterior walls of ashlars with a fill of mortar and small stones is little known and less characteristic in the region of Upper Galilee. From the architectural analysis, it would appear that the structure was one complete unit. The ground floor included the vaulted chamber, apparently used for burial, and the water reservoir, which were constructed for no other reason than to support the church built above. The

Ḥorvat Ḥesheq: mosaic floor of central apse

burial chamber and the water reservoir created an oblong building in order to bear the mass of the superstructure. Since no remains of a staircase were found on the west side of the church where the difference in elevation is approximately 3 m, it would appear that the entrance to the church was from the north. Here, there is a chamber that extends along the entire length of the building and provides access both to the atrium and the narthex. The second chamber, located between the vestibule and the church proper, apparently served as a staircase leading up to the galleries, since there are no signs of any staircase inside the church.

In our opinion, the church at Ḥorvat Ḥesheq was built as a family memorial and was in some way connected with the vaulted burial chamber beneath the center apse. Perhaps even before the construction of the church, there had been a tomb or sarcophagus in the vicinity. The well-dressed natural rock of the north wall of the burial chamber supports such a hypothesis. One gains the impression that the reliquary in the central apse was roughly fashioned to create the impression that it was part of the natural rock (or perhaps was even hewn out of the wall of the vaulted chamber).

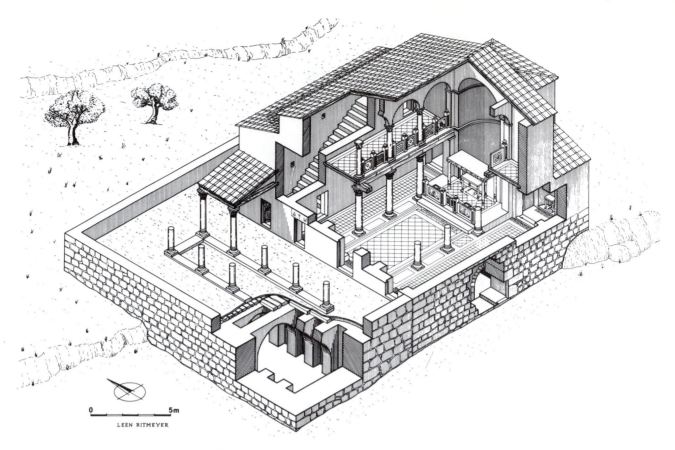

Ḥorvat Ḥesheq: reconstruction of church

In four Greek inscriptions (deciphered and discussed by L. Di Segni; see below) discovered in the church, the names of Demetrius, the deacon, and his son Georgius are mentioned. The main inscription, which is also the largest, is connected with the dedication of the church to St. George (Georgius). It is located exactly above the hewn rock of the vaulted chamber and perhaps suggests that the person buried there was the reason for building the church.

The dedication of the church to St. George may have stemmed from a local tradition connecting the saint (or his relics) to this vicinity, although to date, no other churches dedicated to St. George have been discovered in the region. Nevertheless, during the Crusader period, there was a fortified monastery in the village of Baeinah named St. George de Lebeyne. The remains of this monastery are today located in the Arab village of Deir el-ᶜAsad and nearby is a Muslim holy site named el-Khader. The practice of changing the name of a Christian holy site from St. George to el-

Khader is known elsewhere in this country. Another possible explanation may be that Demetrius, the deacon, having named his son Georgius after the saint, decided to build a family church above the tomb (of his father Somas?) in honor of St. George. At the dedication ceremony, a sacred object related to St. George was placed inside the large reliquary of the middle apse. The inscriptions provides us with the lineage of Demetrius, the deacon, who built this church.

The name Demetrius was common throughout the regions under Seleucid rule, and Somas is probably of Semitic origin.

Two saints were venerated in the church. There can be no doubt that the church was dedicated first and foremost to St. George. Inscription no. 4, however, also mentions Sergius, a saint whose center of veneration was far from the Galilee. Procopius mentions a church dedicated to him at Acre.

Inscription no. 3 informs us of the date of the establishment of the church: the month of April in the year 582 falling within the twelfth

64

indiction. This date, as also indicated by the finds, corresponds to 519 C.E. according to the Pompeian era (64–63 B.C.). The Pompeian era was not adopted by the nearby cities of Acre and Tyre; it would seem, therefore, that Ḥorvat Ḥesheq was not included in one of these territories. The era adopted would be that of Scythopolis (Beth-shean) which was the provincial capital of *Palaestina Secunda*. Apparently Sepphoris, the regional capital, followed the provincial capital. This proposal explains the chronology; on the other hand, however, it necessitates the reclarification of the borders and territories of Upper Galilee. These are shown on the schematic map below together with the division of ethnic and religious elements: Jews in the east, and Christians in the west.

From the excavations of numerous churches in the Galilee region, we learn that nearly all were destroyed within the short period of time between the Persian invasion in 614 C.E. and the Arab conquest around 637. It may, therefore, be correct to assume that the greatest damage inflicted on the Christian villages occurred during the Persian invasion. This was also evident from the results of the archaeological survey of Western Upper Galilee where material dating from the Early Arab period was meager. From the remains at Ḥorvat Ḥesheq, it appears that the church was abandoned in an orderly fashion. The lid of the reliquary of the southern apse was found in place with the fastening clasps in an open position, but the reliquary itself was empty. It does not seem feasible that looters, after damaging the holy object, would have taken the time to return the lid to its proper place. Furthermore, the limited finds at the site

Territories of Upper Galilee showing division of ethnic and religious elements

show that it was vacated in an orderly manner. The thin layer of earth covering the mosaic floor beneath the debris of the collapsed second floor bears witness that the church lay deserted for a short period. Later on, damage was inflicted especially on those panels with human or animal depictions. The ceiling beams were then set on fire, which ultimately caused their collapse. It seems that during the Ottoman period, the church ruins, visible on the surface, caught the attention of treasure hunters who began to dig in the vicinity of the apse, damaging the mosaic.

The Greek Inscriptions at Ḥorvat Ḥesheq

Leah Di Segni

Five Greek inscriptions were found inset in the mosaic floor of of the church.[1] All mention the names of two donors, father and son, who had "erected the holy building" and "completed the whole work." It is thus apparent that the laying of the mosaics was achieved as part of the construction work and that the five inscriptions were dictated at the same time. All are traced with black tesserae and are set into rectangular frames made of tesserae of the same color, except for Inscription no. 5 which is unframed. A sixth inscription, worded in Latin, was found engraved on a miniature altar of the Roman period found in secondary use in the church; it is not discussed here.

Inscription no. 1. This inscription is set into a frame 2.8 m long and 0.4 m wide, in front of the *bema*, facing east. The average height of the letters is 8 cm. The text began and ended with a cross, but the initial cross has disappeared.

It reads as follows:

Ḥorvat Ḥesheq: inscription no. 1

Ḥorvat Ḥesheq: drawing of inscription no. 1

+Κ(ύρι)ε ὁ Θ(εὸ)ς τοῦ ἁγίου καὶ ἐνδόξου μάρτυρος Γεωργίου μνήσθητι εἰς ἀγαθὸν τοῦ δούλου σοῦ Δημητρίου διακ(όνου) τοῦ κτίσαντος τῶν ἅγιον οἶκον τοῦτον καὶ Γεωργίου υἱοῦ καὶ παν (τὸς) τοῦ οἶκου αὐτῶν. +

O Lord God of the holy and glorious martyr Georgius, remember for good Thy servant Demetrius the deacon who built this holy building, and Georgius (his) son and all their household.

The martyr to whom the church was dedi-

[1] For a full discussion on the inscriptions, see L. Di Segni, "Ḥorvath Ḥesheq: The Inscriptions," *CAHL*, pp. 379–390.

cated is Georgius or St. George, the soldier martyr. He was much venerated in Palestine and Arabia, as well as in Egypt and throughout the Near East; by the beginning of the sixth century his cult had reached Constantinople and even far-off Gallia. It is hard to say whether there were any relics of the saint buried in the church — in the vaulted tomb or in the *reliquiaria*. St. George was, however, chosen as a patron by Demetrius who also named his son after the martyr.

Demetrius was a rare name in Byzantine times: this and other Seleucid names (Antiochus, Seleucus) had enjoyed limited popularity in the Roman period and, it seems, only in the areas that had been under Seleucid rule.

Demetrius was a deacon and probably as such he was responsible for the custody of this church, since no priest is mentioned in the inscriptions discovered until now; being rather isolated, the building may not have had a resident priest of its own.

Inscription no. 2. This inscription is located in the southern apse, in front of the *reliquiarium* (see above). It is set in a rectangular frame 1.2 m long and 35 cm wide; the average height of the letters is 6 cm.

The text reads as follows:

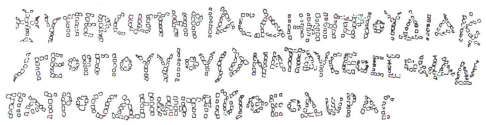

Ḥorvat Ḥesheq: drawing of inscription no. 2

Ḥorvat Ḥesheq: inscription no. 2

67

+'Υπὲρ σωτηρίας Δημητρίου διακ(όνου) (καὶ) Γεωργίου υἱοῦ (καὶ) ἀναπαύσεος Σόμαδ(ος) πατρὸς (καὶ) Δημητρίου (καὶ) Θεοδώρας τ(έκν)ων.

For the salvation of Demetrius the deacon and of Georgius (his) son, and for the rest of Somas (his) father and of Demetrius and Theodora (his) children.

The name Somas is uncommon; it may be Semitic, not necessarily related to the Latin (or Latinized?) Summus. It is mentioned in a church dedicatory inscription said to come from Kh. ͨAlya, less than 10 km north of Ḥorvat Ḥesheq, which implores rest for Count Somas. It is most unlikely, though not impossible, that the references are to the same person, but the two may have been relatives, both belonging to a local family of some standing and wealth.

Demetrius and Theodora were deceased children of the donor.

Inscription no. 3. This inscription is located in the central nave, facing east. It is set in a rectangular frame 1.1 m long and 40 cm wide; the average height of the letters is 6 cm.

The text reads as follows:

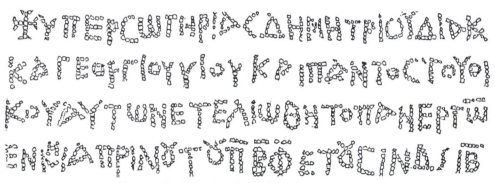

Ḥorvat Ḥesheq: drawing of inscription no. 3

Ḥorvat Ḥesheq: inscription no. 3

68

+ Ὑπὲρ σωτηρίας Δημητρίου διακ(όνου) κα(ὶ)
Γεωργίου υἱοῦ καὶ παντὸς τοῦ οἴκου αὐτῶν
ἐτελ(ε)ιώθη τὸ πᾶν ἔργω(ν) ἐν μη(νὶ) Ἀπριλίου
τοῦ πβφ' ἔτους ἰνδ(ικτιῶνος) ιβ'

For the salvation of Demetrius the deacon and of Georgius (his) son and of all their household, the whole work was completed in the month of April of the year 582, indiction 12.

This inscription provides us with the date of completion of the building, given by month, year and indiction. What remains to be established is the era which was used. Ḥorvat Ḥesheq is located on the border between the provinces of *Phoenicia Prima* and *Palaestina Secunda*, very near to the territories of Tyre and Ptolemais (Acre). In Phoenicia, we would expect adherence to the era of Tyre (126 B.C.E.), which was the one commonly employed in northwestern Galilean inscriptions, or that of Ptolemais (49 B.C.E.), found in inscriptions along the seacoast. In *Palaestina Secunda*, however, the era used was that of Scythopolis (64 B.C.E.). The date, reckoned by the era of Tyre, would fall in 456/457 C.E. which is too early and does not fit the datum of the indiction. The use of the era of Ptolemais gives a date of 535 C.E. in the twelfth indiction, which is possible but unlikely in view of the distance of the site from the city of Acre-Ptolemais. On the other hand, on the basis of the era of *Palaestina Secunda*, one arrives at April 519 C.E. in the twelfth indiction. Ḥorvat Ḥesheq is located inland in central Galilee; thus it is very probable that its region was included in the diocese of Sepphoris in *Palaestina Secunda*.

Inscription no. 4. This inscription is located at the entrance of the southern apse. It is bordered by a frame 1.4 m long and 25 cm wide; the average height of the letters is 6 cm.

The text reads as follows:

Ḥorvat Ḥesheq: drawing of inscription no. 4

Ḥorvat Ḥesheq: inscription no. 4

Κ(ύρι)ε ὁ Θ(εὸ)ς τοῦ ἁγίου Σεργίου ἐλέησον τοῦ δούλου σοῦ Δημήτρι(ο)ν δ(ιάκονον) (καὶ) Γεόργι(ο)ν υἱὸν καὶ παντὸς τοῦ οἴκου αὐτῶ(ν).

O Lord God of Saint Sergius, have pity of Thy servant Demetrius the deacon and Georgius (his) son and of all their household.

A different saint is mentioned here: though the church itself was dedicated in all probability to the martyr Georgius, the southern apse was consecrated to the cult of St. Sergius, and the *reliquiarium* placed here must have contained his relics. St. Sergius' cult had its center at Resapha-Sergioupolis in the Syrian desert and was very popular throughout the Near East.

Inscription no. 5. The inscription is set in the mosaic floor near the southern entrance to the church. Its measures 80 × 32 cm, and is unframed. The height of the letters is 7–8 cm.

The text opens and closes with crosses, and reads as follows:

Ḥorvat Ḥesheq: drawing of inscription no. 5

’Αγαπᾶ Κ(ύριο)ς τὰς πύλας Σιὼν υἱὼν ὑπὲ(ρ) πάντα τὰ σκενό(μ) ατα' Ιαλώβ +

The Lord loves the gates of Sion more than all the dwelling-places of Jacob.

This is an extract from Psalm 87:2, uncommon in inscriptions. The only two cases known to me in Palestine and its vicinity are from Transjordan: in the entrance of the eighth-century church on the acropolis at Maʿin, and in the church of Bishop Sergius at Um el-Rasâs dated to 587 C.E.

The Church of the House of St. Peter at Capernaum

Virgilio Corbo, O.F.M.

After an interval of more than forty years, excavations at Capernaum were resumed in April 1968.[1] In 1921, Father Gaudence Orfali, O.F.M., had discovered an octagonal structure of Byzantine date, to the south of the synagogue; he cleared all but its eastern part, an omission which prevented him from identifying the nature of the building.[2] With only an incomplete plan before him, Orfali, unable to appreciate what he had found, was forced to contrive the theory of a *kolymbethra*, "pool," to explain it.[3] Subsequent to recent excavations, the structure can now be identified as a church marking the site of the House of St. Peter.

Renewed work in the octagonal building commenced in 1968 with the removal of the surviving mosaics for restoration and installation in new beds. This enabled not only the excavation of the entire building but the extension of investigation into the levels beneath. Houses from the Roman and even Hellenistic periods were discovered — among them a *domus ecclesia*, "church house," of the first century C.E. To facilitate comprehension of these discoveries — one of the highlights of Christian archaeology in Israel — we shall trace the sequence of Christian shrines at this site, from the first century *domus ecclesia*, through its remodeling in the fourth century C.E., to the erection of the final octagonal church over it.

The *Domus Ecclesia* of the First Century C.E. The Synoptic Gospels often mention the House of Simon-Peter at Capernaum, where Jesus often stayed during his public career. After the resurrection, the Jewish-Christian community at Capernaum began using the house as a meeting place. This, then, became the *domus ecclesia* or, as the Jewish-Christian community came to call it, the *beit-knesset* (Hebrew for "synagogue"). This Christian meetinghouse, within the more spacious House of Simon-Peter, was brought to light during our first and second seasons of excavation (April–June and September–November 1968).

The *domus ecclesia* is situated within the main courtyard of the house, near the entrance from the main street of the town. Prior to its transformation into a place of worship, the house had two rooms; when the wall separating them was removed, a large, square room was obtained, measuring ca. 7 sq m. The outer face of the western wall of the building is preserved for its full length of 8.35 m and its remains reach a height of 0.4–1 m above the pavement of the courtyard. The average thickness of the walls is ca. 0.6 m. Doorways in the original two rooms opened onto both the northern and the southern parts of the courtyard. When the house was modified for worship, its rough basalt walls were plastered over, and the smooth surfaces were painted with Jewish-Christian symbols. The original floors, which were of basalt pebbles, were then also coated with plaster, and large fragments of the floor in the northeast have been found *in situ*. Three successive layers of plas-

[1] Cf. the preliminary report in V. Corbo, *The House of St. Peter at Capharnaum* (Jerusalem, 1969, repr. 1972); and the final report in V. Corbo, *Cafarnao* I: *Gli edifici della citta* (Jerusalem, 1975), pp. 25–111. The excavations were directed by Fathers Corbo and Loffreda on behalf of the Studium Biblicum Franciscanum, Jerusalem.

[2] Cf. G. Orfali, *Capharnaum et ses ruines* (Paris, 1922), pp. 103–109, and Pls. I and II.

[3] Ibid., p. 107.

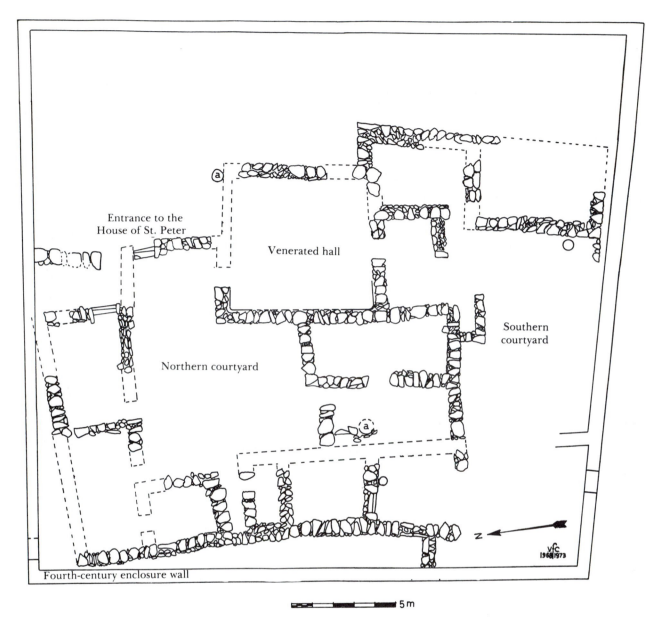

Capernaum: domus ecclesia of the first century C.E.

ter are evident, between which fragments of Herodian lamps were found. During our excavations, thousands of decorated fragments from the plastered walls were collected, including over a hundred bearing religious graffiti written in Greek, Latin, Aramaic and Syriac (Estrangelo). Both the floors[4] and the

graffitti show that already in the first century C.E. the site was revered in association with Jesus' sojourn there.

The Rebuilt *Domus Ecclesia* of the Fourth Century C.E.
The most recent seasons of excavation (1983–1984) at the site have revealed the entire extent of the *insula*, or quarter, of which Simon-Peter's house was part. This *insula* lay between the lake and the synagogue and was

[4] These plastered floors resemble those in the *konistra* or orchestra of the Herodian theater at Caesarea Maritima, or the more modest floors in the Herodian fortress at Machairus; see *LA* 31 (1981): 257–286.

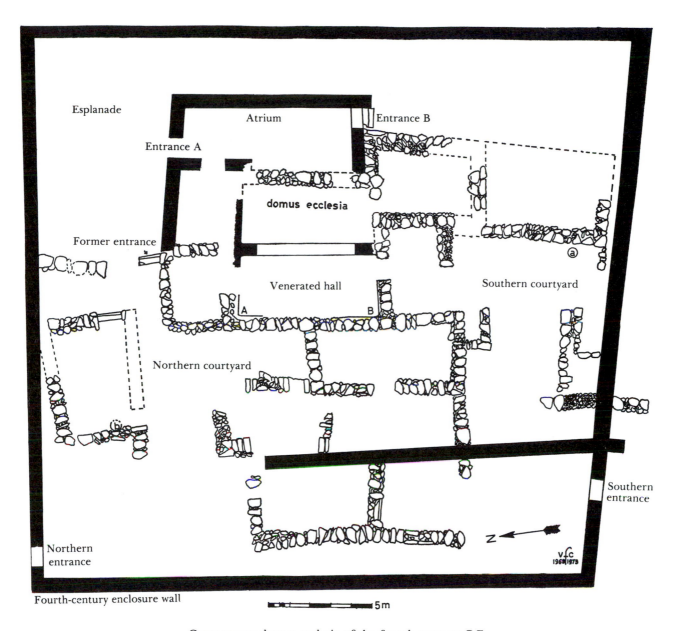

Esplanade

Atrium

Entrance B

Entrance A

domus ecclesia

Former entrance

Venerated hall

Southern courtyard

Northern courtyard

Southern entrance

Northern entrance

Fourth-century enclosure wall

5m

Capernaum: domus ecclesia of the fourth century C.E.

transformed radically during the fourth-century renovations at the shrine. The testimony of Epiphanius (*Adversus Haereses* 30, 11), referring to the Comes Joseph of Tiberias, a friend of the Emperor Constantine, facilitates the understanding of how the building was transformed into an entirely walled-in enclosure, within a city quarter. The process involved the following alterations: (1) the house was isolated within a precinct, protected by an outer wall; (2) a new street (*decumanus*) was

created north of the precinct; (3) the original entrance on the east, from the esplanade of the main street, was eliminated, and two new entrances were introduced on the north and south; and (4) an atrium was added on the eastern side of the house, with a sacristy on the north. At the same time a new roof was erected, supported by an intermediate arch, and a polychrome floor was installed.

Although the venerated site was remodeled, the rooms of St. Peter's house around

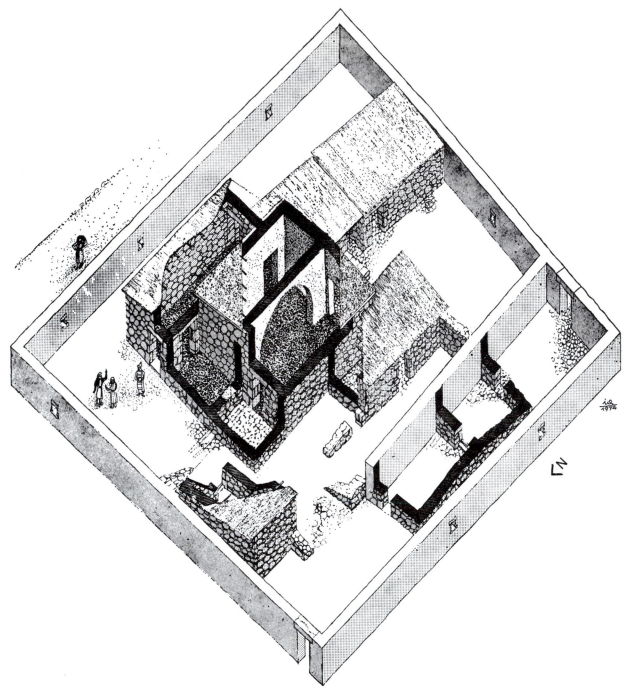

Capernaum: isometric reconstruction of the fourth century C.E. domus ecclesia

the *domus ecclesia* remained intact, and Peter's descendants continued to dwell there. The esplanade overlooking the main street, as noted, had disappeared almost entirely in the remodelling process.

The Octagonal Church Erected in the Fifth Century C.E. above the *Domus Ecclesia*

In the fourth century C.E., the Gentile clergy — imbued with a Hellenistic-Roman background — began to prevail over the Jewish-Christian elements within the Church, resulting, *inter alia*, in basic changes in the architecture of the places holy to Christianity. The splendid buildings erected by Constantine the Great at the Holy Sepulchre, at Bethlehem and on the Mt. of Olives — all based on Western architectural forms — marked the

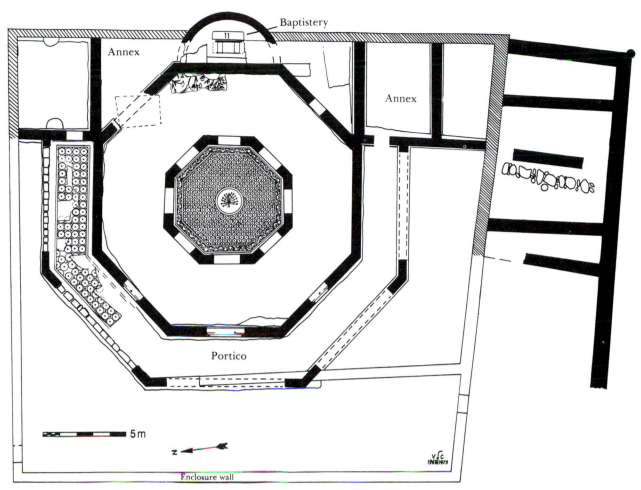

Capernaum: octagonal church erected above the domus ecclesia in the fifth century C.E.

beginning of a new fashion in sacred Christian architecture. This is reflected, too, at Capernaum, where the erstwhile meetinghouse was demolished to make way for a new, more impressive structure — the first church of octagonal plan to be built in the Holy Land. This new building, as uncovered in our excavations, is dated by its finds to the first half of the fifth century C.E. Concentric in plan, it spreads out from a central octagon (maximum diameter: 7.9 m) to a larger octagon (maximum diameter: 16.53 m), in turn surrounded on five sides by a portico which gave access to both the church as well as to several annexes on the east. In its original phase, the plan did not include an apse, which was added later along with a baptismal font. The flanking corner annexes were interconnected by a narrow passageway, and also had openings leading directly to the greater octagon.

Several clear guiding principles are evident in the plan of this concentric building. Although the central octagon is set exactly over the walls of the erstwhile house traditionally associated with Simon-Peter, the external dimensions of the new church were determined by the lay of the outer wall of the fourth-century enclosure. Only after the octagonal building was completed were the apse and baptistery added, on the east, thus blocking direct access between the two annexes (10 and 12), and incorporating a part of the enclosed wall in the apse itself. At the center of the octagonal church there were small arches resting upon white stone pillars, and the entire structure was roofed over with clay tiles — fragments of which were found in the earlier excavations. The three main doorways on the west were also of white stone, and their massive thresholds were found in situ; how-

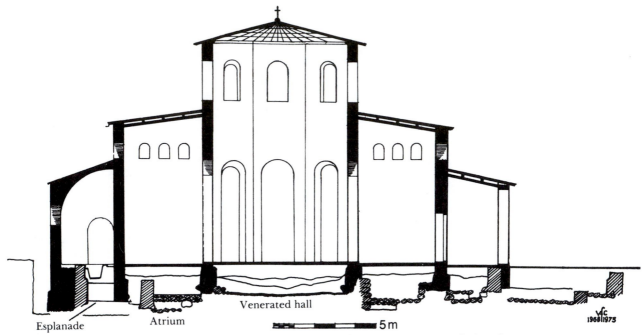

Esplanade   Atrium   Venerated hall

5 m

Capernaum: reconstruction of the fifth-century octagonal church

ever, the walls of the building were most probably built of local basalt stone.

The entire church was paved with mosaics. Those in the portico, extensively preserved on the north, form a carpet of rosettes or roundels. Those in the large octagon are of nilotic character, but only sparse fragments remain. The mosaics in the central octagon are better preserved; at the center, within a medallion frame, is a large peacock whose tail is extended. Surrounding the medallion is an overall diaper imbrication, each scale containing a small flower.

The baptistery, within the apse, has flanking steps leading down into the small font. This form of baptistery indicates that baptism was administered by immersion at Capernaum in the fifth century C.E.

Sometime after the Arab Conquest, during the ninth century C.E., Capernaum was abandoned, and decayed under a heap of ruins only to be rediscovered over a millennium later.

The Early Christian Monastery at Kursi

Vassilios Tzaferis

In 1970, during the construction of a new road on the Sea of Galilee's eastern shore, ancient remains were unearthed approximately 300 m to the east of Tell e-Kursi. During the three excavation seasons that ensued (between the years 1970–1973),[1] the ruins of a large monastery and an impressive early Christian basilica were uncovered.

Three main settlement periods were identified. The earliest, from the late fifth to the early sixth century C.E., marked the foundation of the monastery and basilica. During the second period, which continued from 585 C.E. until the Persian invasion in 614 C.E., the basilica underwent several alterations, probably due to changing liturgical customs. The third and final period, which lasted until the late seventh or early eighth century C.E., was marked by the destruction wreaked by the Persian invasion. Many of the buildings were severely damaged, but the site was not completely destroyed. Although the place continued to be populated, and living standards even improved significantly, the church did not regain its monumental character and the complex was greatly reduced in size. The construction of new buildings in the monastery's living quarters was less refined. During the late seventh or early eighth century C.E., the site was destroyed — possibly by an earthquake — and abandoned.

The Monastery

The monastery complex (see Pl. III), measuring 140 × 120 m, was enclosed by well-preserved plastered walls. Random excavation

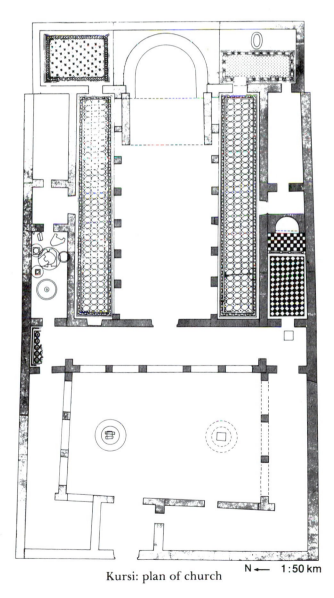

Kursi: plan of church

N ←— 1:50 km

[1] The excavations were carried out under the direction of the author on behalf of the Israel Department of Antiquities and Museums. For further details, see the final report by V. Tzaferis, *The Excavations of Kursi-Gergesa. ʿAtiqot* (English Series) 16 (Jerusalem, 1984).

Kursi: general view of church, looking east

Kursi: reconstructed apse and southern aisle

probes indicated that the living quarters were constructed around the basilica. During the earliest period, there were entrances on all four sides of the monastery compound. However, in the final stage of use, only the main western entrance, overlooking the Sea of Galilee, was employed. An 8-m-wide street led from that entrance to an open courtyard in front of the church.

The basilica. Like other large, important early Christian churches, the spacious 1,125 sq-m basilica consisted of a number of elements: a large basilican prayer hall, *pastophoria* flanking the apse, a narthex, an atrium and two lateral wings containing auxiliary rooms, chapels and a crypt.

The rectangular, monumental church compound, measuring 45 × 25 m, is comparable to some of the most important early Christian churches excavated to date in the Holy Land.

The porticoes of the atrium, the prayer hall and the chapels in the lateral wings were all paved with brightly colored mosaics (see Pl. IIIb). These contained geometrical patterns and designs of flowers, fruits, plants, birds and fish. The best-preserved mosaics are in the two aisles; they are decorated with various motifs encompassed within rectangular medallions.

Most of the animal representations were systematically destroyed, leaving gaping holes in the mosaics. The few that escaped defacement had been covered by fallen columns. Although the identity of the mosaics' destroyers is unknown, the defacement may have been connected with the iconoclastic movement in the early eighth century C.E., following the edict of the Muslim caliph, Yazid II.

The Site's Significance
The site's particular importance stems from its possible association with Jesus. The gospels (Matthew 8:28–34; Mark 5:1–20 and Luke 8:26–39) and other ancient sources relate that Jesus sailed from Capernaum to some point on the other side of the Lake of Galilee. Three

different names are given for the region in which the events took place: "the land of Gadarenes," "the land of Gerasenes" and "the land of Gergesenes." "The land of Gadarenes" and "the land of Gerasenes" refer to places located at a considerable distance from the Sea of Galilee: Gadara in the northeast and Gerasa in Transjordan. "The land of the Gergesenes" is the most likely identification for the spot in question.

The term "Gergese" raises a number of questions. Was this a district in the region of the Sea of Galilee, and if so, where was its exact location? Apparently, there was a place of this name on the eastern shore, which was known locally as "Kursi." This word, which appears several times in talmudic sources, was probably a local Semitic version of "Gergesa." The same spot may also have been mentioned in the *Sabae Vita* of Cyril of Scythopolis (Bethshean) as "Chorsia," in his description of St. Sabas' tour to holy places around the Sea of Galilee. "Gergesa," "Kursi," and "Chorsia" appear to be one and the same.

Kursi can be pinpointed: it is situated on the shore of the Sea of Galilee, in the Wadi Samekh delta, not 200 m from the excavated church and monastery. The topographical features of Wadi e-Kursi, coupled with the archaeological finds, point to a correspondence with the site mentioned in the Gospel story.

The early Christians by no means ignored the topographical features: they built their monastery at the foot of a steep hill, like the one described in the epistles in connection with the Miracle of the Swine. The remains of a tower, enclosing a natural pillar of rock and concurring with the church and monastery in period, were uncovered midway up the steep incline. A small chapel behind the pillar was partly built and partly hewn out of the rock. The chapel was paved with mosaics.

There can be no doubt that the early Christians intended that this structure, together with the tower and the pillar of rock, be a landmark indicating where the Miracle of the Swine had taken place. Noting the topographical similarity between the site and that in the gospel account, the fifth- and sixth-century Christians venerated it as the holy site where Jesus had performed the Miracle of the Swine, regardless of whether it was, in actual fact, the same place.

CHURCHES IN SAMARIA
AND ON
THE MEDITERRANEAN COAST

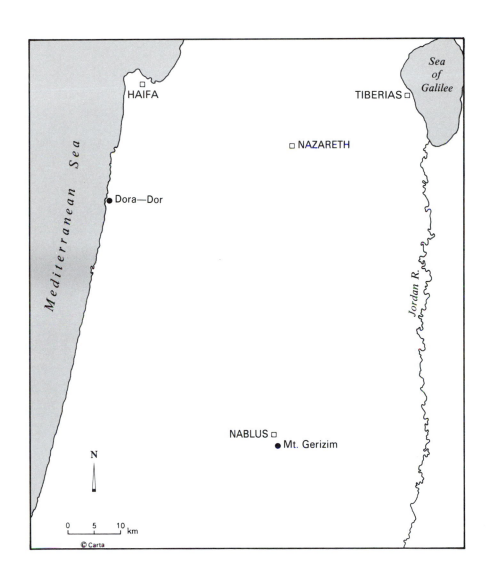

The Church of Mary Theotokos on Mt. Gerizim

Yitzhak Magen

A large Byzantine enclosure surrounded by a wall and towers is located on the highest peak of Mt. Gerizim, the sacred mount of the Samaritans. It is known in Arabic as *el-Qala^c*, "the Citadel." In the center of the enclosure is an octagonal church named after Mary Mother of God (*Theotokos*).

The site was surveyed several times by travelers in the nineteenth century. During the 1930s archaeological excavations of the church were conducted by the German scholar M. Schneider.[1] A recent survey and excavation of the church has revealed new finds.[2]

History of the Site

The erection of the church on Mt. Gerizim has been recorded in Christian as well as Samaritan sources.

The most complete historical report concerning the events which led to the construction of the church and surrounding fortifications is that by Procopius.[3] He writes that initially the Samaritans were allowed to ascend Mt. Gerizim and pray there freely, undisturbed by the Byzantine authorities. As part of his description, Procopius recalls the conversation between Jesus and the Samaritan woman (John 4:20–21). He goes on to describe the conflict between the Samaritans and the Christians that arose due to Zeno's decision to build a church on the mountain and to dedicate it to the Mother of God. In 484 C.E. Zeno fortified the site with a wall and detached ten soldiers to guard it. During the reign of Anastasius, the Samaritans ascended Mt. Gerizim, killed the soldiers, and probably damaged the church itself. During Justinian's reign an additional outer wall was built in order to strengthen the defenses.

According to the Byzantine writer Malalas,[4] the Samaritans in Palestine revolted during Zeno's reign, and Zeno converted their synagogue on Mt. Gerizim into a house of prayer and named it after Holy Mary, Mother of God. A similar reference, which is actually from the same source, is found in the *Chronicon Paschale*.[5]

In the Samaritan Chronicles,[6] we find a parallel story:

> In the twelfth year of Netanel's term as High Priest, Zeno, King of Edom (= Byzantium) came to the holy city of Shechem and oppressed the children of Israel ... and went to the synagogue built by Babah Rabah on the chosen site of Mt. Gerizim and inquired as to the ownership of the place ... and took the mountain within its full boundaries and the water pool and erected a large building and dug a tomb for himself.

[1] A.M. Schneider, "Römische und Byzantinische Bauten auf dem Garizim," *ZDPV* 68 (1951): 210–234. See also J. Wilkinson, "Architectural Procedures in Byzantine Palestine," *Levant* 13 (1981): 156–172; R. Krautheimer, *Early Christian and Byzantine Architecture* (Harmonsworth, Middlesex, 1965), pp. 116–117; B. Bagatti, *Antichi villaggi cristiani di Samaria* (Jerusalem, 1979), pp. 57–58.

[2] This article is based on the author's more detailed report, "The Church of Mary Theotokos on Mt. Grizim," *CAHL*, pp. 333–342.

[3] Procopius of Caesarea, *Buildings* V, VII, tr. H. B. Dewing (London, 1954).

[4] John Malalas, *Chronographia*, ed. L. Dindorf (Bonn, 1831), pp. 382–383.

[5] *Chronicon Paschale*, tr. M. Whitby (Liverpool, 1989).

[6] E.N. Adler and M. Seligsohn, "Une Nouvelle Chronique Samaritaine", *Revue des études juives* 45 (1902), No. 4876.

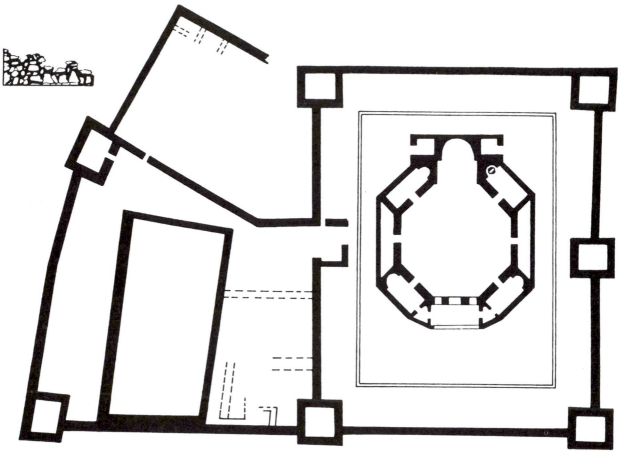

Mt. Gerizim: general plan of Byzantine enclosure

Mt. Gerizim: aerial photograph of Byzantine enclosure

The Samaritan revolts, which took place in the fifth and sixth centuries, began with the erection of the Church of Mary on Mt. Gerizim in the year 484 C.E. It has a centralized form typical of commemorative churches (*martyria*). The construction of the church on the Samaritan holy site indicates that the Christians now looked upon Mt. Gerizim as a *locus sanctus*. It also signifies the submission of the Samaritans and their conversion to Christianity; the Samaritans regarded the act as a desecration of their Holy of Holies.

The continuous Samaritan attempts to damage the church compelled Justinian to protect it with an outer wall. Learning from the experience of earlier rebellions, he also fortified the city of Neapolis (Shechem).[7]

Description of the Site

The site (100 × 83 m) is made up of two parts. In the south, there is a square enclosure (71 × 56 m) surrounded by a fortified wall, in the center of which stands an octagonal church, while in the north, there is an irregular fortified enclosure with a rectangular building, probably a large water pool, called in Arabic *Bir er-Rasâs*.

The Southern Enclosure

The southern enclosure has four square corner towers (8.6 × 8 m) and an additional one in the southern wall. In the northern wall there is an elaborately built gatehouse featuring four building phases. The two later phases are probably from the Arab period. The gate's dimensions are 9.6 × 8.6 m. It has massive walls, the outer faces of which are built of finely hewn stones. The 3-m-wide entrance could be closed by a massive wooden door. The gateway floor is made of well-fitted flagstones. In addition to the direct entranceway leading to the surrounding enclosure, there is another wide entrance leading to the staircase that apparently ascends to a tower in the wall guarding the gateway. Above the remains of

Mt. Gerizim: northern enclosure wall (Phase 1)

the hewn stone construction, the walls of the second phase can be clearly discerned. In the next phase, apparently during the Muslim period, the gate was made narrower and a wide staircase was built next to it.

The walls of the enclosure are built of large dressed stones with margins and a protruding central boss. The walls are preserved to a height of 4 m in some places; originally they were some 7 m high. Within the enclosure there are various rooms, some of which were built at a later date.

The peristyle around the church. The church is surrounded by a peristyle (53 × 39 m) comprising square piers (1 × 0.6 m) built of well-hewn stones which resemble those of the church and gateway. Peristyle piers were uncovered in the north and west wings of the church; it is assumed, therefore, that originally they completely surrounded the building.

The area around the peristyle was not entirely excavated. Along the northern wall it is possible to discern rooms adjoining the outer wall, but the plan of the area outside the peristyle is unclear. The area between the peristyle and the church was entirely paved with well-fitted flagstones which neatly abut the church walls on the one side and the peristyle on the other. It appears, therefore, that the peristyle, the paving, the church and the gateway were built as one unit. To the

[7] M. Avi-Yonah, "The Samaritan Revolts Against the Byzantine Empire," *EI* 4 (1956), pp. 127–132 (Hebrew) and English summary on p. ix.

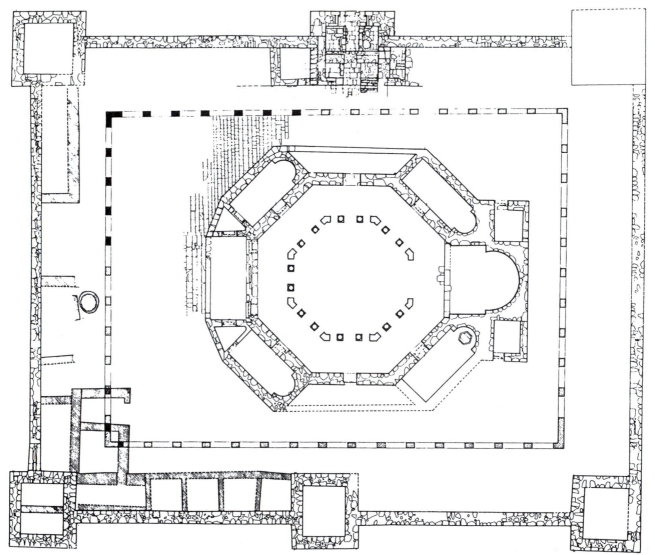

Mt. Gerizim: plan of church and enclosure from the time of Zeno (484 C.E.; Phase 1)

west of the church there is a large cistern into which water from the paved area drained.

The church. The church has an octagonal ground plan (the outer dimensions are 37.4 × 30 m). It comprises double walls which create rooms and chapels. In the east a protrusion encloses an apse. The entrance to the church is in the west, where the open room serves as a narthex, probably paved with marble slabs. Three openings led from it into the church, the central one being the largest. The narthex provides access to a side chapel on either side. Another two chapels flank the apse. Entrance from the narthex to the chapels on either of

its sides is through triangular rooms. The chapels have an additional opening onto the main hall of the church. The chapels flanking the apse are larger than those on the west. The walls of the southeastern one were coated with marble slabs as indicated by the negative imprints in the recesses on the chapel walls and the numerous marble fragments found in the church. In the apse of the chapel there is a hexagonal stone installation which cannot be a baptistery because of its small dimensions. Thus we prefer to identify it as a place for a reliquary. At both the north and south sides, between the chapels, there is a narrow elongated trapezoid-shaped room, connected to

86

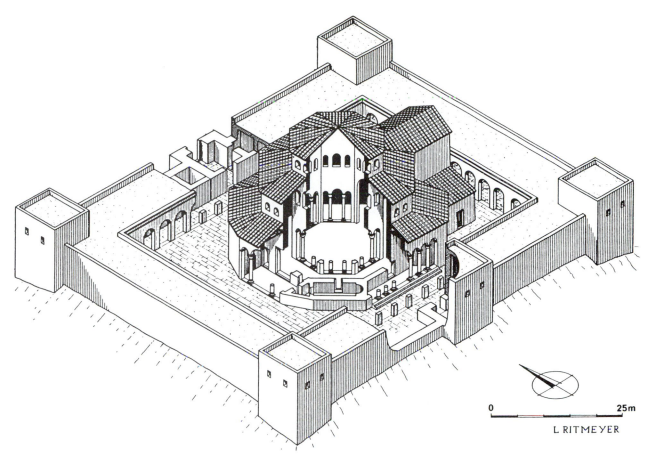

Mt. Gerizim: reconstruction of church and enclosure from the time of Zeno (484 C.E.; Phase 1)

the main hall of the church. Their function is unknown; perhaps they served as treasuries. At either side of the large elevated apse is a small square room, the entrance to which is from outside the church.

It is unclear how the floors of the church and apse were paved. Perhaps in the earliest building phase, they were paved with marble slabs and mosaics; some mosaic tesserae and fragments of marble paving slabs were found in the excavation.

In the center of the church there is an octagon of bases of piers and columns which supported the central dome (see reconstruction). Only a few column fragments made of red limestone have been preserved.

The Northern Enclosure
The northern wall of the enclosure is built of dressed stones with margins and a central protruding boss, as in the wall of the southern enclosure. A wall starting at a square tower at the northwestern corner continues to the east

and has another larger tower at its middle point. This tower is located opposite the gate tower of the southern enclosure, to which, apparently, it was connected by a paved way. We are inclined to assume that the gate tower was the central entranceway to the northern enclosure as well as to the entire church complex (although this does not appear as such in the reconstruction). This is not at all surprising, as the main road leading to Mt. Gerizim comes from the north, the direction of Shechem-Neapolis. From the central tower the wall continues to the east, creating an irregular corner.

In the northern enclosure there is a large structure, probably a water pool. Plaster fragments can still be seen on the walls and water collects at the bottom in the winter. At first sight the pool does not appear to be an organic part of the Byzantine construction. The building and stone-dressing techniques are different from those of the rest of the enclosure so perhaps it dates to a phase earlier than the Byzantine enclosure and the church.

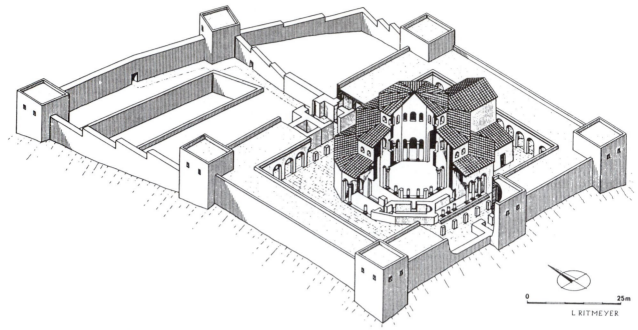

Mt. Gerizim: reconstruction of church and northern enclosure (Phase 2)

The Finds

The archaeological finds in the excavation were relatively meager. A small number of coins, some late pottery objects, marble, mosaic, and early ceramic fragments were revealed. Architectural elements like columns, Corinthian capitals, and cross-ornamented capitals were found. In Schneider's excavation, inscriptions and an altar slab were uncovered. Among the interesting finds of our recent excavation were six dedicatory inscriptions carved on stone slabs deciphered by L. Di Segni.[8] Two inscriptions were installed in later floor pavements and the other four were found in the debris. At least five of the six inscriptions were identified as inscriptions of Samaritans who brought donations to their sanctuary, previously located in close proximity. Only a few inscriptions from Mt. Gerizim belong to the Christian edifice. The most significant, found by Schneider in the 1930s, is that which mentions an important relic deposited there: "A stone from the Golgotha."

[8] L. Di Segni, "The Church of Mary Theotokos on Mount Gerizim: The Inscriptions," *CAHL*, pp. 343–350.

Analysis of the Excavations in the Light of Historical Sources

From Procopius' writings we have learnt about two phases in the history of the church and the surrounding enclosure:

Phase 1: The church and perhaps the surrounding wall were built during the reign of Zeno.

Phase 2: An additional outer wall was erected to protect the site during the reign of Justinian.

Until the present research, it was assumed that the church was constructed by Zeno while the walls and towers around it were built by Justinian. The discovery of the gate and peristyle and the fact that they were built as an integral part of the church and the fortifications, imply that both the church and the enclosure were built at the same time by Zeno. It should be noted that a gateway of such dimensions is of no value without a fortified wall to defend it. The question that arises, therefore, is what did Justinian build? We assume that the northern enclosure, which seems to be different from the rest of the construction, is his addition. This enclosure abuts the southern one and technically, at least, appears to be from a later period. It was built at the most vulnerable section of the site adjacent to the gate and the main road from Neapolis in the north. This supposition not only corresponds to the archaeological data but also clarifies Procopius' words. It is difficult to conjecture that an isolated church would be built on a mountaintop without proper means of defense, and in the excavations, as we have noted, no remains of an earlier fortification were found.

It is doubtful that a synagogue stood on the site, the existence of which is mentioned by Malalas and the *Chronicon Paschale*. As of now there is no evidence whatsoever of the existence of such a synagogue. It is possible that the intention of these sources was to indicate that the church was built to replace a synagogue which was situated on Mt. Gerizim, but not necessarily on the same site.

The erection of the church on Mt. Gerizim and the conflict between the Samaritans and the Christians again raises the question of the location of the Samaritan temple during the Hellenistic period and the site of the Holy of Holies of the Samaritan community. As a result of R. Bull's excavations at Tel er-Rasâs[9] and his supposed discovery of remains of a Samaritan temple beneath the Roman one (Temple B), he assumed that the Samaritan temple, built according to the plan of the Temple in Jerusalem during the time of Sanballat, the governor of Samaria (Flavius Josephus, *Antiquities* XIII, 254–256), was the one he found on the northern peak of the mountain. A reappraisal of Bull's finds, however, and especially the discovery of a Hellenistic town on Mt. Gerizim in the center of which the church site is located, illustrate the need for a renewed search for the Samaritan holy place and temple in the area of the church. In a sounding made in the center of the church, remains of a Hellenistic structure were revealed. This evidence refutes Schneider's conclusion that no Hellenistic remnants were found in the church. It is of interest that the three holy Samaritan sites, the "Twelve Stones," "Hill of Eternity," and the place of the "Offering of Isaac," surround the church. We believe, therefore, that a Samaritan shrine was located in this area and its existence was forgotten as a result of the church's construction and Christian desecration. If some of the inscriptions discovered in the area of the church can be truly dated before the fifth century, there would be good reason to consider a continuous Samaritan cult at this spot from the Hellenistic age until the Christian occupation of the site.

9   R.J. Bull, "Field XII," *BASOR* 180 (1965): 37–41; R.J. Bull and W. Wright, "Newly Discovered Temples on Mt. Gerizim in Jordan," *Harvard Theological Review* 58 (1965): 234–237.

Dora-Dor: A Station for Pilgrims in the Byzantine Period on Their Way to Jerusalem

Claudine Dauphin

Pilgrimage Routes

The excavation of the church center of Dora-Dor, the ancient coastal city north of Caesarea, has been renewed and expanded in recent years. Our work has revealed that this was not merely a religious, administrative, urban, or regional center, but an important station for pilgrims on their way to Jerusalem.

The route to Jerusalem was arduous, and a pilgrimage to the Holy City involved a laborious journey by land and sea. The pilgrims suffered prolonged delays, storms at sea and shipwrecks, and were tossed around on the decks of merchant vessels that sailed from Western Europe to the coast of Syria and Palestine.

Monks and pilgrims flocked to the Holy Land not only from the West, but even from Mesopotamia and more distant eastern lands. St. Jerome relates that every day he greeted monks from India, Persia, and Ethiopia in his monastery in Bethlehem.[1] The best-documented pilgrimage, however, is that from the West. Pilgrims from Constantinople, if they did not come by sea, followed the "Pilgrims' Road" across Asia Minor — to Tarsus and Antioch in Cilicia. In every case their route was along the major coastal road, the "Via Maris" which connected Antioch with Alexandria.

When the pilgrims reached the Holy Land at the port of Caesarea, Jerusalem was still seventy-three Roman miles away, a three-day journey. On an average day, they would have progressed twenty to twenty-five Roman miles, a figure based on the detailed testimony of the Bordeaux traveler, who made his way from Gaul to Jerusalem. He left Chalcedon on the east coast of the Sea of Marmara (between Constantinople and the Dardanelles) on May 30, 333, and returned to Constantinople on December 26 of that year; thus he remained outside the imperial capital for seven months. On his way to Jerusalem the pilgrim from Bordeaux stayed in fifty-eight hostels (mansiones). Assuming he spent one night in each hostel, it took him slightly more than eight weeks to travel the 1,200 miles from Constantinople to Jerusalem — an average of twenty-one miles a day.

No pilgrim could manage without taking advantage of the well-organized stations for changing horses (mutationes) and the hostels for overnight lodging (mansiones) located along the main roads of the empire. The Roman and Byzantine mansio, like its successors, the Turkish khan and caravanserai, contained a large courtyard with stables. Around it were rooms, in which the travelers ate and rested, and lodging areas on the upper story. If there was no room at the mansio, the pilgrim was forced to join other travelers at a local inn, or taverna. The mansiones and tavernae had a poor reputation among the Christians as well as among the upper echelons of pagan Roman society. In particular, church ordinances forbade clerics to enter these establishments, which Gregory of Nyssa viewed as dangerous and a source of corruption for Christian pilgrims. To cater for the needs of Christian travelers, church-sanctioned hospices or official inns (xenodochia), supervised by the clergy and often associated with monasteries, sprang up in cities along the main

---

[1] Hieronymus, *Epistulae*, 107, 2, 3, in *Corpus Scriptorum Ecclesiasticorum Latinorum*, ed. I.A. Hilberg (Vienna, 1910–1918), pp. 54–56.

pilgrimage routes. During the 80s of the fourth century, Gregory of Nyssa relates that such inns were scattered throughout all the eastern provinces,[2] and in the year 437 we hear that on the road between Constantinople and Jerusalem there were numerous hospices and inns (pandocheia) intended for pilgrims.

Despite all the arrangements described above, the pilgrim's road was beset with difficulties, especially if he adopted a life of asceticism and abstinence that weakened his resistance to the hardships and climatic changes on the way. Thus, for example, in 437, Melania the Younger made her way in deep snow from Constantinople to Jerusalem. In summer the travelers had to withstand drought and dust in Anatolia, followed by heat and humidity on the coast of Cilicia; these climatic trials weighed heavily on St. Jerome during his journey to the East in 374. He himself managed to survive the hardships, but his companion, Innocentius, died when they reached Antioch. Pilgrims arriving via Egypt also encountered deserts, which caused much suffering to women like Melania or Egeria, who were raised and educated amid the comforts of the Western aristocracy. Egeria, Mother Superior of a Convent in Galicia in northwestern Spain, made her way toward the Holy Land between 381 and 384; she endured the arduous climb to the summit of Mt. Sinai, and even scaled Mt. Nebo, sustained, if we may rely on her diary, by her unremitting yearning to visit the holy site. Her longing for the sacred places also helped her triumph over the physical and mental challenges of her pilgrimage to the Holy City. The pilgrims' strong desire to see with their own eyes the sites and landscapes where the events well-known to them from the Bible had occurred drove them over mountains and through wilderness.

Every pilgrim's "travel kit" included two essential items: a Bible and travel books based on the Onomasticon, a volume identifying the sites in Palestine mentioned in Scripture, writ-ten in Greek by Eusebius, Bishop of Caesarea, and translated into Latin by St. Jerome around 390. Accompanied by these works the pilgrims made their way toward Jerusalem, visiting the sites mentioned in the Holy Scriptures. Sometimes they joined groups of pilgrim-guides, who, in addition to narrating the well-founded traditions, occasionally tended to provide the naive pilgrims with incorrect identifications of places and feed them romantic tales.

Dor

One spot to be visited on the coastal route was the episcopal basilica of Dora-Dor, which was uncovered in archaeological excavations beginning in 1979. This church is of great interest not just in itself, but because it exemplifies a complex used by many pilgrims on their way to Jerusalem. The findings at Dor make tangible the structure of a station concentrated around a religious site.

Ancient Dor lies some 10 km north of Caesarea, on the Mediterranean coast. It was a flourishing city from the Canaanite period until Roman times. St. Jerome, in his translation of Eusebius' Onomasticon, describes Dor of the early fourth century as "now deserted" (nunc deserta),[3] and in Epistle 108, dated to 404, in connection with the first journey of the pilgrim Paula around 386 C.E., he writes: "... She marvelled in the ruins of Dor, a city once very powerful."[4] Both comments have, in the past, too often been understood literally. They are rather to be judged in the light of Jerome's interest in sites as fossilized embodiments of biblical events. That Dor, a border town between the provinces of Phoenicia and Palaestina Prima ("First Palestine"), was an episcopal see subject to the authority of the metropolitan Archbishop of neighboring Caesarea, the capital of "First Palestine," was not worth a mention by Jerome, since his Onomasticon aimed not at describing contemporary

---

[2] Gregory of Nyssa, Epistulae, ed. G. Pasquali (Leiden, 1959), 2.

[3] Eusebius, Onomasticon, ed. E. Klostermann (Leipzig-Berlin, 1904 [repr. 1966]), 78, 9. This edition includes Jerome's Latin translation of the work.

[4] Hieronymus, Epistulae, 108, 8, 2 (see note 1).

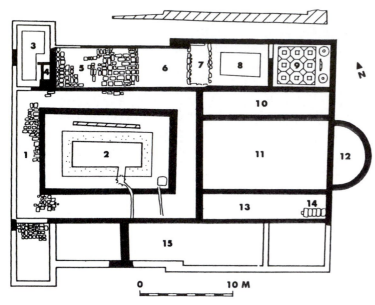

Dora-Dor: plan of church — 1) Atrium; 2) Cistern; 3) Northwestern tower(?); 4) Staircase; 5) Atrium; 6) Vestibule; 7) *Piscina*; 8) Room 1; 9) Room 2; 10) Northern aisle; 11) Nave; 12) Apse; 13) Southern aisle; 14) Saints' tomb; 15) External southern aisle (Hellenistic walls are hatched-in) (S. Gibson)

cities, but merely indicated to pilgrims biblical archaeological remains worth visiting. The mention of Dor in Byzantine geographical treatises and in the reports of its bishops, who participated in church councils in the fifth through seventh centuries C.E., testifies to its importance during that period.

The population appears to have abandoned the summit of Tel Dor where, during the Byzantine period, there remained only a military observation point, as suggested by the excavations since 1980 directed by Prof. E. Stern of The Hebrew University of Jerusalem. The contemporary settlement was located on the northeastern slope of the tel and at its base, where Kibbutz Naḥsholim was built in 1948. While preparing the ground for new construction in the kibbutz, ancient remains came to light and were partially excavated during a salvage dig conducted by Dr. J. Leibovitch in February 1952 under the auspices of the Israel Department of Antiquities and Museums. These excavations unearthed the apse of a large basilican church and the mosaic floor of its northern aisle. The structure was

apparently quite large, and Dr. Leibovitch was probably correct in assuming that this had been an episcopal basilica, the seat of the bishop of Byzantine Dor. Also uncovered during these excavations was a bishop's ivory scepter, terminating in the shape of a hand with the three middle fingers extended in the characteristic episcopal benediction — symbolizing the Holy Trinity; one finger was adorned by an ivory ring.

Following Dr. Leibovitch's death, the excavations were stopped, the site was neglected, and weeds grew over the mosaics, threatening them with complete ruin. Because of the site's importance, the Israel Department of Antiquities and Museums decided to resume the excavation of the church of Dor, under the direction of the present author.[5] There have been three seasons of excavation, in June–July of 1979 and 1980, and September–October 1983.

Two periods of occupation were discerned: 1) the Byzantine period (fourth–seventh centuries C.E.); and 2) the Ottoman period (seventeenth–eighteenth centuries).

The Byzantine church complex covered some 1,000 sq m. Its nucleus was a basilica with three aisles, 18.5 m long and 14 m wide. The nave is 7.5 m wide, and terminates in the east in a semicircular apse, whose outer radius is 4 m. On each side of the nave is a 2.5-m-wide built aisle. The walls are 60 cm thick, and were built of ashlars 35–100 cm long. Occasionally the ashlars were laid out as headers and stretchers. The height of the courses varied between 20 and 28 cm. The walls had a 1-cm-thick layer of plaster on the inside, which in some places was preserved on the upper face of the foundation course, suggesting that the courses were joined by plaster.

The nave and both aisles were paved with mosaics, of which only small patches have so far been found. The tesserae are 1.1 × 1.1 cm, with eighty-five per sq dm.

Outside each aisle was an additional row of

[5] The excavations were carried out under the auspices of the Israel Department of Antiquities and Museums, the Russell Trust (Scotland) and the European Science Foundation.

Dora-Dor: general view of the church from the northwest (Z. Radovan)

rooms, a kind of outer aisle, 4 m wide in the west widening to 4.5 m in the east, extending along the entire length of the building. The northern outer aisle was laterally subdivided into various segments. At its western end was a room (6 × 3.3 m) paved with crude white mosaics. In its southeastern corner the base of a staircase was uncovered; it probably enabled access to an upper story or gallery. This room was perhaps the ground floor of a small tower and was used as lodgings by the sexton. From the west, the other segments of the northern outer aisle were: an atrium, 8.7 m long, paved with stone slabs which led into an antechamber, 5.2 m long, whose plaster floor was originally paved with marble slabs; this gave access to a shallow plaster-lined, rectangular basin or baptismal *piscina*, 4.4 m long, 2.1 m wide and 97 cm deep. The eastern and western edges consisted of two steps, each

12 cm high. These zones were followed by two mosaic-paved rooms. Room no. 1 measured 6 m east–west × 4.5 m north–south. Its mosaic was decorated by 60 red-ochre rose buds each enclosed in a dark gray calyx, spread out in six north–south rows of ten buds each, on a white ground. At the eastern end of the panel a fragmentary *tabula ansata* marked the central axis. The pavement of Room no. 2, 6 m long and 4.5 m wide, had a pattern of irregular red-ochre octagons on a white ground, each containing a gray-black, yellow-ochre and red-ochre square, and stepped lozenges in the same colors. To the east of this, a stone step probably gave access to an elevated area — chancel or altar — now destroyed. Marble screens encased it on its northern and southern faces. The mosaic floor of Room no. 2 extended eastwards on either side of the stone step. Its decorative motif repeated itself sym-

93

metrically on either side of the step. It consisted of a red-ochre circle, 1 m in diameter, enclosing five interlocking red-ochre circles with five black petals in the center.

The southern outer aisle was almost entirely destroyed by modern building activity. Its mosaic pavement has survived in small patches south of the southern wall of the southern aisle. In both outer aisles, the tesserae measured 1.1 × 1.1 × 1.1 cm and were laid to a density of forty-seven per sq dm. At the northwestern corner of the southern outer aisle there may have been a tower comparable with the tower at the western end of the northern outer aisle.

To the west, the church was preceded by a rectangular atrium paved with stone slabs, 18.5 m long and 13.25 m wide, with a peristyle. Along the east–west axis of the apse and occupying most of the width of the atrium, the floor slabs covered the collapsed vault of a large cistern, 7.4 m long, 3.15 m wide and 3 m deep. Its plaster lining covered even its pavement of crude white tesserae, each 2 × 2 cm. Three pairs of corbels or projections protruded from the internal northern and southern faces of the cistern. Water entered through three plaster-lined channels which led from the wall south of the cistern, and gutters probably directed water from the roof. A shaft was hewn in the solid rock beside the cistern. It was 90 cm in diameter and 3 m deep, plaster-lined, and with seven footholds at 25 cm intervals carved into its eastern and western sides. It was connected to the cistern by a doorway, 73 cm wide and 1.79 m high, cut into the southern wall of the cistern.

At the end of the first season of excavation we hypothesized that the church had been built in the fourth or at the beginning of the fifth century C.E. This hypothesis was based on coins from the third and fourth centuries found within the sand fill under the church floor, and on a fifth-century coin found in the cross-section north of the southern wall of the northern outer aisle. Our hypothesis was confirmed in the 1980 season, when a mosaic floor with a geometric pattern was uncovered at the eastern end of Room no. 1. The dimen-

Dora-Dor: southern side of peristyle court and southern aisle, from the west (Z. Radovan)

sions of this lower mosaic floor, located 38 cm below the upper one, were 4.5 m north–south and 2.75 m east–west. The design in red-ochre and yellow-ochre against a yellowish-white background consisted of a trellis of large squares set in diagonal rows across the pavement, joined by smaller squares at right angles to the pavement, and enclosing small stepped squares. The tesserae measured 1.5 × 1.3 and 1.7 × 1.2 cm, and their density to the sq dm was sixty-seven.

A bronze tremessis coin of Emperor Constantine II (337–361 C.E.) minted at Cyzicus was found on the pavement. The building of the first stage of the church must therefore be assigned at the earliest to the first half of the fourth century. To the early basilica belonged the lower mosaic pavements of Rooms nos. 1 and 2, the lower floor of slabs and pebbles of the antechamber in the northern outer aisle, the lower plaster floors of the *piscina*, the peristyle court, the aisles, the nave, the apse and the southern outer aisle. The lower pavement of Room no. 1 was burnt at its northern end; similarly, a fire destroyed the slab-and-pebble floor of the antechamber, an event which preceded the erection of the upper building in the fifth century.

In the second phase, mosaics (a higher floor) were laid in the outer aisles, in the inner ones, and in the nave. About 2 m north of the northern outer aisle stands the southern wall of a monumental edifice, which we uncovered for a length of 22 m. Only one course of stones and a section of stone paving have been preserved. This building is late Hellenistic or Roman, judging from its masonry and pottery assemblage. Its paving stones were removed and reused by the builders of the nearby basilica.

The plan of the basilica is unique for Palestine. Its only parallels are the churches of el-Ḥosn at el-Bara and Church A at Dair Solaib in Syria from the fifth century C.E. The location of the *piscina* adjacent to the atrium, within the church complex rather than outside it, is unusual. This phenomenon is echoed in the Syrian volume of canon law, *Testamentum Domini Nostri Jesu Christi*, from the second half of the fifth century, which stipulates regulations regarding the building and design of churches. According to its instructions, the baptistery must be connected to the atrium. In the sixth century C.E., the rhetor, Choricius of Gaza, in a sermon in praise of Bishop Marcian (*Laudatio Marciani*), describes a long portico on the north side of St. Sergius' Church in Gaza. This portico contained the baptistery. The northern outer aisle of the basilica in Dor, with its tripartite division, corresponds to the first three stages of the baptismal liturgy, as described in the Mystagogical Catheceses or Sermons by Cyril, bishop of Jerusalem in the middle of the fourth century. Those about to undergo baptism stood in an antechamber at the western end, considered the "region of Darkness"; from there they advanced eastward in the direction of the "divine Light," into the "inner chamber," which at Dor is Room no. 1. There they undressed and were anointed with oil, and one by one walked into the *piscina*. They recited the Act of Faith and were immersed three times, or had holy water sprinkled on their foreheads. Immediately after the baptism they were anointed a second time by the bishop, and wrapped themselves in white robes. Cyril does not mention a specific room connected with the anointing ceremony, but this probably took place at the eastern end of the northern portico, where the newly baptized participated for the first time in the Eucharist, and partook of the host. The steps leading to the raised apse or *bema* in Room no. 2 indicate that the sacred mysteries were conducted here.

The southern outer aisle of the basilica probably served a different purpose. It is possible that this is where sick persons seeking cures gathered during their incubation — a period of prayers, fasting, and often deprivation of sleep. This custom of incubation was well known already in ancient Greek medicine, and was widespread mainly in the temples of Asclepius, the god of medicine, such as those in Epidauros and Pergamon. It was adopted by the Christians; evidence of this can be found in biographies of saints, especially in the tales of the miracles attributed to St. Artemios in the sixth century C.E. This saint appeared before the sick in their sleep, in the porticoes of the church in Constantinople bearing his name, and cured them or prescribed them a treatment. At Dor, the sick gathered around the remains of two saints whose names are unknown to us, but whose grave lies at the eastern end of the southern aisle. Their grave was covered with five slabs laid across it in an east–west direction. There was a small hole, with a diameter of 16–18 cm, at the western end of the easternmost stone slab, and in the hole, a clay pipe, whose sides were 7 cm in diameter, was found. We suspected that this pipe was used to pour oil into the grave. The oil, on coming into contact with the saints' remains, became holy. From there it drained into a plastered basin 2 m long and 1.4 m wide, located between the grave and the northern wall of the southern aisle, whence the oil was taken for curing the sick. This assumption was verified with the discovery of oily deposits around the lower parts of the eastern wall of the southern side aisle.

In Syria the bones of saints were usually deposited in stone reliquaries; these were boxes shaped like small sarcophagi. Oil was poured into a hole pierced in the stone cover of the reliquary; after becoming sanctified through contact with the holy remains, it was drained out through an additional hole at the bottom of the box. The reliquary-grave at Dor is the first of its kind discovered in Palestine. Holy oil collected from the tombs of saints was taken back home by pilgrims in small ampoules, which were small clay flasks made in molds, or hammered metal flasks, bearing a description of the holy places where the oil was sanctified, and usually also the Greek word Εὐλογία ("blessing"). Famous examples are the thirty-six metal ampoules which stand today in the treasury rooms of the cathedrals of Bobbio and Monza in Italy. These ampoules, originating in Jerusalem, bear descriptions of the Cave of the Nativity in Bethlehem, the Cross of Calvary, and the Holy Sepulchre in Jerusalem.

Both theologians and pilgrims believed that holy oil could protect them from the devil's temptations. One of the worst temptations was drunkenness, about which St. John Chrysostom ("of the golden mouth") commented:

> Take holy oil and anoint your entire body with it, your tongue, your lips, your neck, and your eyes, and you shall never fall prey to drunkenness, for the oil with its delicate smell reminds you of the struggles of the martyrs, restrains licentiousness, strengthens faith, and puts an end to all diseases of the soul.

Throughout the Byzantine period pilgrims to the Holy Land, both high-born and lowly, eagerly sought to acquire holy relics to take back with them to their homes. This phenomenon is illustrated by Egeria's story of an enthusiastic pilgrim who bit off a piece of the Holy Cross in the Church of the Holy Sepulchre while kissing it, and made off with it in his mouth. And indeed the tomb of the ancient saints at Dor also attracted pilgrims. In the 1952 excavations a gray marble column was found about 100 m east of the basilica. Carved 92 cm above the column's base was a Greek inscription in three lines: Τοῦ ἁγίου Γολγόθα λίθος, "A stone from the Holy Golgotha." Below the inscription was a hollow cross with a square 5 × 5 cm hole in its center. Carved at the end of each of its four arms was a small cross. The square hole probably contained a cruciform metal reliquary, affixed to the column, with a stone fragment from Golgotha inside it.[6] This sacred stone was also a prime source of attraction for the pilgrims passing through Dor.

Those traveling by sea disembarked in the excellent harbor of Dor, built in two sections — north and south — on either side of the ancient tel. This provided protection against wind from all directions. Dor had proper docking facilities along a coast almost devoid of ports, as there are no more than two or three natural harbors between Egypt and Lebanon. Dor's position as a major port and a crossroad on the commercial and pilgrim routes from Egypt and North Africa to Syria and Cilicia is illustrated by the large quantities of various imported ceramics uncovered in the excavation of the basilica. We found white Egyptian storage jars, "Late Roman" and "African Red Slip" bowls and plates, as well as storage jars from Asia Minor.

To accommodate the large crowd of worshippers and the stream of pilgrims, the need arose to plan a spacious courtyard with a large cistern in the basilica of Dor (as was done in the Constantinian churches of Jerusalem and Bethlehem). Although there is no lack of fresh water in the vicinity, it was essential to collect water in a cistern within the church complex where it would not evaporate, so as

6 J. Leibovitch, "The Reliquary Column of Dor," *Christian News in Israel* 5 (1953): 22–23.

to meet the current water needs of the church and its attendants, and of the pilgrims and the sick. A canon law (erroneously attributed to the Council of Nicaea in 325 C.E.) indicates that the atrium would have been surrounded by buildings to provide food and lodging for pilgrims, a residence for the bishop, gardens, bathhouses, porticoes, and colonnades. It may be, however, that the mammoth complex described in the canon was not intended for every locality, but as a guideline for the building of the "new city" that was erected outside of Caesarea in Cappadocia (today Kayseri in Turkey), on the "Pilgrims' Road."[7]

The pilgrims greatly appreciated the stations near the holy places on their way to Jerusalem. Melania, for example, prayed throughout the night in the Martyrium of Leontius in Tripoli in Lebanon, and Egeria stayed in the convent adjacent to the sacred site of St. Thecla near Seleucia in Cilicia. The holy relics uncovered in Dor indicate that it too served as a religious center of this kind. We hope that in future excavations in the area we will be able to reveal part of the complex connected with the church, which will make it possible to reconstruct the daily life of pilgrims in a provincial pilgrimage center in Palestine.

A layer of ashes and collapsed rubble clearly indicates that Dor was destroyed by fire. The excavations uncovered slabs of wall plaster, tiles, and fragments of vessels, window panes and glass chandeliers — mixed with melted iron nails, door bolts, and fragments of a lead chandelier (*polycandelon*). Unlike the devastation of the church sites of Byzantine Palestine, this destruction does not date to the Persian invasion of 613–614 C.E., nor even to the Arab Conquest in 636.[8]

At the Lateran Council, which convened in the Church of the Lateran in Rome in 649 C.E., the Bishop of Dor, Stephanus, appeared before Pope Martin and was introduced as the "first among the council of the Church of Jerusalem." His function as the deputy of the Jerusalem Patriarchate was to install bishops, priests, and deacons, so long as there was no way to appoint a Patriarch in Jerusalem following its conquest by the Arabs. Stephanus acted in place of the Jerusalem Patriarch, a post left vacant by the death of Sophronius I in 645 C.E. and not filled again until the year 705. This position was granted him both on account of the importance of the district of Dor and because he was the apostolic legate of Pope Theodorus, Martin's predecessor. Due to Church intrigues, Pope Martin appointed John of Philadelphia (Amman) as his apostolic legate. Following this transfer of authority, which took place in 649, we hear no more of the region of Dor until the twelfth century, when the Crusaders built a Christian village called Le Merle around the harbor, which again assumed an important role as one of the ports of the Crusader Kingdom of Jerusalem.

After a long period of abandonment, the site of the basilica of Dor became in the early seventeenth century and until the end of the eighteenth century the Muslim cemetery of the neighboring Arab village of Tantura. The first graves were dug into the upper mosaic pavement of the northern outer aisle. Alternating layers of graves and sand gradually formed a mound covering the ruins of the Byzantine church.

[7] See E.D. Hunt, *Holy Land Pilgrimage in the Later Roman Empire, AD 312–460* (Oxford, 1982), pp. 65–66.

[8] See G. Dahl, *The Materials for the History of Dor* (New Haven, 1915), pp. 113–120.

CHURCHES IN JERUSALEM

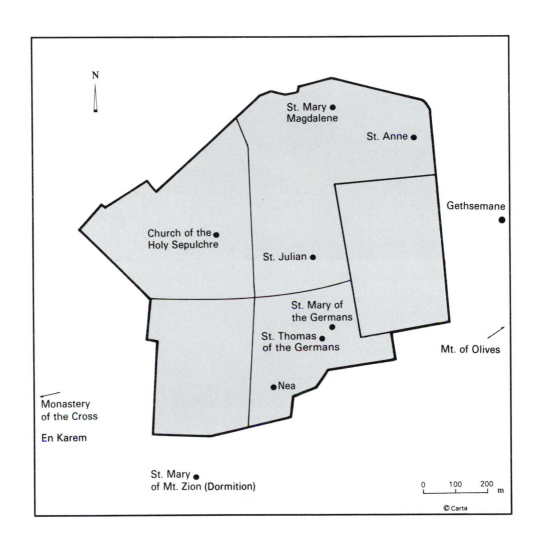

N

St. Mary ● Magdalene

St. Anne ●

Gethsemane ●

Church of the ● Holy Sepulchre

St. Julian ●

St. Mary of the Germans ●

St. Thomas ● of the Germans

Mt. of Olives

● Nea

Monastery of the Cross

En Karem

St. Mary ● of Mt. Zion (Dormition)

0   100   200
                        m

© Carta

The Church of the Holy Sepulchre: facade (above); rooftop (below) (Z Radovan)

The Early Church of the Holy Sepulchre in the Light of Excavations and Restoration

Joseph Patrich

The results of twenty years of excavation and research in the Church of the Holy Sepulchre following the restoration works, which had previously been reported on in various articles, have now been published in two books. The first to appear, in 1974, was by Charles Coüasnon, one of the architects responsible for the restoration of the church.[1] It comprises a series of lectures he delivered to the British Academy in 1972. Finds uncovered in subsequent excavations are not included. In 1981–1982, the archaeologist Virgilio Corbo[2] published an all encompassing work in three volumes. Corbo was in charge of archaeological research for the Latin Patriarchate, and since 1963 had also enjoyed the cooperation of the Greeks and Armenians. These two major works refute some of the conclusions of Fathers Vincent and Abel, whose study of this complex of buildings had hitherto been the most comprehensive,[3] and even today scholars will find essential and extremely useful information in their *Jérusalem nouvelle*, especially with regard to the literary sources and to the structure as it exists today.

The archaeological research was usually a by-product of restoration and preservation activity, and not an end in itself. This fact, together with the fragmentation of responsibility and supervision among the various de-nominations, has had its adverse effect; a considerable number of questions have been left unanswered, or clouded by controversy. Thus, for example, there are substantial differences of opinion between Corbo and Coüasnon regarding the reconstruction of the Constantinian Rotunda or the Anastasis.

A team of architects, known as the "Joint Technical Bureau," with representatives of the three large communities which control the Church of the Holy Sepulchre — the Roman Catholics, the Greek Orthodox, and the Armenians — supervised the restoration work in accordance with a program approved by all. In 1961, thirteen trenches were dug at various points in the building to explore the foundations, as well as a drainage tunnel on a north–south axis, from the Franciscan monastery to the large cistern under the entrance plaza (*parvis*) of the church. These trenches, although originally not intended for archaeological research, provided important finds, and some of them were widened. In certain places, archaeological excavations per se were carried out, but not all of them have received adequate publication.

Between 1960 and 1969, Corbo, under the auspices of the Custodia Terra Sancta, supervised excavations throughout the parts of the church belonging to the Catholics: in the northern vestibule of the Anastasis and in the gallery above it; in the Chapel of the Apparition to the Virgin and in all the rooms of the Franciscan monastery adjacent to it on the north and east; in the northern gallery over the "Virgin's Pillars"; and in the Chapel of the Finding of the True Cross. In 1970, the Greek Church instigated excavations in the area of the Katholikon, under the supervision of the

[1] Ch. Coüasnon, *The Church of the Holy Sepulchre* (Jerusalem/London, 1974).

[2] V.C. Corbo, *Il Santo Sepolcro de Gerusalemme, Aspetti arceologici dalle origini al periodo crociato*, I–III (Jerusalem, 1981–1982). An English summary of the Italian text is provided by Stanislav Loffreda, and the plates and photographs have both Italian and English captions.

[3] L.H. Vincent and F.M. Abel, *Jérusalem Nouvelle* (Paris, 1914–1924) (hereafter *JN*), pp. 89–300.

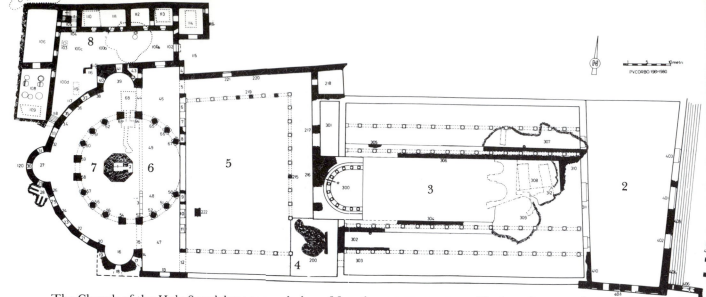

The Church of the Holy Sepulchre: ground plan of fourth-century structure. Blackened areas refer to architectural units discussed in article — 1) Cardo Maximus; 2) Atrium; 3) Martyrium (Basilica); 4) Golgotha (Calvary); 5) Tri-portico (Inner Atrium); 6) Anastasis (Rotunda); 7) Hewn rock and Jesus' tomb; 8) Patriarch's palace (Corbo, *Sepolchro*, Pl. 3)

architect Anastasios Economopoulos,[4] and on the eastern side of the Rock of Golgotha, under the direction of the latter and his colleague, Christos Katsimbinis (June–August, October–December 1977).[5] In 1966, the Armenians carried out minor exploration on the southern side of the Anastasis, which they control, and also east of the Chapel of St. Helena, where the Chapel of St. Vartan was later built. The excavations there, begun in October 1975, continued until February 1981. From November 1975 to February 1976, they were supervised by Magen Broshi; and in 1981, after the excavation site was extended, Gabriel Barkay took measurements and photographs.[6] The Spanish Father, Florentino Diaz Fernandez, also examined this work, especially in its latter stages, as well as the excavations east of the Golgotha.[7]

Topography of the Crucifixion Site and the Sepulchre

The Gospels relate that the place of the crucifixion — Golgoltha or Golgotha — was situated outside the city wall (the second wall). Nearby was a garden with a new tomb, which Joseph of Arimathea had dug for himself, and in which he buried Jesus.

The excavations show that this site, situated on a hillock, which is possibly the scriptural hill Gareb (Jeremiah 31:39), was from the ninth century B.C.E. on a royal stone quarry. The Rock of Golgotha protruded from within it. It is most probable that the latter was indeed shaped like a human skull, *Golgoltha* in Aramaic (*kranion* in Greek, and *calvaria* in Latin), from which it derives its name. After the quarry was abandoned, it was partially filled with soil and became a garden — the garden that is mentioned in the story of Jesus' crucifixion and burial. Several tombs have been discovered in the walls of the quarry. The facade of that in which Jesus was buried was located in the western bedrock wall of the quarry. Nearby, a catacomb discovered at the end of the previous century is now known as the Tomb of Joseph of Arimathea (no. 28 on the plan).[8]

[4] A. Economopoulos, *La Terra Santa* (April 1971): 111.

[5] Ch. Katsimbinis, "The Uncovering of the Eastern Side of the Hill of Calvary and Its Base," *LA* 27 (1977): 197–208, Pls. 19–38.

[6] M. Broshi and G. Barkay, "Excavations in the Chapel of St. Vartan in the Holy Sepulchre," *IEJ* 35 (1985): 108–128, Pl. 17; and in this volume, M. Broshi, "Excavations in the Holy Sepulchre in the Chapel of St. Vartan and the Armenian Martyrs," pp. 118–122.

[7] F. Diaz Fernandez, "La Recherche Archéologique," *Le Monde de la Bible* 33 (March–April 1984): 28–36.

[8] Ch. Clermont-Ganneau, *Archaeological Researches in Palestine* I (London, 1899), pp. 242–245.

The Remains from the Period of Aelia Capitolina

Eusebius, in describing Constantine's deeds, mentions that Hadrian erected a temple to Aphrodite on the site of Jesus' tomb. Like all Roman temples, it was built on a raised platform (*podium*) and thus it hid the tomb, but left it intact. After the temple and the earthfill in the foundations were removed, the tomb was revealed. Reconstructions of the town plan of the Roman city usually site the open Forum at the northeast corner of the main crossroads, and the temple would have been located at the northern edge of this square. Alongside it, it is possible that here too, there was a civic Basilica, as was customary in many Roman cities. In this case, late-Roman ruins on the site can safely be attributed to these two buildings.[9]

On the basis of previous excavations and surveys, the following remains are attributed to the period of Aelia Capitolina:

1. The corner of a building, parts of which are preserved in the Russian Alexander Hospice and in the nearby Zalatimo's bakery (the part that is located inside the bakery is today closed off by a wall built in 1984). The bakery, which faces Beit Ha-Bad Street ("The Street of the Oil Press"; Tariq Han ez-Zeit), is situated alongside the stairway that leads up to the Deir es-Sultan or the Ethiopian grounds. There is no alignment between these walls and those of the Constantinian basilica, and between the former and the Hadrianic wall described below, north of the large cistern. In Corbo's opinion, this remnant is from the facade of the boundary wall around Hadrian's temple (the *temenos*), Herodian stones being reused in it, while other researchers hold the view that during Hadrian's period it formed part of the civic Basilica and not of the temple.[10] Perhaps it is the ruins of a building from

the Second Temple period. Its external facade shows the same type of integrated posts as the upper section of the Temple Mount retaining wall and the wall around the Cave of Machpelah in Hebron.

2. The remains of the walls that were discovered under the Constantinian buildings in excavations within the Katholikon (Wall E in the photograph below) and the northern and southern vestibules of the Rotunda. Corbo maintains that the temple had a triple sanctuary (*cella*), in line with a Capitoline temple, and that this is the "Trikamaron" mentioned in the *Chronicon Paschale*. On the basis of a coin of Aelia Capitolina from the reign of Antoninus Pius, he also reconstructs six columns at the facade of the temple. Coüasnon relates most parts of these remains to the first

The Church of the Holy Sepulchre: excavations in the Katholikon (see previous illustration no. 300), looking west (Corbo, *Sepolchro*, Photo 88)

[9] See for example the map of Aelia Capitolina in Y. Tsafrir, *Eretz-Israel from the Destruction of the Second Temple to the Moslem Conquest*, II: *Archaeology and Art* (Jerusalem, 1984), p. 60 (Hebrew; English edition in press).

[10] *JN* (see note 3), pp. 40–70; Coüasnon, *The Church of the Holy Sepulchre* (see note 1), p. 45.

The Church of the Holy Sepulchre: northern wall of the northern Constantinian cistern under the parvis, looking northeast. The wall belongs to the Hadrianic temenos (Corbo, *Sepolchro*, Photo 1)

stage of the Constantinian Anastasis (see below).

3. A subterranean barrel vault north of the Sepulchre (no. 68 on the plan), built of stones with low bosses within marginal drafts. In Corbo's opinion, this was an underground store of utensils of the pagan temple no longer in use (*favisa*). During the Constantinian period, a vertical shaft and a short tunnel were dug to drain rainwater from the surface of the Anastasis to this pit. When the Rotunda was erected the vault was partially blocked by the foundations of the northern pair of columns.

4. The northern wall of the large cistern under the *parvis*. It has been suggested that this belongs to the Hadrian *temenos*. It has the characteristic stone dressing — a central low boss within marginal drafts. In some places the drafts divide a long stone into smaller units, so that it seems as if the wall is built of more or less uniform stones. This building technique, which was also common in the Byzantine period, is different from that employed in the walls and foundations of the Constantinian complex. Corbo suggests that this Hadrianic wall was covered over with a thick layer of plaster only in the fourth century, when the cistern was built. However, one can hardly believe that the site was left as an unroofed gaping pit within the area of the forum of Aelia Capitolina south of the *temenos* walls. It would make more sense to date the cistern to the Roman period, and likewise the large cistern that is currently located under the New Greek Building (Abraham's Hostel).[11]

An additional section of this wall can be seen further to the east, on the ground floor of Abraham's Hostel. As noted above, these walls are not aligned with the southern wall mentioned in no. 1 above. The stones are also different in size and dressing. These ruins, therefore, should be attributed to two different buildings: the temple on the west, and the civic Basilica east of it.

5. Walls and signs of quarrying in the *parvis* area, with a north-facing apse.

6. Two walls in a general east–west direction. The first is in the area of the Coptic Patriarchate, and the second, south of it, near the Crusader refectory.[12] They are more or less aligned with the southern wall of the Russian Hospice.

7. Walls that were uncovered during the excavations at St. Vartan's Chapel. (See in this volume, M. Broshi, "Excavations in the Holy Sepulchre in the Chapel of St. Vartan and the Armenian Martyrs," pp. 118–122.)

8. Various remains that were uncovered in excavations east of the Golgotha Rock: a small cave in the latter's eastern side, in which a wall was built; an oven and some dilapidated walls (see plan on p. 109). The connection between

[11] C. Schick, "Large Cistern under the New Greek Building Southeast of the Holy Sepulchre," *PEFQST* (1889): 110–112; *JN* (see note 3), Pl. XII, Cistern XI.
[12] Coüasnon, *Holy Sepulchre* (see note 1), p. 47.

104

these and Aphrodite's Temple or the Forum is not clear.

A real attempt to locate all these ruins on a single ground plan, indicating their elevations and those of the Rock, has yet to be made. Therefore, in any matter relating to the site and its buildings in Roman times we are more ignorant than otherwise. What is certain, however, is that the intensive construction by Constantine destroyed large portions of the former buildings, as Eusebius' writings and the few remains that have come to light in excavations testify.

Construction Works in the Fourth Century

The Emperor Constantine, encouraged by his mother Helena and aided by Macarius, the Patriarch of Jerusalem, enthusiastically embarked on erecting a church and monument on the site of Jesus' tomb. First the pagan temple was demolished, as has been stated, to once again reveal the Holy Sepulchre. After that, the basilica was constructed with great pomp and ceremony. At the same time, the rock of the hill was hewn away in order to isolate the Sepulchre within a circular plaza.

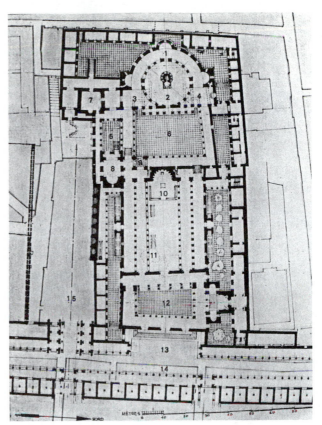

The Church of the Holy Sepulchre: reconstructed plan of the fourth-century complex 1) Ambulatory; 2) Rotunda; 3) and 4) Lateral vestibules; 5) Southern atrium; 6) Courtyard of the Rotunda; 7) Baptistery; 8) Church of the Golgotha; 9) Church of the Cross; 10) Basilica of Constantine; 11) Crypt of St. Helena; 12) Eastern atrium; 13) Entrance; 14) Cardo Maximus; 15) Site of Hadrian's forum (Coüasnon, Pl. VIII)

Within the complex of buildings that make up the Holy Sepulchre, the following can be distinguished (from west to east):

1. The Holy Sepulchre itself and the surrounding structure, known as the Anastasis ("Resurrection") or Rotunda because of its circular shape.

2. An inner courtyard (surrounded on the north, south, and east by columns — hence, the term "Triportico"), stretching east of the facade of the Anastasis.

3. A large basilica-type church, designated in the contemporaneous sources as the "Martyrium."

4. The entrance courtyard to the church — the atrium — the front of which leads into the main Cardo of the city.

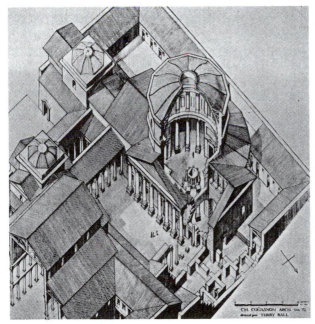

The Church of the Holy Sepulchre: reconstructed plan of the fourth-century church after the completion of the Rotunda. Below left, the Basilica and the dome of the Chapel of the Golgotha. (Coüasnon, Pl. XVII)

The Church of the Holy Sepulchre: broken columns of the Constantinian Triportico (see ground plan, pilasters 521 and 525) under the Crusader pavement, looking west from above (Corbo, *Sepolchro*, Photo 20)

In addition to these four buildings, which Eusebius also mentions, two other structures can be discerned:

5. An additional building north of the Anastasis and the inner courtyard, designated by Coüasnon as monastic cells, while Corbo proposed to identify it as the Patriarch's residence. It has two stories, and extends north and west of a narrow, elongated courtyard.

6. The Baptistery, apparently south of the Anastasis, where now three Greek Orthodox chapels stand. The foundations of the latter may preserve the remnants of the Baptistery,

which in turn may have been erected on the site of an older Roman bathhouse with its standard three sections.

We will now review the remains of these various components as revealed by their architectural survey and during the archaeological excavations.

The Anastasis (Rotunda)

Eusebius relates that the Holy Sepulchre was adorned with beautiful columns. He makes no reference to a closed building surrounding the tomb. Eusebius' testimony, and the ancient walls that were discovered under the pavement of the Anastasis, led Coüasnon to posit the existence of two stages, both of them dating to the fourth century C.E. In the first phase, still during the time of Eusebius and Constantine, the Sepulchre stood as a relatively simple mausoleum in an open courtyard, measuring around 15 × 15 m, surrounded by columns. During this time, the planned Anastasis was being built behind the Sepulchre (see reconstruction on p. 102), and it was apparently completed only toward the middle of the century. In 381–384 C.E., when the pilgrim Egeria visited Jerusalem, the Holy Sepulchre was already located inside an enclosed building. Corbo rejects this view. He does not regard the literary source as conclusive proof, and is of the opinion that the Anastasis was built in one stage as a roofed building, already in Constantine's time.

The enclosing wall, which rests on the rock, is 1.2 m thick. It was built of superbly hewn polished stones, and has been preserved intact to a height of more than 11 m all around the Rotunda. This level is today above that of the gallery pavement. The inner facade of the enclosing wall had a round contour, whereas the outer one had a polygonal contour for the entire height of the original wall. Higher up it is also rounded at present. This upper part of the wall was built in the eleventh century. Several courses of bricks separate it from the lower Constantinian wall, as if by design.

The enclosing wall has three apses, the western one protruding beyond the wall. Its lower courses, to a height of 4 m, are built against the rock of the hill, which was leveled and hewn away when the Rotunda was built. The northern and southern apses are sunk in square projections beyond the rounded facade of the wall, so that their existence is not evident from the outside.

Each apse is illuminated through three arched windows, 1.4 m wide, and in each section of wall between the apses, three more 2.1-m-wide arched windows were built. On the inner side of the enclosing wall and the apses, up to the level of the window sills, are the projections that held the marble facing of the walls in place. The semi-domes of the apses retain traces of the layer of plaster that underlay the wall mosaics.

The tomb, which, according to the Pilgrim from Placentia (ca. 570 C.E.) and Arculf (some date between 679 and 688 C.E.), was hewn from a single block of stone, stands inside a round plaza about 35 m in diameter, enclosed by the ring wall. Above the tomb there was a canopy supported by pillars.

Concentric with the ring wall, twelve pillars in groups of three surround the Sepulchre in a circle about 20 m in diameter. Each group of three stands between pairs of piers in the north, south, and west. According to Coüasnon, the piers in each pair were connected by a wall segment erected above a lintelled doorway in order to reinforce the structure.

The Sepulchre does not lie in the center of this inner circle, but at a point to its west, at the junction of the axes that pass through the centers of the three apses. Between the northern and southern apses and the facade of the Anastasis, north and south of the circle of pillars and piers, were two square spaces — the northern and southern vestibules (nos. 46 and 47). Their outer walls, which were a continuation of the outer ring, have been preserved to a height of 11 m. Between the ring wall and the circle of pillars, there ran a peripheral corridor (ambulatory), which connected the two lateral vestibules.

The facade of the Anastasis, which faced east, had a wide main entrance and four secondary entrances on either side. The main entrance and the three inner ones on either of its sides connected the lateral vestibules to the inner courtyard (Triportico), which separated the Anastasis from the Martyrium; while the two outer openings connected the lateral vestibules to the northern and southern porticoes of the courtyard.

In excavations in the Armenian section, slightly east of the facade, a segment of a thick wall (no. 222) was discovered. Coüasnon sought to deduce from this that in front of the facade of the Anastasis there stood a colonnade projecting into the courtyard, and that this stretch of wall belongs to its plinth or stylobate. Corbo rejects this proposition on the grounds that the colonnade thus obtained is too shallow, but he does not offer any alternative explanation for this section of wall.

Another section of wall uncovered in excavations, extending from column 53 in the plan northward, was identified by Corbo as the stylobate of a chancel screen or *cancellus* that bordered the western section of the Rotunda. He learnt of the existence of such a *cancellus* from the description of the pilgrim Egeria.[13]

Corbo and Coüasnon are also in disagreement about the reconstruction of the upper part of the Rotunda during the fourth century, although they are in accord regarding the ground plan. It appears that two of the current columns of the Rotunda, whose shafts are about 3.5–3.6 m high, originally formed a single column twice as tall. Coüasnon is of the opinion that these lofty columns belonged to the fourth-century Rotunda, and were sawn in two during the eleventh-century restoration and reconstruction of the building. Corbo, on the other hand, believes that the column was sawn already in Constantine's time, and that the six columns originally formed part of the facade of the pagan temple.

According to Coüasnon's reconstruction (see above, p. 105), the Rotunda columns (approximate diameter: 1.03–1.12 m) rose to a height of 7.15 m. They stood on a plinth 1.78 m high. There was no gallery above the ambu-

---

13 P. Maraval (ed. and tr.), *Egerie, Journal de Voyage* (Sources Chretiennes 296, 24.2), p. 236.15.

107

latory; instead a roof was mounted on light wooden rafters. This roof also covered, on the same level, the northern and southern vestibules of the Rotunda. The round central space above the Sepulchre rose to a great height, and was crowned with a kind of cupola, which also rested on wooden rafters — a form of roofing typical of early Christian architecture. A reconstruction of this sort corresponds to a Roman mausoleum and is well attested in the architecture of the period. Round *mausolea* were built in Rome over the tomb of Constantia, daughter of Constantine, and over that of Helena, his mother. Another major building — octagonal in shape — was built by Constantine over the Cave of the Nativity in Bethlehem, as part of the basilican church. In other words, this type of structure for the preservation of holy places was common in those times.

Corbo, on the other hand, maintains that in Constantine's days the columns of the Rotunda rose to a height of only 3.5 m above the plinth (their height today). In his reconstruction, a gallery — similar to the structure of the Anastasis as it is today and has been since the eleventh century — ran round the ambulatory, but was supported by wooden rafters at the time and not by stone vaults. This architectural reconstruction does not have parallels in contemporaneous *mausolea*, nor does it seem to contend with the fact that the ancient ring wall, which has been preserved to a height of more than 11 m above the current gallery pavement, belonged in its entirety to the ground floor of the Anastasis. There are no remains of a hypothetical Constantinian gallery. The estimated height of the columns — 10.5 m including plinth and capital — corresponds to that to which the ring wall has been preserved, and supports Coüasnon's reconstruction.

The Inner Courtyard (Triportico)
The collapsed columns of the Constantinian portico were found in Trench III, in the area of the "Virgin's arches." Three of the original pillars of the "Virgin's arches" stand *in situ* (no. 219 on the plan). The original northern wall of the Triportico has been also preserved to a height of ca. 11 m (no. 220 on the plan). In Trench V, the base of a column belonging to the eastern portico was discovered *in situ* (no. 215 on the plan; see also the photograph on p. 106).

The Golgotha and the Golgotha Chapel
The Rock of Golgotha — a bare rock, jutting to a height of approximately 5 m — was included in the southeast corner of the inner courtyard. It was surrounded by a metal screen, and surmounted by a large cross — in memory of the crucifixion.

Excavations east of Golgotha indicate that the original southern aisle of the Basilica was blocked off on the west by a wall, so that there was no direct access to the Rock from this direction. According to the *Breviarius* ["The Short Description of Jerusalem" (early sixth century C.E.)], a golden cross inlaid with precious stones was placed at the top of the Rock. This was the *crux gemmata* donated by Theodosius II in the year 420 C.E. According to the same source and the testimony of the Pilgrim of Placentia, the cross on the Rock was in the open air, and the Rock was surrounded by railings adorned with silver and gold. According to Theodosius (518–530 C.E.), there were steps leading up to the top of the Hill of Golgotha. The remains of this staircase, parts of which have been removed or are today blocked off, are located north of the Rock. During the time of the Crusaders, an outer entrance was built on the south, from the *parvis* to the chapel atop the Golgotha, via the Chapel of the Franks. This door is blocked now, having been converted into a window. Today, the chapels above the Golgotha are entered via a staircase that was built in the wake of the fire of 1808. This staircase blocks the eastern of the two Crusader entrance gates to the Church of the Holy Sepulchre.

A canopy over the Golgotha was first erected in the days of Modestus, who rebuilt the churches of Jerusalem after the Persian Conquest of 614 C.E., and later became its Patriarch. This was originally a simple intersecting vault, standing on four piers. In the

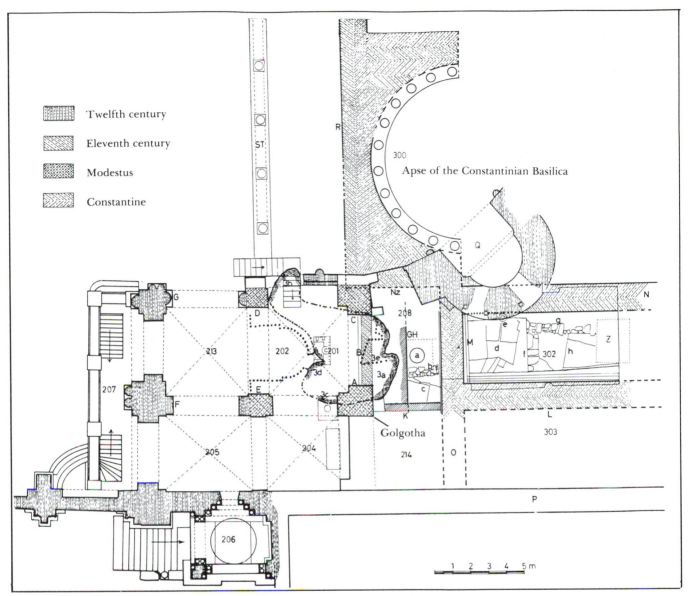

Twelfth century

Eleventh century

Modestus

Constantine

Apse of the Constantinian Basilica

Golgotha

1 2 3 4 5 m

The Church of the Holy Sepulchre: development of the area of the Golgotha. In the days of Constantine, the rock was uncovered. Modestus erected a canopy (pillars A, C, D and E bear an intersecting vault). At the same time, Adam's Chapel with its apse (202) was built to the west. The Crusaders extended the Chapel of Golgotha westward by adding columns F and G and cells 205 and 213. The northern staircase rests on projection 3b. The southern one, adjacent to the Franks' Chapel (206), dates to Crusader times. The staircase (207) in use today was built after the 1808 fire and sealed off the eastern entrance to the church. Excavations in area 302 uncovered: a small cave (3e), an eleventh-century wall that blocks Modestus' eastern arch (B); a revetment east of the Rock (GH); a round bas-relief (a); a wall of uncut stones (b); foundations of a Crusader wall (N); carvings in the rock (d, e, h); low walls (f, g); foundations of the Basilica of Constantine (N, M, L) (Corbo, *Sepolchro*, Pl. 40)

eleventh century the eastern side of the canopy was closed off by a wall.

A Christian tradition, which connects the Rock of Golgotha with Adam's grave, is already related by Origen in the third century C.E. It is only from the early sixth century,

however, that the Byzantine sources mention Adam's Chapel or Abraham's altar under the Rock of Golgotha. According to Arculf, memorial masses were held at the altar of this chapel for important persons prior to their burial, while their bodies were laid out in the

The Church of the Holy Sepulchre: cross-section of the Golgotha and adjacent structures, looking south — Adam's Chapel (202) with column and arch; rock surface under the Constantinian pavement (1a); Crusader column (1c) extending Adam's Chapel westward; location of tombs of the Crusader kings (1e) over which staircase 207 was built in 1808; entrance to area 1e (1f); The Greek Chapel of Golgotha (201, 213); columns dating to Modestus (A, E); eleventh-century wall blocking the eastern arch (B); rock fissure in Adam's Chapel (3d); small cave in the eastern side of the Golgotha (3e); revetment for Rock of Golgotha (GH); round bas-relief (a); rock carvings (c); Constantinian Basilica walls (a); later cistern (aa); two Crusader arches (above); bedrock and earth fill in quarry (d, h) (Corbo, *Sepolchro*, Pl. 41)

courtyard in front of the entrance to the Church of Golgotha. The Crusaders extended Adam's Chapel eastward, and the site served as the mausoleum of several Crusader kings.

According to Egeria's description, Arculf, and other sources, rites were performed in a church located next to the Rock of Golgotha, which is not the Basilica of Constantine. Coüasnon reconstructs this church in the northeast corner of the *parvis*, detached from the Rock of Golgotha, where the Ethiopian Chapel of the Archangel Michael stands today. Corbo does not refer to this question in his plans.

The Basilica of Constantine

The foundations of the Basilica were discovered during excavations in the Chapel of St. Vartan, in the crypt of St. Helena, and east of the Golgotha (see plan, and drawings on p. 105). A section of the apse was uncovered in

excavations in the Katholikon. On the basis of these remains, and Eusebius' description of the Basilica, a fairly precise reconstruction of the latter can be made. The foundations were sunk deep into the ground, as far as bedrock or the earthfill of the quarry. In certain places, they cross older walls from the Roman period. The foundations were built of hewn stones with polished surfaces, without margins.

In St. Vartan's Chapel, the following Latin inscription was discovered: DOMINE IVI-MUS, "Lord, we have gone," alongside a picture of a ship. It was suggested that this refers to the Latin version of Psalms 122:1: "I rejoiced when they said to me, We are going to the house of the Lord," and that it was drawn by Christian pilgrims that came to venerate the holy tomb when the foundations of the Basilica were still being built (see in this volume, M. Broshi, "Excavations in the Holy Sepulchre in the Chapel of St. Vartan and the Armenian Martyrs," pp. 118–122).

110

The portion of the apse discovered in 1970 in Trench V in the Katholikon (see photograph on p.103) made it possible to determine the Basilica's axis. This does not coincide with that of the Anastasis, but runs slightly south of it. The internal apse of the Basilica faces west toward the Sepulchre. The width of the nave is about 15 m (the width of the subterranean St. Helena's Chapel is 13.5 m). Portions of the stylobates supporting the two rows of columns on either side of the nave were uncovered, flanking St Helena's Chapel. Father Vincent was of the opinion that this Chapel was originally a crypt of the Basilica.[14] However, excavations behind the wall of its apse indicate that the latter was built in the twelfth century, during the Crusader period, at which time the crypt was also constructed. Only the lateral walls were earlier. Coüasnon shares Corbo's conclusion on this matter. However, he suggested that the northern lateral wall, which goes down to bedrock, was erected in the time of Hadrian, forming the foundations of the civic Basilica. But the excavations in the Chapel of St. Vartan proved that this is a Constantinian foundation.

From Eusebius' description in his book, *The Life of Constantine*, we know a lot of details about the appearance of the Basilica. The nave was flanked by two aisles on each side. The Basilica was entered from the east, via three entrances. Opposite, at the western end, was the apse, with its twelve pillars corresponding to the twelve apostles, surmounted by silver capitals. The nave rose to a substantial height, and was covered by a lead roof supported by wooden rafters. The aisles were bordered by two inner rows of columns beyond which were two rows of square pillars, with galleries above. Coüasnon[15] suggests that the ground-floor columns were approximately 4.8 m high, and the gallery columns approximately 3.6 m high. The ceilings of the nave, aisles, and galleries were made of gold-plated coffers. The inner walls of the Basilica were covered with marble and colored stones.

The Church of the Holy Sepulchre: Wall L east of Golgotha, looking southeast. Note the typical stone dressing and stepped foundations belonging to the first southern aisle of the Basilica (Corbo, *Sepolchro*, Photo 101)

Corbo believes that the Basilica measured ca. 40 × 58 m (outer dimensions) while Coüasnon's reconstruction shows its length as only ca. 49 m. Coüasnon also reconstructs a height of 22 m from the floor to the ceiling of the nave. According to Corbo, each aisle had sixteen freestanding columns, while Coüasnon thought that there were only fourteen. The northernmost aisle was aligned with the present-day road leading to the Coptic Patriarchate, the northern wall of the Basilica being preserved in the wall enclosing the Coptic monastery from the south. A 15-m-long section of its southern external wall can be seen in the Ethiopian Chapel. The two inner aisles were blocked by a wall at their western end, but the two outer ones apparently opened

---

[14] *JN* (see note 3), Pl. XXXIII.
[15] Coüasnon, *Holy Sepulchre* (see note 1), p. 44.

onto the Triportico at the west, in order to afford worshippers easy access to the various parts of the Holy Sepulchre complex. Coüasnon depicts outer staircases north and south of the Basilica leading up to its gallery level. Corbo's plan makes no reference to these.

A small section of the facade of the Basilica is found in the Russian Hospice. It is not perpendicular to the lateral walls of the Basilica — so that the shape of the atrium resembles an equilateral trapezoid oriented north–south, 41 m long and with bases measuring 20 and 18 m (Corbo's outer dimensions). Coüasnon depicts the trapezoid as having bases measuring only 28 and 22 m, since he assumed that the wall that encloses the courtyard of the Ethiopians from the east coincides with the facade wall of the Basilica.

The Atrium
Eusebius' description mentions colonnades in the area of the atrium, but their remains have not yet been discovered. Two of the three front gates, which also appear on the Madaba Map, have been preserved in the Russian Hospice and in Zalatimo's Bakery. As stated above, the corner of a Hadrianic or Herodian structure was incorporated here. The parallel rows of projections on the walls evidence that the latter were marble-faced. A majestic and broad staircase, also featured on the Madaba Map, led from the Cardo Maximus to the front entrances. A Kufic-Arabic inscription, discovered here in the last century, indicates, according to several scholars, that this was the site of a mosque that commemorated Omar's prayers on the stairs of the Church of the Holy Sepulchre, as related by Muslim sources.[16]

According to the *Breviarius* and the Pilgrim of Placentia, the treasury of the Holy Sepulchre was in the area of the atrium, left of the entrance into the Basilica. This room contained holy objects: Jesus' true cross (made of hazelwood); the reed and sponge mentioned in the story of the crucifixion; the grail which Jesus blessed and gave to his disciples to drink

from, saying, "This is my body and my blood"; and the placard bearing the words "The King of the Jews." It was customary to take the cross from this room to display to the worshippers in the courtyard. Relics connected with the Virgin Mary were also kept here.

The Southern Atrium (*Parvis*) and the Baptistery
According to Coüasnon's reconstruction, the northern part of the *parvis* served as an atrium to the Church of Golgotha. Two large cisterns are located under the *parvis* (see photograph on p. 104).

Various Byzantine sources — the Pilgrim of Bordeaux (330 C.E.), Cyril of Jerusalem (347–348 C.E.), the pilgrim Egeria, and others — speak of the existence of a baptistery attached to the Church of the Holy Sepulchre. Coüasnon[17] follows the traditional interpretation and places the baptistery south of the Anastasis, on the western side of the *parvis*, on the site of the three eleventh-century Greek chapels. Adequate research, however, has yet to be carried out at this spot. Corbo, on the basis of various remains, including a baptismal font, suggests that the Constantinian baptistery lay north of the Anastasis in area 100d (see plan on p. 102),[18] and that only in the eleventh century was a baptistery erected to the south of the Anastasis (see below, p. 114). However, Corbo's area — a mere passageway between courtyards 100 and 120 — is not suitable to serve as a baptistery for conversion to Christianity or for christening babies. A place opening onto the open *parvis* would apparently have been more appropriate.

The Patriarch's Residence
A two-storied row of rooms north and west of the Anastasis, beyond courtyard 100, is identified by Corbo as the Patriarch's residence.[19] It seems, however, that in the Byzan-

---

[16] *JN* (see note 3), Pl. VI; idem, *RB* 6 (1897): 643ff.
[17] Coüasnon, *Holy Sepulchre* (see note 1), p. 46–50.
[18] See also C. Tinelli, "Il battistero del S. Sepolcro in Gerusalemme," *LA* 23 (1973): 95–104.
[19] Corbo, *Il Santo Sepolcro de Gerusalemme* (see note 2), Pls. 59–65.

tine period this palace was located in the area of the current Greek Patriarchate — an opinion held by many scholars. The wing that surrounds courtyard 100 was a service wing of the Church of the Holy Sepulchre, with an oil press, storage rooms, and accommodations for some of the church's attendants. In the days of Patriarch Elias (494–518 C.E.), a special monastery was built alongside the Patriarch's residence to house the monks of the Church [the "*Spoudaioi* (Devotee) of the Holy Sepulchre"]. This monastery is conventionally located on the site of the Greek monastery next to the present-day Patriarchate.

The Persian Conquest and Modestus' Restoration

The Persian Conquest of Jerusalem in 614 C.E. brought in its wake much bloodshed; many churches and monasteries were destroyed. The Holy Sepulchre, however, was not razed to the ground. The remains of the True Cross, the most precious relic of the church, were taken to the Persian capital, Ctesiphon, together with many captives, including the Patriarch of Jerusalem, Zacharias. After the victory of the Emperor Heraclius in 628, the Cross was returned to the church. The grandiose project of rebuilding the church was already begun in the time of the Persian regime. It was entrusted to Modestus, abbot of St. Theodosius' Monastery in the Judean Desert, and subsequently Patriarch of Jerusalem.

The Muslim conquest of Jerusalem in 638 was not accompanied by acts of destruction, so that Arculf's description (some time between 679 and 688 C.E) can be taken as referring to Modestus' restoration. This source, excavations, and architectural research indicate that the latter work consisted mainly in reinforcing the structures and replacing the wooden roofs that had been burnt by flat vaults supported on consoles projecting from the walls. Apart from this, all parts of the Holy Sepulchre complex remained intact. Arculf also mentions the Church of the Virgin Mary, to the right of the Anastasis. According to the ancient illustrations accompanying the manuscripts, this was situated south of the Chapel of Golgotha, but the text is not definitely clear on this point.

Within the Anastasis, which is described as a circular church, Arculf mentions three walls, and in the illustrations of the various manuscripts these are depicted as concentric circles. No trace of them, however, has been discovered in excavations, and it would appear that the text is referring to the three wall segments between the piers in each of the three pairs; Coüasnon suggests that the manuscript illustrators misunderstood the text and erred. According to Arculf, the main entrance at the front of the Anastasis had been blocked off, while the four secondary ones on either side of it remained in use. There was an altar in each of the three apses. A large church — of which the Rock of Golgotha was apparently part — is mentioned at the site of the Golgotha. East of the Chapel of Golgotha is the Basilica of Constantine, and between them is Abraham's altar. The grail and the sponge were kept in the inner courtyard between the Martyrium and the Anastasis, and not in the atrium of the Basilica. The spear and the cross, on the other hand, were housed in the stoa of the Basilica. The fact that the city was under Muslim rule meant that rites formerly conducted in the outer atrium were now performed in the inner courtyard, or inside the Basilica itself.

The magnificent Basilica met its end under the programed demolition of the complex ordered by the Fatimid Caliph al-Ḥakim bn-Amr Allah in 1009 C.E.[20] The destruction was almost total. First the utensils and furniture were smashed; then the liturgical vessels and treasures were confiscated; finally the Basilica of Constantine was razed, and the Rock of Golgotha and the Sepulchre itself damaged. From that time the Sepulchre ceased to be a monolith with a tomb hewn into it, and became a structure whose upper part was built. The ancient Basilica has never been restored since then. Attention was directed toward re-

---

[20] M. Canard, "Déstruction de l'Église de la Résurrection," *Byzantion* (1965): 16–43.

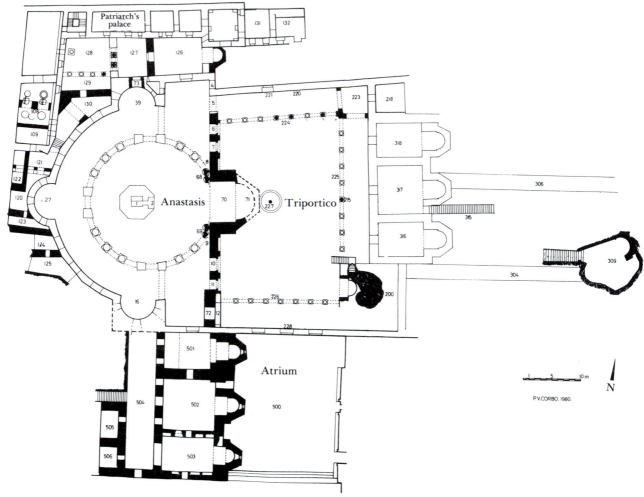

The Church of the Holy Sepulchre: plan a of eleventh-century ground-floor remains (Corbo, *Sepolchro*, Pl. 4)

storing the building over the Sepulchre — the Anastasis — and the Golgotha. Reconstruction began in 1030, under the aegis of the Byzantine court of Constantinople and with the permission of the Muslim rulers of Cairo. The work was completed in 1048 by the Emperor Constantine IX Monomachus (1042–1055 C.E.).

The Edifice of Constantine Monomachus in the Eleventh Century

The remains of the eleventh-century edifice are reasonably clear. A distinctive feature is the presence of courses of brick. The main part of the building — the Anastasis — was incorporated almost intact into the later Romanesque Crusader church built in the twelfth century to the east of the Rotunda; it is

in this form that it stands to this day. The Anastasis was shaped like a round church with a gallery, with a large apse on the east, unlike a mausoleum, whose center is higher than its circumference, and whose facade is straight. The ambulatory and gallery had intersecting stone vaulted roofs, rather than light wooden rafters. The gallery was open to the central space through a series of alternating columns and piers divided by three pairs of heavier piers on the north, south, and west. Slightly pointed arches spanned the piers and columns on both stories.

On the gallery level an entrance was opened through the western side of the ring wall that surrounded the Anastasis, above the western apse (no. 86 on the plan of the gallery level). This entrance, which directly connected the

114

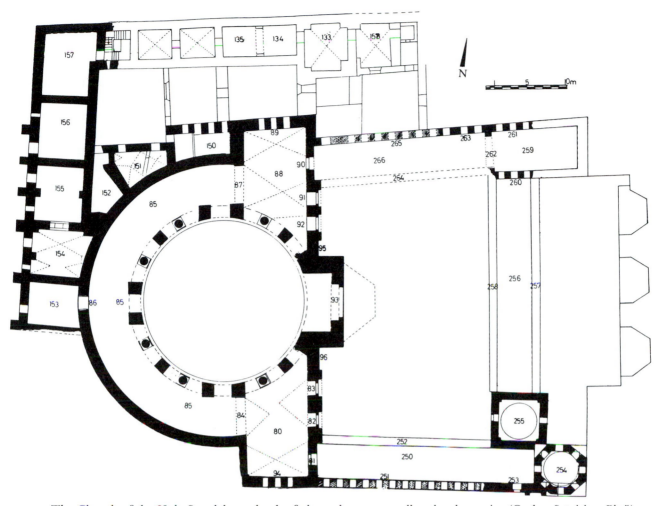

The Church of the Holy Sepulchre: plan b of eleventh-century gallery-level remains (Corbo, *Sepolchro*, Pl. 5)

street (currently Christian Quarter Street) to the level of the galleries, is mentioned in Nasir-i-Khosro's description of 1047 C.E. The apse that was erected on the eastern side of this round church rose in a wide arch to the ceiling of the galleries. To this day the arch links the Rotunda to the Katholikon. The entrances in the facade of the Anastasis on either side of the apse were sealed during the construction in order to reinforce its arch. In the northern and southern apses of the Anastasis, pavements of small marble slabs in a geometric design have been preserved. Remains of similar pavements have been found in the northern vestibule of the Anastasis (geometric motifs) and in its gallery (with pictures of birds and fish). An entrance was breached in the northern apse to connect

the Rotunda to the narthex of Mary's Chapel.

The edifice surrounding the Holy Garden followed in its ground plan the fourth-century Triportico, except that now it was a two-story building supported by piers and columns, rather than the simple single-story Triportico that had surrounded the courtyard in the fourth century. Only the columns of the northern portico remain *in situ* to this day, as part of the Crusader building. These are the so-called "Virgin's arches." The Rock of Golgotha was incorporated into the southeast corner of the Holy Garden. Atop it stood a chapel entered by a staircase from the north, with another chapel below, on its western side.

The main entrance into the complex was no longer in the east, but in the south, through the plaza of the present-day *parvis*. Over the

The Church of the Holy Sepulchre: eleventh-century pavement of small marble slabs in northern apse of the Anastasis (Corbo, *Sepolchro*, Photo 153)

The Church of the Holy Sepulchre: reconstruction of the structure rebuilt in 1048 by Constantine Monomachus (Coüasnon, Pl. XXV)

southeast corner of the complex loomed an octagonal spire with a brick "squinch dome."

The Eleventh-Century Chapels

Three chapels mentioned in the sources have been reconstructed in the east of the Holy Garden. Their foundations, however, are buried today under a Crusader building, and have not been uncovered. Further east, outside the area of the eleventh-century edifice, an ancient cistern was converted into the subterranean Chapel of the Finding of the True Cross. A staircase led down into this chapel where a wall picture from the Crusader period was discovered around the altar. In the area of courtyard 100, north of the Anastasis, a chapel was built as a memorial to St. Mary (no. 126 on plan a of the eleventh century). This was done by roofing the courtyard with a stone vault, supported by the Constantinian walls on either side, and building a new apse on the site of entrance, 102 (plan, p. 102), which led from courtyard 100 into courtyard 115. West of chapel 126 was narthex 127, bordered on the west by a pair of columns. Further west was the chapel courtyard, 128, as an atrium with a single row of columns in the south, of which only the easternmost one has survived. In the Crusader period, a staircase was built in this courtyard, leading from the "Patriarch's Gate," a new gate which connected Patriarch Street with the Holy Sepulchre. The gate, located on Christian Quarter Street near the junction with Greek Patriarchate Street, is today blocked, but its decorations are visible.

Three chapels were built on the west side of the southern atrium: the Chapel of John the Evangelist or the Forty Martyrs of Sebastia (no. 501 on plan b of the eleventh century); a baptistery (no. 502) which perhaps replaced an ancient one; and the Chapel of St. James the Less (no. 503). Entrance to these chapels was from the west, via a common narthex, which is still reached by a staircase that leads down from the area of the Greek Patriarchate.

In the area of the Holy Garden, east of the apse, "the navel of the world" (*Omphalos*) was displayed inside a special aedicule. In the Byzantine period, since the time of Cyril of Jerusalem (347–348 C.E.), the Rock of Golgotha, situated farther to the southeast, was considered the navel of the world.

The Church of the Crusaders to Recent Times

On July 15, 1099, Jerusalem was conquered by the Crusaders. Now that the Christians were once again masters of the site, it befitted them to erect a larger and more magnificent house of worship. The apse of the Rotunda was removed; in its place, on the east side of the Rotunda, a tall structure of intersecting vaults was built in Romanesque style, in the area of the Holy Garden, along the same axis as the Anastasis. The resulting edifice brought the Sepulchre, the Rock of Golgotha, the *Chorus Dominorum*, and various chapels under one roof. The new structure was inaugurated on the fiftieth anniversary of the Crusader conquest, July 15, 1149. This is basically the building we know today. To its east, on the site of the Constantinian Martyrium, a monastery for the church canons was erected.

The structure has suffered much impairment since its inauguration — earthquakes, fires, and intentional destruction. Serious damage was caused in the great fire of 1808, which spread from the Armenian Chapel in the southern section of the Anastasis gallery. The dome of the Anastasis was destroyed, and the tomb and the marble pavement were severely impaired. The repairs, which were authorized by a special edict (*firman*) obtained by the Greeks from the Sultan Maḥmud II, were supervised by the Greek architect Comnenus of Mytilene. Further renovation of the Rotunda was carried out in 1863–1868 under the aegis of the French and Russian governments, and supervised by the architect Mauss. Under Mauss' supervision, a small prayer niche, which had stood on the roof of the Rotunda, was rebuilt in the courtyard of the Monastery of the White Fathers, next to the Church of Saint Anne, where it can be seen today.

The 1927 earthquake also took its toll on the church. As a result, the dome of the Katholikon was repaired, and the facade reinforced by steel girders. In 1935, under the British Mandate, Harvey undertook an architectural survey in order to examine the structural condition of the building.[21] However, due to controversies between the various communities, the restoration work was delayed for another twenty-five years. In 1955 an international conference of architects was held on the subject of conservation of the Holy Sepulchre. Representatives from England, Belgium, Spain, the United States, France, Greece, Italy, and Lebanon were present. In 1960 an agreed-upon plan was authorized, and the "Joint Technical Bureau" was established and initiated the work that is currently drawing to its close.

[21] W. Harvey, *Church of the Holy Sepulchre, Jerusalem — Structural Survey, Final Report* (London, 1935).

Excavations in the Holy Sepulchre in the Chapel of St. Vartan and the Armenian Martyrs

Magen Broshi

The Church of the Holy Sepulchre is a large complex located in the heart of the Christian Quarter of Jerusalem's Old City. It originated in the days of Constantine the Great, in the fourth century C.E.; since that time, it has undergone various phases of destruction, reconstruction, and entirely new construction. Most of the extant complex dates from the Crusader period.

In 1960 extensive restoration work was begun in the Holy Sepulchre, which included archaeological excavations. The first general review, incorporating data stemming from these excavations, was published by Father C. Coüasnon,[1] and a well-illustrated final report, in three volumes, has recently been published by Father V. Corbo.[2] Of course, the main point of interest was the uncovering of the church building from the Byzantine and medieval periods. Remains from earlier epochs, including the end of the Israelite period, were also found here.

Description of the Excavations

The Chapel of St. Helena (Constantine's mother) is situated at the eastern edge of the church complex. It is reached by descending a stairway from the main level of the church. St. Helena's chapel is in the custody of the Armenians, who call it the Chapel of St. Krikor (Gregory). An additional stairway leads down, eastward, to a rock-hewn cave known as the Chapel of the Invention of the Cross.

In 1970 the Armenian Patriarchate sought to clarify whether, beyond the apses of St.

Helena's chapel, to the east, there was a sealed space or, as was generally suspected, merely bedrock. A brief excavation revealed that indeed there was a space that had been blocked already in antiquity.[3] This continuation of the Chapel of the Invention of the Cross was excavated by the Armenian Patriarchate, and was subsequently fitted out as a chapel, today called the Chapel of St. Vartan and the Armenian Martyrs.

Remains from the Roman and Byzantine Periods

In describing the architectural remains of the space now known as the Chapel of St. Vartan, the chronological order here will be reversed as the later finds serve as a point of departure in determining the dates. Walls W4 and W6 belong to the Constantinian basilica, known in antiquity as the the Martyrium. W4 is the foundation of the northern stylobate of the nave, and W6 was intended to support the ceiling of the quarry, which forms the rock ledge on which the facade was erected. Numerous fragments survive from this early church, enabling a fairly accurate reconstruction of its plan.

It is possible to follow the length of the southern face of W4 for 39 m (in the space under discussion and its continuation in the Chapel of St. Helena), and that of its northern face for 21.75 m. The wall is 2.82 m thick and is preserved to a height of 12 m. It was built in two parts: a lower section of fourteen courses and an upper portion, slightly set back, of six

[1] C. Coüasnon, O.P., *The Church of the Holy Sepulchre in Jerusalem* (London, 1974).
[2] V.C. Corbo, O.F.M., *Il Santo Sepolcro de Gerusalemme*, 1–3 (Jerusalem, 1981–1982).

[3] The clearance was conducted by several laborers on behalf of the Armenian Patriarchate. We wish to express our gratitude to Bishop Guregh Kapikian, who invited the author to oversee this work.

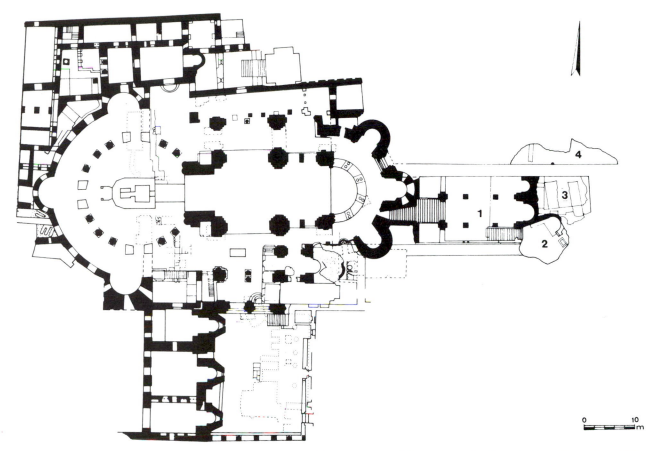

Plan of the Holy Sepulchre complex: 1) Chapel of St. Helena (Chapel of St. Krikor); 2) Chapel of the Invention of the Cross; 3) Chapel of St. Vartan and the Armenian Martyrs; 4) The northern space

courses. Its foundation was constructed of fieldstones, with ashlars above. Some of the stones were taken from earlier buildings — smoothly dressed stones (apparently from Hadrianic structures), Second Temple period stones with marginal drafts, and three smooth column drums. The well-cut ashlars had been coated over with a gray plaster, a few traces of which are still visible. Although it does not seem that this wall was intended to be exposed to view when the basilica was in use, its craftsmanship is fine. It is the most attractive and the best preserved part of the Martyrium and of the entire Constantinian complex.

Chapel of St. Vartan and the Armenian Martyrs: the space to the north, looking north

119

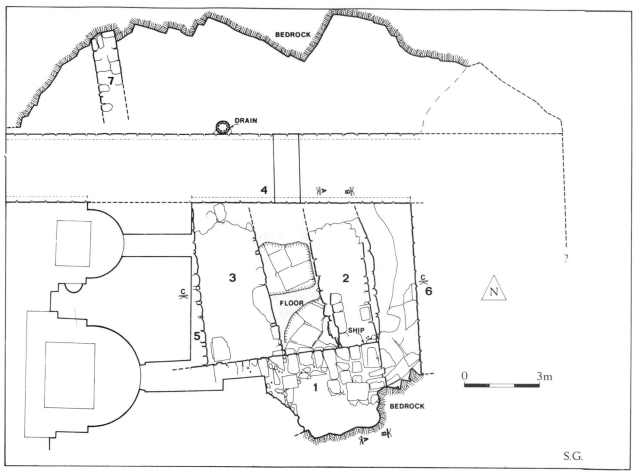

Chapel of St. Vartan and the Armenian Martyrs: plan of the excavated area. The numbers relate to walls

Wall W6, as noted, was intended to support the ceiling of the quarry — the *mizzi ḥilou* limestone stratum left by the Iron Age quarrymen after they removed the high-quality *meleke* stone they were seeking. The facade of the church was constructed over this space, and thus a massive means of support was required within the 13-m gap. This wall was built like W4 — of ashlars, some of them in secondary use from the Hadrianic and Second Temple periods. There is almost no doubt that both walls were erected by the builders of the Constantinian basilica using Hadrianic stones, but there is no reason to assume that they utilized Hadrianic walls that had been found here, as has been suggested (albeit with caution) by Coüasnon. There is considerable similarity between the style of construction of these two walls and that of the other walls of

the Constantinian basilica. W4 and W6 are situated in full agreement with the orientation of the Constantinian apse.

W2 and W3 are earlier than the Constantinian walls and, for several reasons, should probably be ascribed to Hadrianic buildings. In our opinion these massive walls are the remains of a structure (probably a vault) that supported the floor of the complex of the Temple of Aphrodite, which Corbo calls the *Capitolium*. We know of this temple from the literary sources (mainly Eusebius, *Vita Constant.* III, 25–26) and from occasional archaeological remains. W2, which is 2.3 m thick in its lower part and 1.6 m thick in its upper portion, was built onto the Iron Age floor, slightly above bedrock. W3, whose assumed thickness is 2.75 m, is founded on bedrock. Like most walls not intended to be seen, both

120

were built, without esthetic considerations, of mixed fieldstones and ashlars in secondary use. The source of the ashlars was probably the destroyed buildings of Second Temple Jerusalem. That these walls were later than Second Temple times is indicated by stones with marginal drafting and protruding bosses, generally dated to the Second Temple period, which are clearly in secondary use here. Further evidence for ascribing these walls to the period of Aelia Capitolina is the tiles stamped with the mark of the Roman Tenth Legion, probably from the third century, that were recovered from the adjacent fill.

As already noted, W2 and W3 were probably built as part of a vault to support the floor of the Hadrianic temenos. It can be assumed that the vault's closest parallels are those in the huge cistern beneath the neighboring Monastery of St. Abraham, which are generally considered Hadrianic. The height of the tallest of the piers in that cistern is similar to the assumed height of the vault under consideration.

Wall W7 in the northern space is also apparently Hadrianic. It, too, was transected by the builders of the Constantinian W4; the manner of its construction resembles that of W2 and W3, although it is much narrower (only 1 m wide).

It seems that W1 is also Hadrianic, although its dating is less certain than in the case of W2, W3, and W7. W1's ascription to the period of the three latter walls is indicated by several points of similarity (dry-built courses and the mixing of fieldstones and ashlars in secondary use), and by a stone block that bears a drawing of a ship and an inscription (see below). The drawing was probably added in the days of the foundation of the Constantinian basilica, to a then-existing wall. However, there is also a possibility — although an unlikely one — that W1 is from the eleventh–twelfth centuries C.E., that it was built to set apart the Cave of the Invention of the Cross, and that the painted stone block was integrated into it in secondary use. Wall W5 is definitely from the Crusader period, when it delineated the Chapel of St. Helena on the east.

North of W4 a cistern existed in the Constantinian period. In the northern part of this area, a blocked entry can be discerned which formerly led to a cistern which is still in use today. Its function is indicated by a drainpipe constructed of 18 stone segments (visible to a height of 9.5 m) that abuts W4 and descends to the rock floor. The diameter of the segments is 0.46 m and each is 0.53 m high.

In conclusion, the architectural remains in the Chapel of St. Vartan and the Armenian Martyrs are listed in chronological order:

1. Quarry: Iron Age II.
2. Beaten-earth floor: Iron Age II.
3. W2, W3, W7, and apparently also W1: Hadrianic period.
4. W4 and W6 and the cistern and drainpipe: Constantinian period.
5. W5: Crusader period.

The Inscription and Drawing: Their Date and Significance

A smooth stone block, 0.65 × 0.31 m, is set in the eastern corner of W1. On this block is a drawing of a ship and, below it, in Latin, the words: DOMINE IVIMVS, "Lord, we have gone." To where and from where are not mentioned. This may be an allusion to the Latin version of Psalms 121:1: *In domum Domini ibimus*, "Let us go to the house of the Lord."[4] This change between "v" and "b" (i.e., from the past to the future tense) is known in Christian and in Vulgar Latin inscriptions.[5] The phrase is also found in the New Testament, in John 6:68: *Domine, ad quem ibimus?* "Lord, to whom shall we go?" The use of a verse from the classical psalms of pilgrims to Jerusalem indicates that our text was probably inscribed by the earliest Christians in relation to their journey to Jerusalem, where they could express their Christian feelings overtly. The use of Latin indicates that these pilgrims were from countries in the western part of the

---

[4] The author is grateful to the late Father P. Benoit for this reference.

[5] The author thanks Prof. V. Väänänen, of the Historical-Philosophical Institute of the University of Helsinki, for his comments.

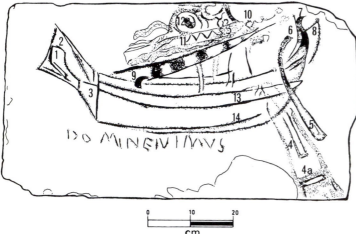

Chapel of St. Vartan and the Armenian Martyrs:
drawing and photograph of ship and the inscription

The lowered mast (No. 9) is of the composite type, as is indicated by its tapering form and especially by the wooldings, or lashings, that bind its several parts. The Roman parallels are supplemented by the ship depicted at Beth-sheᶜarim from the third century or first half of the fourth century C.E.[7] The mainsail is apparently furled (Nos. 10, 12) above the mast, with the shrouding and the sheets around the yardarm (No. 11). The side wales run back to the stern, providing a housing for the oars (No. 13). There may also have been triangular topsails above the square material.

Was the unstepped mast a retractable type belonging to a small coasting vessel, or did it represent a fixed one of a large ship? The latter possibility seems more likely. If the mast was retractable it would be unusual for the ship to also have a foresail; in all other known depictions of vessels with retractable masts, a foresail is not illustrated.[8] An additional factor supporting the assumption that this was a large ship is the Latin language of the accompanying inscription. If the writer had indeed come from the western Mediterranean, the journey would have required a relatively large ship and not a small coaster. It further suggests that the pilgrims responsible for the drawing and the inscription had faced some great peril, such as a storm, which broke the mast of their ship and could have caused its sinking. By means of this drawing and inscription they expressed gratitude for their salvation.[9]

Roman Empire — Italy, Gaul, Spain, or North Africa.

The ship is depicted with its bow to the left, it stern to the right, and its mast unstepped and lying on its side. It is a small merchant sailing vessel typical of the Roman period, for which there are numerous parallels.[6] A foresail, or *artemon*, is shown above the bow (No. 1). The upper line is apparently the raked foremast. The artist depicted two rudders; only the lower part (No. 4) of the one on the left is visible, while the one on the right is seen in full (No. 5) with its tiller (No. 6). There is a detail drawn around the left-hand rudder (No. 4a) that defies interpretation. On the stern is a *chiniscus*, a goose-headed ornament common on ships from this period, with the sternpost behind and supporting it (No. 8).

[6] L. Casson, *Ships and Seamanship in the Ancient World* (Princeton, 1971).

[7] M. Pliner, "The Sailing Ship of Beth-Shearim," *Sefunim* 1 (1966): 23–24 (Hebrew).

[8] Casson, *Ships and Seamanship* (see note 6), p. 329, n. 3. The author thanks Lionel Casson and Abner Raban, for their assistance in identifying the various parts of the ship.

[9] The drawing of the ship and its inscription have been discussed by Bennett and Humphreys, Testa, Helms and the author. For a bibliography and details of the controversy over their reading and interpretations, see C.M. Bennett and and C.S. Humphreys, "The Jerusalem Ship," *International Journal of Nautical Archaeology* 3 (1974): 307–310; I. Testa, "Il Golgota, Porta dell Quiete" in *Studia Hierosolymitana in Onore di P.B. Bagatti*, I (Jerusalem, 1976), pp. 197–244, especially pp. 219–224; S.W. Helms, "The Jerusalem Ship, ISIS MYRIONYMOS and the True Cross," *International Journal of Nautical Archaeology* 9 (1980): 119; and M. Broshi and G. Barkay, "Excavations in the Chapel of St. Vartan," *IEJ* 35 (1985): 108–128.

Recently-Discovered Crusader Churches in Jerusalem

Dan Bahat

Research into the medieval city of Jerusalem was resumed in 1967 following a 41-year-long lull since the publication of Vincent and Abel's study.[1] It was as if these two scholars had brought the subject to a close, and no further attempt was made to verify the location and identification of the Crusader churches of the city.

In 1967, substantial building activity began in the Old City of Jerusalem and its immediate vicinity, the lion's share focusing on the Jewish Quarter which has since been extensively surveyed and excavated. The discovery and identification of some important landmarks in laic Jerusalem also resulted in a better understanding of the Crusader city, although many problems remained to be solved. The building of churches was undoubtedly of great importance to the conquering Crusaders (see Pl. IVa). Some of these churches have been located and explored while others are either misidentified or remain to be found.

A number of Crusader churches were uncovered within the area of the Jewish Quarter of the Old City of Jerusalem. The first to be mentioned is a typical medium-sized church called St. Mary of the Germans (Sancta Maria Alemannorum) which was discovered in 1968.[2] It was built on the eastern slope of the German Quarter of the Crusader city, which today is occupied by the Jewish Quarter. When Mr. C.F. Tyrwhitt-Drake, Dr. T. Chap-

lin and Captain C.R. Conder, surveyors of the Palestine Exploration Fund (henceforth PEF), inspected the structure in 1872,[3] and correctly identified it, it was inhabited by some families.

Not far from this German center, another religious edifice was discovered, which was also visited by the PEF team[4] and tentatively identified by it as the Church of St. Thomae Alemannorum. The most prominent features noted by the PEF scholars were the two apses, then used as cupboards. This church was reexamined after 1967, and the two apses visible in the nineteenth century, and a third apse, were cleaned. All three were located in the eastern wall of the church. The running cornice, an almost regular feature of Crusader architecture in the Holy Land, was also revealed, as were two columns with their capitals which originally had stood at the the eastern extremity of a row of four or more columns. (Another column was sighted in 1969 but has since vanished.) One of the capitals carries a very crude floral design, whereas the other is plain, either having been defaced in antiquity or having been brought to the site as a rough, unworked block of stone.

All that remained of the Church of St. Thomae Alemannorum was incorporated in a private dwelling and whitewashed (see Pl. IVc), making further study of the site impossible. The size of the church must have been 8.9 × 12 m, which was less than the average for medium-size churches of the city. The church's size was very similar to that of

[1] C.H. Vincent and F.M. Abel, *Jerusalem Nouvelle* (Paris, 1922–1926).

[2] For a detailed description of this church, see in this volume, A. Ovadiah, "A Crusader Church in the Jewish Quarter of the Old City of Jerusalem," pp. 136–139; and M. Ben-Dov, "The Restoration of St. Mary's Church of the German Knights in Jerusalem," pp. 140–142.

[3] See *Survey of Western Palestine, Jerusalem* (London, 1889), pp. 272.

[4] Ibid.

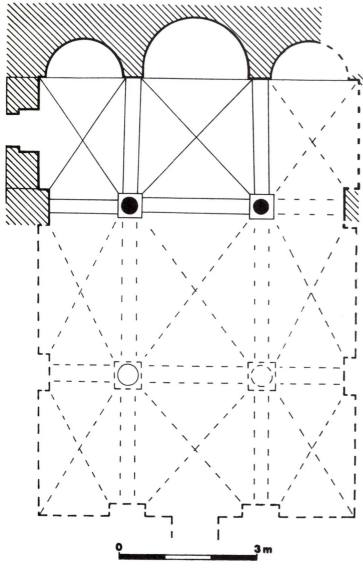

St. Thomas of the Germans: plan of church

the Church of St. Agnes and other small religious edifices in Jerusalem.

This church is mentioned in two documents, one dating to the twelfth century, and the other to the thirteenth century C.E. From these sources, it is very difficult to determine its precise location. However, since no other Crusader church is known in what is today the Jewish Quarter of Jerusalem, the identification of the remains noted here with the Church St. Thomae Alemannorum (St. Thomas of the Germans) is extremely feasible.

A basic outstanding question concerns the location of the church on the second story of the building and not, as normally expected, on the ground level. The PEF surveyors mentioned some ancient remains on the first floor which were not discernible in the recent study. At this stage of the research, the only possible explanation for this phenomenon is that the church was part of a larger monastic complex.

A third ecclesiastical building found in the Jewish Quarter, at its southernmost limit, may be identified with the Armenian Church of St. Stephen mentioned in a document dated to 1334 C.E., although Crusader sources record the existence of another church, St. Petrus ad Vincula ("St. Peter in Chains") in this part of the city in the twelfth century, with which it should be identified. John of Würzburg, the most prominent of the twelfth-century German pilgrims to visit Jerusalem, referred to a chapel named St. Petrus, "... whose crypt, which is very deep and dark, is said to have been the prison in which St. Peter ... being bound with iron chains ..." was incarcerated. From later sources we know that it became a bakery in the fifteenth century and eventually a Turkish prison.

Following the discovery of the famous New Church of St. Mary, the "Nea," the southern wall of the Church of St. Peter was studied by the Jewish Quarter archaeological expedition. A Crusader structure, 62 m long, was attached to this long and massive wall. It was preserved to a considerable height and consisted of a series of rooms of various dimensions, although all were of equal width (approximately 11.5 m). Of special note is a hall built with the characteristic architectural features of Crusader Jerusalem such as elbow-shaped consoles on which Crusader capitals were mounted. From some of the finds it is clear that there was originally a second story, and we can deduce that the remains uncovered actually belong to the basement of the building. The excellent workmanship and size of this structure (its height alone reached 7.4 m) imply that it had a public function. As this church abuts the southern retaining wall of the Nea Church, and undoubtedly covered the latter's surface, it probably had a crypt.

124

The building of a Crusader church over or adjoining a Byzantine church is a well-known phenomenon of Christian Jerusalem. After the Crusader period, probably in the time of the Mamluks, parts of the building were incorporated into installations such as basins and canals utilized in various kinds of workshops.

On adjacent Mt. Zion, a modern addition to the German Church of the Dormition provided the opportunity for further exploration of the two superimposed churches that existed there in antiquity, the Byzantine Church of Holy Sion and the later Crusader building. The Crusader structure was razed to the ground in the thirteenth century and only parts of it, including the Caenaculum, were later restored. In recent excavations, the northwestern corner of the church was unearthed. Remains include not only its northern and western walls, but also some of the pillars which formed the base of the arches that marked at least six bays of the church. The dimensions of the church, until then thought to have been about 66 × 36 m, proved to actually have been 72 m long and 36 m wide. Of great significance was the discovery that the Crusader remains rested on those of the Byzantine and even Second Temple periods. As it was believed that all traces of this church had been removed during the construction of the modern building in the begin-

ning of our century, the discovery of material — however fragmentary — is a vital indication that more information regarding Crusader religious architecture may be revealed in studies of other churches on Mt. Zion.

The Muslim Quarter, the least-known area of the city, has also yielded Crusader ecclesiastical remains. In the heart of that quarter a church, discovered on Khaldiyah Street, today serves as a blacksmith's workshop.[5] Surprisingly enough it had succeeded in escaping

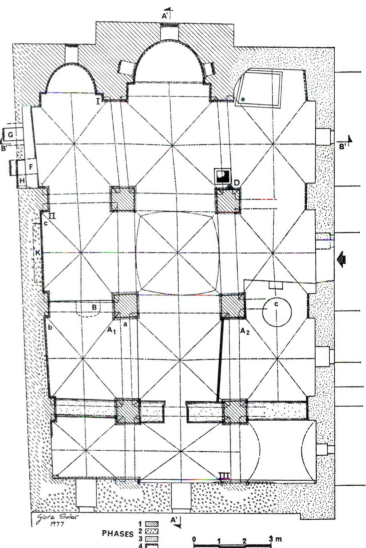

St. Julian in the Moslem Quarter: plan of church

The twelfth-century(?) Caenaculum

[5] D. Bahat, "A Smithy in a Crusader Church," *Biblical Archaeology Review* 6/2 (1980): 46.

125

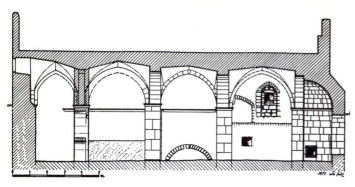

St Julian in the Moslem Quarter:
east-west cross-section, looking north

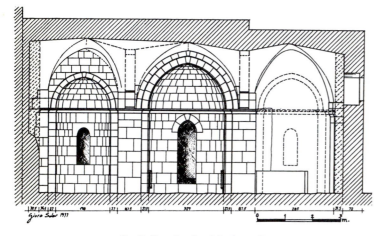

St. Julian in the Moslem Quarter:
north-south cross-section, looking west

the scholars' notice; the access to the church was direct from the street. It was basilican in plan; the two rows of columns, each comprising six pillars and twelve bays, supported a roof with cross vaults (one bay — the southwestern one — had a barrel vault). According to the dimensions of this basilica, 14.8 × 10.5 m, it may be classified among the medium-size churches of Crusader Jerusalem. Its slightly bent axis suggests that the builders were limited by the location of already existing buildings in the vicinity. The only decorative elements of the interior are the three apses, beautifully executed and molded in the shape of a running cornice (see Pl. IVd). Outside, the rectangular chevet on the eastern wall is easily discerned from the courtyard adjacent to the smithy.

Since the Crusades this church has housed various workshops and as a result many of its features, such as the original floor, have vanished. To this day, the forge comprises various installations which indicate its function in the past. None of the present doors or windows are new. Alterations suggest that the church had more than one phase of existence. The original construction dates to the twelfth century C.E., and the rebuilding of the northern and western walls is the essential representation of the second phase. At this time, a running cornice of inferior quality was also attached, indicating that the structure apparently still functioned as a church under Christian rule in Jerusalem of the thirteenth century C.E. The third phase is marked by the reconstruction of the southern wall, also probably carried out by worshippers, and finally the church was converted into a workshop. The dating of these last two phases is very difficult to determine.

Our building cannot readily be identified with any specific church mentioned in historical sources. The most feasible probability is the Church of St. Julian, known from a document from 1177. In accordance with this suggestion, today's Khaldiyah Street, in which the church is located, may be identified with St. Julian Street.

New discoveries have also been made in the northwestern sector of the Old City, where Crusader remains were already known. The Church of St. Mary the Magdalene is among these.[6] Its ruins were visible until World War I when it was demolished and a school building was erected on its foundations. The church was a twelfth-century reconstruction of a structure built during the Arab period and served the Eastern Church exclusively — namely the Copts and the Jakobites. The Crusader building dates from the early days of Crusader rule in Jerusalem.

The Church of St. Mary the Magdalene was rediscovered in 1978 when a shelter was dug for the school mentioned above, unearthing the cloister. It was a rectangular structure of which the western side was entirely exposed. Parts of the northern and southern arcades were also revealed, enabling us to deduce the

[6] D. Bahat, "The Church of Mary Magdalene and Its Quarter," *EI* 18 (Jerusalem, 1985), pp. 5–7 (Hebrew).

126

width of the inner cloister's yard as 7.2 m. The western arches and bays were found to be intact. This discovery, which extends the church's complex further northward, solved a former enigma involving the topography of Jerusalem: historical documents mention a postern near the church and because of an early text describing this opening, modern scholars had tended to mark an inner wall adjacent to the church. Now, with the discovery of the northern aisle of this ecclesiastic complex, there is no reason for not assuming that this postern, which is also mentioned in later thirteenth-century sources, is what is today Herod's Gate.

A study of a lithograph from 1817 depicting a Crusader church and a monastery, named "Sainte Mary of the Seven Sorrows" by the author of the book in which it appears, is of considerable significance.[7] The church can clearly be identified as actually being the Church of Sainte Anne, which is well known to every visitor to the city. The lithograph, which illustrates the medieval monastery attached to the church, is the only precise de-

The Church of St. Anne depicted in a lithograph from 1817 (*Jérusalem nouvelle*, Fig. 423)

scription of the latter before it was completely demolished, and provides a minimal knowledge of the site as it was before the alterations made by the French in the 1850s.

Thus we can see that Jerusalem, the capital of the Latin Kingdom, has contributed — in the last two decades — a considerable amount to our knowledge of the Christian churches in the Holy Land.

[7] D. Bahat, "A Propos de 'l'Église de Sept-Douleures' à Jerusalem," *RB* 85 (1978): 81–83.

The Nea:
Justinian's Church of St. Mary, Mother of God, Discovered in the Old City of Jerusalem

Nahman Avigad

With the victory of Constantine the Great over his enemies in the East in 324 C.E., Christianity received official status throughout the Roman Empire. The Holy Land, hitherto a remote district within the province of Syria-Palestine, suddenly assumed a new importance, and Jerusalem, whose past splendor had long since tarnished, once again emerged as a religious center — this time Christian, the target of pilgrimages and the object of lavish building projects: churches, monasteries, and hostels. It was under Justinian (527–565 C.E.), however, that Byzantine Jerusalem truly flourished. He was famous for his enormous construction efforts throughout the empire, and his largest project in Jerusalem was the "New Church of St. Mary, Mother of God (*Theotokos*)," known simply as the Nea ("new" in Greek).

Interestingly, the Nea Church and the Holy Sepulchre are the only churches specifically depicted on Jerusalem's Cardo in the famous mosaic map discovered in 1884 in a Byzantine church at Madaba, Transjordan. The map graphically portrays the Holy Land and its

various towns and villages, with Jerusalem at its center shown larger and in more detail than the other localities. The depiction is "three-dimensional" and the artist sought to achieve a certain realism. Despite its schematic execution and the ideological motivation of the artist, we have before us a reliable representation of Jerusalem and its various outstanding features as they were in the sixth century C.E. This is the oldest known pictorial map of Jerusalem, giving a bird's-eye view of the city.

On the map of Madaba, the Nea (designated by the letter H). and the Holy Sepulchre (G) are shown as lying on the Cardo (I), the main artery of the city. The archaeological evidence from the southern part of this road also dates to the time of Justinian, and it would seem that it, together with the Nea, evoked the force behind the building and development activities which raised Byzantine Jerusalem to its greatest heights. Perhaps one of the motives behind the construction of the southern part of the Cardo was to link the "new church" to that of the Holy Sepulchre which lies on the northern, Roman part of the Cardo, and it would seem that the artist of the Madaba map sought to commemorate this new architectural project.

The Nea Church was famous in the annals of Byzantine Jerusalem, for it was one of the largest and most magnificent churches in the city. Its construction is described and lauded by the Byzantine historian Procopius in his book on Justinian's building projects. He begins his description as follows: "And in Jerusalem he [the Emperor Justinian] dedicated to the Mother of God a shrine with which no other can be compared. This is called by the

Schematic drawing of Jerusalem in the
Madaba mosaic map

natives, the 'Nea Church.'"[1] All trace of this edifice, however, in its immensity, splendor and beauty, disappeared as if it had never been.

The Nea was inaugurated in 543 C.E. Procopius notes that the stones for its construction had to be brought by special means and that its enormous columns were wrought by miracle. He also states that the building site had to be expanded artificially, for it was too narrow to accommodate the entire structure, which included a monastery, a hostel, a hospital and, according to other sources, a library. The construction of this church was an imperial enterprise of monumental proportions, and its execution was entrusted to Theodoros, an architect from Constantinople. As Procopius relates:[2]

> The Emperor Justinian gave orders that it be built on the highest of the hills, specifying what the length and breadth of the building should be, as well as the other details. However, the hill did not satisfy the requirements of the project, according to the Emperor's specifications, but a fourth part of the church, facing the south and the east, was left unsupported, that part in which the priests are wont to perform the rites. Consequently those in charge of this work hit upon the following plan. They threw the foundations out as far as the rock. And when they had raised this up level with the rock they set vaults upon the supporting walls, and joined this substructure to the other foundation of the church. Thus the church is partly based upon living rock, and partly carried in the air by a great extension artificially added to the hill by the Emperor's power.

The conjectured location of the Nea had long been based on two sources. Early Christian pilgrims related that it stood at a high spot opposite the southwestern corner of the Temple Mount — in other words, somewhere in the modern Jewish Quarter. The second source was, as mentioned above, the Madaba map, which shows a large structure in the area of today's Jewish Quarter. On the basis of the pilgrims' reports, this structure was generally identified with the Nea Church.

When we began our excavations in the Jewish Quarter, we viewed the Nea as a legendary edifice, that only by some odd chance we might come across.[3] For us excavators, therefore, its discovery was to be a unique experience. We successfully brought a long-standing quest to a close by piecing together over several years fragments and clues which culminated in the certain identification of our discovery with the Nea. Our conclusions were then confirmed by an epigraphic find which served to identify the structure almost by name. Such integration of all possible documentary factors — literary, pictorial, architectural and epigraphic — is a dream of every excavator, only rarely realized.

In the previous century, during the foundation of the Batei Maḥse complex in the southern part of the Jewish Quarter, an ancient wall built of large stones was discovered together with a marble pavement. Plans for the building of a residential building in this area drew us to excavate there in June 1970. We encountered what seemed to be the continuation of that same wall, running from north to south. We uncovered a stretch 13 m long and 6.5 m thick, with foundations descending to bedrock at a depth of 8 m. Its outer face was built of large, dressed stones with irregular margins and rough central bosses. Within this thick wall was an inscribed apse, 5 m in diameter, orientated to the east. The direction of the apse would indicate that it belonged to a

---

[1] Procopius, *Buildings* V, 6, Loeb edition ed. by H.B. Dewing and G. Downey, London, 1954), pp. 342–243.

[2] Ibid.

[3] Excavations in the Jewish Quarter of the Old City of Jerusalem were begun in 1969 following the reunification of the city in 1967 and as part of the reconstruction of the quarter as a residential area. The project, which continued until 1983, was directed by the author under the auspices of The Hebrew University of Jerusalem, the Israel Exploration Society and the Israel Department of Antiquities and Museums. Its results have been published in N. Avigad, *Discovering Jerusalem* (Nashville, 1983).

The Nea: eastern wall with northern lateral apse

point of reference. A large open space some 100 m west of the apse became available for excavation. After digging down through five or six meters of rubble and debris, as well as modern foundations, we reached an archaeological stratum containing Byzantine pottery. Here we found the thick, deeply-set foundations of a building, with the threshold of a doorway whose original width was 5.4 m. The door gave access to a large space at the east, which was paved with white marble flagstones. All these were remains of a very large structure, the major part of which lay to the east opposite the wall with the apse and parallel to it. Since the building with the apse stretched to the west, and these latter remains were orientated to the east, it was obvious that both parts belonged to one and the same huge building. Substantiating the identification with the Nea Church was the fact that our building in the west reached the edge of the Cardo exactly as depicted on the Madaba mosaic map.

church, and that it was not the main apse but a smaller, lateral one. The extreme thickness of the wall points to a structure of huge dimensions. It was clear that a church of such size, at this particular location, could only be the famed Nea Church. The legendary Nea had become a tangible reality.

The summer of 1973 awarded us with an opportunity to search for further remains of the building of which we now had a concrete

Further details of the Nea Church were revealed in a discovery made in 1973, south of the Batei Maḥse, outside the city walls at a spot where the Jerusalem Foundation was preparing a public park along the city wall. During the preparatory work there, a clearance directed by Meir Ben-Dov revealed the corner of a massive structure below the present city wall north of Burj Kibrit, the tower at at its southeastern corner. It was built of large, drafted stones resembling those of the wall containing the apse, in the courtyard of Batei Maḥse; it was exactly in line with the wall of the apse some 35 m to the north. This was certainly the southeastern corner of the Nea Church. Its discovery was important for the revealing of the extent of the church proper. The southern internal apse near it was also uncovered in 1982 during the construction work near the Turkish wall performed by the East Jerusalem Development Corporation. The shape of the central apse has not yet been determined, since it is partly destroyed and partly hidden underneath modern structures. The preserved remains of the wall seem to indicate that it was an internal apse of approx-

The Nea: the southeastern corner

imately 12 m in diameter with a minor projection beyond the eastern line of the wall.

Procopius described the Nea as a basilica surrounded by porticoes on all flanks except the eastern one, and that two huge columns stood in front of the entrance. A narrow corridor led from the basilica to an atrium which was also surrounded by an inner row of columns; in front of the atrium was a round courtyard, connected with the gate structure. This depiction presents a very complex plan of unparalleled form. The archaeological remains are too sparse to enable us to verify if such a layout could in fact be accommodated by the given space. The simplified plan drawn by us comprises a basilica with two rows of columns and complies with the existing remains. Admittedly, four rows of columns would be more fitting for the great width of this church, but they do not correspond with the finds. Some other subdivision of the huge space should be considered.

The nave terminated in a large apse and there was a chamber at the end of each aisle. These two rooms have a smaller apse inscribed in their eastern walls. The interior of the church was about 100 m long and 52 m wide, making it the largest known basilica in Palestine. At the west there is the narthex which contains the only preserved doorway leading into the southern aisle. The total length of the exposed building remains is 116 m. Further west a narrow atrium seems to have bordered the Cardo.

As mentioned above, the Nea was actually a complex of buildings spread over a large area beyond the church itself. In 1976–1977 we excavated an area adjacent to the southern city wall intended for an underground parking lot. Some 40 m north of the city wall, we encountered an east–west wall (no. 3 on the plan), 66 m long and 7.6 m high, which contained a series of vaulted openings with relieving arches above; abutting it was a building of the Crusader period. It soon became clear that the long wall was actually the southern revetment of the Nea Church complex; such a wall was necessary to support the earth fill which had been used to expand the level area

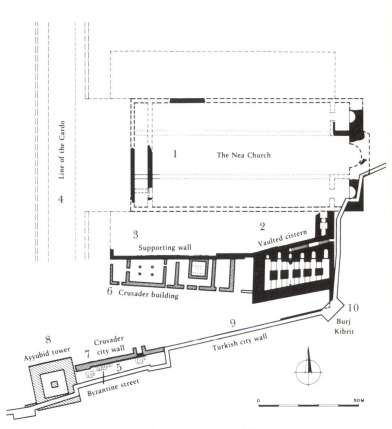

Plan of Byzantine, Crusader and Arab building remains in the southern area of the Jewish Quarter

of the construction site for the church on its southern flank. Assuming that the general plan was symmetrical, the revetment enabled us to estimate that the overall width of the complex extending to the north was about 105 m.

The most dramatic development in our discovery of the Nea Church was still to come. Our work brought us to the inner angle of the above-mentioned Burj Kibrit (no. 10 on the plan), as a garden theater was to be built there. The task of excavating here was difficult and drawn out, primarily because of the danger that the tower debris which formed a steep scarp here might collapse. We cleared the upper, modern debris with mechanical tools; the tractor hit a subterranean structure, breaking a hole through it into the interior. This was believed to be a cistern but proved to be exceptionally deep. When we descended with a rope ladder some 10 m into the interior, the sight was overwhelming — entirely-plastered enormous vaulted halls with arches

The Nea: one of the intact vaults
(no. 1 in illustration below), looking north

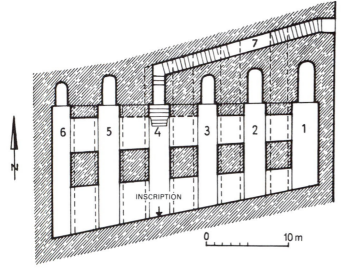

The Nea: plan of the vaulted cistern

resting upon massive pillars and deep niches built into the walls. Two such halls were intact but we were to learn that the continuation to the west, which seemed to be destroyed, contained another four vaults. To the north a sort of long corridor led down into this structure. The plastered walls suggested some sort of huge water reservoir. Only later did we learn that earlier explorers of Jerusalem[4] had visited this spot a century before, when the entire series of six vaults was still intact. The structure particularly occupied our attention because of its close ties with the Nea Church.

The interior of this structure (no. 2 on the plan on p. 131) spread over an area of some 9.5–17 × 33 m. The archways connecting the vaulted halls are borne on massive pillars, 3.5 × 5 m. The entire structure was built of compacted rubble covered over with a strong, pinkish plaster. In the northern wall there were two tiers of deep niches, behind which was a long, stepped gallery leading down into the cistern. The upper doorway of the gallery was blocked by the collapse of the ceiling, but we have cleared the debris and opened it up.

All the evidence, in particular the specially plastered walls, and two pottery pipes, indicate that this structure had been used for the storage of water. But this was not its main function; such a massive and complex construction would have been built primarily as a substructure for some building rising above it. Indeed above the vaulting we did find remains of walls and pavements. These walls were built in alternating courses of stone and brick, a technique also used in the northern part of the vaults below and one very typical of the

[4] T. Lewin, *Siege of Jerusalem by Titus* (London, 1863), pp. 221–224, relates how he and his companion, Dr. Barclay, were lowered by rope into the "subterranean depths" and landed upon a large wooden board afloat in the water. They explored the vaulted chambers. Lewin ascribed the impressive structure to the House of Ananias, High Priest in the days of the Second Temple. C. Warren, *Excavations at Jerusalem, 1867–1870* (London, 1884), Pl. XXXVI, published a schematic plan of the cistern which, for some unknown reason, he called a "columbarium" (dovecote), but he gave no description. C. Schick, *PEFQSt* (1898): 79–81, also knew of the cistern, and reported the collapse of several of its vaults.

The Nea: wall above the vaults built of alternating strips of stone and brick

Byzantine buildings of Constantinople from where it was apparently brought by builders familiar with it. This led us to associate the vaulted cistern with the Byzantine Nea Church close by to the north (no. 1 on the plan on p. 132). Moreover, in 1981 the brick-and-stone constructions were found to continue to the north, thus connecting the vault complex with the building of the church. In this context, we assume that the cistern was originally intended to support one of the wings of the Nea Church complex, built over the slope.

Procopius' description corresponds precisely with this archaeological evidence: the local topography, the remains of the Nea Church founded upon bedrock, the vaulting built on the southern slope with traces of construction above it, and the supporting wall of the terrace on the south. There is little doubt that our subterranean vaulting is identical with the vaulted substructures mentioned by Procopius.

The vaulted substructure of the Nea Church was apparently considered to be a particularly worthy achievement. Not only did it receive full credit in Procopius' writings, but its builders saw fit to commemorate its construction in a monumental inscription fixed on one of the walls of the cistern. The discovery of this inscription was the climax of our investigations of the Nea Church.

At the top of the southern wall of Vault 4 was a large 1.58-m-long *tabula ansata* containing a Greek inscription in large, clear letters, 8–10 cm high. The letters were applied on the plaster, modelled in bold relief, and painted red. Only a few were partly damaged or had "slipped" off the surface, leaving traces on the plaster. The inscription terminates with a

133

The Nea: initial treatment of the Justinian inscription discovered on southern wall of Vault 4

small cross. Underneath the *tabula ansata* there is a large cross. The inscription reads as follows:

Κ(αὶ) τοῦτο τὸ ἔργον ἐφιλοτιμή
σατο ὁ εὐσεβ(έστατος) ἤμων βασι
λεὺς Φλ(άουιος) Ἰουστινίανος προνοί
α χ(αὶ) απουδὶ Κωνσταντίνου
ὁσιωτά (του) πρεσβ (υτέρου) χ(αὶ) ἡγουμέ (νου)
ἰνδ(ικτιῶνος) ιγ′ +

And this is the work which our most pious Emperor Flavius Justinianus carried out with munificence, under the care and devotion of the most holy Constantinus, Priest and Hegumen, in the thirteenth [year of the] indiction.[5]

5 The author is indebted to Y. Tsafrir for valuable remarks and bibliographic references.

The inscription thus commemorates the building of a structure undertaken on behalf of Justinian, its patron and donor, under the direction of Constantine, abbot of the monastery. The mode of dating, according to the indiction, was based on a 15-year cycle between assessments of property for taxation purposes throughout the Byzantine empire. There were three indictions during Justinian's reign: in 534/535, in 549/550 and in 564/565 C.E. The second one occurred six years after the dedication of the Nea Church and this is most likely the date of construction of this associated structure.

The word ἔργον ("work") obviously refers to the construction of the cistern where the inscription was fixed or, more likely, both the cistern and the building which it supported. The location of the inscription, in almost total darkness some 8 m above the floor within a

A. Church of the Nativity: interior view

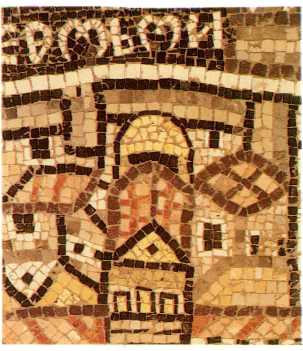

C. Church of the Holy Sepulchre in the Madaba mosaic
map

◁ B. Church of St. Catherine, Mt. Sinai: interior view

PL. I

A. Nahariya: central rosette

C. Nahariya: a sheep

B. Nahariya: bird catcher

PL. II

Kursi: A. General view of monastery (above); B. View of church, from the north (below)

A. Crusader Jerusalem: Cambrai map

C. Crusader Jerusalem: Caenaculum

B. Crusader Church of Thomas of the Germans today

D. Crusader Jerusalem: triapsidal Church of St. Julian

A. Monastery of the Cross: interior of church

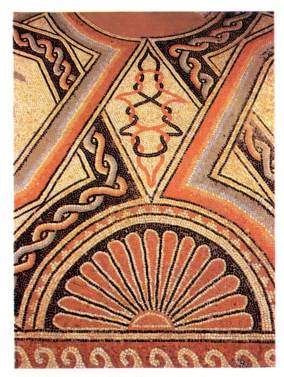

B. Monastery of the Cross: mosaic pavement

C. Monastery of the Cross: fresco (thirteenth cent.) ▷

A. Judean Desert: cliff laura at Pharan

B. Judean Desert: cliff laura at Pharan

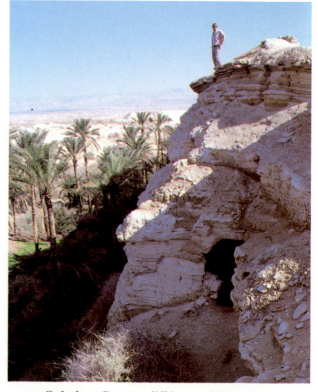

C. Judean Desert: cliff laura of Gerasimus

A. Khirbet el-Beiyûdât: southern amphora in apse mosaic

D. Khirbet el-Beiyûdât: detail of panel in southern aisle

B. Khirbet el-Beiyûdât: medallion in apse mosaic

E. Khirbet el-Beiyûdât: panel in southern aisle

C. Khirbet el-Beiyûdât: panel in southern aisle

F. Khirbet el-Beiyûdât: detail of panel in southern aisle

A. Khirbet el-Beiyûdât: inscription no. 2

B. Khirbet el-Beiyûdât: inscription no. 4

The Nea: the Justinian inscription

ΚΤΟΥΤΟΤΟΕΡΓΟΝΕΦΙΛΟΤΙΜΗ
CΑΤΟΟΕΥCΕΒˢΗΜΩΝΒΑCΙ
ΛΕΥCΦΛˢΙΟCΤΙΝΙΑΝΟCΠΡΟΝΟΙ
ΑΚCΠΟΥΔΙΚΩΝCΤΑΝΤΙΝΟΥ
OCΙΩΤΠΡΕCΒˢΚΗΓΟΜΙΝΔˢΠ +

The Nea: line drawing of the Justinian inscription

subterranean cistern, indicates that it was not
intended to be displayed, and thus, it had
escaped the attention of our predecessors who
investigated the cistern a century ago. It
should be considered as a foundation inscription which was unveiled and seen only during
the inauguration ceremony. It is reasonable to
suggest that the building concerned was the
monastery, part of the Nea complex, of which
Constantine was the superior.

We are fortunate that this "hegumen" Constantine can be identified, and his association
with the Nea Church confirmed. He was one
of the abbots of the Nea Church and is mentioned in Patristic literature in the late sixth
and early seventh century C.E. as ὁ ἀββᾶς
Κωνσταντίνος ὁ ἡγούμενος τῆς ἁγίας Μαρίας τῆς
Θεοτόκου τῆς Νέας, "Abba Constantinus the
Hegumen of the [Church of the] Holy Maria,
Mother of God, the Nea."[6] The inscription
renders both the connection between Constantine and the Nea Church as well as that
between the vaulted cistern and the church
complex.

It may be said that our inscription is one of
the very rare building inscriptions in this
country related to the Emperor Justinian[7] and
by far the most monumental and revealing
one of this period which has come to light.
Found *in situ*, in association with remnants
of the famous Nea built by this emperor, it
constitutes a significant contribution to the
history of the holy city of Jerusalem.

[6] Johannes Moschus, in *Patrologiae Graecae*, LXXXVII, col.
2857 A. See also J. Milik, "La topographie de Jérusalem vers la
fin de l'époque Byzantine," *Mélanges de l'Université Saint Joseph*
37 (1960–1961): 145–151, esp. 146, n. 2.

[7] For two inscriptions in Sinai, see I. Ševčenko, "The Early
Period of the Sinai Monastery in the Light of Its Inscriptions,"
DOP 20 (1966): 255–264, inscriptions nos. 1 and 5, and plates.
See also P. de Bas and W.H. Waddington, *Voyage archéologique en
Grèce et en Asie Mineure, Inscriptions Greques et Latines*, III (Paris,
1870), p. 463, No. 1916.

A Crusader Church in the Jewish Quarter of the Old City of Jerusalem

Asher Ovadiah

The course of restoration work in the Jewish Quarter of the Old City of Jerusalem involved the carrying out of a number of archaeological excavations. One of these was undertaken in 1968, on a site being cleared of ruins in order to lay a new road giving access to the Western Wall. It was here that a Crusader church together with its adjoining complex was discovered.[1]

The church is situated at the eastern edge of the hill on which the Jewish Quarter is located, facing the southwest corner of the Temple Mount.[2] Parts of the building were still preserved above ground level, and the west wing even served as living quarters for a number of families. The church is part of a larger complex including halls (an upper and a lower one) to its south and adjoining structures to its north. The latter have not yet been examined.

The church had the basilican shape typical of most Crusader churches in the Holy Land. Two colonnades of three square-shaped piers divided the structure into three spaces — a central nave and two aisles. Only the eastern piers of the northern and southern rows were found *in situ*, but their location enables us to

determine the exact placement of the others. These are solid, square piers, their sides measuring about 1 m, with dressed edges; only their lower parts have been preserved. The nave and the aisles were demarcated on the east by three semicircular internal apses, each having a window.

The window of the central apse was short and broad, its width on the outside measuring 1.1 m and on the inside 1.3 m; in height it was 1.5 m. The windows of the side apses, on the other hand, were narrow and long, their inside width having being 60 cm at the top and 48 cm at the bottom, while on the outside they measured 30 and 35 cm respectively. The side windows were approximately 3 m high. Similar windows, all of which narrowed toward the outside and are typical of the Crusader period, are also known from the Church of the Annunciation in Nazareth, the church at el-Qubeibeh ("Emmaus"), the Ramla church, and elsewhere.

The northern apse alone was entirely revealed, the other two having been preserved to the beginning of the roof structure only. It is likely that originally an altar stood in each apse, as in the Church of Sainte Anne in Jerusalem and elsewhere. The chancel was elevated above the main floor level by one step. It was impossible to determine the form of the chancel screen. The stones from which the apse was built were smoothly dressed and laid on a foundation of unhewn stones. Adjacent to the inner walls of the apses, there were apparently stone benches, built to the height of the rough-stone foundations.

There were three entrances in the western wall of the church. The central one was tall and broad, probably 2.9 × 1.15 m. The jambs

---

[1] The excavation was carried out on behalf of the Israel Department of Antiquities and Museums under the direction of the architect, E. Netzer, and the writer. See A. Ovadiah, "A Crusader Church in the Jewish Quarter of Jerusalem," *EI* 11 (1973), pp. 208–212, Pls. 39–40 (Hebrew); idem, "A Restored Complex of the 13th Century in Jerusalem," *Actes du XVe Congrès International d'Études Byzantines* (*Athènes 1976*) II (Athens, 1981), pp. 585–596. The plan was prepared by the Company for the Restoration of the Jewish Quarter, and the photographs were taken by W. Braun and W. Kaneti.

[2] H. Vincent and F.M. Abel, *Jérusalem nouvelle*, II, Part 4 (Paris, 1926), pp. 952–953.

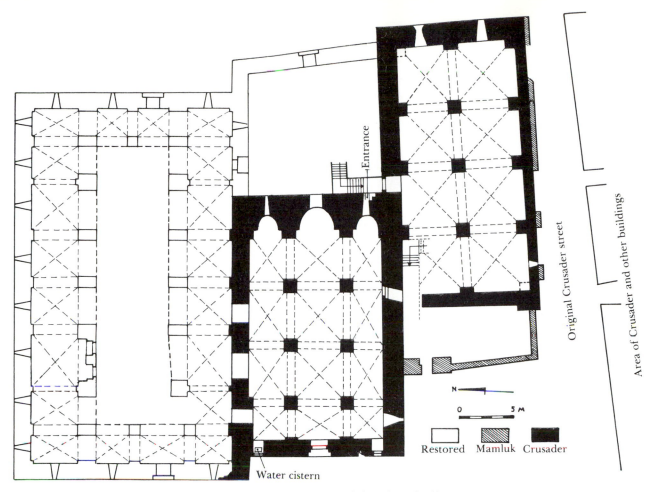

St. Mary's of the German Knights: plan of church and adjacent structures

are of Romanesque style, i.e., rounded into a semicylindrical type of column. The two side entrances were lower and simpler, and measured 2.2 m in height by 80 cm in width. Both the central and southern openings stood to mid-height, while the northern one was completely preserved. The latter was built above a water cistern, 10 m deep, hewn from the rock but with a narrower constructed neck.

Four additional openings were set in the northern wall of the church, leading to the northern complex of buildings. They were blocked. One of them was built in typical Romanesque style: a rounded archway with jambs comprising two single columns decorated at their tops. These, however, had been uprooted. In the southern wall, a wide opening with three steps gave access to the structures south of the church. On one of its jambs, a bolt socket had been hewn. All the thresholds remained intact. The northern en-

trances, from west to east, measured 1.18 m (in width) × 2.22 m (in height), 2.2 m × 3.2 m, 1.6 m × 2.5 m, and 0.8 m × 1.6 m. The

St. Mary's of the German Knights: facade of church prior to construction in the area

137

southern ones had a width of about 1.2 m and an approximate height of 2.2 m

At the southwestern corner, a section of wall about 2 m wide, made of unhewn stones, was uncovered. Apparently it served as the foundation of the southern wall of the atrium to the west of the church.

The original roof of the church did not survive. It may be assumed that it was gabled, as was usual in that period, perhaps even with a bell-tower at its western side, which collapsed over the years.

The internal dimensions of the church were approximately 20 × 12 m and the walls were between 1.5 and 2 m thick. The width of the nave and aisles was 5 m and 3.5 m respectively; the distance between the pillars (axis to axis) was 4 m. The depth of the central apse was 2.6 m with a chord length of 3.8 m. The northern apse was 2 m deep with a chord length of 2.4 m.

The church was constructed of smoothly-worked limestone blocks, and its southeastern corner featured typical Crusader dressing: prominent central bosses with smoothed margins. In a number of sections, additions dating to the Arab period were evident.

In the external wall of the southern apse, a large niche was found, but its original function remains obscure; it may merely have been a form of decoration. Its jambs were modeled, and above them were two carved consoles supporting a handsome arch, only half of which remains. The niche is not on the same axis as the apse, and the relation between the two is not clear. At a later stage it was broken through, providing access to the southern apse. The niche was 1.2 m in width by 2.6 m in height while the opening extended to its full height but was only about 1 m wide. Below the *bema* is a 5-m-high vaulted structure, which modern-day inhabitants had put to use as a cistern for collecting rainwater, but it was originally used for other purposes. This underground structure was obviously erected to support the *bema* area of the church because of the topographical conditions of the area. In its eastern wall there is a wide and high pointed portal.

There were two stages of construction in the church, as evidenced by the two floor levels. Only the base of the original floor made of hard-beaten clay is preserved. The second floor was about 0.5 m higher and was paved with white tesserae, approximately 0.2 × 0.2 m in size. It remained intact in the eastern and central parts of the building.

On the lower part of the northern apse, frescoes have survived, although it is difficult to date them and determine their style. Their color is dark brown on a white background.

Among the Crusader period remains discovered south of the church was a double-storied hall:

1. The lower hall had an east-west axis and included two aisles; it was roofed by a ribbed vault. There was a window in the southern wall of the southern aisle, facing the street. Two more windows, narrowing toward the outside, existed in the eastern walls of each aisle. Entry to this lower floor was by way of a stepped passageway in the south wall of the church, where we discerned the former location of five stairs which had been torn out, and the remains of a plastered ceiling.

2. The upper story comprised colonnades, bearing arches and ribbed vaulting. Although only three square piers and two bases with rounded corners have survived, we are able to reconstruct the entire story. The bases rested upon a stylobate, 1.1 m wide × 2.5 m deep, which was founded on the remains of Hellenistic walls. In a later period (Mamluk?), a fairly thick plastered wall, preserved almost in its entirety, was erected on these bases. Most prominent on the surviving piers are knee-shaped colonnettes with a foliage motif on their capitals (stylized Corinthian capitals) which formed part of the cornice work and supported a series of arches.

From the existing remains, the entire story can be visualized as constituting square pillars that supported arches and a ribbed vaulting. The distance between the piers was approximately 3 m.

The descriptions of three pilgrims from the twelfth century refer to the structure: John of Würzburg (1160–1170), Jacques de Vitry

(1180) and the anonymous author of *The City of Jerusalem*. On the basis of these three historical sources and the cumulative archaeological evidence, the present church is identified with the Church of St. Mary of the Germans (of the Teutonic Order), erected near the Hospital and/or Hospice of the Germans. The historical texts do not make it clear whether the structure to the south of the basilica was a hospital or a hospice. From a comparison to similar plans of buildings in contemporary Europe, we conclude that the two-storied structure south of the church was a hospital (while its upper story was used as a cerremonial hall), and that the building located north of the church was a hospice.

The church was built by a German pilgrim in the first half of the twelfth century. Its history is summarized by J. Prawer.[3] It belonged to a group of German-speaking knights which formed a branch of the Order of the Hospitallers. This group of knights was organized already in 1127–1128 and was concentrated in the Church of St. Mary, located in the area of the present Jewish Quarter of the Old City of Jerusalem. This church became a center for German pilgrims to Jerusalem who were not acquainted with other languages commonly spoken by the Crusaders.

The church was already referred to by Tobler,[4] in addition to other scholars, and its identification with the Crusader Church of St. Mary is beyond doubt. The archaeological and stylistic data relate in the main to the architectural elements characteristic of the twelfth century, namely ribbed vaultings, and pipe- or knee-shaped pillars with stylized Corinthian capitals, etc. These and other typically Romanesque elements were incor-

St. Mary's of the German Knights: general view of the lower story of the hospital

porated by the Crusaders into the buildings they erected in Palestine.

It is difficult to determine the date of the destruction of the church and the hospital and/or hospice, but one may assume that they were damaged in 1187 (or 1188) when Salaḥ ad-Din's armies conquered Jerusalem. A Crusader street, approximately 3 m wide, runs to the south of the hospital.[5] Various remains, especially the Crusader consoles fixed in the walls, enable us to state with certainty that the thoroughfare was covered with a series of arches. The street itself followed the natural slope at the eastern edge of the quarter. The excavations revealed its paving consisting of medium-sized rectangular blocks.

South of the Crusader street, more Crusader remains were discovered, some *in situ* and some in secondary use. These included typical Crusader masonry, arches, columns, and vaults.

[3] Y. Prawer, *A History of the Latin Kingdom of Jerusalem*, I (Jerusalem, 1963), p. 395 (Hebrew).

[4] T. Tobler, *Topographie*, I (Berlin, 1953), pp. 416–417.

[5] This street, west of the church, can be clearly seen on the map of Crusader Jerusalem; see Prawer, *Crusader Kingdom* (note 3).

The Restoration of St. Mary's Church of the German Knights in Jerusalem

Meir Ben Dov

In the seventh decade of the twelfth century C.E., a Crusader named John of Würzburg visited Jerusalem. The journal of his travels[1] contains some marvelous descriptions of the city. He writes:

> Following that street [the Street of the Chain], to the right of the gate leading to the Temple, is a passage through a boulevard of columns, and on that street are a hospice and a church built recently in honor of St. Mary but popularly called the German building, for only German-speaking pilgrims are accepted there.

This compound was damaged in the destruction of the city by al-Malik al-Muatem after previously being captured by Salah ed-Din's forces and converted into a Muslim structure. When Frederick II, the Holy Roman Emperor, was given authority over Jerusalem by virtue of the peace pact with al-Malik al-Kamil, the Crusaders began restoring the ruined buildings of the city, and since he was a German, German property was given first preference. However, after Jerusalem returned to Muslim control under the Mamluks, this particular church was demolished; it remained as a memory for over seven hundred years. Nevertheless, from the descriptions left by John of Würzburg and others, scholars realized that all these German structures were located under the houses of the Jewish Quarter in the Old City of Jerusalem. It was only after the Six-Day War, however, when the rebuilding of the Jewish Quarter led to the clearing of the ruins and

old houses, that the remains of this compound were uncovered. While these operations were in progress, a beautiful capital was revealed on a wall. This find was brought to my knowledge. From just a glimpse, it was clear that it belonged to a structure dating from the Crusader period. It was first studied by A. Ovadiah[2] and E. Netzer who correctly identified it as a part of the complex of German buildings known from historical documents. Mayor Teddy Kollek subsequently asked me to excavate and reconstruct the entire site.

Firstly, we decided to dismantle most of the later rooms and stables in order to clarify the plan of the building. We preserved what seemed worthwhile and restored several walls so as to strengthen the adjacent ones which were in danger of collapsing.

The story of the entire complex of buildings uncovered by the excavations is as follows. In the early part of the twelfth century C.E., shortly after the establishment of the Hospitaller Order of St. John, a separate group of German knights emerged within it. They set themselves the important task of caring for the German pilgrims who did not understand French, the language then prevalent in Jerusalem. Other national groups, both from Europe and the East, established separate hospices for compatriot pilgrims. One such example is the Hungarian Hospice.

The church was named after Mary, Mother of Jesus, perhaps in memory of the New Church of Mary built by the Byzantines in that area. It was situated in the middle of the compound which included a service wing and

---

[1] M. Ben-Dov, *In the Shadow of the Temple. The Discovery of Ancient Jerusalem* (Jerusalem, 1985), pp. 348–353.

[2] See in this volume, A. Ovadiah, "A Crusader Church in the Jewish Quarter of the Old City of Jerusalem," pp. 136–139.

St. Mary's of the German Knights: the three apses

St. Mary's of the German Knights: facade, looking west

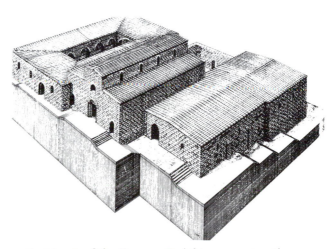

St. Mary's of the German Knights: reconstruction

141

hospice, as well as a hospital with a ceremonial hall located above it. Contemporary witnesses note the poverty of the German group, and indeed this is confirmed by the simplicity of the structure. The chronicles of the period also tell of the Germans' unceasing desire to relinquish the auspices of the French Hospitaller Order and establish a new German-national group. However, under pressure from the Hospitallers, the popes objected strongly. It was only during the Third Crusade (ca. 1190) that the foundations were established for an independent German military order, officially called St. Mary of the Teutons.

As mentioned above, the church was located in the center of the German compound. It was built in the Romanesque style, measured 21 × 12 m, and included a nave and two aisles. Three semicircular apses were in the eastern wall. Their upper part was decorated with a cornice featuring a simple geometric decoration. Each apse had windows. The church was entered through a gate in its western wall, adjoining a street leading northward to the Street of the Chain. The gateposts were worked in the style of the period and there was a window on either side of the gate opposite the two aisles. A decorated niche in the northern wall apparently held relics or other sacred artifacts. In the western part of this wall there was also a door leading to the hospital quarters. This wing comprised two stories with a stairway leading from its ground floor (the hospital) to its upper one (the ceremonial hall). Its ground floor housed the sick, while the upper story was used for ceremonies. The hospice on the northern side of the church compound was also built in the style of the time — a central courtyard surrounded by rooms. Another courtyard was located in the east and an additional room lay beneath the church.

In spite of the compound's proximity to an aqueduct, five cisterns had been dug to collect rainwater. We excavated and cleared one of them, uncovering dozens of pottery pieces, mainly from the thirteenth century. Among these were numerous bowl and dish sherds, mostly glazed, which originated in public dining halls. Vessels had apparently been collected during the cleaning and vacating of the premises during the Mamluk period, and thrown into the cistern which became a refuse dump. Most of the vessels found had been made by local potters; there were some eastern imports, but none had been produced in Europe. This is a well-known phenomenon in the Crusader world in Palestine. The Crusaders customarily purchased their everyday household wares locally and did not need to import similar goods from Europe.

Beneath the flagstones of the hospital hall we discovered vestiges of a typical sixth-century Byzantine mosaic floor. The remains of a cistern coated with gray plaster must be associated with the residential quarter located there in the Second Temple period. The Crusader construction, whose foundations reached bedrock, destroyed all remains of the past. A superficial and unsystematic survey carried out on the four sides of the compound revealed that it had been surrounded by Crusader buildings, many of them undamaged and occupied by residents of the Old City right up to the beginning of the Jewish Quarter restoration work.

The Monastery of the Cross in Jerusalem

Vassilios Tzaferis

The Monastery of the Cross, standing like a mighty fortress in the midst of the Valley of the Cross, is one of the earliest structures in western Jerusalem.[1]

A beautiful internal courtyard and a basilica-shaped church are located in the center of the building, surrounded by a five-story structure containing over one hundred rooms, halls, various workrooms, chapels, a library and auxiliary chambers. The two top floors were added in the mid-nineteenth century, while the lower ones, including the central church structure, are of earlier origin (see Pl. Va).

The beginnings of construction are shrouded in the distant past, and as often happens with similar ancient buildings, many legends and traditions have developed around it in an attempt to unravel and explain the secrets of its sanctity and its origins. The single, central theme of all these traditions relates to the spot where the tree grew from which Jesus' cross was made. The church was constructed to commemorate the place, and thus the monastery received its name.

There is, for instance, one legend, originating in the twelfth century and combining elements of a well-known biblical tale (Genesis 18–19) with a Christian legend of a later date. According to this tradition, Lot, in order to gain forgiveness for the sin he had committed with his daughters (Genesis 19:31–41), was commanded by Abraham to plant three staves left behind by the three angels who had visited him (Genesis 18:1–15), and water them from the Jordan River. If it came to pass that the staves grew into a tree, it meant that the sin had been expiated. According to Christian tradition, the place of planting was in the present-day Valley of the Cross. Lot did as Abraham had commanded him, and wonder of wonders, the three staves took root and grew into a miraculous tree having three different branches — Cypress, Pine and Cedar. In the reign of King Solomon, the tree was cut down, to be used in the construction of the Temple. However, it was subsequently rejected as unsuitable, because the builders were unable to fit it to their needs. Hundreds of years later, this accursed tree became the cross upon which Jesus of Nazareth was crucified.

Another legend, from the mid-thirteenth century, comprises a number of elements from the New Testament. Accordingly, Adam, seeing the end of his days approaching, requested and received a twig from the Tree of Knowledge. He placed the twig in his mouth at the moment of his demise, and from it sprang the tree from which Jesus' cross was made, bringing atonement for the original sin. The burial of the first man and the sprouting of the tree all took place, as tradition has it, in the Valley of the Cross.

Many legends and widely-varying tales have been woven over the years about the actual date of the monastery's construction. Some of them are entirely imaginary, while others are based on various historical events. Thus, several illustrious names have been associated with the building's foundations: Queen He-

---

[1] See A. Economopoulos, "Fresh Data Resulting from the Excavations in the Church of the Monastery of the Holy Cross," *Actes du X⁰ congrès international d'archéologie Chrétienne*, vol. II (Citta de Vaticano-Thessalonique, 1984), pp. 377–390. The author suggests a rather earlier dating for the foundation of the monastery within the Byzantine period. See also V. Tzaferis, *The Monastery of the Cross in Jerusalem* (Athens, 1987).

The Monastery of the Cross, looking northeast

lena (fourth century), Tatianus, King of Georgia (fifth century), Emperor Justinian (sixth century), Emperor Heraclius (seventh century) and the Emperors Michael IV (1034–1041) and Constantine IX Monomachus (1040–1050). Of all these versions, the one linking the name of Emperor Heraclius with the founding of the monastery is the most widespread. According to it, the Emperor erected the monastery as a monument in memory of and thanksgiving for his brilliant victory over the Persians.

As is well known, the Persians captured Jerusalem in 614, looting it and taking the Holy Cross to Ctesiphon, their capital. Fifteen years later, Heraclius routed the Persians and restored the Cross to its original site in the Church of the Holy Sepulchre. Tradition holds that to commemorate this momentous occasion, the Emperor founded the Monastery of the Cross on Jerusalem's western outskirts.

The majority of dates suggested here with respect to the founding of the monastery do not seem to be reasonable from the point of view of historical circumstances and the conditions prevailing in the Holy Land at the times proposed. Thus, linkage with the names of Queen Helena and King Tatianus appears to be rather tendentious. On the other hand, the reign of Heraclius after the the Persian invasion of Palestine does not seem to be

The Monastery of the Cross: interior courtyard

opportune for the construction of a new monastery in Jerusalem since most of the other monasteries and churches had been destroyed during this inroad. The same may be said of the beginning of the eleventh century, during the rule of the Emperors Michael IV and Constantine IX, when most of the churches and monasteries in Jerusalem had been completely or partially destroyed by the mad Egyptian Caliph, al-Ḥakim (996–1021). Instead of building a new monastery it would have been more feasible to repair more important ones.

In the few research works written in Greek or Georgian, an opinion was put forward suggesting that the monastery had been built at the beginning of the eleventh century by the Georgian monk Prochorus who arrived in Jerusalem from the monasteries of Mt. Athos in northern Greece. However, a 1936 Georgian manuscript in the library of the Greek Patriarchate describes Prochorus not as the founder, but only as the restorer.

Of all the dates proposed for the construction of the monastery, therefore, the sixth century C.E. seems to be the most acceptable.

Without involving the name of Emperor Justinian, it seems reasonable to assume that the monastery, like other important ones in the Holy Land, was erected in the sixth, or even around the end of the fifth century C.E. Support of this hypothesis comes from a new source — an archaeological discovery, recently made on the site.

In the mid-1970s, the Greek Patriarchate, to whom the monastery belongs, undertook extensive renovation and restoration of the entire structure, both inside and out. In the course of the work, the eleventh-century mosaic floor of the main church was uplifted for repair and reinforcement. To the great surprise of the restoration team, headed by the architect Economopoulos, another colorful, more ancient mosaic floor was revealed beneath it (see Pl. Vb). The team also found clay vessels and rings dating from the Byzantine period, i.e. the fifth–sixth centuries C.E. These archaeological discoveries have not yet been published, but the writer had the good

fortune to be present when they were made, and thus was able to closely examine the artifacts on the spot. There was no doubt that the mosaics and the other finds belonged to the Byzantine period.

In view of the archaeological finds and what was said above, it is possible to summarize the historical beginnings of the Monastery of the Cross as follows: it was founded sometime in the Byzantine period, perhaps in the sixth century, during the rule of Emperor Justinian. It was damaged in the course of the Persian invasion and conquest of Jerusalem, as were other monasteries and religious institutions, and restored upon the return of Byzantine rule under Emperor Heraclius. At the beginning of the eleventh century, the monastery again suffered serious impairment at the hand of the Egyptian Caliph, al-Ḥakim. A short while later, apparently during the reigns of the Byzantine Emperors Michael IV and Constantine IX, it was again rebuilt and restored, this time at the initiative of the Georgian monk Prochorus. Since then, the Monastery of the Cross has come to be known as "The Georgian Monastery."

From this period onward in the annals of the monastery, as supported by a wealth of historical and literary evidence over many hundreds of years following its renovation, its fate was tied to that of the Georgian monks living in the Holy Land. Many came to Palestine as far back as in Byzantine times, and even in the early Arab period. After the expulsion of the Crusaders, however, and throughout the Mamluk reign, their status improved and their numbers increased due to the good political relations prevailing between their native country, Georgia, and the Mamluks. Many Georgian rulers of the Bagrat dynasty, such as David II (1089–1125) and Queen Tamar (1189–1212), aided and supported the Georgian nuns in the Holy Land, transferring sums of money for the construction of monasteries and purchase of land.

The eleventh to the fourteenth centuries, then, were the best and the most glorious in the monastery's history. During this time, it served as a spiritual and religious center for the many and varied activities of the monks and nuns based there. All the surrounding lands were also purchased, becoming the property of the monastery, to be worked by farmers brought from Georgia. The nearby village of Malḥa was in fact also settled by Georgian farmers in those years.

At the beginning of the thirteenth century, an emissary of Queen Tamar arrived. He was the monk and poet Shouta Roustaveli, who had always been active in the organization of Georgian monks and nuns in the Holy Land in general, and in the Monastery of the Cross in particular. It was during his tenure that the church walls were adorned with beautiful murals, depicting many saints and holy figures, together with Greek philosophers such as Plato, Socrates, Aristotle, Plutarch, Solon the Athenian and others (see Pl. Vc).

It was during the thirteenth century that the Monastery of the Cross reached the zenith of its glory. Within its walls, in its dozens of rooms, dwelt many monks, among them theologians, poets and scholars, producing various manuscripts or copying documents into such languages as Greek, Georgian, Russian, Arabic and Armenian. A large number of these have been preserved, and can today be found in the central library of the Greek Patriarchate.

But with the decline of Mamluk rule in Palestine, the position of the Georgian holy men was also undermined. The fifteenth century witnessed various groups of monks becoming entangled in internal quarrels and conflicts, causing splits in their ranks and weakening them to a point where their continued existence was gravely endangered. The Monastery of the Cross was overwhelmed by the burden of tremendous financial debts, and there was concern that it may fall into neglect.

In the mid-seventeenth century, while Niceophorus held office as head of the monastery, a last desperate attempt was made to save the institution, reorganize it and restore it to its former status. According to a bilingual inscription still preserved in the monastery, written in Greek and Georgian and bearing the date 1643, the entire monastery was reno-

vated and the murals in the church restored. However, Niceophorus' efforts were of no avail. The financial contributions from Georgia dried up completely and the numbers of the monks and nuns dwindled. Worst of all, the monastery sank into debt to such an extent that it was unable to make repayment. Most of the properties and lands which it had previously acquired now had to be sold. Even then, the proceeds were insufficient to cover the liabilities. Many Jerusalem monasteries were sold, while others were forcibly seized by the creditors. It was in this difficult hour that the Greek Patriarchate, their only ally, came to the aid of the Georgian monks and nuns. Patriarch Dosithius (1669–1707), after strenuous effort and wearying journeys to many lands, finally managed to raise the funds needed to redeem a large part of the Georgians' huge debts. Among others, he repaid those sums owed by the Monastery of the Cross, and from that time onward, it came under the religious authority of the Greek Patriarchate of Jerusalem.

In 1841, the Russian Church requested the Greek Patriarchate to return the church to its possession, wishing to convert it into the Russian Mission center of the Holy Land. The Patriarchate refused, and in order to forestall any similar future appeals, decided to turn the monastery into a theological seminary. After a number of years of preparation and further renovation, adapting the building to its new function, the monastery was reopened in October 1855 to serve as a school for novice priests.

In the course of time, the monastery became renown as one of the best and most important schools in the Orthodox Christian world; but in 1908, again due to financial difficulties, the institution was closed, and reverted once more to a monastery — lonely and neglected.

In the 1970s the building was again restored and renovated by the Greek Patriarchate with the aim of turning it into a residential institute for theological and archaeological research. Today it is also being used to accommodate pilgrim visitors.

CHURCHES IN JUDEA
AND IN
THE JUDEAN DESERT

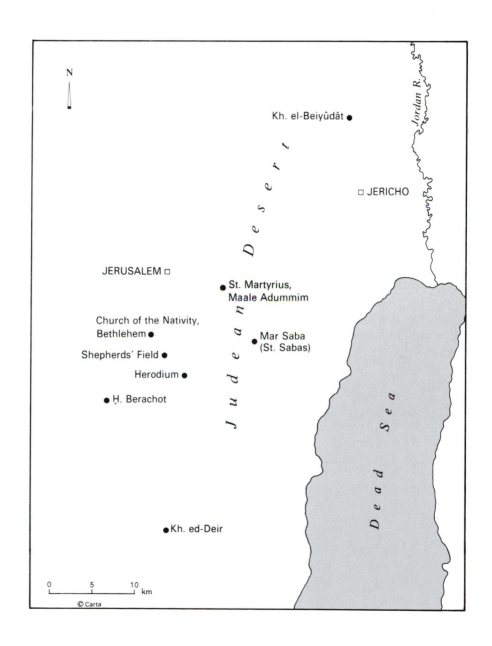

Monasteries and Churches in the Judean Desert in the Byzantine Period

Yizhar Hirschfeld

At the height of monastic activity in the Judean Desert in the fifth to seventh centuries C.E., there were approximately seventy monasteries in existence,[1] most of them concentrated in two regions: one in the northwest, and the other in the Jericho valley. Along the desert's western margin, some forty-five monasteries and monastic sites (hermitages, etc.) can be counted, while on the plain between Jericho and the Jordan River, there are remains of another twenty-five.

Three chronological stages can be distinguished in the development of monasticism in the Judean Desert. The founding stage during the fourth century, the expansion in the fifth century, and the zenith, from the end of the fifth to the beginning of the seventh centuries. The Arab Conquest in 638 marks a process of decline among the Judean Desert monasteries.

The Founding Stage

Chariton, a native of the city of Iconium (Konya) in Asia Minor is considered to be the pioneer of the monastic movement in the Judean Desert. He arrived there in the fourth decade of the fourth century C.E., and founded three lauras: Pharan, Douka and Souka (see map). A laura may be defined as a community of recluses living in isolation during the week and meeting for common prayer on weekends. The three lauras founded by Chariton possessed the features which ensured the continued existence of the monasteries during the initial stages of their

establishment in the desert: a source of available water (a spring), cliffs abounding in caves and natural rock cover, and reasonable proximity to civilian settlements on the desert periphery.

The Expansion

Euthymius is thought to be the real founder of monasticism in the Judean Desert. A native of Melitene (today Malatia), capital of Armenia, he came to the Judean Desert in the year 405, and remained there for seventy years. During that time, he was party to the setting up of three monasteries. The first two, Theoctistus in Naḥal ʿOg (Wadi Mukallik) and Caparbaricha in the Ziff region, are located on the outer margin of the area later occupied by other monasteries. Euthymius' third monastery, named after him, was built at Meshor Adummim, close to the Jerusalem–Jericho road. It produced a line of well-known monks, such as Martyrius, Elias and Sabas, who were prominent both as Church leaders and as monastery founders in their own right. In Euthymius' time, the nature of Judean Desert monasticism underwent a change, raising it from near anonymity to a position of high prestige and involvement in the Church establishment in Jerusalem. His biography, and those of the leaders of other monasteries in the fifth and sixth centuries, such as Sabas and Theodosius, are known to us from the book of Cyril of Scythopolis, who practised monasticism in the Judean Desert in the same period and was witness to events.

The Zenith

In the fifth, sixth and the beginning of the seventh centuries, Judean Desert monasticism

---

[1] Y. Hirschfeld, "List of the Byzantine Monasteries in the Judean Desert," *CAHL*, pp. 1–90; idem, *The Judean Desert Monasteries in the Byzantine Period* (New Haven/London, 1992).

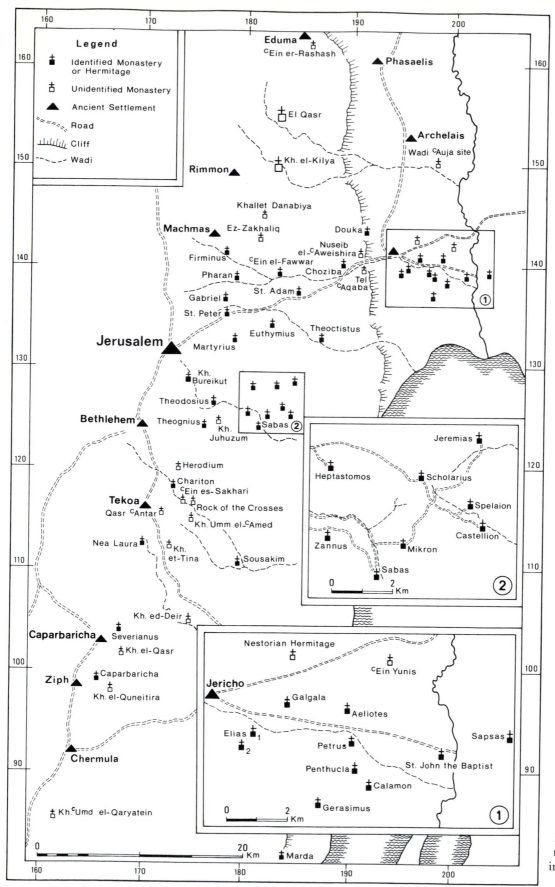

Legend

■ Identified Monastery or Hermitage

⊥ Unidentified Monastery

▲ Ancient Settlement

═══ Road

⊥⊥⊥⊥ Cliff

– – – Wadi

Eduma ▲
ᶜEin er-Rashash

Phasaelis ▲

⊥ El Qasr

Archelais ▲
Wadi ᶜAuja site ⊥

⊥ Kh. el-Kilya

Rimmon ▲

Khallet Danabiya ⊥

Machmas ▲ Ez-Zakhaliq

Douka ■

Firminus ■ ᶜEin el-Fawwar ⊥ Nuseib el-ᶜAweishira ■

Pharan ■ Choziba ■

St. Adam ⊥ Tel ᶜAqaba ■

Gabriel ■

St. Peter ■ Euthymius ⊥ Theoctistus ⊥

Jerusalem ▲ Martyrius ⊥

Kh. Bureikut ■

Theodosius ■

Bethlehem ▲ Theognius ■ Kh. Juhuzum Sabas ② ⊥

Herodium ⊥

Chariton ■
ᶜEin es-Sakhari

Tekoa ▲ Rock of the Crosses ⊥
Qasr ᶜAntar ⊥ Kh. Umm el-ᶜAmed ⊥

Nea Laura ⊥ Kh. et-Tina ⊥ Sousakim ⊥

Kh. ed-Deir ⊥

Caparbaricha ▲ Severianus ⊥
Kh. el-Qasr ⊥

Ziph ▲ Caparbaricha ■
Kh. el-Quneitira ⊥

Chermula ▲

Kh. ᶜUmd el-Qaryatein ⊥

Marda ⊥

Inset ②

Jeremias ⊥

Heptastomos ⊥ Scholarius ⊥

Spelaion ⊥

Zannus ⊥ Mikron ■ Castellion ■

Sabas ■

0   2
═══ Km

②

Inset ①

Nestorian Hermitage ⊥

ᶜEin Yunis ⊥

Jericho ▲ Galgala ⊥

Aeliotes ■

Elias ■₁ Petrus ⊥ Sapsas ■
₂ St. John the Baptist ⊥

Penthucla ⊥

Calamon ⊥

Gerasimus ■

0   2
═══ Km

①

0   20
═══════════ Km

Location of monasteries in the Judean Desert

150

Monastery of Theoctistus

Laura of Theodosius

reached its zenith to which are linked the names of Theodosius and Sabas. The former founded the largest communal monastery in the Judean Desert and the latter established the largest laura, known as The Great Laura, in the Kidron Valley. In 494 C.E., the two were elected to head the monks. Theodosius directed the cenobitic monasteries in the Jerusalem region, while Sabas was in charge of all the Palestinian lauras and the anchorites.[2] These appointments indicate the recognition of the authority of both monks as leaders of the monastic movement in the Judean Desert.

Theodosius, of the province of Caesaria, capital of Cappadocia in Asia Minor, set up a *coenobium* around the year 476. Lying to the east of Bethlehem, it was the largest of all the monasteries in the Judean Desert, having 400 inhabitants and being renowned for its tradi-

tion of hospitality and social awareness. Its monastic system was based on that of Basil the Great, of Cappadocia.

Theodosius' journey from Jerusalem to the site he chose for his monastery was not arduous. Sabas, on the other hand, was described as a hermit who secluded himself deep in the desert. His monastery began to develop around his isolated cave in Naḥal Kidron (Wadi en-Nar), where he had come to settle in 478 C.E., and gradually increased in size, until it came to be known as The Great Laura (today, Mar Saba). Sabas was an ardent builder. He established some ten monasteries, eight of them in the Judean Desert. All of Sabas' desert monasteries, except The New Laura south of Tekoah, are located in the vicinity of The Great Laura in the Kidron Valley. The proximity of these monasteries symbolizes their bond to Sabas, and indirectly serves as evidence of his impressive leadership

[2] D.J. Chitty, *The Desert City* (Oxford, 1966), p. 86.

151

The Great Laura (Mar Saba)

Monastery of St. George (Choziba)

and ability as a founder and builder of monasteries.

Parallel to the floruit in monasticism on the desert heights, there was a similar impressive increase in the number of monasteries near the Jordan River, which apparently was linked to the multitude of pilgrims flocking to the holy places near the Jordan in the Byzantine period. On the road descending from Jerusalem to Jericho, four memorial churches and adjacent monasteries were erected, providing services to the pilgrims. The best known and most important was the Monastery of John the Baptist, on the west bank of the Jordan. Two other monasteries on the road also flourished. One is the Monastery of Martyrius, mentioned above, the size and wealth of which surpassed that of any previously-known monastery.[3] The other was Choziba, more commonly known as the Monastery of St. George, in Naḥal Prat (Wadi Kelt). Toward the end of the fifth century, this monastery changed from a hermitage to a *coenobium*, and its gates were opened to female visitors. These developments indicate the willingness of the monks to welcome pilgrims and travelers.

The process of growth and prosperity was halted by the Persian invasion in 614, and especially by the Muslim Conquest around 638 C.E. The isolation from the centers of the Byzantine Empire and cessation of the flow of pilgrims seriously effected the monasteries. The archaeological evidence has revealed that most of the monasteries in the Judean Desert were abandoned. The monastic movement, which in its prime had embraced tens of monasteries, shrank to a mere handful — only the most important ones and those located close to the road from Jerusalem to the Jordan. Judean Desert monasticism did not cease to exist, but the scope and power it had enjoyed during the Byzantine period was never regained.

[3] See in this volume, Y. Magen, "The Monastery of St. Martyrius at Maᶜale Adummim," pp. 170–196.

Types of Monasteries
in the Judean Desert

The main factor shaping the architecture of the monasteries was geography. About half of those known to us from within the bounds of the Judean Desert were constructed in close proximity to rock cliffs or steep areas. On the basis of this fact, several scholars have suggested that a differentiation should be made between the regular and the cliff types of monasteries. The shape of the regular type is defined by its name; its representatives are to be found mainly around Jericho and its internal layout is symmetrical. On the other hand, in the monasteries built in the cliff areas of the desert heights, there were many architectural deviations, stemming from a need to adapt the structure to the steep topography.

Typologically, the monasteries of the Judean Desert may be classified into two main groups: lauras and *coenobia*.

Lauras. By definition, a laura is a monastery of recluses, each monk living alone in his cell, meeting with the others only on Saturdays and Sundays for prayer and to stock up on food and other necessities. The Greek term "laura" means "lane" and apparently relates to the location of the cells along a path leading to the main building. Every laura is composed of these two elements: the central building containing a church and other utilitarian structures, and the monks' cells. According to the various sources and archaeological findings, in the Judean Desert during the Byzantine period there were some twenty lauras. About half were of the cliff type and half of the regular type. Chronologically, the cliff lauras are older. The first three monasteries erected in the Judean Desert in the fourth century C.E., Pharan (see Pl. VIa–b), Douka and Souka, were cliff lauras. The first regular-type lauras, on the other hand, were built only a hundred years later.

The lauras are generously proportioned in area. A few of them, like the Laura of Firminus in Naḥal Michmaš or The New Laura, spread over dozens of acres. Their boundaries are marked by the most distant cells, so that

Douka (Deir Quarantal) cliff laura

the major part is open, undeveloped space. The distances between the cells varied according to topographic conditions and the number of members in the community, but our survey indicated that the average distance was 33 m.

The most notable differences between the two types of lauras relate to the form and size of the nucleus. The core of the regularly-shaped type is usually fairly large, while that of the cliff monastery is smaller, the spread of the buildings being dictated by topography. In some of them, such as The New Laura or the Laura of Firminus, an attempt was made to separate the church complex from the other service buildings.

Coenobia. Here the monks practise communal life (κοιηὸς βίος), sharing a daily routine of prayer, work and dining. In the Judean Desert, there are some forty identified cenobitic monasteries. Twenty-five are of the regular type, while the other fifteen are cliff *coenobia*. The regular-type *coenobium* is characterized by a generally square plan and is surrounded by walls giving it the appearance of a fortress or a well-fortified estate. Building wings are arranged around an inner courtyard which also serves as a source of light and ventilation. In the internal layout of the monastery, there is a tendency to separate the service areas (stores, stables) from the living quarters of the monks where they carry out their daily work. The auxiliary rooms are usually located close to the entrance gate of the monastery, for reasons of both convenience (loading and unloading) and sanitation.

An element common to most cenobitic monasteries is the passageway leading directly from the church to the refectory. The partaking of the common meal in the refectory was a direct continuation of the prayer ceremony in the church. Accordingly, the refectory was always located in the vicinity of the church and connected with it by means of some sort of architectural element, such as a covered passageway or an open courtyard. In several *coenobia*, for instance the Monastery of Martyrius at Maᶜale Adummimm, and the monastery at Khirbet ed-Deir, the founder's grave is located in close proximity to the passage joining the church and the refectory.[4]

The architecture of the cliff-type *coenobia* usually took advantage of the surrounding physical landscape. Most of them were constructed on terraces, the walls of the lower buildings serving as foundations for the structures erected on top of them. In most cases, the monasteries were built on the southern or southeastern slope. This choice, also characteristic of the cliff-type lauras, afforded maximum exposure to sunlight, yet gave the inhabitants protection from the strong winds prevalent in that region during the winter.

Monastery Churches in the Judean Desert
The church was an essential element of every monastery. Its existence was an expression of the monks' desire to come together and participate in common prayer and liturgy. The larger monasteries had more than one church. In the Theodosius monastery, for instance, there was a central church, and nearby, three smaller ones; later, in the early

sixth century, a fifth was added, dedicated to the Virgin Mary.

The monastery churches were not different from other churches in the country. The apse was located in the east; in front of it, there was a raised chancel (*bema*) separated from the nave by a chancel screen. In the center of the *bema* stood the altar, usually of marble.

Often, other adjacent rooms were used in the cult. An almost permanent fixture was the *diaconicon*, mentioned in the monastic literature of the Judean Desert. Another element found in several churches was the baptistery. Apparently, the main purpose of the construction of the baptismal fonts in the monasteries was to baptize the local population.

The monastery churches in the Judean Desert are divided into two main types: the monastery-chapel type, and the cave-church type. The first is the most common both in the Judean Desert and elsewhere. The dimensions of the chapels vary, but all consist of a long, narrow prayer hall facing a single apse. Apparently, the simplicity of the construction and the absence of internal partition by means of galleries and columns suited the monks' requirements. In most cases, we find that the opening between the church and the chapel is located in the southern wall which faces the courtyard.

The cave type, where the cave's internal space was converted into a church, is found in several monasteries of the Judean Desert. The caves were usually located in the center of the monastery, and were exceptional for their internal spaciousness and relatively good illumination. A good example is the cave-church at Khirbet ed-Deir, mentioned above. The well-known basilican church, whose internal space was divided by two rows of columns, is quite rare and found only in later monasteries. A good example is the church uncovered in the Euthymius monastery which was rebuilt after the Byzantine period.[5]

---

[4] See in this volume, Y. Hirschfeld, "The Cave-Church at Khirbet ed-Deir," pp. 244–258.

[5] Hirschfeld, *CAHL* (see note 1), pp. 15–18.

The Byzantine Church at Khirbet el-Beiyûdât in the Lower Jordan Valley

Hananya Hizmi

In June–July 1986 the author directed a rescue excavation at Khirbet el-Beiyûdât on behalf of the Archaeological Officer of Judea and Samaria.[1] The site (Grid Ref. 1945/1522) is some 12 km north of Jericho. It is situated in the runoff delta of Wadi ʿAujah in a fertile agricultural area.[2] Though archaeological research in the region has revealed a great many finds associated with the Byzantine period,[3] contemporary literary sources make no mention of any settlement in this particular area.[4]

The Church Complex

Excavation revealed a basilica church divided into three parts by two rows of columns. Its external dimensions are 23.6 × 15.5 m, with the apse projecting to the east. The walls (0.8 m thick) are preserved to an average height of some 2 m; the outer face of the western, northern and eastern walls is composed of hewn stones while the inner face was made of small to medium-sized fieldstones. Plaster was applied in two layers to the inner face: the first coat was some 2–3 cm thick and contained ribbed pottery sherds decorated with white slip; the second layer was thin (generally not exceeding 0.5 cm) and finely sieved. In a few places — mostly in the apse — patches of red-colored plaster were found.

The narthex is longer than the width of the church; though its southern wall has not yet been discovered, the wall of the southern aisle does not continue to close it off. The narthex was exposed only to the level of the tops of the walls. The arrangement of the doors of this vestibule is not yet clear. We also lack information regarding the atrium. If there was, in fact, such an atrium, the main part of its area is covered by the modern Jericho–Beth-shean

---

[1] The site was damaged in two places during the laying of telephone lines (see the plan). The following participated in the excavation: Y. Levy, A. Kaapaḥ (area supervisors), A. Toledo (registrar), A. Tsur, A. Tsaʾalah (administration), P. Gertovski (surveying), T. Slotska, R. Tsion (drawings), and L. Ritmeyer (reconstruction). Photographs was taken by the author. I wish to thank Dr. Y. Magen, the Archaeological Officer for Judea and Samaria, for his assistance. This article is based on H. Hizmi, "The Byzantine Church at Khirbet el-Beiyûdât: Preliminary Report," *CAHL*, pp. 245–264.

[2] Khirbet el-Beiyûdât was first named as the best candidate for identification as Archelais by Guthe: H. Guthe, "Beitrage zur Ortskunde Palästinas", *Mitteilungen und Nachrichten des Deutschen Palästina-Vereins* 17 (1911): 68–69. J. Porath, in his doctoral thesis adopted this identification: J. Porath, *Ancient Irrigation Agriculture in the Arid Zones of Eretz Israel* (Tel Aviv, 1985), p. 55 (Hebrew). Archelais is mentioned in the following sources: 1. Josephus, *Ant.* 17.340, 18.31, relates that Archelaus, son of Herod, built the village and gave it his name. Josephus also mentions that Archelaus diverted water to Archelais from the irrigation canal, which ran to the village of Naʿaran. 2. Pliny recounts that Archelais was a village which lay between Jericho and Phasaelis; he also relates that it was one of the more famous date-growing districts (Pliny, N.H., V. 13,44.3). 3. The Peutinger Map places Archelais some 19 km north of Jericho [see K. Miller, *Die Peutingerische Tafel* (Stuttgart 1962)]. 4. The Madaba Map depicts Archelais as a fortified village whose wall contained three towers and a central gate. The village is shown as being located between Elisha's church in Jericho and Phasaelis.

[3] A number of surveys of the area have been made: see *SWP*, v. 2; M. Kochavi (ed.), *Judaea, Samaria and the Golan. Archaeological Survey 1967–1968* (Jerusalem, 1972), pp. 108–109; Porath,

Ancient Irrigation Agriculture (see note 2), p. 55 and the bibliography given there.

[4] Notwithstanding Russel's reading of Archelais in a Syrian document and his dating of the earthquake to 363 C.E., excavations have not, as yet, revealed any traces of a settlement from the early Byzantine period. I should like to thank N. Applebaum who directed my attention to this source [K.W. Russel, "The Earthquake of May 19, A.D. 363," *BASOR* 238 (1980): 50].

Khirbet el-Beiyûdât: general view of church,
looking north

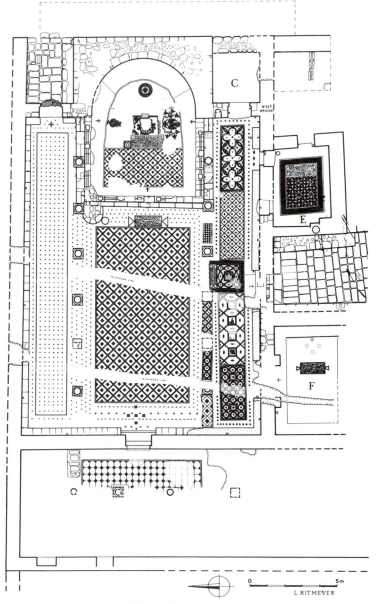

0   5m

L RITMEYER

Khirbet el-Beiyûdât: plan of church

road. The narthex was 6.2 m wide and was divided lengthwise by a row of columns, the bases of four of which were discovered. These are all 50 cm wide but of different styles. The partial excavation of this area has revealed a number of white, finely plastered columns of different heights ranging from 1 to 1.5 m; however, all have the same diameter corresponding to that of the column bases.

The narthex floor was paved with a geometric mosaic, the full size of which is, as yet, unknown. The panel is decorated with a net of squares (35 × 35 cm each), the corners of which are colored (red and black in alternate rows) to form diamonds. Two of the four column bases were found set into the mosaic, each one surrounded by a black border measuring 1 × 1 m. The two borders are not identical, probably due to poor workmanship.

Between the northernmost column base and the eastern wall of the narthex, a tomb was dug into the mosaic probably in the later phase of the church.[5] It is 1.5 m long, 40 cm wide and 60 cm deep. It has brick and pebble walls. The deceased, a woman, aged between 25 and 35 and some 1.5 m tall, was laid supine with her head toward the west.

An opening some 1.3 cm wide leads from the narthex to the nave. As mentioned above, two rows of columns divided the church into a nave and two aisles; each row consisted of six columns whose bases, with diameters of 60 cm, were 2.8 m apart. Most of the bases have remained *in situ*. It is noteworthy that excavation did not reveal even a single column fragment, probably due to the secondary use of the columns in a later period, somewhere in the vicinity of the church.[6]

[5] The tomb was excavated with the help of J. Zias, the anthropologist of the Israel Antiquities Authority, whose findings are presented here, and his assistant, R. Abu-Di'ab. I wish to thank them both for their help.

[6] Though marble columns are often used as raw material in the production of lime, no lime pit has been discovered in the immediate vicinity. It should be noted, however, that in the fourth layer of Hisham's Palace (Khirbet el-Mafjar) architectural items made of marble and bitumen were discovered, some of which were decorated with crosses; it is possible that they were taken from Khirbet el-Beiyûdât.

Khirbet el-Beiyûdât: general view of church

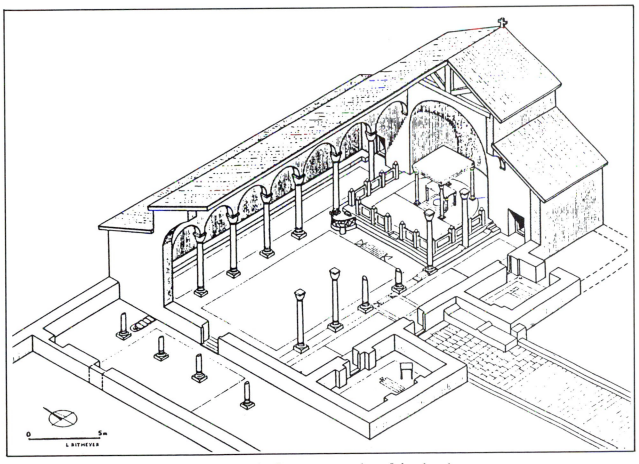

0   5m
L RITMEYER

Khirbet el-Beiyûdât: reconstruction of the church

The northern aisle is 17.8 m long on the inside and 3.3 m wide to the middle of the column bases. A plastered bench, 40 cm wide and 30 cm high, runs along its northern and western walls; it is made mostly of sandstone blocks, sometimes in secondary use. The entire length of the aisle is paved with a mosaic consisting of a panel, generally measuring 1.8 m in width and made of tesserae averaging about 1 cm in size. The panel is composed of a simple black frame, enclosing a repetitive pattern of squares arranged in 63 rows of six. At the eastern end there is a cross-shaped blossom in red, contrasting with the black and white of the other parts of the mosaic.

The opening leading out of the church at the eastern end of the aisle is 80 cm wide. It was later blocked with bricks and rough stones. The area outside the church, up to the line of the eastern wall of the apse, is paved with stone slabs measuring 60 × 40 cm on average. In this paved area a stone cross was found. It may have originated from the upper part of the church's facade.

The main part of the mosaic floor of the nave comprises a 10 × 5.5 m panel decorated with a simple geometric pattern: a net of diamonds formed by rows of intersecting diagonal lines. Each of these diagonals is made up of four rows of tesserae; the two inner

being red and the two outer, black. At the center of each diamond is another smaller diamond of the same colors. A few centimeters above the floor level, excavation revealed a burnt layer, probably the remains of wooden roof beams. (Evidence of fire was also found in other places.)

The area between the nave's main panel and the two rows of columns is paved in a pattern similar to that of the northern aisle — black squares on a white background, while the space on the west features a combination of different patterns: five squares forming a cross lie directly in front of the entrance; the rest of the ornamentation comprises alternate rows of squares and flower buds. The nave and the northern aisle seem to have constituted a single unit, including the bench around the walls and the column bases.

At the eastern edge of the nave, at the foot of the *bema*, there is an inscription enclosed in a *tabula ansata*.[7] "Porphyrius the episcopus and Eglon the priest," to whom, as those responsible for paving the church, the inscription was dedicated, are not mentioned in any of the literary sources of the period.

The *bema* is 8 m wide, 5.2 m long and raised some 60 cm above the floor level of the nave. There are three openings in the projecting part of the *bema*. One, 60 cm wide, leads to the nave, while the other two, of similar width, provide access to the aisles. The mosaic floor of the *bema* near the side entrances contains crosses. The entrance leading to the northern aisle seems to have fallen into disuse at the time when the eastern entrance to the northern aisle was blocked up. The *bema* was surrounded by a chancel screen, the posts of which were approximately 1 m apart. Only the sockets were found. An *ambo* (pulpit) protrudes from the northwestern corner of the platform. Only one course of the *ambo* survives: it is made of stones finely hewn on the

Khirbet el-Beiyûdât: the bema, looking east

[7] I should like to thank L. Di Segni who translated the inscriptions (see in this volume, L. Di Segni, "The Inscriptions at Khirbet el-Beiyûdât," pp. 164–169). I am also indebted to Dr. V. Tzaferis for his preliminary reading of two of the inscriptions.

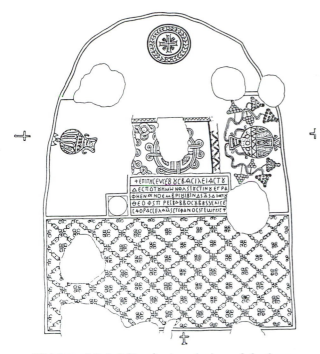

Khirbet el-Beiyûdât: the inscription of the bema

outside and built in the shape of a semicircle, 1.1 m wide and 1.1 m deep.

A column drum in secondary use, set into the mosaic, was found to the south of the *ambo*. The column section is 50 cm in diameter and of about the same height. Beside it a two-handled stone bowl was found upside down — it presumably stood on the column section and was meant to hold the holy water. To the west of the *ambo*, there was a burnt patch on the floor — presumably remains of the wooden upper portion of the pulpit.

The apse, 6 m wide and 3.2 m deep, is made of curved stones which were finely hewn on their outer face. It is preserved to a height of 2–3 courses and traces of red plaster remain on the few curved stones in the center. The eastern facade of the church behind it is formed by a straight wall of stones hewn on their outer face, which is preserved to a height of six courses above the three of the foundation. This wall is very thick — its narrowest point being some 1.2 m — as it supported the semi-vault of the apse.

A column base (30 cm in diameter) was found *in situ* in the apse and the damaged mosaic floor bore traces of a further three bases, 2.4 m apart, which surrounded the altar. (A similar column base was found in

Room C, south of the apse.) These bases could have supported columns no more than 2.5 m high; therefore, the altar was presumably covered by a canopy or *ciborium*.

The floor of the *bema* is covered by three layers of mosaics. Probes made at three spots where the uppermost mosaic was damaged revealed the first phase, a white mosaic floor. Another probe, at the edge of the altar, exposed a limestone chest which had been inserted into the mosaic with the use of white plaster. This *reliquiarium* was found empty.

During the second stage, the floor level was raised some 10 cm and a new mosaic laid, only a portion of which is preserved. In its center there is a rectangular carpet containing an interlaced circle which is divided into quarters filled with quadrants. It seems that this was the place where the altar table was erected.

The third and final stage consists of two separate colored mosaic panels, one covering the apse and the other the *bema*. The rectangular panel on the *bema*, measuring 4.6 × 2 m,

Khirbet el-Beiyûdât: the northern amphora in mosaic floor of the bema

is surrounded by a 1-cm-wide black, double border. The pattern consists of diamonds, the sides of which are made up of flower buds. The center of each diamond is filled by four buds in black and red on a white background. The second panel lies within the apse and is shaped accordingly. At its foot, between the two column bases, is an inscription (1.85 × 0.75 m). The inscription was dedicated to Abbosoubbos the priest (among others), as he was responsible for the mosaic paving of the floor. It is the only inscription with a date: the fourth year of the indiction of the Emperor Flavius Justinus (either Justin I, who ruled from 518 to 527, or Justin II, 565–578). Thus the fourth year of the indiction might have been either 525 or 570. The later date is to be preferred because the inscription cannot be dated before the mid-sixth century on palaeographic grounds.[8]

In the mosaic floor of the apse, on either side of the altar, is a colorful amphora: one is located in front of the stairs leading to the *bema* from the southern aisle and the other lies in the same position on the northern side of the altar. The southern amphora (see Pl. VIIa) has two handles and trailing vines and is of geometrical design, in black, red and mustard-yellow colors. The northern amphora has a more elegant shape: the body is slightly less rounded and the shoulders are less inclined; the colors are red, white and mustard-yellow. It is somewhat surprising that this vessel lacks the vines of the first amphora. The two amphoras are of different shape and more than one artist seems to have been involved in their execution, as well as that of other parts of the mosaics of the *bema*.

At the eastern edge of the apse, the mosaic floor contains a medallion (see Pl. VIIb), 80 cm in diameter, made of two concentric circles with flower buds between them. In the middle of the medallion there is a black cross, outlined in red. Between its arms sprout four flower buds.

The southern aisle is identical to its northern counterpart in width. Its southern wall has four bench sections separated by three entrances: two lead to side-rooms, while the central, wide one opens onto a road which ran southward probably to the nearby settlement.

The mosaic floor of the southern aisle differs completely in character from those of the rest of the church: it has rich and complicated patterns and is made up of smaller tesserae of a different kind. It is clear that it was paved separately from the mosaic of the nave. There is a sequence of five different panels in the southern aisle (see Pl. VIIc–f). The central panel, opposite the central entrance to the church, contains an inscription in a *tabula ansata* in its northern part. The border of this panel is some 20 cm wide and consists of a braid-like intertwining pattern in three colors. The main ornamentation consists of alternating circles and pointed oval units which enclose a square. Unfortunately, the design inside the square has not been preserved. The inscription was dedicated to the priests and their assistants who have either Greek or Semitic names. The names of two priests, Aphleos and Lukas, are recorded.

The four remaining panels have geometric and floral motifs. They are encompassed by a row of tiny diamonds. The easternmost panel incorporates three quatrefoil units, each with a single diamond at its center, and eight small flower buds. The remaining space in the panel is filled with petal shapes creating a pattern of minute diamonds and triangles. The second panel from the east contains a net of diamonds enclosing smaller diamonds. The two panels to the west of the central panel are of different sizes and have of more complicated patterns. The larger one is filled with a design of overlapping octagons within each of which is a pattern of four hexagons enclosing a square. The center of each hexagon contains a small lozenge. Of the squares, only two are preserved: one features a cluster of grapes, and the other two intertwining elipses.

---

[8] The mosaic on the *bema* was dated to the fifth century C.E. by R. Talgam. This would lead to the conclusion that the earliest stages of the church building are to be dated to the beginning of the fifth century, if not earlier. This proposition is hard to accept in the light of the finds: architectural, ceramic and palaeographic.

The eastern part of the fourth panel was covered with a layer of black ash, while the western edge was hidden under a pile of building stones, some of them still covered with white plaster. The panel's pattern comprises eighteen circles and three squares. The center of each circle is marked by four buds sprouting from a central point and the squares are decorated with a lozenge motif. Similar buds fill the space between the circles and the frame.

The intercolumniations are decorated with simple geometric patterns such as circles, diamonds, a chess pattern, and a continuous design of four-petaled rosettes. On the northern side of these panels, damage to the border during renovations can be discerned in several places.

At the eastern end of the southern aisle there is an opening, 1.1 m wide, leading to a room (C on the plan) beside the apse. The floor of this room is paved with a plain white mosaic. The northern wall is built of stones and the others of bricks. This room and the southern wing in general are of poor quality and are of a later date.

The side-rooms. As mentioned above, two side-rooms are located in the south adjacent to the southern aisle from which they were entered. The eastern one (E on the plan) is 3.2 m wide and 4.4 m long in its internal dimensions. Its walls are built of brick on stone foundations. The room is paved with a colored geometric mosaic floor, 3.2 m long and 2.5 m wide, with a frame some 30 cm wide. It has a complicated pattern of interlaced circles, forming Maltese crosses. There is an inscription in a *tabula ansata*, enclosed in a 138 × 68 cm frame, in the eastern part of the panel. It was dedicated to Lukas, presumably because he not only funded the mosaic but also the construction of the room as a whole. Lukas the priest is also mentioned in another mosaic — that found in the southern aisle.

The southwestern side-room (F on the plan) has internal dimensions of 6.2 × 4.2 m. Its walls are made of bricks on a stone foundation and are preserved to a height of about 1 m.

The entrance was damaged by the digging of a telephone trench. The floor in this entrance is paved with a white mosaic with a cross-shaped pattern. Two square pillar-bases were found *in situ* in the room on either side of the entrance. They may well have borne arches supporting the roof of this chamber. It should be mentioned that the excavations revealed no fragments of tiles or any other roofing material apart from bricks, and it seems that the roofing system consisted of wooden beams and pressed dried mud.

The southwestern room is paved with a simple, white mosaic with a black frame-like band, 4.8 × 2.9 cm in size. In the eastern part of the floor parts of four legs (10 × 10 cm) of a table remain *in situ*, sunk into the mosaic. The table, standing as it did at one end of the room, was probably used for various religious ceremonies. In the floor in front of where the table had stood there is an inscription in a 142 × 62 cm frame, dedicated to John the priest and Abbosoubbos [the deacon(?)]. The latter is also mentioned in the inscription found in the apse.

The finds. An important discovery was made on the road outside of the church: a column drum, 50 cm in height and diameter, the top of which was shaped into a conic sundial. This finely-designed piece is obviously the work of a skilled craftsman. Its lower part features the figure of a bearded man lying on his side. Under the figure, in a simple frame, is an inscription, the middle of which has been damaged. The sundial is dated to the Roman period.

The principal raw material used by the builders of the church was local limestone. Other significant finds during the excavation were mostly architectural elements made of marble, bituminous limestone and sandstone The chancel screen posts and the table legs were made of blackish bituminous limestone (Nebi Mussa stone), and sandstone was used for doorposts and regular building blocks. Of special interest is an architrave decorated with leaves and an egg and dart (*ovolo*) pattern. Few marble objects were found: fragments of ves-

Khirbet el-Beiyûdât: drawing and photograph of Roman sundial

sels, some of the chancel screen posts and panels, parts of pillars and the *reliquiarium*.

Little pottery was collected: mostly sherds of amphoras, bowls, cooking pots and lamps. Several coins were also found, but their bad condition does not enable identification.

Conclusions

It is possible to distinguish three major phases in the construction of the church, as well as intermediate phases when rooms were added.

First phase. When first constructed, the church was in the form of a basilica with the apse protruding to the east. The location of the church was probably influenced by the amount of potential building materials (i.e., walls, column drums) in the area of the earlier Roman village of Archelais. The main entrance of the church faced the nearby road to the south. To the east of this access there was an additional entrance to the southern aisle, but this was later blocked. The entrance from the narthex, too, is to be associated with this phase, as are the mosaic floor in the southern apse and the inscription dedicated to the priests Aphleos and Lukas who were

probably involved in the initial construction of the church. The white mosaic floor under the present level of the apse and the *bema* is also to be included in the first phase.

Some time after this, a side-room (room E) was added to the south of the southern aisle. It was built on the initiative of the priest Lukas, who is to be identified with the priest of the same name mentioned in inscription no. 1 (see L. Di Segni, "The Inscriptions at Kirbet el-Beiyûdât," pp. 164–169). This first phase can be dated to the end of the fifth and the beginning of the sixth centuries C.E.

Second phase. This is the most important phase of the church's construction. The nave was made slightly smaller and the narthex was built. A service room for the priests (Room C) was erected to the south of the apse and entered through the southern aisle. Two benches were also built on the southern side of the wall dividing the apse from the southern aisle. A doorway was breached in the eastern wall of the northern aisle, opening onto a paved passage leading out of the church. This entrance was later blocked and, in fact, seems to have been temporary, being

162

used only during the replacement of the mosaics throughout the church (apart from the southern aisle). On the *bema* and in the apse, a new mosaic was laid on top of the earlier floor; only a small part of this second mosaic now remains in the middle of the *bema*. The tesserae which were removed were dumped in a large pile in the outer court to the north of the apse. Other alterations included the construction of a bench along the walls of the church and the addition of an *ambo*.

These changes may be attributed to the period of Bishop Porphyrius and Eglon the priest who are mentioned in the inscription at the foot of the *bema*. Porphyrius probably served in the mid-sixth century.

At a later stage a second side-room was added to the southwestern corner of the southern aisle. The table legs found in the room, built on the initiative of John the priest and his assistant Abbosoubbos, seem to indicate that it might have been used as a chapel.

Third and final phase. The changes carried out during this phase were centered around the apse and the *bema*. The most important was the replacement of the mosaic floor, during which the altar table remained in place and a five-line inscription was inserted in front of it. According to this inscription, the work was carried out during the fourth year of the indiction of the Emperor Flavius Justinus. For the reasons given above, it seems more likely that this refers to Justin II and that the year in question is 570/1. The church was abandoned a number of decades after this: this seems to have occurred in an orderly fashion, as indicated by the meagre finds. The church was later burnt down, as evidenced by the charred beams and accumulations of ash in various places on its floor.

Finally, since the builders of the church appear to have made use of material available in the vicinity, there may well have been an earlier settlement on the site. The architectural elements that were in secondary use in the Byzantine period, as well as the Roman pottery found both on the surface and in soundings, would seem to corroborate the hypothesis that Khirbet al-Beiyûdât is to be identified as the site of the village Archelais.

The Inscriptions at Khirbet el-Beiyûdât

Leah Di Segni

The five inscriptions[1] discovered in the church belong to at least three building phases. The earliest is undoubtedly the small four-line inscription squeezed into an intercolumniation between the nave and the southern aisle, whose mosaic pavement was left untouched. One of the two priests mentioned in this inscription, Lukas, appears as donor in the dedication of the room in the southeastern corner of the church. The script in the two texts is quite different: on purely palaeographic grounds, it would be possible to date the inscription in the southern aisle a little earlier than the one in the adjacent room. As a matter of fact, this chamber may belong to a successive stage, when additions were made to both sides of the apse. In any event, if the priest Lukas mentioned in both dedications is one and the same man, the inference is that no great length of time lapsed between the execution of the two inscriptions.

Some time later, a new floor was laid in the nave and the northern aisle. No precise date for this development is given, but the inscription inset in the new pavement, at the eastern end of the nave, records the names of the bishop under whose rule the work was carried out, and of the priest who supervised it: he was called Eglon and must have been in charge of the church after Lukas' time. Another priest is mentioned in the fourth inscription, which also contains the only precise chronological information in the church; it is set in the uppermost floor of the *bema* and dates the last stage of the building to the reign of Justin

(undoubtedly Justin II). This new mosaic pavement was laid around the altar and was inaugurated on November 12, 570: this is the *terminus ad quem* for all the building stages and the inscriptions in the church. The priest mentioned in this inscription is called Abbosoubbos, a rather rare name which recurs in inscription no. 5: in the latter Abbosoubbos, probably the same man, is mentioned together with the priest John, but does not bear any title. Possibly he was then only a deacon and was later promoted to the priesthood, succeeding John as the clergyman in charge of the church. If this was the case, inscription no. 5 must antedate no. 4 by a few years.

Inscription no. 1. This inscription is framed in a small *tabula ansata*, 1.08 m long and 0.38 m wide, in an intercolumniation between the nave and the southern aisle. The four lines of its text are very cramped, giving the inscription an unelegant appearance, but the script is regular enough. Its narrow, angular characters (6–7 cm high) belong to the Byzantine square alphabet and point to a date in the fifth or at the very beginning of the sixth century C.E.

The text begins with a cross and reads as follows:

> Κύ(ριε) βοήθισον τοὺς δούλου(ς) (σου)
> Ἀφλεος καὶ Λούκας πρεσβι-
> τέρους καὶ Στέφ(ανον) καὶ Σαμα(ιον?)
> καὶ Ἐλισέος καὶ Λύπων.

Lord, help (Thy) servants Aphleos and Lukas the priests, and Stephanus and Sama(ios?) and Eliseos and Lypon.

---

[1] This article is based on L. Di Segni's expanded discussion, "Khirbet el-Beiyûdât: The Inscriptions," *CAHL*, pp. 265–273.

Khirbet el-Beiyûdât: inscription no. 1

The text includes the usual vulgarisms, so common in Byzantine inscriptions, especially those of a popular kind: the phonetic spellings *boethison* for *boetheson*, *presbiterous* for *presbyterous*, etc. Most of the names, like those in the other inscriptions, are Semitic. The only truly Greek name here is Stephanus.

As for the names themselves, besides the evangelic Stephanus and Lukas and the biblical Eliseos (Elisha), we find Aphleos, probably the Arabic name Haphal, and Sama(..), possibly standing for Samaios, the Greek transcription of the Jewish and Arabic name Shamay. The origin of Lypon is doubtful: it may be a modified Greek name, derived from the common Alypius.

Inscription no. 2. (See Pl. VIIIa.) This inscription is framed in a *tabula ansata* at the eastern end of the mosaic pavement in the southeastern room. The frame, 1.38 m long and

Khirbet el-Beiyûdât: drawing of inscription no. 1

165

Khirbet el-Beiyûdât: inscription no. 2

0.68 m wide, is beautifully designed in blue tesserae; rows of red cubes mark a division between the four lines of the script, and the characters are shaped in blue. The lettering is remarkably neat and well spaced and belongs mostly to the Byzantine round alphabet:

Κ(ύρι)ε μνήσθι(τι) Λούκα
τοῦ πρεσβ(υτέρου) ὅτι
ἐκ τῶν καμάτων
αὐτοῦ ἐψηφώθη.

Lord, remember Lukas the priest, because (this room) was paved at his expenses.

Inscription no. 3. This inscription is set in the mosaic pavement of the nave, in front of the *bema*. It is framed within a *tabula ansata* 1.6 m long and 0.7 m wide; both the frame and the letters are made of blue tesserae. The characters average 9–10 cm in height and are beautifully shaped and regularly spaced; they belong to the round alphabet:

Ἐπὶ τοῦ ἁγιωτ(άτου) καὶ ὁσιωτ(άτου)
ἡμῶν Πορφυρίου ἐπισκό-
που ἐψηφώθη ὁ ναὸς οὗ-
τος σπουδῆς Ἐγλῶνος πρεσβ(υτέρου)
κ(αὶ) ὑπὲρ σωτηρίας τῶν καρποφορ(ούντων).

In the time of our most holy and pious bishop Porphyrius, this church was paved, owing to the zeal of the priest Eglon and for the salvation of the benefactors.

According to its geographical location, the village must have been included within the diocese of Jericho, of which Porphyrius was the bishop sometime during the sixth century C.E.

Inscription no. 4. (See Pl. VIIIb.) This inscrip-

166

A. St. Martyrius: general view of monastery

B. St. Martyrius, church's vestibule: mosaic floor and Paul's tomb

St. Martyrius: A. Mosaic floor in narthex (above); B. Mosaic pavement of refectory (below)

A. St. Martyrius: panel in mosaic floor of kitchen

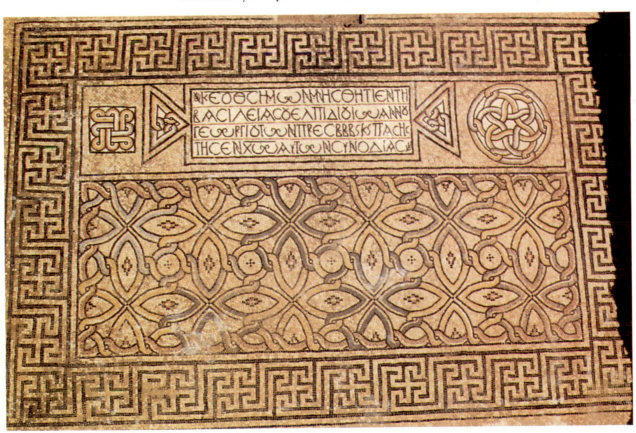

B. St. Martyrius, Chapel of the Three Priests: mosaic floor and inscription

A. Church of the Nativity, north wall mosaics: Council of Sardika

B. Church of the Nativity, south wall: Jacob from the row of Christ's ancestors

C. Church of the Nativity, transept: Apostle James in Transfiguration

D. Church of the Nativity, north wall: Syriac inscription

A. Church of the Nativity, north wall: candelabrum

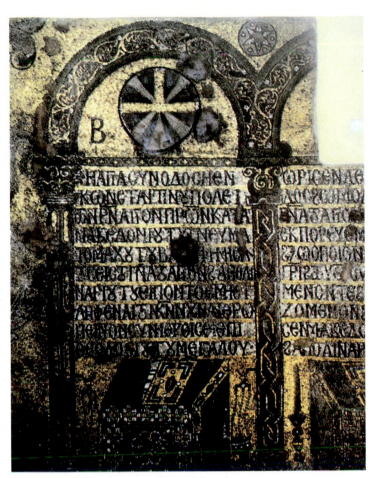

C. Church of the Nativity, south wall: Council of Constantinople

B. Church of the Nativity, south wall: candelabrum

D. Church of the Nativity, north wall: populated scrolls

PL. XIII

A. Church of the Nativity, north wall: angel

B. Church of the Nativity, column painting: Apostle James the Elder

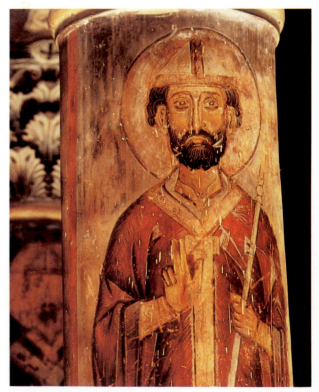

C. Church of the Nativity, column painting: Pope Leo

A. Ḥorvat Brachot, nave mosaic: beribboned bird

C. Ḥorvat Brachot, nave mosaic: buffalo

B. Ḥorvat Brachot, crypt: mosaic floor

D. Ḥorvat Brachot, nave mosaic: lion

A. Herodium, the northern church: nave

C. Herodium, the northern church: dedication inscription in narthex

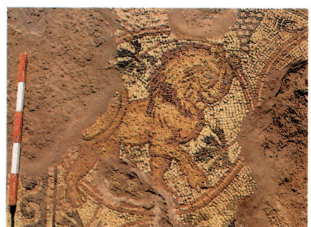

D. Herodium, the eastern church: lion in nave's mosaic

◁ B. Herodium, the central church: nave

Khirbet el-Beiyûdât: drawing of inscription no. 3

Khirbet el-Beiyûdât: drawing of inscription no. 4

tion is set in a rectangular frame, 1.85 m long and 0.75 m wide, on the *bema* in front of the altar: it overlaps the central motif of the earlier pavement, which was left untouched under the altar table. The frame and the letters are made of blue tesserae, while the horizontal rows of cubes that separate the four lines of script are red.

The text begins with a cross and reads:

Ἐπὶ τῆς εὐσεβοῦς βασιλείας τοῦ
δεσπότου ἡμῶν Φλ(αουίου) Ἰουστίνου ἐγρά-
φη ἐν μη(νὶ) Νοεμβρίου ιβ ἰνδ(ικτιῶνος) δ (καὶ) διὰ τοῦ
θεοφ(ιλεστάτου) πρεσβ(υτέρου) Ἀββοσούβ-
β(ου) (καὶ) Ἐλισέ[ου]
Σαορας Σελαμ(άνου) (καὶ) Στέφανος (καὶ)
Γεωργ(ίου) ἐψ(ηφώθη).

Under the pious reign of our master Flavius Iustinus, (this inscription) was written, in the month of November, 12,

of the 4th indiction, and the mosaic was made thanks to the God-loving priest Abbosoubbos and to Eliseos son of Saoras son of Salamanes, and to Stephanus and to Georgius.

On palaeographic grounds it can be established that the emperor mentioned here can only be Justin II, Justinian's successor, who reigned from 565 to 578 C.E. He is also mentioned in a funerary inscription from Jericho, dated December 13, 562, which, although somewhat neater, shows some palaeographic similarity to ours. The fourth year of the indictional cycle fell only once during Justin II's reign, in 570/1: the date of the inscription is therefore November 12, 570.

The priest then in charge of the church was Abbosoubbos (or Abbosobos as in Inscription no. 5), a rather uncommon name, who heads

167

Khirbet el-Beiyûdât: inscription no. 4

the list of individuals under whose care the new mosaic pavement was laid.

Saoras was most probably the name of Eliseos' father, and Selam(anes) that of his grandfather. The mention of both father and grandfather is not uncommon, and in any case it was perhaps necessary here since another Eliseos appears in the earlier inscription, no. 1. He was some three generations older than Saoras' son: the mention of the younger Eliseos' genealogy served to emphasize the fact that the older Eliseos was not his direct ancestor. Since the honor of appearing in the church inscriptions obviously reflected not only on the person mentioned, but also on his family, it is easy to understand how important it was to clearly identify the individual involved — especially in a village community, with its petty jealousies.

All the names in Eliseos' family are Semitic: Saoras, from the Arabic Sahar, appears in several Greek inscriptions. Selam with the abbreviation sign cannot be Selam or Selēm, but is probably Selamanēs. The other two individuals, Stephanus and Georgius, had Greek names which were also very common among the non-Greek population.

Inscription no. 5. The room attached to the southwestern corner of the church may have been a service room or a small subsidiary chapel: the inscription does not provide any clear indication. It is framed within a *tabula ansata* in the white mosaic pavement in front of the table or altar, facing east. The frame (1.42 m long and 0.62 m wide), the dividing lines and the script are black on a white background.

The inscription is divided into five lines. The script is well spaced and calligraphic. Some of the characters are unusually elegant in shape and enable an approximate dating.

168

Khirbet el-Beiyûdât: drawing of inscription no. 5

The text begins with a cross and reads as follows:

Κ(ύρι)ε Ἰ(ησο)ῦ Χ(ριστ)ὲ πρόσδεξε τὴν
καρποφορίαν τῶν δούλω(ν)
σοῦ Ἰωάννου τοῦ πρ(εσβυτέρ)ου καὶ
Ἀββοσόβου ὅτι ἐξ ἰδίων κό-
πων ἤγιραν τὸν οἶκον τοῦτον.

O Lord Jesus Christ, receive the offering of Thy servants, John the priest and Abbosobbos, for they erected this room by their exertions.

There is no doubt that "by their exertions" in this text refers to "at their expense" as in inscription no. 2 and not to physical labor.

169

The Monastery of St. Martyrius at Maᶜale Adummim

Yitzhak Magen

Salvage excavations carried out in the center of the town of Maᶜale Adummim (coordinates 178/133) unearthed a large Byzantine monastery known in Arabic as Khirbet el-Muraṣṣaṣ[1] (see Pl. IXa). The excavations were conducted under difficult conditions and presented a considerable logistic and scientific challenge due to their location within a dense urban settlement. Consequently, it was necessary to complete the work as quickly as possible. The entire site was exposed, a fact which was to have a far-reaching impact on the research of Byzantine monasteries. The ground plan of the monastery has been completely preserved and was found to include all the components of such buildings known from the sources.

The structure stands on the summit of a low hill overlooking the main Jericho-Jerusalem road. Below it spreads the mystifying and untamed landscape of the Judean Desert. Extending over some two and a half acres, the monastery was surrounded by a vast agricul-tural area, irrigated by cisterns, which supplied most of the needs of the inhabitants.

The site was composed of three parts: the monastery complex, an open courtyard, and a hospice for pilgrims. The monastery complex was enclosed by a defensive wall, 70.6 m long on the east, 77.4 m on the south, 65.4 m on the west and 79 m on the north. The open courtyard, which adjoined the western wall, served to collect rainwater and had a cistern in its center. Drainage channels conveyed the water from the courtyard to cisterns inside the monastery. The hospice, which is a separate structure, is situated northeast of the main building. In addition to guest rooms, it contained all the necessary auxiliary rooms as well as a chapel and a stable.

History of the Site

The identification of Khirbet el-Muraṣṣaṣ with the Monastery of Martyrius is based on the phonetic similarity between the two names and on the description of the establishment of the latter in the *Life of Euthymius* by Cyril (Kyrillos) of Scythopolis,[2] a monk who lived in the Judean Desert in the sixth century C.E.

> Two anchorites worthy of mention departed from Mt. Nitria [in Egypt], arrived in Palestine and came to Euthy-mius, the miracle worker, and attracted by his glory, which was universally ack-nowledged, remained with him, each in a separate cell. One was a man of Cappadoc-ian origin known as Martyrius and the other, called Elias, came from Arabia. Euthymius, spiritually enlightened, felt

---

[1] The salvage excavations were carried out over a period of twenty months in 1983–1984 by the the Archaeological Officer of Judea and Samaria assisted by Hananya Hizmi. The excavations were financed by the Israel Ministry of Housing with the cooperation of the Maᶜale Adummim municipality. The following participated in the excavations: Haim Goldfuss, Dorit Kirshner, Saif Adin Hadad, Uri Dinur, Daphna Shwiki, Zephania Shmuel, Tali Karinkin, André Okonov, Beni Levin-stein, Tania Slutzki (surveyor), Leen Ritmeyer (restorer) and Zeev Radovan (photographer). Joseph Zias of the Israel Anti-quities Authority carried out the anthropological studies. The manuscript was read by my colleagues Dr. Vasilios Tzaferis, Dr. Yizhar Hirschfeld and Rina Ben-Yair-Talgam, who made help-ful comments. I wish to express my gratitude to all of them. See also Y. Magen and R. Talgam, "The Monastery of Martyrius at Maᶜale Adummim (Khirbet el-Muraṣṣaṣ) and Its Mosaics," *CAHL*, pp. 91–152; L. Di Segni, "The Monastery of Martyrius at Maᶜale Adummim (Khirbet el-Muraṣṣaṣ): The Inscriptions," *ibid.*, pp. 153–164.

[2] Cyril of Scythopolis, *Life of Euthymius*, 32, ed. E. Schwartz (Leipzig, 1939), p. 51.

Maᶜale Adummim: aerial photograph of monastery

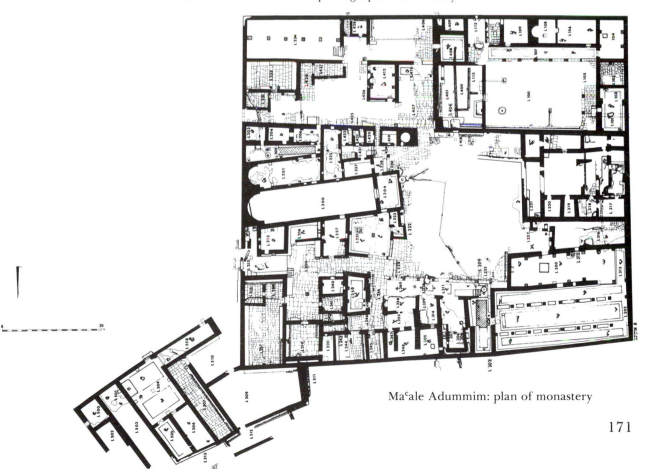

Maᶜale Adummim: plan of monastery

171

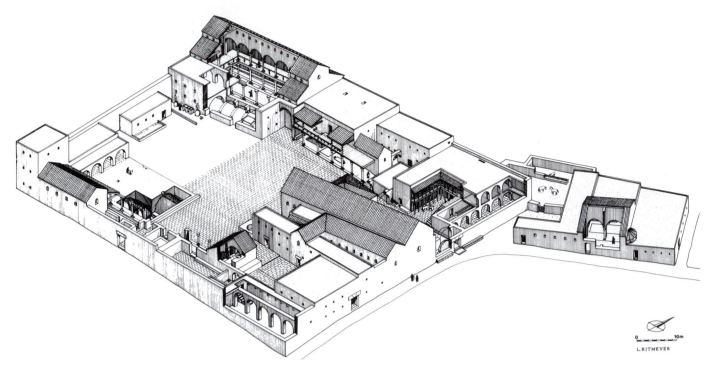

Ma^cale Adummim: reconstruction of monastery

great affection for the two and frequently invited them for talks, especially since he foresaw with his clairvoyant powers that they would eventually inherit the throne of James, the holy apostle, each in his own time. The Saint took them to the Coutila Desert and the Rouba Desert on the fourteenth day of the month of January and they remained with him until Palm Sunday in the company of the illustrious Gerasimus and the other anchorites who assembled on Sundays to receive Communion at the hands of the revered Euthymius. Finding the cells of the laura very narrow and uncomfortable — for so had Euthymius ordered them to be constructed — Elias went down to Jericho some time later and built a cell for himself outside the city, on the spot on which today stand his sacred and famous monasteries, while Martyrius found a cave about fifteen *stadia* west of the laura and went into seclusion there. With God's help he also established there a most famous monastery.

A distance of fifteen *stadia* is equivalent to slightly less than 3 km. Though the Monastery of Martyrius is in fact 4 km (as the crow flies) from that of Euthymius, it is the only such structure west of the latter; consequently its identification is universally accepted. Martyrius and Elias did not continue an eremitic way of life but joined the religious establishment and in the course of time both became patriarchs of Jerusalem, Martyrius in 478–486 and Elias in 494–516.

Only near the termination of our excavations were we able to corroborate the identity of Khirbet Muraşşaş with the Monastery of Martyrius by means of a tomb inscription. This inscription, engraved on a fine, red-colored stone slab, mentions Paul, priest and archimandrite (see below). Who was this Paul and what was his connection with the Monastery of Martyrius? According to Cyril's *Life of Theodosius*:[3]

---

[3] Cyril of Scythopolis, *Life of Theodosius*, ed. E. Schwartz (Leipzig, 1939), p. 239.

When Martyrius, the Holy Father, gave up the spirit, all the monks of the Judean Desert assembled before the ailing Patriarch Salustius and unanimously elected the great Theodosius head of all the cenobitic monasteries in the district of the Holy City in place of Gerontius of the monastery of St. Melania, and as his deputy they appointed Holy Paul, abbot of the monastery of Father Martyrius.

The appointment of Theodosius as "head of all the cenobitic monasteries" took place in the year 492 C.E. From the above quotation, it appears that the monastery on Khirbet Muraṣṣaṣ was named after Martyrius in the Byzantine period, and from this and the preceding passage, Martyrius seems to have not only lived in a cave but to have built a monastery. The fact that Paul was designated Theodosius' deputy implies that the monastery was a very large and important one. The elevation of a monk to high office was dependent not only on his qualifications but also on the eminence of his monastery. In the *Life of St. Sabas*, Cyril of Scythopolis mentions the arrival in Constantinople in 536 C.E. of the abbot of the Monastery of Martyrius, Domitianus, together with other monks.

A Greek dedicatory inscription in the refectory of the monastery contains the date of its completion and of other buildings there:

In the days of our pious father Genesius, priest and archimandrite, this work too was done for his salvation and for his community (synod) in Christ. It was completed on the fourth day of the month of March, in the first (year of the) indiction.

The indiction referred to was a fifteen-year period between property evaluations of the inhabitants of the Roman Empire for the purpose of tax collection. Dating according to indictions is not completely possible unless other corroborating historical evidence is available or the chronological span of the specific indiction is known. The initial years of the indictions in the period in question fell in 522, 537, 552, etc. The construction of the refectory and the renovation of the monastery could therefore have taken place during one of these years. The artistic and archaeological evidence reveals that at the time that the monastery underwent a thorough renovation, the church was rebuilt, and several major buildings were added, including the magnificent refectory, several of the chapels and the hospice outside the monastery wall. Construction on such an extensive scale is consistent with the reign of Justinian who contributed much to the strengthening of the monasteries in the Judean Desert and to Christianity in Palestine in general, even though Procopius fails to mention the rebuilding of the Monastery of Martyrius among Justinian's construction projects. It may have been renovated following Sabas's visit to Justinian in 531, at which time numerous building projects in the monasteries in the Judean Desert were initiated. It seems, therefore, that the monastery's floruit terminated in March 553, but a later date of March 568 or 583 is also possible.

Three main phases in the history of the monastery can therefore be distinguished:

1. Its establishment by Martyrius. Under the central church, an earlier church was found. This is the original nucleus out of which, in time, the monastery complex developed. The orientation of the monastery's outer walls does not conform with the axis of the early church. The cave which was later converted into a burial site was probably the one in which Martyrius dwelt after he left Euthymius' monastery. During this phase the monastery was unwalled and of limited size.

2. The enlargement of the complex and its transformation into a major monastery of the Judean Desert in the days of Paul. This was a large monastery which essentially had the same plan as the structure we uncovered. In its center was a court, 29 m long and 20 m wide, with a flagstone pavement. Paved lanes led to this court from the two gates in the eastern wall. Between these lanes stood the church complex which had undergone a fundamental change in this period. The monastery was now enclosed by a defensive wall and large stables were installed near the gates in

Ma'ale Adummim: paved lane leading to northern gate
in eastern wall, looking west

the eastern wall. A wing consisting of a central
court surrounded by living quarters and
service rooms was also added on the southeast.
It could not be established whether the pilgrim's hospice already existed during this
phase, though it is possible that there was an
original nucleus that was considerably
expanded in the following, third phase.

Despite the limitations imposed by the existence of the original church and the position
of the gates in the eastern wall, the monastery
had a meticulous plan designed to meet the
needs of the monks. Each of its various
elements, constructed around a main court,
fulfilled a different function. During this
phase too the magnificent water system was
installed.

3. The floruit of the monastery during the
days of the archimandrite Genesius. Genesius
is not mentioned by Cyril of Scythopolis

despite the fact that they were contemporaries. This phase can therefore be assigned to
the first year of one of the indiction cycles in
the second half of the sixth century. Numerous alterations, though not major ones, were
made, but the basic plan was retained. The
pilgrim's hospice was erected, probably above
an earlier one. The stable area was reduced in
size in the northeast and southeast wings and
changes were made in the latter. The church
complex was considerably renovated, a colored pavement being added, and to its south a
chapel, which also had a colored floor, was
built. The Chapel of the Three Priests was
erected to the southwest of the church complex. The southwest wing was also reconstructed: several rooms were combined and a
new chapel was built. The bathhouse in the
north wall may also date to this period. The
north and west walls were rebuilt. The most
prominent addition in this phase was the construction of the imposing refectory which
warranted a foundation inscription. It was
probably erected above a smaller refectory
from the previous phase. Several alterations
were made in the buildings in the north wing
and the cave of Martyrius was converted into a
tomb for the monks. It contained only a few
burials, which attest to the brevity of its use. A
notable feature of this phase is the installation
of the large mosaic pavements.

The monastery was apparently damaged
during the Persian invasion of 614 C.E.,
though traces of burning of the gates of the
main church were the only signs of destruction discerned.

Several coins were found in a pottery jug in
one of the rooms of the church. The latest
coins, except for one from between 750 and
760, date to the third year of the reign of
Emperor Heraclius (612/3 C.E.), i.e., only
one year before the Persian Conquest. It
seems, therefore, that the monastery was
abandoned after the Persian invasion.

In the Arab period, a square building was
constructed above the ruins in the center of
the monastery. Secondary use was made of
remaining stones. The finds, including a coin,
were from the Early Arab period.

The monastery was apparently plundered at that time, and much of its masonry was dismantled, especially roof tiles, architectural elements and mosaics.

The Monastery Complex

The complex was enclosed by a strong wall, 0.7 m thick, built of large, partially-dressed ashlars. The wall was preserved in several spots to a height of 1–2 m, but it was originally 4–5 m high. It was renovated over the years. Its western section was constructed of very well-dressed stones, especially in the north-western corner. This section was probably rebuilt when the refectory was erected. On the outer side of the wall the spaces between the stones were filled with mortar, while the inner face was built of small stones and gray cement. The base of the northern and western walls was coated with a reddish water-resistant plaster to prevent rainwater from penetrating into the monastery, a technique commonly employed during the Byzantine period.

The complex in which the monastery was built consisted of the following components: 1) the north gate in the eastern wall and the stable area; 2) the church complex; 3) the northern wing and the cave of Martyrius; 4) the refectory; 5) the southwestern wing and the farm area; 6) the southeastern wing and the Chapel of the Three Priests; 7) the bath-house; and 8) the early Arab building.

The north gate in the eastern wall and the stable area. This gate reflects the deterioration in security in the area, probably in the wake of Saracen incursions. Outside the wall there was an open area with a flagstone pavement and benches on either side for the comfort of visitors. To the right of this area extended a drainage channel which drew off rainwater from the entrance. The gate was 1.8 m wide and had a stepped threshold which contained two sockets to secure the posts of its wooden doors. In addition to these doors, the entrance could also be sealed on the inside by a rolling stone, 2.5 m in diameter, that moved in a rock-cut track between the wall of the

Maᶜale Adummim: northern opening in eastern wall; on the right — the rolling stone; in the foreground — roller used to compress the roofs

Maᶜale Adummim: rolling stone which closed northern gate

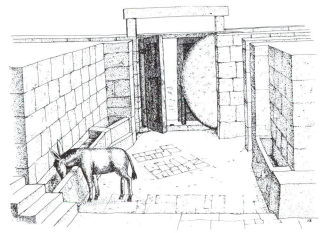

Maᶜale Adummim: reconstruction of northern gate and its wooden doors, rolling stone and troughs

monastery and a specially built inner wall. In the wall there was a recess into which the rolling stone was pushed when the entrance was closed, while at the end of the cut track there was a depression to prevent it from sliding. The use of such stones is well known in Palestine from the Second Temple period and later, but they have been found only in tombs, such as those of Queen Helene and Herod's family in Jerusalem and the tombs at Khirbet Midras in the Judean Shephela (foothills) and at Ḥeshbon in Transjordan. In the Byzantine period, however, the rolling stone appears in ordinary buildings, e.g., at Ḥorvat ᶜAdir in southern Hebron hills and more recently in the synagogue at Susiya. These sites are all situated on the fringe of the desert and were apparently subject to constant raids by Bedouins. The rolling stone was not intended for regular use but only for times of emergency, when there was a threat of attack by marauders.

The gate led to an open square (213), 8.4 m long and 3.8 m wide. The bedrock was leveled and had a few indentations cut into it to secure the paving stones. In the northern and southern walls there were plastered troughs; the water spilt by the animals while drinking was drained off through a small adjacent channel. It is interesting that the troughs were installed in the entrance area to the monastery and not in the stables. From the entrance one turned left to a narrow passageway (210) which was equipped with an installation for drinking water.

The entrance area (213) gave access to a room (212) which had a mosaic floor. This room was probably the post of the monastery's gatekeeper who supervised entries and exits and tended the mules. Area 213 opened onto a square paved with large flagstones which extended west toward the main courtyard and north toward the stables. Left of the entrance there is an oblong-shaped room (216). A bench and bed made of stone and an installation for washing feet were located along the southern wall of the courtyard. Outside Room 216 were remains of feeding troughs. Perhaps this room served as a rest-

ing-place for the animals' attendants and for the servants of visitors. A staircase near the entrance indicated that this wing had a second story.

The stable area north of the entrance consisted of an extremely large stable (217) and a smaller one (219) and adjacent to them various service rooms for the cattle and their keepers. Monks did these duties; even Sabas, the great monastic father, was, during his youth, a donkey driver in the Monastery of Theoctistus in the Judean Desert. In the center of Square 230, in front of the stables, there was a stone-cut trough and an inverted stone with a ring at the end for tethering an animal while it drank. Another staircase in the corner near the entrance led to a second story above the large stable (217), which was supported by arches. This stable, 18 m long and 9 m wide, was paved with large flagstones. The presence of a stable inside the monastery called for strict hygienic measures, and the flagstones could be washed very easily. The water was drained via a channel in the center of the floor. There were troughs along all the walls except the northern one; each was very carefully constructed, especially that along the southern wall which also had iron hooks, reinforced with lead, for tethering animals. Piers in these troughs were also equipped with iron rings. The troughs in the small stable, which were higher, were also well preserved. In the second building phase, one of the

Maᶜale Adummim: stone-cut trough and inverted stone
with ring for tethering

176

rooms (245) was incorporated into the enlarged stable area, but it later went out of use.

Beyond the stables, toward the center of the monastery, there was a passageway and adjacent to it, a stone bed at the head of which a cross was carved. A guard was probably stationed in this passageway. The nearby room (240) appears to have been his post. A niche surmounted by a painted plaster couch was built in a corner of Room 259. A column in the floor supported a stone tablet on which stood a vessel for ablutions prior to entry into the monastery and the main church. Opposite this installation was the entrance to the martyrium — the memorial chamber — of the main church.

The church. The church was situated in the middle of the eastern wall of the compound between the two gates. It consisted of a church (200), chapel (201), narthex (209), entrance hall (221) and auxiliary rooms. Various building stages could be distinguished, as would be expected in a structure which existed for a period of more than 130 years, during which time various alterations would have been essential. The sanctity of the site would have required always erecting the church on the same spot.

Several building stages were revealed in a sounding dug in the church. Some 50 cm beneath the present floor, an earlier mosaic was uncovered; it had not been destroyed by the later construction. This earlier church probably dates from the time of Martyrius before he was appointed patriarch of Jerusalem. The north and south walls of the later church were part of the earlier structure. They were partly built of ashlars with marginal dressing. Rooms 212 and 216 north of the church also belong to the original nucleus. The complex, in its present form, represents the latest phase of the monastery from the second half of the sixth century, but its overall plan dates to the second stage, to the time of Paul.

The church had two entrances, a main one in the north and a secondary, but quite wide

Maᶜale Adummim: stable area, looking north; left — northern area and its chapel and entrance to burial tomb

Maᶜale Adummim: stable area in second phase, looking north

doorway in the south for the use of the clergy. The main entrance was reached through a square-shaped hall (221), 8 × 8 m, which had a colored mosaic floor. This hall was entered both from the west, through an opening with two steps, and from the north, directly from the paved lane leading from the north gate. The hall remained open but the door between

177

Ma^cale Adummim: small service room adjacent to Martyrium in which two rows of roof tiles were found

it and the narthex could be locked. To the west of the hall were two small service rooms: in one of them (223) two rows of roof tiles were found, while the other (222) had a mosaic pavement. Plastered benches, about 40 cm high, were built along the eastern, northern and southern walls of the entrance hall.

In the center of the hall (see Pl. IXb) lay a reddish tombstone, 90 cm long and 77 cm wide. It bore a Greek inscription which reads: "Tomb of Paul, the priest and archiman-

Ma^cale Adummim: tombstone with Greek inscription, "Tomb of Paul, the priest and archimandrite"

drite." A cross was carved between two date palms in the center of the inscription. The tomb beneath it was rectangular in shape and had plastered sides. Upon opening the tomb we were surprised to discover that in addition to Paul, nine other persons — eight men and perhaps one woman — had been interred there, one on top of the other.

Two phases were distinguished in the entrance hall:

1. Its construction and the interment of Paul. The tomb was sealed by a stone and the entire floor of the hall was later paved with colored mosaics. There is no relationship between the location of the tomb and the mosaics though there may have been some sign to mark the former. The custom of burial beneath a mosaic floor is also known from the Byzantine monastery near Rimonim (Khirbet Kilia) in the Samarian Hills.

2. In the sixth century the tomb was opened, probably in order to bury the abbots of the monastery. The fine tombstone was then laid over it and surrounded by square flagstones to facilitate access to its opening. In this phase another bench was added in the north part of the room.

Because of the sensitive nature of excavating the remains of Christian saints, we requested the help of the heads of the Monastery of el-^cAzariya (Bethany) and afterwards transferred the remains there for reburial.

The entrance hall was paved with five colored mosaic panels: two large ones with a square pattern in the northern part, and three smaller ones in the south. Alterations had been made to the small mosaic in the southeastern corner; another tomb may be located beneath it.

Access to the narthex from the entrance hall was through a wide passage. The narthex, 6.5 m long and 4 m wide, had undergone numerous changes. Its western side was enlarged in the sixth century and benches were installed along its long western side and in its north- and southwestern corners. In time a new wall separating the narthex from the nave was built above the mosaics, thus damaging them. The threshold between the narthex and nave was apparently added after the mosaic had been laid in the latter. The jambs of the door leading onto the nave were destroyed by fire, probably when the monastery was damaged in the Persian conquest (614 C.E.). Another, narrow doorway in the southern wall led to the service rooms.

The mosaic discovered in the narthex (see Pl. Xa) is a remnant of a larger one which was destroyed during the rebuilding of the church. In its center is an amphora with a vine trellis emerging from it. Flanking the amphora are gazelles and above them, birds and a rabbit eating a bunch of grapes. The central carpet is surrounded by a band containing medallions in which birds and flowers are depicted. The style of the mosaic and the stratigraphic evidence indicate that it was laid in the second building phase and the alterations are to be attributed to the third stage.

The nave (200) was 25.5 m long and 6.6 m wide. It was paved with a richly colored mosaic which had been almost completely dismantled by robbers. Its ornamentation consisted of round and hexagonal medallions containing various animals. We have succeeded thus far in identifying an elephant, a

Ma‘ale Adummim: nave and narthex of church, later threshold and wall and drawing of narthex's mosaic

fish, a cock, a duck, a barn owl, a partridge, a donkey and a rabbit. It was possible to restore the mosaic with great accuracy by tracing the preparatory painting applied to the mortar layer before the tesserae were laid.

The church had a raised *bema* with a Greek inscription (found damaged) in front of it. Both the *bema* and the apse were originally paved with mosaics, but nothing has remained of them. The fragmentary inscription men-

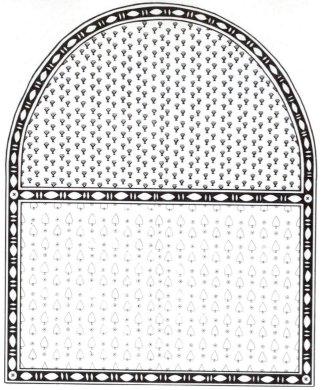

Maᶜale Adummim: drawing of mosaic pavement of southern chapel's apse

tions Genesius, the priest referred to in the foundation inscription in the refectory, who is associated with the last phase of the monastery. It reads: "(In the days of our pious father) Genesius priest and archimandrite (also this work was done) ... for the memory and rest of ... John, John...."

We do not know whether this John is the same one whose name appears in the Chapel of the Three Priests or whether the reference is to one of the abbots who died before Genesius' appointment.

North of the nave was a large room (227) in which changes dating from the last building phase were discerned. This was probably the *prothesis*, the room in which the Eucharistic elements were prepared and displayed to the congregation. The room had a white mosaic pavement on which were found ceramic, glass and metal vessels. Another large room (225), south of the nave, had a colored mosaic pavement laid in three panels. Here too alterations had been made. This room apparently had a tiled roof. It may have served as the *diaconicon*, in which the priests and deacons kept their vestments, sacred vessels and the offerings brought to the church.

South of the nave is a chapel (201), 15 m long and 4.6 m wide. Most of its mosaic pavement had been pillaged. It had two entrances, one leading to the nave and the other to what was probably the baptistery (205); in any event the latter contained a well. A large, octagonal baptismal font found in the western court, which is reminiscent of that discovered in the monastery at Tekoa, may have been taken from this room. The apse of the chapel was decorated with colored mosaics comprising a border with a geometric design enclosing a rectangular section with a repeated heart pattern and a semicircular area with a repeated plant motif. Adjacent to the apse was a fragment of what seems to originally have been a long Greek inscription. We did not succeed in reconstructing it.

In rooms 203, 204 and 206, changes were introduced in the early phase. Rooms 206 and 203, and perhaps also 204, were originally a single room; partition walls were later added, causing damage to the mosaic floor. The southern gate could be reached through a doorway in Room 206. Several rooms southwest of the narthex may have been reserved for the use of the deacons and guards of the church.

The north wing and the cave of Martyrius. As mentioned above, in its original form, the entire eastern block of the north wing was an integral part of the monastery's entrance. In Room 245 it is still possible to see a stable preserved from the earlier phase. In the third stage of renovation the stable area was reduced in size and changes were made in some of the rooms. Room 259 underwent a complete transformation; it was paved and linked with the living quarters. Beyond it, to the west, was a passageway (254) with a mosaic floor which was incorporated into the flagstone pavement of the central courtyard. It terminated in a series of pillars which form part of a portico facing the latter. Further west, is a group of rooms with white mosaic floors; some of them may have been dwellings.

In the last building phase, this locality was transformed into the burial area of the monas-

Ma'ale Adummim: northern wing; center — burial cave and inscription of the three priests; right — the chapel

Ma'ale Adummim: northern wing and central courtyard, from the west

tery. Cave 314 was perhaps the one which Martyrius occupied when he first arrived at the site. In the second phase, it may have been converted into a cistern and in the third phase it was enlarged to serve for burials. The meager remains found in the cave indicate that it was used for this purpose only for a brief time. The main cemetery was apparently located outside the walls; only the most distinguished persons merited interment within the confines of the monastery. A *tabula ansata* in the mosaic floor above the cave contains a Greek inscription in four lines of which only part has been preserved; the words that can be clearly deciphered read: "Lord, shall be remembered in Thy kingdom, Elpidius, John, George ... and the other priests who rest here...." These three names also appear in the Chapel of the Three Priests at the southern edge of the monastery. The remains of infants under the age of six were also discovered in the cave; their presence can probably be explained by the fact that the cave was open in the Early Arab period and the family living at the site used it to bury their dead.

A staircase, partly built and partly hewn, led down to the cave, which was coated all over with plaster. At one stage, the cave was entered through a porch — probably of wood — whose posts may have been set in the four depressions at the entrance to Room 304. It was altered to accommodate the two gutters of the refectory which conveyed water to the large cistern in the north. It seems that a chapel (258) was built next to the cave which was connected with the revered monks who

were buried nearby. A stone lintel decorated with a cross and other motifs was found in secondary use in the western wall of the cave.

The refectory. The refectory was a magnificent structure. It is the first time that a building of this type, together with its mosaics and vessels, has been found in a good state of preservation. Not only were meals taken in the refectory but the monks probably also assembled there for study and for certain religious rites that were held outside the church.

The refectory represents the zenith of the last building phase of the monastery and the foundation inscription for the entire undertaking was therefore laid there. As mentioned above, this imposing structure may have been partly erected above an earlier refectory of more modest size. The overall length of the complex was about 31 m and it was about 25 m wide. It comprised several units: a basilica-

Ma'ale Adummim: refectory, from the east

181

shaped main hall, a kitchen, the vestibule of the main hall, rooms for cooking and storage, and a large cellar, probably for storing wine. A second story, above the kitchen, was paved with a colored mosaic.

The main hall (302) of the refectory, 26.5 m long and 12 m wide, was situated in the north-western corner of the monastery. Its outer walls were built of large ashlars. The north and west walls of the monastery were apparently rebuilt at the time of construction of the refectory.

Two rows of seven columns divided the hall into a nave and two aisles. Most of the column bases were found *in situ*, but none of the columns had survived, apart from one which had been broken during its removal and had sunk into the mosaic floor. Four capitals were uncovered, each of a different style, a common feature in the Byzantine period. The hall had a tiled gabled roof which also spanned the vestibule (303). In Room 304, at the eastern end of the vestibule, were two plastered channels which collected rainwater from the roof via gutters and conveyed it to a large cistern north of the monastery.

A stone bench, about 40 cm high, ran along the walls of the hall. The walls, except for that part immediately above the bench, were both plastered and whitewashed, while the bench and adjacent wall section were only coated with gray hydraulic plaster in contrast with the white plaster of the rest of the walls. This was probably to prevent the soiling of the monks' habits by the regular white and softer plaster. The walls were coated with two layers of plaster and decorated with paintings, mostly inscriptions in red paint. A passageway (315) in the southwestern corner of the hall, paved with white mosaics, had gone out of use and the bench at its southern end had been removed. The reason for this became clear when we excavated the kitchen and found a small window between it and this hall, through which food trays could be passed. Near this window in the hall, was a large marble table set on a wooden stand. Broken panes of glass attest that windows in the outer walls served for illumination.

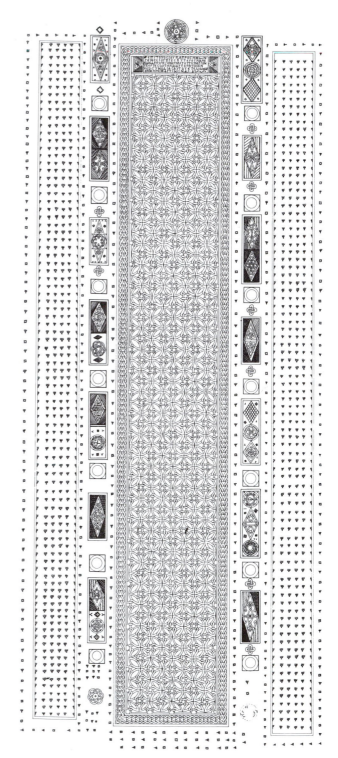

Ma‘ale Adummim: drawing of refectory's central mosaic

The entire mosaic pavement covering the refectory (see Pl. Xb) was preserved in its full splendor. It consists of three panels. A border with rows of floral motifs against a white background extends the length of the two

182

aisles. The nave contains a very large and elaborate colored mosaic with a guilloche in the form of stylized circles and crosses. This design is enclosed by a wide border containing a rope ornament which forms a pattern of hearts. This pattern also appears in the Chapel of the Three Priests and in the hospice's chapel. At the eastern extremity of the nave is a *tabula ansata* containing the foundation inscription (see above).

At the entrance to the nave is a guilloche which is less impressive than the rest of the mosaic. A drainage channel runs beneath the threshold. In the intercolumniations are fourteen small mosaic panels containing either lozenges within borders, or a pair of lozenges flanked by round medallions. Each panel exhibits a different design. The mosaics in the intercolumniations are made of smaller tesserae than those in the nave.

The refectory was entered through a roughly oblong vestibule (303), 11 m long and 4 m wide. Two separate rooms were originally located here, and the vestibule thus contains two different mosaic panels. The first panel consists of squares in a frame and the second features rows of flowers within a border. Benches ran along the walls of the vestibule. It was probably an annex of the refectory, perhaps for lay monks. It was entered from the south; near the entrance was a round mosaic medallion. Water for cleaning the floor was drained through stone apertures in the floor. A trial trench revealed that there was an earlier mosaic beneath this one, indicating that alterations had been made in the two rooms in the last building phase and that the construction of this part of the refectory dates to the preceding phase.

After uncovering the main hall of the refectory, we conjectured that the large room to its south (300) was the kitchen and this indeed proved to be the case. It soon became evident that not only had the refectory been preserved in its entirety but even the vessels used by the monks: plates, cups, bowls, storage jars and trays, some made of bronze. The kitchen, 21 m long and 6 m wide, was about 1.2 m higher than the main hall. It had two

Maᶜale Adummim: kitchen south of refectory. Note mosaic segments from upper floor and central voussoir which collapsed together with upper floor; in center of white mosaic pavement, there is a colored mosaic

entrances on its south side and a small window for serving food in its northwestern corner. Its roof was constructed of six arches which spanned the room. One of these arches was found collapsed. Beside it lay a molded threshold and the lock of the door of the second story. This upper story also had a magnificent colored mosaic floor which had fallen into the kitchen in sections large enough to allow us to reconstruct its designs. Some of the numerous vessels originated from the second floor, as they were found scattered above the upper mosaic. It is thus evident that this second story was an integral part of the refectory — perhaps an open porch facing its main hall — so that the monks dining upstairs could also take part in the events in the main hall. The second story could also be reached by means of a wide staircase in the entrance of the vestibule (303), which also may have had an upper story. Changes were also made in the north wall of the building and in the all-white

Ma'ale Adummim: southwestern wing, area of chapel and cistern

mosaic floor of the kitchen. On the eastern side of the latter, opposite the door, a mosaic was laid in a square panel consisting of large red and black tesserae within a double border. In the center of the panel is depicted an amphora from which emerges a vine with bunches of grapes; the vine immediately above the amphora envelopes a bird (see Pl. XIa).

The doorways on the south led to an open space with several of drainage channels; this was probably the cooking and utility area. Near the west door was the entrance to the cellar which was undoubtedly reached by means of a wooden ladder. This cellar, partly built and partly hewn in the rock, was used, as evidenced by the numerous potsherds, for storing wine.

Hundreds of vessels were found in the kitchen and adjoining rooms. They included mainly drinking cups and plates, large storage jars, mortars and cooking pots. Also uncovered were large marble serving trays and

metal utensils. One of the cooking pots contained eggshells.

The southwestern wing and the Early Arab agricultural area. Another wing, in the southwestern corner of the monastery, was built around a large central court (100) paved with crude mosaics; a section made of large white tesserae was revealed. The court was 22 m long and 14 m wide. Beneath it was a large rock-hewn cistern which was completely coated with reddish hydraulic plaster. A row of piers in the center of the cistern supported arches forming the ceiling. The cistern was about 10 m deep. Four openings drained the water in the paved court and the runoff flowing in channels to the monastery from the west (see discussion of the water supply system, below).

West of the paved court there was a paved portico (105) as evidenced by the bases of piers. Changes were made in three rooms in the area (101, 103, 104) after the destruction of the monastery. The first room (101), 8.5 m long and 6.5 m wide, with its entrance in the east, was paved with a white mosaic enclosed in a colored border. Room 103 had a flagstone pavement as in the adjoining portico. Room 104, in the southwest, measured 9 m long and 6.5 m wide. Its floor had been plundered by robbers. In this room were found piles of bases and capitals of columns which had been dismantled and prepared for transport. They probably were stacked here sometime during the Early Arab period when the monastery became a source of building materials. This room was also equipped with a press installation, 1 m long and 90 cm wide. There may have been an upper story of monks' cells above this row of rooms.

In the northeastern corner of Room 104, an opening led to the main passageway (107) which measured 21.5 m long and 2.2 m wide, and had a white mosaic floor surrounded by a black border. In its north wall, facing the paved court, piers supported arches to form a portico. The capitals and bases found in Room 104 undoubtedly belonged to this portico.

Access to Court 100 was gained from the east via Passageway 112 which in turn was entered through a gate in the southern wall of the compound. Passageway 112 had a flagstone floor (partly removed by robbers) which was supported by a barrel vault discovered beneath it. It led to an open area which was also paved with flagstones. In the Early Arab period this space was turned into farmland which was irrigated by means of built channels. Passageway 112 also gave access to the portico with the mosaic floor (107). The agricultural area (loci 113, 400, 401, 404; see below) was originally paved with flagstones. The portico (107) had two doorways on its south side, one leading into Room 109 and the other into the chapel (106, 108). The eastern side of Room 109 was paved with flagstones, while its western part had a mosaic floor.

The southern chapel, which was 13 m long and 4.8 m wide, consisted of two parts: an oblong room (106) with a white mosaic floor, and a raised *bema* (108) which had been bounded by a chancel screen and paved with large flagstones, of which only the impressions have survived. A mosaic pavement was laid near the apse. At the entrance to the chapel a chancel-screen post of reddish limestone was found with the impression of a cross — probably of bronze — at the top. The chapel was erected in the last building phase and seems to have comprised two former rooms which were combined. A new mosaic floor was laid and the piers that had supported arches were dismantled, indicating that the chapel had a tiled gabled roof.

The farmland (113, 400, 401, 404) was irrigated by a well-planned system of channels. The water was obtained from the large cistern and was discharged into a small pool from which it flowed into a network of open stone channels, entering the furrows through apertures in the channels. This system greatly increased the efficiency of agricultural work and allowed a single person to easily irrigate an extensive area. At first we assumed that the farm was part of the monastery of the Byzantine period, but a closer examination revealed that this was not the case. Below the agricultural area pilfered flooring fragments were discovered, indicating that the farmland was laid out after the monastery stones had been removed. Furthermore, the channel which conveyed farmland surplus water into Room 408 lay above the latter's white mosaic. As a result of the preparation of the farmland, two rooms (409, 410) went out of use. A chancel post was converted into a channel, clearly proving that the work was carried out only after the Byzantine period, in the Early Arab period. A channel on the north side of the court conveyed water to the cisterns of the monastery. During the excavation of this part of the court, it was discovered that its northern boundary wall had been constructed in the Early Arab period and partly in even later times. Beneath this wall and the later buildings was found a row of rooms, some paved with mosaics and some with flagstones. We can therefore conclude that this wing had consisted of a group of buildings surrounding an open court.

Ma^cale Adummim: farmland and well-planned system of channel irrigation

The southeastern wing and the Chapel of the Three Priests. This wing had served as the original entrance area of the monastery, as is evidenced by the extensive flagstone pavement and the stables. When the southeastern gate went out of use — perhaps sometime during the Byzantine period — the function of the area was changed and numerous alterations were introduced. In the entrance room of the gate, which was 2.5 m wide, a drainage channel was laid to remove excess water from the cistern in Room 205. A paved lane led from the gate to the main court of the monastery. Along the sides of the lane were partly preserved paved rooms and remains of troughs. The structural changes made in the area in the last phase included the construction of the chapel (412), perhaps above an early stable. A large storeroom (234), 20 m long and 7 m wide, was revealed south of the paved gate area. Six piers in its center originally supported arches. Its floor was unpaved, but the stones may have been

plundered. In its short western wall was a doorway with three steps. Adjoining this storeroom, to its west, was a group of rooms with white mosaic floors; their function has not yet been established. This wing represents the service area of the monastery.

Ma^cale Adummim: southeastern wing, from the west; in the foreground — Chapel of the Three Priests from the third building phase

186

Ma'ale Adummim: drawing of Chapel of the Three Priests' mosaic pavement with its dedicatory inscription

According to the stratigraphic evidence, the chapel (412), which we call the Chapel of the Three Priests, is to be attributed to the monastery's last building phase, when the southeastern gate was blocked. The chapel was 7 m long and 5 m wide. At its eastern end it terminates in an apse which is flanked by plastered piers. Directly in front of the apse was a square area which corresponded to the dimensions of a square limestone table found at the site. Two piers in both the east and west walls had originally supported roofing arches. The chapel was entered from the north by descending one step. In the earlier phase, during which the chapel may have had a stone floor, the entrance had been in the east, through a paved passageway. The chapel we discovered was paved with large, richly-col-ored tesserae forming a bordered panel. The border comprised meanders in a guilloche design, while the inner panel included a round guilloche, identical to those in the refectory and in the church of the hospice. A *tabula ansata* adjacent to the apse contained a Greek inscription; it was flanked by a medallion on one side and a square design on the other (see Pl. XIb). The latter also have parallels in the hospice and the refectory and prove conclusively that all three mosaic pavements were the work of the same artist. The inscription reads: "O Lord our God, remember in Thy kingdom Elpidius, John and George the priests, and all their Holy Community (Synod) in Christ." We have no knowledge of the role played by these three priests in the life of the monastery, nor whether the chapel was erected while they were still alive in gratitude for their deeds or after their death. All that is known is that these priests belonged to the monastery and were buried in the cave there.

The bathhouse. The bathhouse revealed at the site is the first to be uncovered in a monastery. The sources, furthermore, do not mention the existence of bathhouses in monasteries, and our find is therefore of great significance in the study of monasticism in Palestine.

The bathhouse was situated in the middle of the west side of the site. Its dimensions were apparently 9 × 13 m and it was composed of three parts. The floor of the *caldarium* (hot room) is about 1 m above bedrock and rests on brick pillars of the *hypocaust*, which is 6 m long and 2 m wide and partly hewn in the rock. From the south, rock-cut steps lead to a mosaic-paved passageway. In the east wall of the *caldarium* is a round alcove containing a separate compartment. The walls consisted of natural rock faced with bricks. Scorch marks indicate that the furnace of the *hypocaust* was situated north of the *caldarium*. An additional room on the south may have been the *apodyterium* (dressing room). A passageway paved with a colored mosaic in a leaf pattern, similar to the one in the apse of the chapel (201) of the main church, extended the length of the *caldarium*. To the east of the mosaic was a pool which served as the *frigidarium* (cold room). The bathhouse was erected in the vicinity of two main cisterns, one outside the monastery wall and the other in the south wing. A pipe extending from the *caldarium* and the pool conducted the water beyond the limits of the monastery. The ground plan of the bathhouse is not identical with that of the classic bathhouse of the Roman period.

The building from the Early Arab period. A rectangular structure, 18 m long and 15 m wide, with rooms located around and facing a central court, was erected in the center of the west side of the monastery. Its southern wall continued eastward and encompassed the agricultural area, confirming the latter's attribution to this period. This building was constructed of masonry in secondary use, including marble fragments, the baptismal font and other stones incorporated in the walls. It was built in part above the bathhouse. It is interesting to note that Muslim remains were lacking in most of the other sections of the monastery, and it is difficult to understand the need for such a building if the monastery itself could have been inhabited, unless the latter lay largely in ruins at that time, and a new structure near the large cisterns was preferred. (Most of the cisterns continued to be used by the Bedouins up to recent times.) The erection of the building after the looting of the monastery, the presence of pottery of the Khirbet Mefjer type, the Arabic inscriptions incised on stones, and a coin from the year 750 C.E. corroborate the conclusion that its construction should be dated to the end of the eighth century.

The Hospice

The erection of a hospice in close proximity to the monastery can be explained in the light of the popularity of pilgrimage to the Holy Land to visit the sacred places associated with the life of Jesus and the Old and New Testaments.

The stream of pilgrims to the monasteries was in contradiction to the idea of monasticism which prescribed seclusion and withdrawal from society. Nevertheless, the monasteries welcomed the pilgrims who venerated the monastic life and the holy places. Hospices were built which, though located in proximity to the monasteries, were physically separated from them. The hospice of St. Martyrius even had an entrance different from that of the monastery itself.

Situated on the main road between Jerusalem and Jericho, the Monastery of Martyrius was an important stopover for pilgrims traveling along this route. Thus, a large hospice was erected to the northeast of the site.

The hospice, 43 m long and 28 m wide, contained facilities which catered to all the needs of the pilgrims: guest rooms, a church (chapel) and stables for pack animals. Artistic and archaeological evidence indicates that it was constructed during the last building stage of the monastery, at the same time as the refectory. The stables were completely isolated from the guest rooms and the church. Access to the former was from the west while the latter were reached from the south, and perhaps also from the east.

The stables. Four rooms served as stables and when necessary the entrance (512) could also be used for this purpose. L-shaped mangers were built on either side of the entrance which opened onto an irregularly-shaped room (509) with a row of partly preserved mangers in its south side. The floor of the latter chamber was of hard beaten soil. A door in its southern wall led to Stable 510 which also had a row of troughs built in its southern wall. A door in the latter room offered access to yet another stable (507) which differed from the others and more closely resembled the monastery stables. It was 18 m long and 3.6 m wide and was paved with well-fitting flagstones. In its western wall was a long row of troughs. Initially, this seems to have been the only stable in the hospice, but as the number of pilgrims increased, the stable area was enlarged and the forecourts were also employed for lodging animals.

Guest rooms. The living quarters in the hospice were different from those of the monastery. They were long and narrow and unsuitable for permanent habitation. They were evidently built to accommodate a maximum number of persons. All the rooms had crude white mosaic floors; in only one of them was the mosaic surrounded by a black border. Rooms 500–503, 505–506 and 508 were all guest rooms and at a conservative estimate, lodgings for 60–70 persons could be provided in the hospice, assuming that there was no second story.

The chapel. Not only were the pilgrims prevented from lodging in the monastery, but a separate chapel (504) was erected for them in the hospice. It was 11 m long and 8 m wide and was entered from the south. Doors in the

Ma'ale Adummim: hospice of the third phase, from the south; in center — the chapel; left — paved stables

guest rooms to its north (505 and 506) also opened onto it. The chapel was divided by columns into two parts. The southern area was paved with a multicolored mosaic and the northern one with a white mosaic with black lozenges at its center. One pier was located in the middle of each of the chapel's wall and an additional pier was located in the center of the hall. Two basket capitals of delicate workmanship were uncovered there. The splendid colored mosaic floor of the southern side of the chapel contained a guilloche similar to the one in the refectory, and it can therefore be attributed to the same period. The mosaic was enclosed by a wide decorative border containing two round and two square medallions in the four corners, which also displayed a guilloche ornamentation. At the southeastern end of the chapel there was a *bema*, about 30 cm high, decked with a colored mosaic in a floral pattern against a white background. A *tabula ansata* at the the foot of the *bema* was found to contain a floral design instead of the usual dedicatory inscription.

The plan of this chapel was unusual. The fact that access to two of the guest rooms (505 and 506) was gained through the chapel indicates that they were designed to serve as an annex to it — a kind of atrium — in times of overcrowding; in the evening they reverted to their use as sleeping quarters.

The hospice at Ma'ale Adummim is one of

the largest of its kind discovered in Israel and the only example that can be assigned with certainty to the Byzantine period.

The Water Supply

One of the most interesting features at the site is the water supply system which attests to the extraordinary amount of planning and effort invested in conserving the meager rainwater that fell in the area. The average annual rainfall of 300–350 mm, and much less in dry years, was insufficient to meet the daily needs of the numerous inhabitants and pilgrims. The fear that monasteries would be abandoned because of lack of water was an overriding consideration for their monks and planners. This is clearly illustrated in Cyril's account of the consecration of the Laura of Euthymius as a *coenobium* located not far to the east of the Monastery of Martyrius:

> After the construction of the monastery had been completed in all its glory [in the year 482] within three years only, thanks to the great number of laborers and their devotion, the Fathers decided to consecrate the church and the monastery on the day on which the venerated remains of our Holy Father were brought there to be deposited in a new tomb. But there was a problem. There was no water. And since so little rain fell in this desert, there was also no water in the cistern, and it being already May and almost no rain falls in this desert even in the wintertime, as is well known to all those with a great deal of experience in this matter, there was no reason to hope [further] for rain. In their distress the abbot Elias and the deacon Fidus therefore requested from Father Longinus from the monastery below and from Father Paul, abbot of the Monastery of Martyrius, that they send the pack animals from their monasteries, and together with the animals from our monastery, bring water from the Monastery of Pharan, and they made ready to set out that night. But that very night, the great Euthymius appeared before blessed

Elias and said: Entreat Him in faith. Do not send the animals to the water but cast your troubles before the Lord and this day, before the third hour, the two great cisterns will be filled. And [Elias] arose from his sleep and recounted his vision to blessed Fidus and to all the other priests and sent the animals back. At dawn a cloud appeared [in the sky] and a heavy rain poured down around and above the monastery. And before the third hour the two great cisterns filled up and the rain at once ceased.[4]

This account reflects the day-to-day trials which afflicted the monks who with full cognizance undertook to live in the arid wilderness which more than once brought calamity on those who sought refuge there. The planning

Ma{super-c}ale Adummim: large western cistern in southwestern wing

[4] *Life of Euthymius*, 44 (see note 2), pp. 65–66

190

of the water supply system at the monastery at Maᶜale Adummim and the labor invested in its construction demonstrate that the builders had become experts in finding solutions to cope with the reality described above.

Enormous water cisterns are located in the Monastery of Martyrius. A calculation of their combined capacity reveals that some 20,000–30,000 cu m of water could be stored within the area of the monastery — a vast quantity, even by present-day standards. In the monastery proper, there are still some large cisterns, the biggest of which is 22 m long, 14 m wide and 10 m high and has a capacity is 3,000 cu m. Its ceiling is built of vaults supported by wide piers. The cistern was completely coated with a fully preserved reddish hydraulic plaster, the color being due to a mixture of ground potsherds.

Access to this cistern was through four openings in the ceiling from a large court paved with a white mosaic. It was filled by rainwater draining from the roofs of the adjoining porticoes and from the paved court, but mostly by runoff which entered the western court of the monastery and flowed into the cistern through a built conduit measuring 40 × 60 cm. The conduit first supplied the western cistern outside the monastery and then extended eastward under the wall and the rooms of the monastery to discharge its water into the great cistern. Another section of the conduit continued eastward to the cisterns near the main church. Grooves were cut into the channel, in which stone panels were inserted to block the flow — a kind of dam. When one cistern was filled, the influx was thus diverted to the next cistern. By this means flooding was prevented. The large cistern had a kind of "safety valve" through which excess water was discharged into the paved street and then led outside the monastery.

As was noted above, there were two additional cisterns near the church complex: a huge one west of the monastery, and two other large ones to the southeast and north. Others had been dug at a greater distance, in the agricultural area. The digging of a cistern

Maᶜale Adummim: drainage system in mosaic pavement. The openings were closed with stone slabs and opened on rainy days

in antiquity was a complicated and difficult task, and the removal of vast amounts of stone and debris through a narrow aperture called for considerable skill. The monastery's large cistern probably first served as a quarry and only after the stones were extracted and used in the construction of the edifice were the vaults added and the cavity converted into a water reservoir.

In addition to the large cisterns, the monastery itself acted as a kind of enormous collector which was designed to conserve every drop of water. Rainwater falling on the paved courts and the roofs of the buildings — especially the tiled ones of the church, the refectory and the chapels — was discharged into the cisterns. The squares were drained both by above-ground and subterranean stone-cut channels which collected the runoff and conveyed it to the cisterns. As was noted above, the cisterns were fed both by runoff which flowed through the main channels and by rainwater which accumulated within the monastery proper. The gutter system of the refectory is an astonishing invention: two wide gutters, about 40 cm in diameter, collected water from both sides of the sloping tile roof. The water flowed through them to the large cistern north of the monastery.

The immense quantities of water collected in the cisterns were most probably used not

191

Ma'ale Adummim: selection of vessels from kitchen (some of which fell from upper floor)
and marble table from refectory

only by the monks but also for irrigation and as drinking water for the animals. Because the monastery at Maᶜale Adummim was situated on the desert fringe, it was necessary to employ an intensive system of agriculture, i.e., daily irrigation of crops, such as vegetables and fruits, with the water stored in the cisterns.

The Finds

Despite the fact that the monastery had been plundered during the Persian period and dismantled in the Arab period, a large number of finds were uncovered, attesting to its wealth. They include pottery, metal and glass objects and various architectural fragments. We were astonished by both the quantity and the quality of the pottery. Most of the vessels came from the kitchen. An outstanding find was a ceramic bowl of reddish color incised with figures, apparently Jesus and two of his disciples. There were also numerous jars, jugs and juglets, cooking pots, ceramic lamps as well as hundreds of bowls and cups which had been used by the monks in the refectory. The lamps found were not sufficient to illuminate the entire monastery and it can be assumed that light was furnished primarily by metal or glass chandeliers. In the church, in any event, fragments of chandeliers were revealed.

The number of copper and bronze objects found was surprising since metal vessels were usually plundered for melting down. Two bronze jugs were uncovered as well as a chain to which were attached a cross and a part of large vessel or a chandelier in the shape of an

Maᶜale Adummim: bronze jugs

193

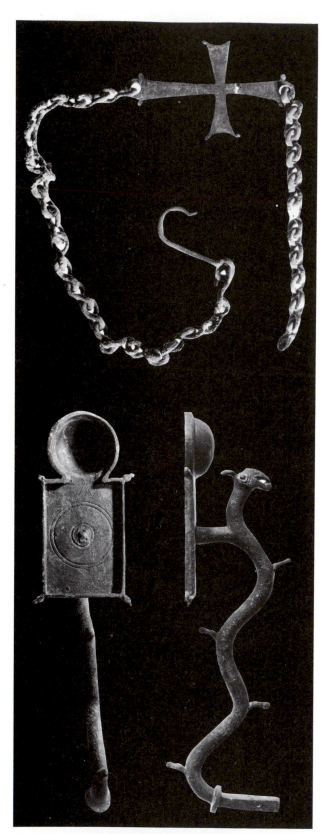

Maᶜale Adummim: basket capital found in hospice's chapel

Maᶜale Adummim: bronze snake-shaped object with griffin's head which supported an incense holder

Maᶜale Adummim: chancel screen post with cruciform incision

Ma ͨale Adummim: four capitals found in refectory

animal's foot. There were also devices to hold oil lamps and two handguards for torches. One of the most interesting discoveries was a griffin-shaped object which supported an incense holder. It terminated at one end in a square rod which could be attached to a wall or to a larger vessel. Only a few coins were uncovered, possibly reflecting the modest way of life of the monks. All the columns and most of the capitals had been despoiled. Four capitals were uncovered in the refectory and two basket capitals were found in the hospice.

Most of the marble masonry had been plundered but the several remnants attest to the splendor of the monastery. These include ornamented chancel screen posts and panels from the church. Several bore traces of bronze crosses. Small marble colonettes and two marble tables, more than 1 m long, were also found. One table came from the kitchen and the other from the refectory. A tray made of black bituminous chalk, which was about 70 cm in diameter, had eight round indentations around the center.

Ma^cale Adummim: one of two sundials discovered in the monastery

An unusual find was two sundials, one of them in the refectory. On both dials the day was divided into twelve hours, and on one of them there was a differentiation between winter and summer. Also uncovered were fragments of frescoes, as well as painted inscriptions, and large glass panes from the windows of the refectory and the church.

Robbery of Antiquities in Ancient Times

The Arab conquest of Palestine in the seventh century C.E. started a process of abandonment of Christian buildings, including monasteries and churches. Many of them became sources of masonry for public and private building. The el-Aksa Mosque, the Omayyad palace south of the Temple Mount, and Hisham's Palace in Jericho all contain architectural elements taken from Christian edifices: columns, marble chancel posts and screens and capitals. Several of the columns still bear crosses, evidence of their origin.

The Byzantine monastery at Ma^cale Adummim was also an inexhaustible source for the pillage of stones. Situated near the road to Jericho, its size and splendor attracted those specializing in dismantling buildings. It was very obvious during the excavations that parts of the monastery had been plundered. In the refectory thirteen columns, ten capitals and one column base were missing. Only one broken column remained. In the southwest corner of the building a number of capitals were found stacked and ready for shipment. Most of the marble artifacts as well, such as chancel posts and screens, were missing. The roof tiles of the refectory, church and various chapels had also been plundered. Of the thousands of tiles that one could have expected to find at the site, only a few — mostly broken — had been left. In Hisham's Palace there is a large room in which roof tiles were stored; these had probably been taken from monasteries.

In addition to its tiles and probably also wooden beams and paving flagstones, small colored tesserae of a high standard of execution were pillaged. These tesserae may also have been used in the Hisham's Palace in Jericho.

The Twelfth-Century Decoration of the Church of the Nativity: Eastern and Western Concord

Gustav Kühnel

History of the Church

Although the Church of the Nativity in Bethlehem was built in several stages, its interior is uniform in appearance.[1] It consists of a nave and four aisles separated by four rows of eleven columns. On the east the nave and aisles terminate in a triconch with all three apses of the same size: two at the end of the transept arms and one at the end of the nave. Although scholars concur that the church has a uniform structure, there is a dispute as to when this uniformity came about.

Between the years 1932–1934, the Department of Antiquities of Palestine conducted excavations there, uncovering an earlier stratum from the Constantinian period, including a floor mosaic, remains of an atrium in the west, and remnants of a polygonal building in the east.[2] Like the present-day church, the Constantinian basilica had a nave and four aisles, but was one bay shorter in the west. It had an atrium, but lacked a narthex. The nave and aisles were attached in the east to an octagonal structure overlying the Grotto

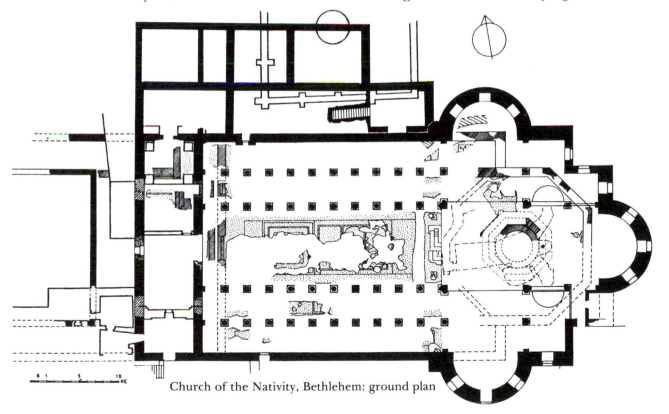

Church of the Nativity, Bethlehem: ground plan

[1] See G. Kühnel, *Wall Painting in the Latin Kingdom of Jerusalem. Frankfurter Forschungen zur Kunst* 14 (1988), esp. pp. 1–5 with earlier bibliography.

[2] For the earlier history of the church, see in this volume, Y. Tsafrir, "The Development of Ecclesiastical Architecture in Palestine," pp. 1–16.

of the Nativity. An opening in the octagonal floor provided a view of the grotto. There was also apparently an *opaion* (*oculus*) aperture in the center of the octagon. This combination of a basilica and a memorial structure is typical of Constantinian architecture, in Rome as well as in the Holy Land (e.g., the Church of the Holy Sepulchre). Father Belarmino Bagatti, who excavated the site during the years 1949–1950, disagrees with this view, claiming that the eastern part of the Constantinian church was a polygonal apse with two side chambers, and without an opening to the grotto.[3]

Regardless of the exact structure of the Constantinian church's eastern part, the question arises as to when it was converted into a triconch. Some scholars argue that the renovations took place during the Justinianian period. This is supported by the fact that the narthex replaced the atrium in the western part during this period. However, the only written source for this assumption is the Patriarch of Alexandria, Euthychius (Ibn al-Batriq) in the tenth century C.E.[4] There is no evidence of destruction of the church to substantiate this theory, nor is it corroborated by Justinian's historian, Procopius, who does not even mention Bethlehem among the emperor's building projects.

Architecturally, the trichonchal structure appears to date to the fifth century C.E., rather than to the Justinianian period. The style of the capitals also points in this direction: those found in Bethlehem are not typical of the latter period. The floor mosaics link the two construction stages. Although their polygonal eastern contours clearly would indicate their belonging to the Constantinian structure, their style would suggest either the late fourth century C.E. or the early fifth century C.E.[5] The date of the church's renov-

ation, involving minor changes to the nave and aisles, far-reaching ones in the eastern extremity and the addition of the narthex, remains uncertain: sometime between the Constantinian and Justinianian periods. Perhaps, as M. Restle suggests, it took place in the second half of the fifth century C.E.[6]

Since then, the church's basic structure has not been modified significantly. Although the building's interior has undergone important changes — the blocking up of the apsidal windows and of the windows of the aisles has altered the lighting, the passages from the aisles to the transept arms have been blocked off, and the *iconostasis* prevents access to the principal apse — these do not alter its basic plan. It can thus be said that the present-day Church of the Nativity still maintains the Early Christian structure with decorations from the Crusader period.

Political Conditions in the Middle Ages

During the years of Muslim rule, the Christians, like the other non-Muslim groups, constituted a *millet*, i.e., a community with religious autonomy, responsible to the caliph for its good behavior. The Christians, however, had always viewed the Byzantine emperor as their political and religious leader; hence the grant of protectorate status by the Byzantine Empire to the Christians in the East, persisting throughout the Muslim rule. Although, in theory, this status applied to individuals rather than to territories, in practice some emperors strove to liberate the holy places. During the pre-Crusader eleventh century C.E., Byzantine protectorship of the Christians in the Holy Land strengthened: Emperor Constantine IX obtained permission to rebuild the Church of the Holy Sepulchre, destroyed by Caliph al-Ḥakim; the Christians living in Jerusalem received permission (apparently in 1036) to erect a wall around

[3] B. Bagatti, *The Church from the Gentiles in Palestine* (Jerusalem, 1971), pp. 175–184, Fig. 48. See also, idem, *Gli antichi edifici sacri di Betlemme* (Jerusalem, 1952).

[4] L. Cheiko (ed.), *Euthychii patriarchae Alexandrini Annales*, I. CSCO 50 (= *Scriptores Arabici, Textus* Ser. III, 6) (Beirut, Paris, Leipzig, 1906), p. 201.

[5] E. Kitzinger, "Evolution stylistique des pavements des mosaïques dans l'Orient grecque depuis l'époque constanti-

nienne et jusqu'à celle de Justinien," in *La mosaïque greco-romaine. Colloque internationaux du CNRS*, I (Paris, 1965), pp. 341–351, Fig. 10.

[6] M. Restle, "Bethlehem," *Reallekicon zur beyzantinischen Kunst*, col. 611.

their quarter; the people of Amalfi residing in Jerusalem recognized the Byzantine emperor's sovereignty. There is also evidence that the Empire's authorities collected taxes in the holy places, giving rise to disputes with the pilgrims from the West.

Conditions changed when dominion over the holy places became Western-Christian, leading to political competition between the new Crusader states and the Byzantine Empire. However, during the reigns of the Byzantine emperor Manuel Comnenus and the Crusader kings Baldwin III and Amalric I, amiable relations prevailed between Byzantium and Crusader Jerusalem — as the marriages of these two kings to Byzantine princesses attest — and Byzantine political and cultural influence over Jerusalem was at a peak.

Manuel Comnenus' policy was based on continued Muslim pressure on the Crusader states, sufficiently powerful to ensure their dependency on him, although not strong enough to crush them. He built up his image as a patron, although it is not clear whether his dependents actually became vassals. Wilhelm of Tyre records warm, friendly meetings between the emperor and the Christian kings at Mopsuestia, Antioch and even Constantinople.[7] Such relations were due to a great extent to Manuel's wish to reunify the Eastern and Western Churches. In a letter in 1171 to the king of France, Louis VII, he promised to recognize Alexander III as the legitimate pope. At the Church Council convened at Constantinople in 1166, Manuel exploited his hold over the Orthodox clergy to adopt certain dogmatic motions in the spirit of their Latin connotations.[8]

This article examines to what extent the

[7] "Wilhelmus Tyrensis, Historia rerum in partibus transmarinis gestarum XVIII, 22–25," in *RHC Hist. occid.*, I (Paris, 1844), p. 912. See also, R.J. Lilie, *Byzanz und die Kreuzfahrerstaaten; Studien zur Politik des byzantinischen Reiches gegenüber den Staaten der Kreuzfahrer in Syrien uns Palästina bis zum vierten Kreuzzug* (Munich, 1981); S. Runciman, "The Visit of King Amalric I to Constantinople in 1171," in B.Z. Kedar, H.E. Mayer and R.C. Smail, *History of the Crusading Kingdom of Jerusalem Presented to J. Prawer* (Jerusalem, 1982), pp. 153–158.

[8] P. Classen, "Das Konzil von Konstantinopel 1166 und die Lateiner," *Byzantinische Zeitschrift* 48 (1955): 339–368.

relations prevailing between the Byzantine Empire and Crusader Jerusalem influenced and found expression in the decorations executed in the Church of the Nativity.

The Church Decoration

The mosaic Greek and Latin inscription on the main apse's southern wall clearly reflects the cooperation between Manuel Comnenus and Amalric I. Its text corroborates the intermingling of Eastern and Western elements apparent in the style and iconography of the mosaics and column paintings. The inscription will be discussed later in this article in an attempt to determine when and by whom the Crusader ornamentation was accomplished.

Two components are discerned in the Crusader decoration program of the Church of the Nativity: the mosaics, parts of which have survived on the walls of the nave and transept, and the column paintings, depicting individually framed figures of saints. These elements should be viewed as two parts of a common decorative plan, originating in the "classical" church of the Middle Byzantine period.

The mosaics and wall paintings in Bethlehem constitute the largest cycle of monumental decorations in the Holy Land still in existence, albeit fragmentary. This cycle is presented in its entirety in this article, based upon existing evidence and written sources. Cleaning and photography conducted by the author over the past few years enabled the reexamination of the Church of the Nativity's decorative scheme. A close analysis of the mosaics elucidated their dating and source, shedding new light upon the controversy regarding their local roots.

The mosaics. The following scenes were depicted at the basilica's eastern extremity. The Virgin appeared in the central apse between the figures of Abraham and King David, and the Annunciation of Mary was represented on this apse's arch. Christ's Nativity was portrayed in the southern apse, and the Adoration of the Magi on its arch. The representation in the northern apse was presumably of that of the Anastasis.

The Doubting Thomas still adorns the wall of the transept's northern arm. Only the lower part of the composition of the Ascension is preserved next to it, showing Mary with two angels (see Pl. XIVa) and the Apostles.

On the eastern wall of the transept's southern arm, Jesus' Entry into Jerusalem is entirely preserved. An adjacent fragment shows James the Apostle from the Transfiguration scene (see Pl. XIIc). The Samaritan woman at the well was featured higher up on the same wall, possibly between the windows. The seated figure of John the Evangelist was depicted higher on this wall, while the figure south of the window was possibly Joachim. There is no doubt that another three evangelists were originally portrayed in corresponding places in the transept, all in the classical pose of an author. The Capture of Jesus was represented on the western wall of the transept's southern arm, and the figure of Anna was depicted south of the window, corresponding to Joachim's position on the opposite wall.

No written source sheds light on the reconstruction of the scenes originally depicted on the western wall of the transept's northern arm, but they were probably from Jesus' Passion: the Washing of the Apostles' Feet, the Last Supper and the Crucifixion.

The nave's western wall was decorated with the Tree of Jesse, showing Jesus' descent from the House of David. The fairly accurate written descriptions indicate that this illustration was purely Western, related to the iconographic type developed toward the middle of the twelfth century C.E. by Abbot Suger of Saint Denis. Its appearance in Bethlehem may well represent this scene's transfer from Western to Byzantine iconography.

The decoration of the nave walls and columns is composed of four levels. The uppermost level, in line with the windows, depicts rows of angels proceeding eastward. Six representations of angels have survived on the northern wall. The artists avoided stereotypical depiction by the use of varying colors, garments and body positions; figures of standing angels alternate with pacing ones, creating the sense of motion toward the apse.

The second highest level comprises representations of the Church Councils: six provincial Councils on the northern wall, and the seven ecumenical ones on the southern wall. An immense decorated cross (*crux gemmata*) is still visible in the center of the northern wall, flanked by two trees signifying the Tree of Life.

Of the original six provincial Councils only the following have survived: the Councils of Antiochia and Sardika (see Pl. XIIa), almost entirely, and fragments of the Councils of Ankyra and Gangara. The provincial Councils were depicted by means of apses and domes resting upon columns and enclosing altars upon which lay Gospel books. The text of the Councils' decisions were inscribed within these representations. Three rich, tree-shaped candelabra — a large candelabrum flanked by two thinner ones — separated the surviving provincial Councils from one another (see Pl. XIIIa–b).

These two highest levels are set apart by a scroll frieze. The 1983 summer cleaning campaign brought to light new details, establishing that this was actually a populated scroll frieze (see Pl. XIIId). The motifs interwoven among the acanthus leaves include diadems, masks, birds, quadrupeds and hybrids, evidencing twelfth-century Western influence in Bethlehem. This frieze is of major importance in the controversy regarding the datings of the two levels, as approached, for example, by the art historian Henri Stern,[9] and is one of the most widely debated questions in the research of the basilica's wall decoration. This being the case, the intermediary frieze was closely examined on site and in the photographs for traces of later adaptations, determining categorically that the tesserae are continuously set. No interruption or alteration is visible between the wall's uppermost level and the level of the provincial Councils.

[9] H. Stern, "Les représentations des Conciles dans l'Eglise de la Nativité à Bethléem," *Byzantion* 11 (1936): 101–152; ibid., 13 (1938): 415–459; idem, "Nouvelles recherches sur les images des Conciles dans l'Eglise de la Nativité à Bethléem," *Cahiers Archéologiques* 3 (1948): 82–105; idem, "Encore les mosaïques de l'Eglise de la Nativité à Bethléem," ibid. 9 (1957): 141–145.

The third level from the top was adorned with rows of Jesus' ancestors, based upon the genealogies in Luke 3:23–28 on the northern wall and in Matthew 1:1–16 on the southern wall. Only some of the ancestral figures on the southern wall are still preserved — Azor, Zadok, Achim, Eleazar, Matthan and Jacob (see Pl. XIIb), all of whom are identified by inscriptions. Here, too, the artists avoided monotony through variations in the color scale, costumes, face type, hair arrangement and other details.

Of the seven ecumenical Councils which had survived intact until the seventeenth century C.E., only a few fragments are still visible: from the Councils of Nicaea, 325; Constantinople, 381 (the best preserved; see Pl. XIIIc); Ephesus, 431; Chalcedon, 451; and Constantinople, 680 C.E. (which stands in isolation close to the wall's western extremity). These Councils are represented as double arches of equal height, each pair containing altars, Gospel books and inscriptions of the Councils' main decisions. Most of the texts are in Greek; the only exception is that pertaining to the Seventh Council at Nicaea, 787, which was in Latin. The representations of the Councils are separated from each other by large candelabra formed by acanthus leaves.

At first glance, the ecumenical Councils appear more linear, flat and abstract than the provincial Councils. Stern's thesis that the ecumenical Councils were twelfth-century C.E. copies of the much earlier provincial Councils, which he dated ca. 700 C.E., is based upon this perception. However, a close examination of both walls following the cleaning campaign repudiates any chronological discrepancy. True, there are obvious stylistic differences between the northern and southern walls. However, they should be considered as the result of different artists or groups of artists consciously using a variety of modes of expression, thus creating the stylistic diversity that is characteristic of the Crusader decoration in the Church of the Nativity.

Careful scrutiny of the cleaned mosaics on the southern wall reveals that although they differ from those on the northern wall in richness and quality, they do not lack originality. The southern-wall mosaics are indeed in a much poorer state, which may explain why they were considered inferior in quality and, therefore, imitative. The identical technique, the same tesserae, the rich color scale uncovered under layers of dirt, and the inventiveness demonstrated by many complex motifs, all demonstrate that the ecumenical Council mosaics concur in time with the entire parietal pattern of the church, i.e., the second and third quarters of the twelfth century C.E.

Other stylistic differences in the church decorations have not led to different datings. The dissimilarities between the mosaics of the two transept arms, for example, are salient in a comparison of the Apostles from the Doubting Thomas scene with the figures greeting Jesus in his Entry into Jerusalem: the dramatically moving lines of the former contrast with the geometric, static masses of the latter. Moreover, differences among the nave's column have not discredited their dating to the twelfth century C.E. The figures of James the Elder and Leo the Great, for example, are clearly rooted in different styles of Byzantine painting: the representation of James the Elder is retrospectively directed toward the Macedonian Renaissance, while that of Leo the Great reflects the contemporary twelfth-century C.E. Comnenian art. The design of the former is soft, diaphanous and light; the latter is linear, stiff and severe.[10]

Such observations are evidence of the diversity of the Church of the Nativity's ornamentation. Although its artists ascribed to different stylistic approaches, they clearly appertain to a common frame. This workshop's singularity lies in the intermingling of local with Byzantine and Crusader elements.

The column paintings. The fourth, lowest level of decoration consists of representations of saints upon the columns of the Church of the Nativity, reflecting the medieval concept of the saint as a pillar of the Church. When a unified church decorative plan took shape in

---

[10] Kühnel, *Wall Painting* (see note 1), esp. pp. 128–147.

post-iconoclastic Byzantine art, paintings of the saints were consistently depicted in the lower parts of the structure, maintaining their original significance as the Church's "support." Bethlehem is the only example known to the author where column paintings were integrated into the "classical" Byzantine church plan. This was due to the church's basilican nature, which was a necessary precondition for the Crusader decoration. A unique solution was found: the "classical" Byzantine decoration scheme was adapted to the existing basilican building, incorporating the traditional medieval identity between the column and the saint.

Twenty-nine saints are painted on twenty-seven of the basilica's forty-four columns. One saint appears on each column in the two rows bordering the central nave. No saints are depicted on the row of columns separating the two northern aisles. On the other hand, two columns in the corresponding row between the southern aisles are adorned with two different representations each. However, other columns in this row have no paintings whatsoever. The order in which the various groups of holy personages are presented in the Church of the Nativity was determined on the basis of the theological writings dealing with the hierarchy of the Christian world, together with the iconographic tradition of the twelfth and preceding centuries.[11]

The most important group comprises the representations of Mary (including depictions of Anna, since typologically she belongs to this group); in second place is a representation of Elijah, the only prophet portrayed in Bethlehem; in third place — Jesus' predecessor and harbinger, John the Baptist, *Prodromos*; the fourth group is that of the Apostles (see Pl. XIVb) and John the Evangelist. All these belong to the heavenly hierarchy, together with the angels depicted in the mosaic between the windows of the nave's walls.

The groups belonging to the earthly hierarchy follow next: the bishops, the deacons, the warrior St. George with St. Leonard on

his heels. They are followed by the ascetics and hermits, the *Anargyroi*, the holy doctors Cosmas and Damianus who cured without payment, the holy women and the holy kings Knute and Olaf.

A separate analysis of each saint's cult and his depiction in Bethlehem suggests a number of cohesive groups of saints, each represented in Crusader Bethlehem for different reasons.

The scenes of Mary clearly belong in a church honoring Christ's birth. A second group consists of the saints who fought Monophysitism. Anthony, Theodosius, Euthymius and Sabas are well known for their struggle against those who believed in the existence of only the divine nature of Jesus. To these we can add the figure of Pope Leo (see Pl. XIVc), who formulated the essay serving as the basis for the dogmatic decision against Monophysitism at the Council of Chalcedon in 451. Strong opposition to Monophysitism in the Church of the Incarnation, where Jesus was born and which is therefore strongly associated with Jesus' human nature, is certainly no coincidence.

The large group of ascetics and hermits honors the founders of Palestinian monasticism, who kept the spark of Christianity alive during the centuries of Muslim rule. Their unique way of life exemplified an unwavering faith, powerful enough to overcome heresy and restore the holy places to Christian hands. Elijah the Prophet and John the Baptist belong in this group by merit of the example they set to monasticism in general. Moreover, Elijah is associated with Palestinian monasticism in particular, as the patron saint of the Carmelites, whose order was founded in Palestine in the twelfth century C.E.

St. George and St. Leonard represent the military aspect of Crusaderdom. St. George is the patron saint of the Crusader armies, while St. Leonard is considered the protector of Crusader prisoners, due to his role in freeing Prince Boemond of Antioch. Kings Knute and Olaf, armed with their shields, can also be viewed as representatives of the various Scandinavian Crusaders.

The depictions of some saints in the Church

---

[11] Ibid., pp. 5–128.

of the Nativity were probably due to their having been commissioned by a pilgrim or group of pilgrims from a specific locality. This is the most likely explanation for the presence of local saints whose cult was limited to narrow boundaries, such as Fusca — revered in Veneto, or Catald — worshipped by the Normans of southern Sicily. This is also true in the case of saints represented with donors at their feet: Mary, Olaf and especially the Apostle James the Elder, whose donors are identified by a shell as pilgrims to Santiago de Compostella. Votive paintings are an intrinsic element in a church so important to pilgrims, and these comprise an integral group among the other groups of saints represented there.

The homogeneity of the saints' depictions upon the two rows of columns bordering the nave — not a single column left unpainted, all figures facing the nave — suggests that they were part of an overall plan, and may even have been painted at once. The representations on the row of columns separating the southern aisles are less uniform; the deviations suggest that they were executed separately. Perhaps more latitude was given to donors' requests and votive paintings in the aisles; the column paintings in the nave, in contrast, primarily express the dictates of the church authorities and planners.

The church's comprehensive decorative plan was intended to emphasize the perfect balance between the two natures of Christ, as formulated by the decisions of the ecumenical and regional Church Councils. Thus, the Councils depicted on the nave walls serve as the focus of the plan. On the western side, the Tree of Jesse demonstrates Jesus' divine origin. On the eastern side various events in his life on earth are shown. The angels of heaven appear above the Church Councils, while below them the saints represent the columns of Christian faith, acting as intermediaries between the faithful and God.

Two dated inscriptions appear in the Crusader decorations: one, painted on the column with the figure of Mary, mentions the year 1130, while the other, a bilingual (Latin and Greek) inscription in the *bema* mosaic, speci-

fies the year 1169 as the date of completion.[12]

The mosaic inscription names the monk Ephrem as artist and the three sponsors: Emperor Manuel Comnenus, King Amalric I and Bishop Raul of Bethlehem. The Latin version highlights King Amalric, beginning with his name and devoting three and a half lines to him, while the Greek version emphasizes Emperor Manuel Comnenus. Notwithstanding the inscription's different emphases and allusions, it reflects the close cooperation between the king of Jerusalem, the Byzantine emperor and the bishop of Bethlehem, expressed in the iconography and style of the Crusader paintings and mosaics. Ephrem, the painter and mosaicist, may have supervised the overall project; however, he was probably aided by many other artists in a workshop which was active for years. The two years 1130 and 1169, mentioned in the inscriptions, may be regarded as the broadest time span of the entire decoration of the church, including the column paintings.

In the course of the author's cleaning and research (carried out in July 1983), a hitherto unknown inscription was discovered, shedding new light upon the identity of the artists who created the mosaics and paintings. It is a Syriac inscription (see Pl. XIId), paralleling the already known Latin inscription "Basilius pictor" accompanying the third angel from the east on the northern wall.[13] The first line reiterates the painter's Latin name in an abbreviated Syriac form (Basil mode): *ṣr bʾsyl*. The second line gives the artist's title and ecclesiastical function — *mšm* (an abbreviated form of *mšmš Diaconus*). The existence of an inscription identifying the artist in what was probably his native language proves that local artists participated in the Bethlehem workshop of the Crusader period. The name "Ephrem" in the *bema* inscription was also common in the Syro-Palestinian region.

---

[12] Ibid., pp. 4f, 146.

[13] G. Kühnel, "Das Ausschmuckungsprogramm der Geburtsbasilika in Bethlehem," *Boreas* 10 (1987): esp. 148. I am most grateful to Professors M. Stone, J.C. Greenfield, and H.J.W. Drijvers for their help in deciphering the inscription.

The Early Christian Holy Site at Shepherds' Field

Vassilios Tzaferis

Shepherds' Field is situated about one kilometer from Bethlehem, in the modern Arab village of Beit Saḥur. According to Christian tradition, it was here that the angel of God announced the birth of Christ to the shepherds "abiding in the field, keeping watch over their flock by night" (Luke 2:8–18).

In 1970 the Greek Orthodox Patriarchate of Jerusalem, which owns the land at the site, made plans to restore the holy place.[1] A clearing revealed ancient remains, the earliest of which, fragments of colored mosaic decorated with crosses, date to the fourth century C.E. The mosaic paved a natural cave, undoubtedly the "Cave of the Shepherds" mentioned in early Christian literary sources.

At the beginning of the fifth century, the cave was enlarged and its roof completely removed to facilitate the construction of a more spacious church. The new building also had a floor of colored mosaics that were laid on top of the old paving. An entrance to the old sanctuary was opened on its southern side, and a flight of about 17 steps was built to it.

At the same time, a small chapel was built on top of the church. This roof chapel seems to have been a kind of memorial, and it too was paved with mosaics whose decorative motif is known from elsewhere in Israel: an amphora out of which emerge vinescrolls with bunches of grapes. Below the amphora are two Greek inscriptions commemorating persons who gave donations for the erection of the chapel.

[1] The site was systematically explored and excavated on behalf of the Department of Antiquities and Museums by the author. For detailed description, see V. Tzaferis, "The Archaeological Excavations at Shepherds' Field," *Liber Annuus* 25 (1975): 5–52.

This church built inside the original natural cave has been completely preserved up to its roof. In the sixth century the entire area was

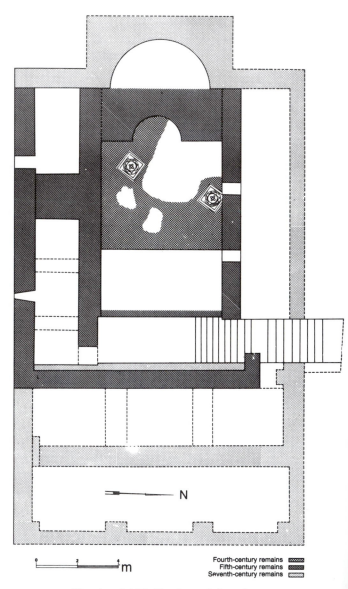

Shepherds' Field: plan of church

Fourth-century remains
Fifth-century remains
Seventh-century remains

completely reconstructed. The small chapel at the top of the church was removed, and the area around it and the lower church was leveled. In their place a magnificent basilica was erected that was supported by white marble columns with Corinthian capitals and paved with colored mosaics. The fifth-century church became an entirely underground building, part of which was walled off and used as a cemetery — probably for the basilica's deceased priests and monks. In this burial place we found more than one hundred skeletons, along with oil lamps, coins, and small crosses worn as pendants, all of which date to the sixth century. The area around the basilica was paved with mosaics and left as an open courtyard.

From a seventh-century calendar of the Christian cult of Jerusalem, we know that the basilica was linked with the early Christians' celebration of Christmas Day. The ceremonies actually began the day before at the "church of the shepherds." From there the priests and worshippers went in solemn procession to the Church of the Nativity in Bethlehem to continue their prayers.

The basilica was destroyed in the seventh century, probably during the Persian invasion in 614 C.E. The Christians replaced it immediately, but with a less magnificent structure. In the Muslim period, when living conditions for the Christians deteriorated, a wall with watchtowers at its corners was built around the site. Once a holy place open to all Christians and pilgrims, it became an enclosed monastery like others in the nearby Judean Desert.

The site was destroyed in the eleventh century. It remained a deserted ruin until our recent excavations brought it to light. Our results were decisive for its identification and reconstruction. The archaeological findings and early Christian sources are in complete agreement about Shepherds' Field and its monuments. The earliest records that mention it as a holy place are the itineraries of Christian pilgrims. From the pilgrimage of Egeria, we learn that by the second half of the fourth century, there was a church here, the

Shepherds' Field: fifth-century mosaic floor in structure above lower church; in the background are remains of basilica

Church of the Shepherds. We also know from this source that a cave within the church was called the "Cave of the Shepherds," or the "Sacred Cave." Christians later connected Shepherds' Field with narratives from the Hebrew Bible. They believed that Jacob pastured his flock there, and that the gracious idyll of Ruth and Boaz, related in the Book of Ruth, occurred at this place. Early Christians also identified Shepherds' Field with Migdal-

Shepherds' Field: southern wall of subterranean church after excavation, and pillars from seventh-century church

Shepherds' Field: general view of seventh-century church

eder, mentioned in Genesis 35:21. According to a legend circulated among Christians at about the beginning of the sixth century, Migdal-eder was founded by Jacob.

It is likely that some of these traditions originated in the local folklore, whereas others were simply invented by Christians as Shepherds' Field became a place of pilgrimage. Their common element is their relationship to the narrative of Jesus' birth — the episode of the shepherds. The stories about Ruth and Jacob may have been considered background to Jesus' birth — according to the Christian belief that Boaz was one of Jesus' forefathers (Matthew 1:5). On the other hand, the identification of Shepherds' Field with Migdal-eder has a relatively concrete basis. Migdal-eder was in Judah; it lay on the main road from Jerusalem to En Gedi, a route that

passed the outskirts of Bethlehem. It is therefore possible that ancient Migdal-eder was within the area of modern Beit Saḥur, as is Shepherds' Field, and that early Christians knew this. However, not only the geographical proximity of the two places suggests that identification: in Hebrew Migdal-eder means "the tower of the flock," a natural association for a story about shepherds.

The records of Christian pilgrims clearly show that Shepherds' Field was an important holy place, highly venerated during the Byzantine period from the fourth through sixth centuries. Even after the Persian invasion it was reestablished and functioned until its final destruction by the Arabs in the eleventh century. For more than one thousand years thereafter, Shepherds' Field lay abandoned and neglected.

206

The Byzantine Church at Ḥorvat Berachot

Yoram Tsafrir and Yizhar Hirschfeld

Ḥorvat Berachot (Kh. Bureikut) is situated east of the Hebron–Jerusalem road, about 3 km east of Kfar Eẓion. It is an expansive hill, on the slopes and summit of which ruins of dwellings, vaulted cellars, rock-cut cisterns, and caves are scattered.

The survey and excavations that have been carried out at the site indicated that the main settlements dated to the Byzantine and the Early Arab periods.

On the southern slope of the hill, a massive rectangular building constructed of relatively large ashlars with margins was detected. This structure, like others on the site, showed signs of plunder, and therefore it was decided to carry out a salvage excavation.[1] A Byzantine church was revealed that had been abandoned in the Early Arab period and converted into a dwelling or storeroom evidenced by the partition walls.

In the course of time, most of the ashlars and all the undamaged roof tiles were plundered. Some of the outer walls are preserved to a height of 2 m, particularly on the eastern slope. Cultivation of the entire area severely damaged the building and especially the mosaic floors.

---

[1] The excavations were carried out in July 1976 on behalf of the Kfar Eẓion Field School, the officer for Archaeology in Judea and Samaria, and the Institute of Archaeology of The Hebrew University of Jerusalem. They were directed by Y. Tsafrir and Y. Hirschfeld, assisted by D. Amit and the instructors at the Field School. The plans and architectural reconstructions were drawn by the architect Giora Solar. Students at the Field School and youth groups of the Bene Akiva "Settlement Movement" participated in the dig. For details of the excavation at the site, see Y. Tsafrir and Y. Hirschfeld, "The Church and Mosaics at Ḥorvat Berachot, Israel," *DOP* 33 (1979): 293–326.

The Church Building

The church has three components: the main hall, the crypt (underground chapel), and an atrium surrounded by rooms (perhaps a monastery). The complex was built on the exposed rock of the southern part of the hill, which slopes fairly gently to the east. Filling and construction work were necessary to raise the eastern part of the church to the same level as the rest of the complex. Topographical conditions made it possible to include a vaulted crypt in the building, under the chancel and apse, by using the natural cave that had served as a place of worship before the church was built. The outer walls are of large ashlars, averaging 60–90 cm in length; some blocks measure more than 1 m. Each course is about 65 cm high; the walls were 70 cm thick on the average.

Most of the stones were crudely dressed on their inner side, which was hidden from sight; only the outer face was carefully cut, usually with smooth margins and a prominent boss in the center. The outer face was probably left exposed, but in order to safeguard the foundations, a sloping revetment of cement and gravel was added to the lower courses. Inside the building the walls were covered with white plaster. We found no traces of colored or painted plaster.

The main hall of the church is basilican in plan and was paved with mosaics. When the vault of the crypt collapsed, the entire eastern part of the church caved in. The destruction was further advanced later when stones were removed for reuse as building material. Nothing has survived of the apse and chancel other than two stones from the former and a few marble fragments. We found some triangular

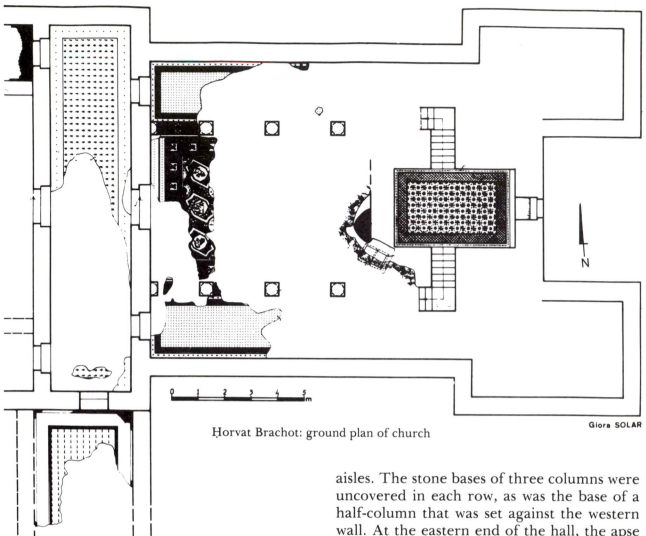

Ḥorvat Brachot: ground plan of church

black stone floor tiles, which may indicate that the chancel was paved with *opus sectile*. Remains of cement adhere to the back of the tiles.

The exterior length of the church, without the narthex, was 15.5 m; its exterior width was 12.5 m. The plan of the church was obviously based on these measurements, as a calculation using the unit current at that time (one foot = ca. 31 cm) gives an exact length of 50 feet and a width of exactly 40 feet. According to the suggested reconstruction, the interior length of the hall, including the apse, was 14.25 m, and its width 11.1 m; the hall without the apse measured 11.1 × 11.75 m — that is, it was almost square. Two rows of columns divided the hall into a nave and two aisles. The stone bases of three columns were uncovered in each row, as was the base of a half-column that was set against the western wall. At the eastern end of the hall, the apse must have been flanked by an additional pair of columns and half-columns. The bases, which measure about 50 × 50 cm, were sunk into the mosaic floor and have shallow sockets to accommodate the columns. Not even a fragment of one of these columns was uncovered in the excavations. The bays between the columns were 1.95 m long; the width of the nave was 6.05 m, measured between the column centers; and the width of the aisles, 2.5–2.55 m.

Only the foundations of the eastern part of the hall, which were below floor level, including the apse and the chancel, remain. The suggested reconstruction is therefore based on the following data: the vault of the crypt, the flights of steps ascending steeply from the crypt to the aisles, the rows of columns, the exterior walls, and especially a profiled stone, probably the base of one of the half-columns

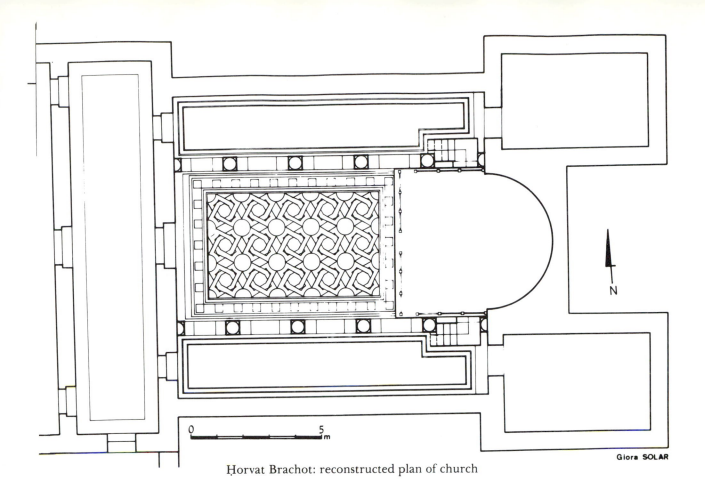

Horvat Brachot: reconstructed plan of church

Giora SOLAR

at the sides of the apse. We recovered one of the concave stones from the apse wall; its preserved length (90 cm) was sufficient to enable us to estimate the span of the apse (5 m) and its depth (2.5 m). These estimated measurements confirm our reconstruction of the apse based on other features. The chancel could be reconstructed as projecting 3.5 m beyond the span of the apse on the basis of various other elements preserved in the church.

The flights of stairs from the crypt to the hall present something of a problem, as the columns partially obstruct access to them. Moreover, these stairs debouch near the nave, thus preventing free circulation in the church. This arrangement gives unobstructed access to the two side rooms that project eastward from the church and implies their special importance. The only remains of these rooms are part of their foundation. We excavated the southeastern room down to bedrock, but the northwestern one only on the outside in order to trace the line of the walls. These side

chambers seem to be independent chapels, not necessarily connected with the daily service in the church.

The three entrances from the narthex into the hall were in the center of the nave and the aisles. In a sounding carried out under the mosaic floor of the hall near the central entrance, we reached bedrock at a depth of 95 cm. The fill layers contained waste from building stones and white tesserae that must have been prepared on the spot. The potsherds we collected in the fill are characteristic of the fifth–sixth centuries C.E. and enabled us to confirm the chronological framework based on other data.

The Mosaic Floors
The mosaic pavement of the church has three main parts: the central "carpet," those in the two aisles, and the layout of the intercolumniations. Only a relatively small part of the mosaic floor has been preserved, at the western end of the hall, but it is sufficient for a reconstruction of the entire pavement.

209

Ḥorvat Brachot: narthex, looking southwest

Ḥorvat Brachot: mosaics of northwest
intercolumniation, looking west

The tesserae in the nave and between the columns are relatively small (about 160 per sq dm) and the execution of the mosaic was of a high technical quality. The tesserae used to pave the aisles are larger (90–100 per sq dm).

The pattern of the mosaic in the aisles consisted of indented squares in white, gray, and red on a white background, bordered with a guilloche in red, orange, white, gray, and red. The "carpet" itself was surrounded by a band of black and gray flower buds.

One of the intercolumniations is almost completely preserved, and surviving fragments of two on the opposite side show that they had similar patterns, although with the alternated colors. Each "carpet" between the columns was 1.55 m long and 0.5 m wide, and had a central rectangular panel flanked by two smaller ones. The main motif in the small panels is a central lozenge that contains two more lozenges, one within the other, each shaded so as to create a three-dimensional effect. In the surviving part dark colors — black and gray — with white and pale blue shading are used in the outer lozenges, whereas the inner one was executed in shades of red, with pinkish-orange and yellow shading. The lozenge inscribed in the central panel contains a nicely designed pattern of "wave crests" in red on a white background; it encloses a central rectangle framed with a black and a white band. Inside this rectangle are two rows of black tesserae surrounded by white, greenish, yellow, orange, and red tesserae.

The motif of a lozenge inscribed in a rectangle is common in mosaics of this period. It gained popularity in the Late Hellenistic and Roman periods, apparently as a depiction of *opus sectile* pavements and of marble dadoes and inlays, somewhat like the imitation of marble in frescoes. This motif also appears frequently on wood and marble plaques and on pottery and glass objects.

Only the northwestern corner of the mosaic of the nave has been preserved, but other surviving fragments enable us to reconstruct the whole composition with a fair measure of certainty. The main border runs between several bands of colored geometric patterns on a

Ḥorvat Brachot: mosaic of nave

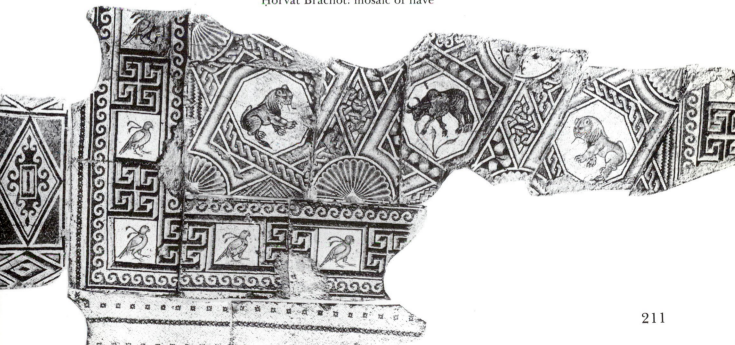

white background and consists of a wide band of squares, alternately featuring beribboned birds and double meanders (see Pl. XVa), each forming a swastika. The meanders are executed in white, gray, red, and shades of blue, brown, and yellow. The artist took care to differentiate between the two intersecting lines making up the meander — one is red-brown and the other gray-blue. Both lines continue for the length of the border. The meanders are skillfully shaded to create a three-dimensional illusion. The birds stand out against a white background, each square measuring 30 × 30 cm. The two-dimensional representation of the birds is in vivid contrast to the three-dimensional meanders. The birds are depicted naturalistically and may be hunting falcons, which often had ribbons knotted around their neck. Other zoological details (although not the colors used) support this identification. Yet, the birds need not belong to a particular species; generic beribboned birds and animals are found in other mosaics from the period, especially at Antioch. The birds here are outlined with dark tesserae; light shades of green and yellow were used for the body; and the beak, legs, and ribbon are red. Borders of double meanders and squares with birds and floral or geometric designs are found in several other mosaics in Israel: at Shellal, Deir Daklah, Mamshit (Kurnub), and in the synagogue at Susiya.

The central design forms the main part of the pavement. It is 3.85 m wide and 6.5 m long (according to our reconstruction). The pattern consists of elongated hexagons with concave ends. Our "carpet" must have contained thirty hexagons, arranged in five rows, with three pairs in each row. One hexagon in each pair is oriented northwest-southeast while the other which interlocks it, is directed northeast-southwest. The northwest-southeast group of hexagons comprises colored bands which are gradually shaded from red on the outer edge, through pink and orange, to white in the center, and from there, through shades of yellow and green, to gray-blue on the inner edge. The range of colors creates an optical illusion. Two of the northeast-southwest or-

ientated hexagons feature a rope pattern in two strands — one red, orange and white, and the other gray and white. In every row the interlocking hexagons create three octagons, while the narrow, concave ends describe circles. Various animals are depicted in both the octagons and circles. Semicircles and quarter-circles, both of which are filled with conches, contact the borders and corners respectively. The outside and inside of the conches are alternately red-brown and gray-blue. Triangles containing colored zigzag lines appear along the border. Similar compositions, rich in patterns and colors, appear frequently on mosaic floors in Israel and Jordan: at Shave-Zion, Suḥmata, Baqᶜa el-Gharbiye, Shiloh, Jericho, Madaba, and Gerasa, for example. The closest parallels to our pavement are those in the Naᶜaran synagogue in the church hall of Maᶜale Adummim.

The animals in the inner hexagons and the medallions are of particular interest. Originally the "carpet" contained twenty-three animals, but only three are completely preserved, all of them in the westernmost row; two fragmentary medallions survive in the row east of it.

Two of the animals in the outer octagons are crouching lions (see Pl. XVd) facing each other. In the central octagon a buffalo (see Pl. XVc) is browsing the leaves of a plant. The southern medallion in the second row has been almost completely destroyed, but the remains of plants and of an animal's feet indicate that here, too, a buffalo or some other herbivore may have been represented.

The animals measure 45–50 cm in length. The depictions of the lions are similar but not identical. They crouch on their hind legs, roaring and ready to leap forward. One front paw is raised and a long, tufted tail twists between their hind legs. Their whiskers are dark red and their bodies are outlined in dark red or gray-black tesserae. Although not well proportioned, the lions' bodies are represented realistically, in a very spirited fashion, using shades of red, brown, orange, yellow, and green, as well as many white patches. The eyes and the inner ear were executed in black

212

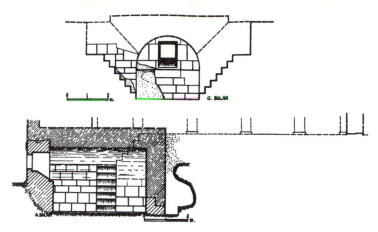

Ḥorvat Brachot: elevations and reconstruction of crypt;
above — looking east; below — section, looking south

Ḥorvat Brachot: south octagon, detail of lion

tesserae, and the ends of the mane and the tail are bluish and gray.

We were unable to find any exact parallels to our lions, although they are among the animals most frequently depicted in mosaic pavements. However, certain selected details, such as the heads and tails, bear a resemblance to those of the lions flanking the menorah in the pavement of the synagogue at Maᶜon, and to some of the features of the leopard in that mosaic — particularly the position of its body, head, and whiskers.

The buffalo in the central part of our mosaic is rendered mainly in dark colors — in shades of gray and black — but some brown and bluish tesserae enliven the representation. The position of the forelegs gives the impression of motion, but the hind legs are those of a stationary animal. The plant the buffalo is eating has red-brown stems and yellow-green leaves. Although we have no exact parallel to this buffalo, stylistically it resembles the donkey from the church at Maᶜale Adummim.

The animals are depicted without any background designs; the heraldic arrangement of

the lions flanking the buffalo and crouching as if to attack suggests movement and drama. The subject, composition, and details of the mosaic are not unique, but the technical accuracy, the wealth of colors and shades, and the three-dimensional effects produced indicate it was laid by a skilled artist.

The Crypt

The most important discovery in the eastern part of the church was the vaulted crypt under the chancel. When the vault collapsed it brought down the entire chancel and possibly also the apse with it.

Our excavations revealed three stages in the development of the crypt and of the church in general. Initially there was a natural cave with plastered walls and a white mosaic floor. Under the floor, at its southwestern end, we uncovered a small tomb (75 × 55 cm), built of limestone slabs. It was sealed with white plaster and contained bones in secondary burial. An anthropological examination[2] revealed three or four skeletons and individual bones of a total of eleven corpses.

In time the crypt expanded over most of the area, making it difficult to estimate the cave's original shape and size. The cave had been a Christian place of worship prior to the construction of the church, and the bones collected in the tomb probably belong to persons who had requested to be buried in a holy place. It was the hallowed significance of the cave that probably led to the erection of the

[2] J. Zias carried out this examination.

213

Ḥorvat Brachot: cave outside west wall of crypt,
looking south

basilica on this site. The construction of
churches to commemorate holy places began
as early as the fourth century C.E. [see the
discussion of the excavation by V. Tsaferis at
Shepherds' Field near Bethlehem (pp. 204–
206)]. No doubt this was part of the continuous effort devoted to finding and revering
holy sites in this part of Palestine from the
time of Constantine onward. The name of our
site and the traditions associated with it are
unknown, because they are not mentioned in
any pilgrim records. Perhaps it was of only
secondary importance. There are numerous
holy sites in the region, and especially in the
neighborhood of Bethlehem: the Cave of the
Nativity, Rachel's Tomb, the tombs of David
and his family, Shepherds' Field, the tomb of
the infants massacred by Herod, the Fountain
of Philip at Beth-Zur, and the oaks at Mamre
and Hebron. Perhaps the tradition of sanctity
attached to our site had some connection with
the Patriarchs' wanderings or with the House
of David.

Near the tomb, we found a pottery lamp
with a bow-shaped nozzle, decorated with two
birds pecking at a cluster of grapes. The type
is characteristic of the fourth century, and

confirms our dating of the first use of the cave
as a shrine.

Together with the church, a vaulted crypt
was built within the cave. Its western wall was
erected on the white mosaic floor and even
partly covered the tomb, blocking access to it
and to the western end of the cave. We found
patches of white plaster. A rectangular window had been built in the eastern wall, and a
cross within a circle was carved on the outer
face of the lintel. The crypt is 4.5 m long and
3 m wide. The base of the eastern wall was
built to a width of 1.1 m because it had to
carry the weight of the apse above it. The
crypt was roofed with a barrel vault that rose
to about 3 m above the floor.

Two flights of steps led into the crypt, one
from the north and one from the south. Nine
of the eleven steps in each flight are preserved. The staircases were 90 cm wide and,
according to our reconstruction of the height,
they were not roofed — at least not from the
first to the seventh step.

The existence of two staircases — one used
to enter and the other to exit the crypt —
shows that the church attracted numerous
pilgrims, and that processions of worshippers
visited the crypt. This conforms with our submission that it was the sanctity of the cave that
led to the erection of the splendid church in
this particular spot, near the foot of the hill
slope and on the outskirts of the village.

Similar entrance-and-exit arrangements, intended to ease the movement of worshippers,
are known from some of the notable commemorative churches in the Holy Land.
Among them the Justinianian phase of the
crypt in the Church of the Nativity in Bethlehem is the most notable. The Church of
Eleona on the Mt. of Olives and the Chapel of
Elianos in Madaba probably also had such a
functional architectural feature.

A particularly close parallel to our crypt is
the northern church at Reḥovot-in-the-Negev
(Kh. Ruḥeibeh) (see below, pp. 294–302), which
is dated to the second half of the fifth century.

The crypt's mosaic floor (see Pl. XVb) is
almost completely preserved. The "carpet" is
surrounded by a border of six-ply guilloche

that is 35 cm wide, and consists of about 160 tesserae per sq dm. The workmanship is good, and the main pattern incorporates rows of three kinds of flowers that appear alternately. The largest flower (12 cm wide) is cruciform and somewhat resembles a four-petaled carnation in bloom. Each petal is divided in half vertically and is colored either with green and black or orange and brown. These green/black and orange/brown flowers alternate in every row. Each is surrounded by four small black and red buds, two of which point toward the flower and two away from it. Alternating with the cross-shaped flowers are round ones — in orange, red, and white — that are divided by a black cross into four parts. The composition is so arranged that the different flowers produce diagonal lines that are identical in shape and color.

This design is very rare and no exact parallels to it have been found to date. Round flowers and buds are relatively common, but the cruciform shape has only been encountered in the southern chapel of the Church of St. John in ʿEn Karem, which was excavated by S. Saller.

During the Arab period the Byzantine stratum in the crypt was sealed by a stamped-earth floor that was laid some 15–20 cm above the mosaic. Between the mosaic and the floor an accumulation of red soil contained a few Byzantine sherds and broken roof tiles. On the mosaic we found a small marble column with a square base that may be one of the altar supports. From the floor, many sherds and tile fragments from the Early Arab period were collected. At that time, in its third phase, the crypt served as a dwelling or storeroom. As the southern staircase was blocked, it must have been entered via the northern one. Among the Early Arab pottery finds, some decorated lamps are of particular interest. They belong to a type that was produced from the eighth century on until the Middle Ages. Our lamps, however, must date to the eighth century as there was no glazed pottery in the levels above the floor from the Arab period.

Thus, it seems that the crypt was occupied for the last time in the Early Arab period. The

Ḥorvat Brachot: cross on outer side of crypt window

most important find related to this time is a three-line Kufic inscription incised on the southern wall of the crypt: "In the name of God the merciful, the compassionate, O God, grant pardon to Yusuf [son of] Yasin."[3] We have no clue to the identity of the writer or to the reason why he was buried in the crypt. It may well be that the tradition of sanctity attached to the place was still remembered in the Early Arab period and was even accepted by the Muslims. If this is so, its origin should perhaps be sought in a biblical belief, common to both religions, and not specifically Christian. The writer may have been one of the Muslim mystics of Palestine in the Ommayad period.

The Narthex and the Atrium

The narthex extends west of the main hall of the church. Its inner dimensions were 3 m in width and 13.75 m in length; it was wider than the hall adjoining it and thus projected on both sides. Three entrances led from the atrium into the narthex. The central one was exactly opposite that leading from the narthex into the hall. Another opening con-

[3] R. and Y. Drory deciphered the inscription.

Ḥorvat Brachot: general view of crypt, looking east

nected the narthex to a large room in the south, which was also paved with mosaics and may have been a vestibule. The entire narthex is paved with fairly coarse, white mosaics (36 tesserae per sq dm) that are framed with a black band and enlivened with rows of black and red flowers and buds. We found many remains of flimsy constructions in the narthex — walls, steps, and stone installations. These stand on a layer of earth several centimeters thick which covered the mosaic floor, and therefore must have been in use after the structure no longer served as a church.

The church complex was completed in the west by the atrium and the rooms adjoining it, which formed a larger unit than the main part of the church itself. We only partially excavated the atrium and the rooms. Under the atrium's central courtyard, a large, deep, rock-cut cistern was uncovered, but as it was

to a great extent destroyed, we could not ascertain its original shape. There was no trace of a pavement in the courtyard itself. It may have been paved with stone slabs of which nothing remains, or alternatively, the bedrock may have been exploited as the pavement.

Porticoes paved with coarse white mosaics enclosed the atrium on the north, the west, and the south. (We discovered remains of a stylobate only on these three sides.) The atrium measured 13.8 m from north to south and 13.4 m from east to west. The porticoes were 2.1 m wide on the north and south, and 2 m wide on the west.

Spacious rooms, or halls, adjoined the atrium on the south and the west. Their outer walls have been dismantled, the stones carried away. However, there is a robber trench that makes it possible to establish the interior width of the western rooms (4.3 m). A surviv-

216

Ḥorvat Brachot: detail of crypt's mosaic floor

Ḥorvat Brachot: Kufic inscription in crypt

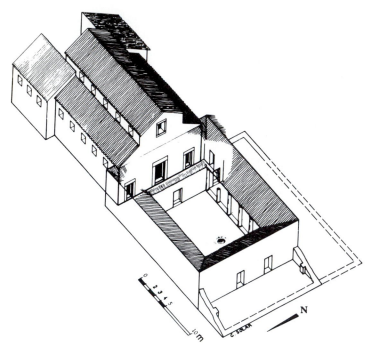

Ḥorvat Brachot: reconstruction of church and atrium

ing strip of mosaic pavement indicates that the width of the southern rooms was 5.3 m. Poor preservation and the limited scale of our excavations did not permit a clear understanding of the internal division of these chambers. Very probably they were part of a monastery adjoining the church. The absence of a main entrance in the western wall is surprising, in view of the splendor of the church and the fine workmanship lavished on its construction.

Chronological Conclusions

In the first phase a natural cave was converted into a shrine by plastering the walls and paving the floor with mosaics. This activity should be dated to the fourth century, probably to its second half.

Because we found no definite chronological data (in written sources, inscriptions or coins), our conclusions rest solely on archaeological considerations and on a comparative analysis of the architecture and the mosaics.

In the second phase, probably in the mid-sixth century, a magnificent church was erected on the site, and the cave was exploited as a crypt. We base this chronology on comparisons with dated sixth-century mosaics, mostly with the later ones found in Martyrius' monastery at Maᶜale Adummim (see pp. 170–196).[4] There is a great similarity in composition, design and technique between the two, and they may have been produced by the same artist.

In the third phase, the church was deserted, apparently in the late seventh century, some time after the Arab Conquest. The main period of Arab occupation at the site should be dated to the first half of the eighth century.

[4] See the discussion by Rina Talgam in Y. Magen and R. Talgam, "The Monastery of Martyrius at Maᶜale Adummim (Khirbet el-Muraṣṣaṣ) and Its Mosaics," *CAHL*, pp. 91–152, especially pp. 148–149; and in this volume, Y. Magen, "The Monastery of St. Martyrius at Maᶜale Adummim," pp. 170–196.

The Churches of Herodium

Ehud Netzer, Rivka Birger-Calderon and Ayala Feller

Herodium, located about 5 km southeast of Bethlehem, is an example of one of the opulent sites built by King Herod, the great builder, and it bears his name. Here he constructed a huge complex comprising a palace, a fortress, a district capital, and the king's burial monument. An unusual round fortified palace was erected at the top of an artificial and modified hill, while the larger part of the complex was located at the base of the latter — in Lower Herodium.

Excavations conducted on the mound by V. Corbo of the Franciscan Biblical School in 1962–1967, exposed, in addition to the Herodian remains, a few ruins from the Byzantine era, including a chapel. The latter was built into the Herodian ruins (its southern and western walls are from Herodian times). The chapel is 7.8 m long and 3.4 m wide. At its eastern extremity is an apse, 2.6 m in diameter, recessed into the eastern wall. However, no traces were found of a mosaic floor or other characteristic features of Byzantine churches. This chapel apparently served a group of monks who chose to make their abode at the top of the round hill.

After the discovery of the Byzantine ruins on the hilltop, the presence of further Byzantine remains was to be expected also among the ruins of Lower Herodium. What was surprising, however, was their quantity and dispersion throughout the site. The crowning glory of the Byzantine finds were three basilica-type churches.[1]

The ruins of Lower Herodium, which extend over 15 hectares (38 acres), provided an excellent base for the settlement in the Byzantine period of new residents at a site that had been abandoned for around 400 years. In some cases the new inhabitants cleared out the ruins and settled within them, making maximum use of every wall, room, and pool. Alternatively, new buildings were erected, some atop and others alongside the ruins, usually exploiting stones taken from them.

The three churches uncovered in Lower Herodium, in the order of their discovery, are:

1. The northern church (excavated in 1973, 1978), located north of the Bethlehem–Tekoa road, atop ruins from the Herodian era.

2. The eastern church (excavated in 1979–1980), located north of the mount upon the ruins of a large structure which almost certainly functioned as a wing of the central palace of Lower Herodium. Some of the structure's original walls served the church building as foundations.

3. The central church (excavated in 1981–1983), adjoining the south of the "monumental building" near the large pool at the heart of Lower Herodium. This church was erected on top of ruins from the Herodian period; its builders reused stones from an elaborate

---

[1] The churches were discovered in 1973–1983 during excavations directed by Ehud Netzer on behalf of the Institute of Archaeology of The Hebrew University of Jerusalem, in cooperation with the archaeology officer of Judea and Samaria and the Israel Exploration Society. Rivka Birger, Rachel Bar-Nathan, Egon Lass, and David Stacey were members of the excavation staff. Surveying was carried out by Ehud Netzer, and photographs were taken by Zev Radovan. We would like to thank Leah Di Segni, who deciphered and studied the inscriptions, and Anat Cohen, who drew the plans. See also E. Netzer, "The Byzantine Churches of Herodion," *CAHL*, pp. 165–176; L. Di Segni, "The Greek Inscriptions in the Northern and Eastern Churches at Herodion," ibid., pp. 17–190.

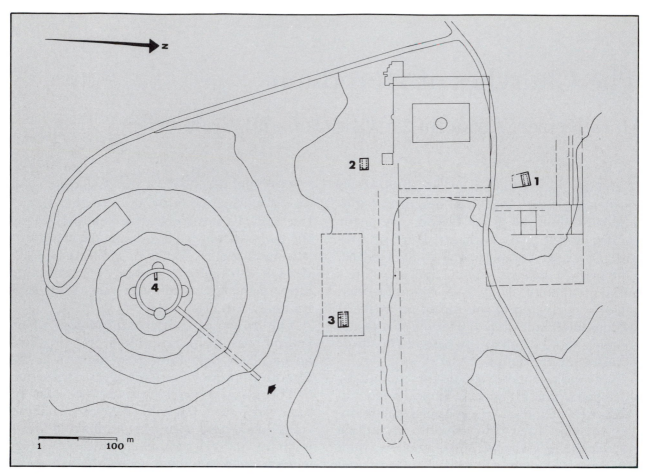

Herodium: location of churches — 1) The northern church; 2) The central church; 3) The eastern church; 4) The chapel built above the fortified palace on the mount

monument whose location has not yet been ascertained, and could possibly have served as Herod's tomb. Unlike the other two churches, this building was preceded by a structure (perhaps a chapel or burial chamber), also from the Byzantine period.

The three churches have several features in common: all were built on a similar scale (moderate size); all have a basilican design and are graced with mosaic floors; all have two small *pastophoria* rooms, on either side of the apse, and all include a baptistery — in two cases in a room located south of the *bema* (*presbyterium*), and in the third, in a chapel-like room adjacent to the south end of the main hall.

The Northern Church

The inner dimensions of the church's hall were 8.5 m in width and 10.4 m in length. The nave, together with the *bema*, was 13.1 m long. The *bema* is rectangular; in place of the regular round apse there is a rectangular room open toward the main hall. On either side of the rectangular *bema* there is a small room. The hall itself is surrounded on three sides (north, south, and west) by a built-in bench, a rare phenomenon in churches from the Byzantine era. Square pillars, four on each side, separated the lateral aisles from the nave. The pillars did not have decorated bases, and apparently lacked capitals. The columns supported stone arcades, evidence of which was found among the building's ruins.

The hall of the church, like its other rooms, had a mosaic floor, most of which has been preserved (see Pl. XVIa). The mosaics were carpetlike; there was one along the nave,

Herodium: general view of the northern church, from the southwest

others along the aisles (one for each aisle), and small mosaic panels in the intercolumniations. The designs comprised simple geometric shapes, each carpet having a different decoration. At the eastern extremity of the large carpet, a five-line Greek dedication inscription was set in a *tabula ansata*. It reads:

> O Lord the Son(?) Christ and holy Michael, receive the offering of Thy servants, the children of Ioulesas, the brothers Saphrica and Anael and their households, and of Salaeos and his children, and of Abraam and his children, and of Zana and Nonna and Nonna's daughter Zana.

The *bema*, too, had a mosaic floor (indicated by the negative impressions of the tesserae in the mortar bed). In its center, evidence of the altar table was found — impressions of two of the altar's four pillars — and below there was a rectangular niche, in which a reliquary had probably been laid. The *bema* was surrounded by a chancel screen, of which no traces remain. There are signs that an *ambo* had originally existed at its northern edge, but it had been removed already during the church's existence.

The small room (1.9 × 2.2 m) south of the *bema* had a basin in its center (approximately 60 × 60 cm), which was built of and coated with mortar and partially sunken into the white mosaic floor. This was most likely a baptismal font, and the room itself was a baptistery. The chamber, similar in size, north of the *bema* also had a mosaic floor, decorated with rows of flowers and other patterns. Its function is not clear; it may have served as a

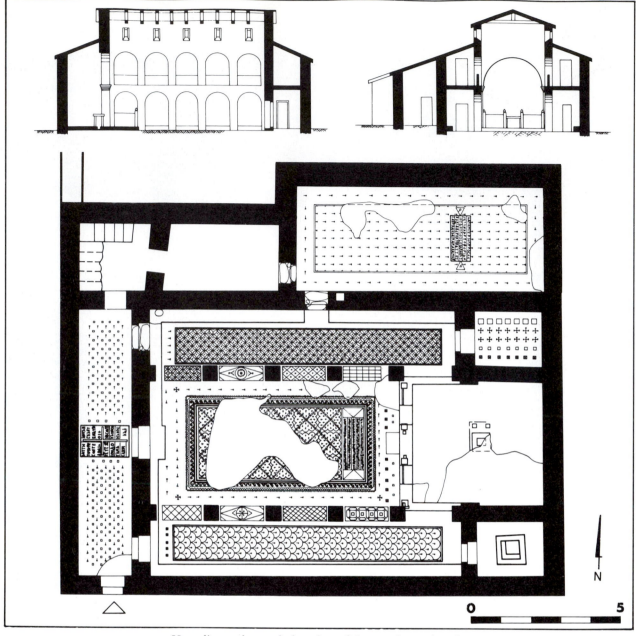

Herodium: plan and elevation of the northern church

prothesis, namely a room for the preparation of the bread and wine for the Eucharist.

The church hall was entered from the west, via the narthex, through three entrances. The central entrance led into the nave, each of the lateral ones led into one of the aisles. The narthex was narrow (1.8 m wide), about as long as the width of the main hall, and was entered from the south (from a courtyard that has not yet been excavated), not from the west as is usual. It was entirely covered with mosaics comprising alternating rows of

flowers and squares. In its center, opposite the central entrance, a dedication inscription in Greek was uncovered (see Pl. XVIc):

> This is the gate to the Lord, the righteous shall enter into it. O Lord the Son, Christ remember Thy servant Anael and Saprica.

The first part is taken from Psalms 117:20 (MT. 118:20), which was commonly inscribed at church entrances. Note that the Saprica mentioned in this inscription is probably not

Herodium: mosaic in southern aisle of
the northern church, looking east

Herodium: narthex of the northern church,
looking south

Herodium: inscription in hall of the northern church

Herodium: inscription in eastern room north of
the northern church's nave, looking east

Saphrica of the first inscription — Anael's
sister — but perhaps his wife. The inscription,
orientated westward, is laid out in an uncon-
ventional manner. It has the appearance of a
gate incorporating a cross which in effect
divides it into four panels, the upper two of
which bear the first part of the inscription,
while the lower two contain its second part.

Three rooms lay alongside the main church
hall and the narthex on the north. The eastern one was the largest (3.5 × 7.6 m). It had a
mosaic floor consisting of rows of flowers, and
in its center a Greek dedication inscription
(also five lines) was laid down in a *tabula
ansata*. It reads:

> Saint Michael, receive the offering of
> your servant Anael and his household,
> Saprica and Mamas. Amen.

In this inscription, the names of Anael and
his wife, Saprica, are joined by that of their
son, Mamas; this text, therefore, may be later
than that in the narthex. Possibly this room,
which was entered directly from the main hall,
served as a chapel. Most of its eastern wall is
destroyed, so that the existence of an apse
there cannot be ascertained.

The westernmost and smallest of the three
rooms had a staircase leading to the upper
story. This room was entered from the
narthex. In any event, the existence of an
upper story is clearly evidenced both above
the lateral aisles (which were colonnaded galleries) and above the narthex. Its remains —
debris comprising tesserae and the mortar on

which they were laid — indicate that it was
also paved with a course, white mosaic. The
third room, situated between the westernmost
chamber and the "chapel," could be entered
from the stairwell. The last two rooms were
paved with white tesserae interspersed with a
few red and black stones, with no pattern.

The mosaic patterns unearthed in the first
church are typical of mosaic floors of the
Byzantine period. The design in the nave
resembles that in the Eshtemoᶜa and Susiya
synagogues, in the first church in Bethany
(fourth–fifth century), in the Church of
Ḥosen (555 C.E.), in the Church of Peter and
Paul in Gerasa (after 533 C.E.), and elsewhere.

The three inscriptions discovered in the
northern church are of considerable interest.
All of them bear the names of the same family
of donors. The first two include the same
form of address: κ(ύρι)ε ΰ(ιο)ς χ(ριστό)ς, "O
Lord, the Son, Christ." Most uncommon is
the appearance of ΰιος, "the Son," and not
the common abridged version, Ἰ(ησοῦ)ς =
"Jesus." It is possible that this is merely a
textual error, but that seems unlikely, as it
appears in both inscriptions. The notation
"the Son" does not correspond to the usual
Orthodox Christian formula. Leah Di Segni,
who read and published the inscriptions,
raised the possibility that it expressed the
belief of non-Orthodox Christians, followers
of a Gnostic Judeo-Christian sect. These sects,
which proliferated in the second and third
centuries C.E., had mostly disappeared by the
fourth century, but groups of them apparently lingered on in the East, at least until the
sixth century C.E. A further indication of
possible Gnostic inspiration was the choice of
the archangel Michael as patron of the
church. The cult of angels was especially
widespread among the Gnostic sects, with particular stress on the role of Michael, who was
identified in certain cases with Jesus himself.
On the other hand, the earlier Orthodox
Church Fathers did not view the angel cult
favorably, and it was only at the start of the
sixth century that the intensification of the
cult among the population, and the disappear-

ance of Gnostic sects, brought about official Church approval of this phenomenon.

The names in the inscriptions are on the whole local or Semitic. Ioulesas is derived from the Roman Julius, but has a local suffix. The name Saphrica, or Saprica, is found chiefly in Egypt and Syria, while Anael-Hanael and Abraam are biblical. Zana was a rare, feminine form of the name Zanos that appears in southern Palestine. The name Nona was particularly common in Palestine, but also in Syria and Egypt. Mamas and Salaeos (Salaḥ) are Semitic connotations that were common in the area.

The donors all belonged to one family. Saphrica and Anael were brother and sister. The other Saprica was Anael's wife (the duplicity of the name may indicate a familial relation). From an epigraphic point of view, the church inscriptions belong to the end of the fifth century or the first half of the sixth century C.E. The fact that the inscription in the room north of the main hall includes the name of the child Mamas may indicate that that chamber, or at least its floor, was an addition to the already built church.

The Eastern Church

The inner dimensions of the main hall were 12.3 m in length and 8.3 m in width. The nave, together with the apse at the end of the *bema*, was approximately 14 m long. As in the northern church, here too there were small rooms on either side of the *bema*, but in this case only part of one, that south of the apse, has survived. Rows of columns — which almost certainly were originally monoliths — separated the aisles from the nave. The columns were stood on roughly worked pedestals. No remnants of their capitals have been uncovered in the excavations.

The main hall (like the other rooms of the church) was decorated with mosaics, which have mostly been destroyed; parts, however, have been preserved, particularly in the west. Here too, mosaic carpets decorated the nave and each of the lateral aisles, and small panels paved the intercolumniations. The most beautiful of these mosaics is that of the nave, which

Herodium: view of southern aisle of the northern church, looking east

has three rows of medallions formed by vine-scrolls with bunches of grapes, leaves, and tendrils. The medallions were filled with animals and birds. In the first row on the west, a peacock faces the central medallion, in which a section of an acanthus leaf has been preserved. The peacock itself has been destroyed, perhaps by iconoclasts, and restored in the shape of a leaf. In the second row, from the left, a lion has been preserved almost in its entirety (see Pl. XVId), and beside it, in this row's central medallion, the top half of an eagle's head. In the third row, only the bottom part of a bird's legs has been preserved. The remaining mosaics in the main hall were decorated with rich geometrical patterns. An unusual phenomenon observed here were signs of red, yellow and green paint on the underfloor beneath the mosaics, in the shape

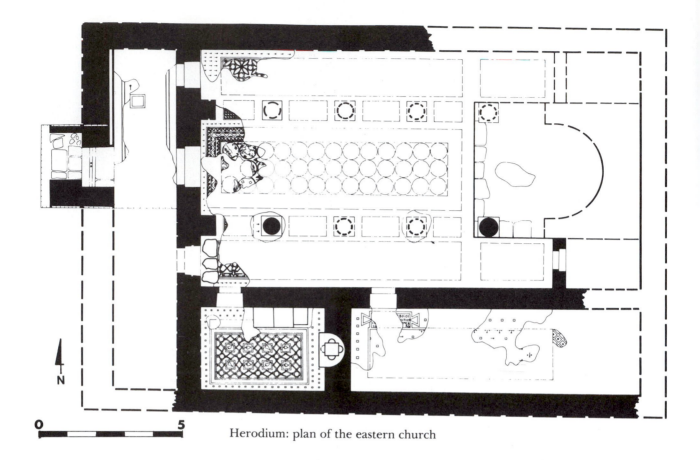

Herodium: plan of the eastern church

Herodium: two southern rooms of the eastern church,
looking east

of the medallions and the figures within them.
These markings helped the mosaicists lay the
tesserae.

The *bema* in this church is mostly destroyed,
and the remains of the apse foundations at its
edge could hardly be discerned. The main hall
was entered through three entrances from a
narrow narthex, as in the northern church.
The latter, which was as long as the church's
width, and 2.5 m wide, was excavated only in
part. A crude mosaic was discovered in the
narthex, with a simple black frame and
flowers.

Two rooms were unearthed south of the
main hall. Both were entered from the southern aisle of the main hall. The western one
(2.9 × 4.5 m) served as a baptistery. Its small
baptismal font was built inside a niche in the
center of the eastern wall; it is plastered and
cruciform. The floor of the room was decorated with a mosaic of unusual geometrical
design — eight squares with leaves and circles

226

enclosing rosettes. Under the floor, in the north, a plundered tomb was unearthed, covered by stone slabs.

The second room — probably a chapel — is larger than the first (about 2.9 m wide and at least 7.8 m long), but destroyed on its eastern side. Its pavement had a black mosaic frame, with patterns of flowers and squares both within and without (here too evidence of colored outlines on the mosaic bed were discovered). Opposite the entrance door a four-line Greek inscription was laid in a *tabula ansata*. Only a small part of it has survived:

> ... for the salvation of those (the benefactors) ... Amen.

The last line may possibly have contained the name of the church. In any case, the letters are quite different from those in the northern church, apparently indicating a later date in the second half of the sixth century (or even the beginning of the seventh century) C.E.

There are indications (rough mosaic stones that fell from above) that the eastern church, like the northern one, also had a gallery above the lateral aisles and the narthex. The stairwell, however, has not yet been discovered.

Mosaics of populated vinescrolls, such as that unearthed in the eastern church at Herodium, were widespread in Palestine in the fifth and sixth centuries C.E. both in churches and synagogues.

The Central Church

Whereas the northern and eastern churches were apparently built as independent structures, the central church was incorporated into a block of buildings which also included the remains of the Herodian "monumental structure," cleared of its ruins and divided into a number of rooms.

The inner dimensions of the main hall were 11.4 m in length and 10.2 m in width. The nave, together with the apse at the edge of the *bema*, was 13.8 m long. Here too the apse was flanked by two small rooms. Between each of the lateral aisles and the nave was a row of four columns, probably monoliths; they stood

Herodium: general view of the central church against the background of the mount

Herodium: general view of the central church, looking west

227

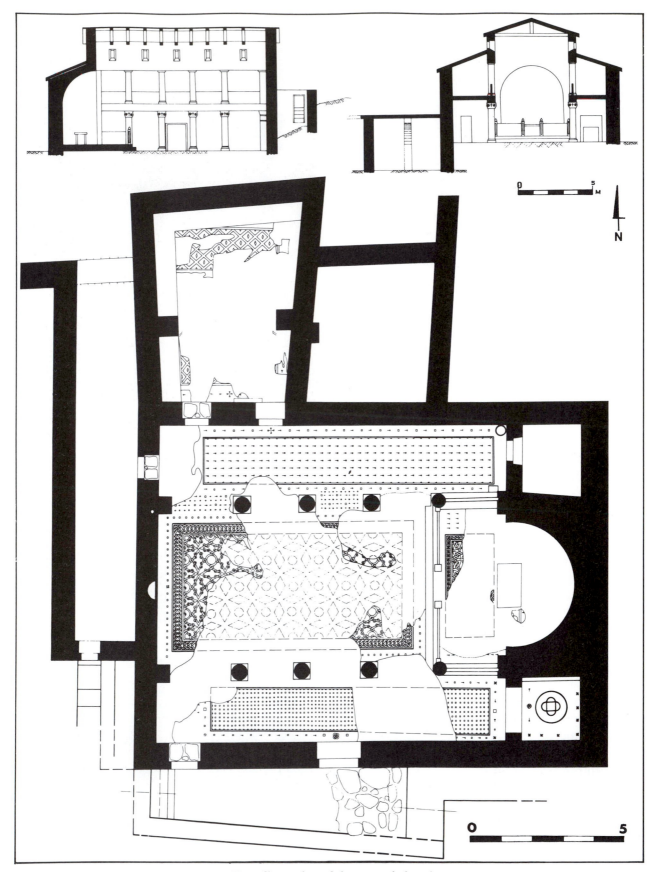

Herodium: plan of the central church

on crudely-worked bases. The excavations unearthed some of the capitals, each different from the others.

The church's main hall was originally covered in mosaics, with a central "carpet" for the nave and an additional "panel" in each aisle; they have been largely preserved. The decoration of the nave's mosaic comprised a complex geometric design, combining lozenges and circles, while in the aisles the patterns were ornamental. Unlike the other two churches, here there were no separate "panels" in the intercolumniations, but instead rows of background pattern (flowers and squares), similar to but more dense than that surrounding the "carpets" of the nave and aisles.

The complex pattern of the nave's mosaic is unusual (see Pl. XVIb). It resembles that of the second church in Bethany (postdating 427 C.E.) but also the mosaics of Khirbet al-Mefjer of the Early Arab period. The patterns in the aisles are representative of common Byzantine designs, such as those in the church of Ḥorvat Berachot.

The *bema* of the central church was also paved with a geometric mosaic, of which only a small part has been preserved. Remains of frescoes with geometrical patterns — and perhaps also vinescrolls — were discerned on the walls of the apse and in the debris. Apparently the entire church was ornamented in a similar manner. Likewise, decorated fragments of plaster were found. The center of the *bema* bears traces of the altar legs. The former was surrounded by a chancel screen, the posts of which, on either side of the entrance to the *bema*, were apparently made of marble, whereas its panels (at least the lateral ones) were built and coated with plaster. In the western wall of the nave, opposite the apse, a small niche was hewn from the natural rock approximately 80 cm above the floor level.

As in the northern church, here too the baptistery was situated in the southern side room (ca. 2 × 2 m) of the apse. In its center stood the baptismal font, hewn out of a single stone, shaped like the drum of a column, 1.1 m

Herodium: baptismal font in the central church

in diameter and 85 cm high. The font was quatrefoil and had a square recess at the bottom. A small cross was engraved in the wall of the font. The mosaic floor of the baptistery, around the font, had a combination of flowers and geometrical shapes, and a cruciform decoration at the front of the font. The baptistery had no door, but opened onto the southern aisle along almost its entire width. North of the apse was another small room (partly destroyed), the floor of which was also mosaic, apparently white.

The main entrance to the church hall was from the south (not the west), and there was no narthex. In front of the entrance was a paved area, rather like a front porch, which apparently had no roof. Unlike the other two churches, which were built under better topographic conditions, the southwest corner of this church was hewn out of natural rock. Thus access from the west was difficult. The location of the main entrance at the south was possibly related to the fact that a large cistern was situated nearby. The latter was apparently built in Herod's time and is still used today.

Another entrance to the main hall was discovered in the west, opposite the northern aisle. This entrance was no doubt of secondary importance, and was later blocked. The area to the west was partly bounded by a corridor, the floor of which was never leveled, but followed the natural contour of the bedrock that sloped from south to north. Possibly there was a second story over this corridor, which led into the galleries (at least the northern one) above the lateral aisles. The topographic layout here was such that it was possible to enter the galleries even without a stairwell. Evidence of a second story above the lateral aisles and perhaps above the corridor on the west as well is provided by the abundant debris of mosaic stones with the plaster on which they were laid.

Only one other room (discounting the two small chambers on either side of the apse) was directly connected to the main hall. This room adjoined the northern aisle near the northwestern corner of the hall. It was trapezoidal in shape and offered access to the main hall via two entrances — one of which was eventually blocked. The room was originally paved with mosaics with geometric designs, which underwent many repairs and modifications. In the course of time, benches were built along two of the walls (on top of the original mosaic floor). These benches incorporated built-in supports for the head or upper part of the body.

As already pointed out, most of the central church was built of stones taken from the nearby Herodian monument. Many had a central boss, and some were even decorated. The two pairs of rooms at the northern end of the church (alongside the room with the benches) were also built of the same material, but they had separate entrances. (No other stones of this type were found anywhere else on the excavation site.)

An earlier building apparently overlapped the western third of the main hall of the church. An opening in the southern wall that was later blocked (the threshold of which is 1.3 m above the church floor) belonged to this building, and an underground trapezoidal cell, discovered underneath the nave, must also have been part of it. There is no doubt that the ceiling of this cell was dismantled, and that the cell itself went out of use once the church was built. It may have served as a tomb earlier in the Byzantine period.

Conclusion

The three churches of Lower Herodium are situated close to one another. Although the presence of a number of churches in one settlement was not an unusual phenomenon, this concentration raises questions. Are we dealing here with a small town, a large village, or was the site in whole or part a monastery, similar to those in the nearby Judean Desert? Furthermore what was the connection between the three churches we excavated and the monastery that was identified on the ruins of the palace of the hill fortress? Was the place in fact inhabited by a Gnostic sect?[2]

The three churches excavated in Herodium have the character of village churches, similar in size and shape to other such edifices in Judea from the Byzantine period. Nonetheless, they do have a number of distinctive features. The northern church has no apse. Instead there is a rectangular room opening onto the main hall along its entire length. This is a somewhat unusual phenomenon in Palestine, although it is occasionally found in chapels, such as those in Mataᶜ or Gibeon. In Syria, on the other hand, this layout is quite common. Butler, the surveyor of the Syrian

[2] The anthropologist J. Zias recently proposed identifying Byzantine Herodium with the "Prodisia" hospital, which, according to Nicephorus Calistus (a late source from the fourteenth century), was built by Empress Eudocia in the mid-fifth century C.E. This source indicates that the hospital was designed to care for 400 sufferers from the "holy disease," that is, leprosy. Zias bases his identification on the phonetic similarity between the Byzantine word "Prodisia" and the Arabic name for Herodium, Jebel Fureidis. The late date of the Calistus source and the lack of proof that "Prodisia" was in fact Herodium render this hypothesis unlikely.

churches, suggests that its profusion resulted from the fact that apseless churches were easier to build.

One of the interesting features of Herodium is the presence of a baptismal font in each of the churches. Usually, when there were a number of churches in one locality, there was a single baptismal font which served all. Another point of interest in this context is the unusual location of two of the baptismal fonts (those in the northern and central churches) in a room flanking the apse, to the south. This phenomenon is known from Kursi, where in 585 C.E. a baptismal font was installed in the room south of the apse. The location in the eastern church, in a chapel south of the main hall, was more conventional. Such a placement is found in the monastery church on Mt. Nebo, where the baptismal font is also extremely similar to that discovered in the central church at Herodium. Similar fonts, fashioned from a monolithic stone, were discovered in Teko^ca, near Herodium, and in Emmaus.

Another extraordinary feature at Herodium are the benches in the northern church along three walls of the main hall. This rare design is known mainly from eastern Transjordan [at Gerasa, there were benches around the entire main hall in the Mortuary Church, and a bench along the northern wall in the "Synagogue" Church; and at Khirbet Mukhayat (Nebo), there was a bench along the western wall of the Church of Amos and Closis]. In any case, we still do not know whether wooden benches were used in churches during this period.

All three churches in Lower Herodium had rooms north or south of the main halls. Their function was connected with the liturgy of the church, and they were usually built at the same time as the rest of the edifice, or shortly thereafter. They occasionally were used as chapels, and in one case as a baptistery. Such rooms may well have served for the collection of offerings (diaconicon) and for preparing the Eucharist.

Only two of the three churches of Lower Herodium (the northern and eastern ones) had a narthex. Apparently its absence in the central church was due to topographic constraints, and not liturgical considerations. The main entrance to two of the churches (the northern and central ones) was in the south, and in the eastern one in the west, as was common.

The great similarity in design of the main halls of the three Herodium churches relates also to their mosaics. The composition of all three employs the same scheme: a central carpet with a main motif and an ornate frame in the nave, carpets with simple frames in the lateral aisles, and (in two churches) small panels in the intercolumniations. Rows of flowers and decorative patterns against a white background surrounded the main carpets. There is also a general resemblance between the mosaics in the rooms adjoining the main halls.

In spite of similarities in general appearance and composition, however, there are clear differences in technique and in the choice of decorative patterns. In the northern church, in the main hall and the narthex, the range of colors is small — four colors and tones — and the tesserae are mainly uniform in size, which gives the mosaics, and in particular the geometric designs, a two-dimensional character. In the eastern church, on the other hand, there is a richer use of color — about twelve colors and shades — and the size of the tesserae varies according to the pattern. As a result, there is greater variety in the mosaics of this church, and a greater play of light and shade. The central church has about nine colors and tones, and here too there are differences in the size of the tesserae in the nave and the lateral aisles, but to a lesser degree than in the eastern church.

This variety may indicate different workshops or periods. The vinescrolls in the eastern church should be assigned to the sixth century C.E., perhaps even to its second half. The mosaics of the northern church, which are notably simpler, apparently predate the eastern church, and may possibly belong to the end of the fifth century or the beginning of the sixth century C.E. We are inclined to

Herodium: mosaic pavement of the central
church's nave

Herodium: mosaic pavement of the northern
church's nave

date the mosaics of the central church to a later stage than the other two churches.

It would seem, thus far, that the best criteria for dating the churches are the mosaic floors and the inscriptions incorporated into them. According to these criteria and to general considerations (such as a comparison of the design of the churches), the churches were apparently built between the end of the fifth century and the middle, or even the end, of the sixth century C.E. Although we cannot ascertain this, it would seem that they were constructed in the following order: first the northern church in the second half of the fifth century, or perhaps in the beginning of the sixth; then the eastern church, in the second half of the sixth century. As to the central church, we cannot be sure whether it was the second or the last to be built, but the latter possibility seems more likely.

All of the churches display signs of renovation, some pertaining to regular maintenance, such as additional layers of plaster or floor repairs, and some to changes and additions, such as the blocking of the entrances. It would appear, therefore, that the churches were in use for a relatively long time, probably including the Early Arab period.

Chapels and Hermitages of St. Sabas' Monastery

Joseph Patrich

The Monastery of St. Sabas (Mar Saba), known in ancient sources as the Great Laura (ηεγίσίη λαύρα), was a colony of anchorites founded by St. Sabas in 478 C.E. on the cliffs of the Kidron Gorge (Wadi en-Nar). The present Mar Saba Monastery is the remnant of that great establishment, and marks the location of the center of the laura (that is, a monastery of hermits). The monastery complex is today comprised of two ancient churches, the tomb of St. Sabas in the courtyard between them, a communal dining room, a kitchen, a bakery, storerooms, about twenty cisterns, dwelling cells for the dozen or so monks who live there, and a hostel that, on the feast day of St. Sabas (December 5), is crowded with about two hundred pilgrims. The remains of the ancient laura extend for approximately 2 km along both banks of the ravine to the south and to the north of Mar Saba. The area close to the center, for about 250 m in both directions, which was more densely built and populated, is at present in a very poor state of preservation. However, farther away dwelling units of hermits have been detected, and in several cases, in which the preservation is surprisingly good, very detailed plans of hermitages have been obtained.

In the archaeological survey conducted in the area in 1982–1983, the remains of about forty-five hermitages of the Laura of St. Sabas were explored (see map on p. 235).[1] The term "hermit cell" cannot generally be applied to them because in many cases they are quite spacious complexes, composed of several components — dwelling chambers, a storage space, a courtyard, and a water system for both collection and storing. Such a compound was usually inhabited by a lone monk, but in several cases it served more than one: an old hermit and his disciple or servant, or monks with the same ethnic origin or common religious approach.

The remains of a chapel, or a private oratory, in about twelve of the complexes were explored in the survey. They are usually distinguished from the regular dwelling chambers by a prayer niche in the eastern wall and by their elaborate decorations.

Small caves are the simplest type of habitation found at the laura. They characterize the first period in its history (478–483 C.E.), when hermits gradually began to gather around St. Sabas, wishing to live under his guidance and spiritual influence. In these a simply-hewn prayer niche was found. This was the case in the cave of St. Sabas, no. 37, on the eastern bank of the ravine.[2] According to the traditions of the Mar Saba monks, his first abode was here. It is a natural cave, 6 m long and up to 3.2 m wide, situated on top of a narrow, vertical rock cleft. A mat was spread on the floor, and an icon portraying Sts. Anthony and Macarius, the fathers of Egyp-

[1] The survey was carried out on behalf of the "Archaeological Survey of Israel." I am indebted to the members of the team: Erez Cohen and Beni Levenshtein (surveyors), and Asaf Ron, Ḥamutal Kishon, and Efrat Shechter. Special thanks are due to Leah Di Segni and to Yad Izhak Ben-Zvi, The Institute for the Research of Eretz Israel, Its People and Cultures, for placing at my disposal a Hebrew translation, yet unpublished, of the

relevant Byzantine sources. See also J. Patrich, "The Monastic Institutions of Saint Sabas — An Archaeological-Historical Research," Ph.D diss., The Hebrew University of Jerusalem, 1989 (Hebrew).

[2] For details of the laura and its structure, see Cyrillus Scythopolitanus (Kyrillos von Skythopolis), *Vita Sabae*, ed. E. Schwartz (Leipzig, 1939), pp. 85–200.

The Great Laura of St. Sabas (Mar Saba)

tian monasticism, was placed inside the niche.

We did find a prayer niche cut into the eastern wall of a dwelling chamber, and not a separate chapel, in Hermitage 15. The niche — 0.8 m wide, 0.5 m deep, and 1.5 m high — is rectangular and was hewn at its top and built at its bottom. The chamber, which is entered from the south, is 5 m long and 2.5 m wide. The niche was not cut in the middle of the eastern wall (as would be expected if it were a chapel), but farther to the north of center. The walls of the chamber and of the prayer niche were covered with white lime plaster. The whole chamber may have been converted into an oratory in a second phase, after an additional dwelling place was built nearby.

Hermitage 43 has a chapel, which measures 2.3 × 3.2 m and is entered from the south.

The chapel is located inside a natural cave, the sides of which were revetted with masonry walls in order to create a balanced space. The prayer niche is rectangular and is sunk into the eastern revetment wall. Two rounded, broader niches were hewn in the northern revetment wall. In several places traces of red paint are preserved on the white lime plaster that covered the walls and the niches.

A proper chapel was built against the cliff in Hermitage 32, which was used by at least two monks. Apparently, due to topographical limitations, it was built as a broadhouse 6 m long and 3 m wide, and was entered from the south through an antechamber 3.5 m long and 3 m wide. A well-made semicircular niche — 1.3 m high, 0.75 m wide, and 0.35 m deep — was hewn in the center of the eastern rock

234

Mar Saba: the first cave of St. Sabas (no. 37)

Mar Saba: prayer niche and mosaic floor in chapel of Hermitage no. 37

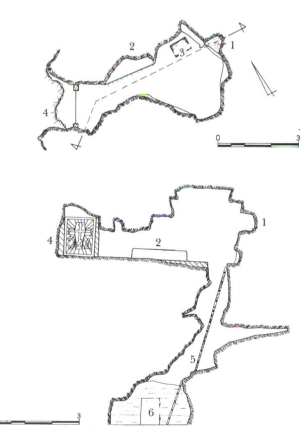

Mar Saba: plan of the first cave of St. Sabas (no. 37) — 1) Prayer niche; 2) bench; 3) Entrance shaft; 4) Iron cancellus; 5) Ladder; 6) Lower entrance

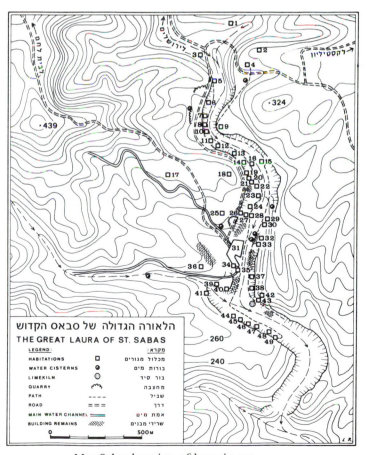

Mar Saba: location of hermitages

wall. The surface of this hemispherical niche is still coated with a plaster composed of lime mixed with crushed potsherds on a layer of flat stone chips. A smaller niche — an irregular square — was cut to the right of the prayer niche. The floor of the chapel was paved with a white mosaic of rather large tesserae. The ceiling was supported by horizontal wooden beams that rested on the eastern rock wall and on the western masonry wall.

When space was limited, a chapel was constructed on a level above the dwelling chamber, as in Hermitage 21, which served a single monk, and Hermitage 29 (see below). The existence of the chapel in Hermitage 21 is indicated by a rounded niche — deep-cut into the upper rock and still partially covered with the original plaster. The reconstructed plan shows a room 2.6 m wide and 3.2 m long that was entered from the west.

In Hermitage 33, which had been inhabited by three monks, the chapel was inside a natural cave, 5.2 m wide at its entrance and 2.8 m deep. In this case, instead of a sunken prayer niche, a rock 1.1 m high and 1.05 m wide, projecting 0.6 m out of the eastern wall, served as an altar. The rock walls and the altar were covered with white lime plaster and the floor was paved with a simple white mosaic.

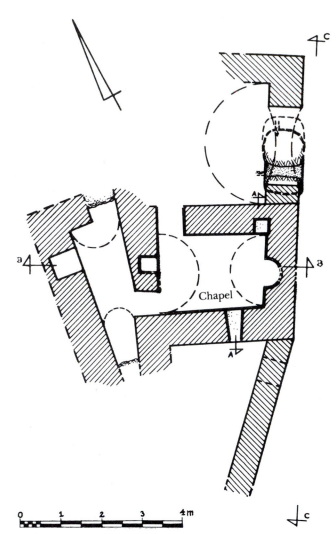

Mar Saba: plan of lower chapel of Hermitage no. 28
(E. Cohen)

A chapel is fully preserved in Hermitage 28, near the very bottom of the western bank of the ravine. It served a small group of monks. It is a rectangular chamber 2.7 m long and 1.8 m wide and is entered from the north. A semicircular prayer niche, now broken through, was hewn out of the eastern wall. To the left, in the northern wall, is a small rectangular niche. The ceiling, perfectly preserved, is a vault of unhewn stones consolidated with clinging mud. The floor is white lime plaster. The walls and the ceiling were covered with mud beneath white lime plaster.

The walls were embellished with colorful frescoes in various floral patterns created by overlapping circles, which were first incised on the white plaster with a compass and then drawn over with red pencil; afterward the

Mar Saba: altar and mosaic floor of chapel in
Hermitage no. 33

236

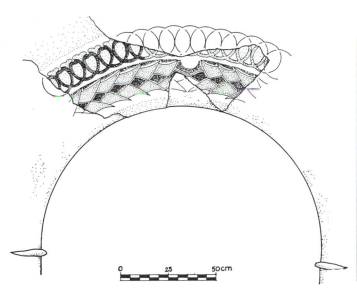

Mar Saba: fresco in lower chapel surrounding prayer niche (E. Cohen)

Mar Saba: two pieces of small concrete altar column, one of which has red cross painted on its white-washed surface (Hermitage no. 28)

areas between them were painted in various colors. The outer edge of the hemispheric dome of the niche, starting from two capital-like plaster projections, was surrounded by a semicircular garland, painted in yellow, green, black, pink, red, and light blue. On the southern wall a fragment is preserved of two interlaced strips, one of which is painted red.

Another chapel, entered from the west, with similar dimensions was traced on the upper story of Hermitage 28, above the chapel described above. Its walls have almost completely disappeared, and generally it is in a very poor state of preservation. The floor was covered with a simple white mosaic that was repaired with fragments of marble and schist plates. In the debris we found fragments of a perforated concrete chancel screen; two pieces of a small concrete altar column, respectively 8 and 7.5 cm in diameter, one of

Mar Saba: window panes in upper chapel (I. Stulman)

237

Mar Saba: remains of mosaic floor in chapel of
Hermitage no. 27

Mar Saba: drawing of mosaic floor in chapel of
Hermitage no. 27

Hermitage 27 is located farther to the west in the cliffs above. It is a vertical complex with six different levels of dwelling chambers and cisterns and was inhabited by several monks. The living quarters have ordinary white mosaic floors, but in what was presumably a chapel, a colorful mosaic floor was laid. Its pattern is carpetlike and composed of squares, lozenges, and triangles around a central "wreath." In each square there is a geometric pattern and in each lozenge and triangle a simple floral design. The emblem in the middle is damaged. The eastern wall of the chapel collapsed, but in the northern rock wall, a hewn rectangular niche 1.45 m high can be discerned.

Hermitage 29, on the opposite bank of the Kidron Gorge is attributed in local tradition to St. Johannes Hesychastes — once a bishop of Colonia in Armenia and one of the most distinguished of the laura's hermits, who lived there from 491 until 559 C.E. His biography is included in the writings of Cyril of Scythopolis, the hagiographer of the Palestinian desert monks.[3] The hermitage was hewn into a vertical cleft. Although it was extensive, it was built for a single monk. The chapel, which is very elaborate and has a wide apse, is situated above the 4-m-long and 2.7-m-wide dwelling cell. Two distinct building phases can be detected in the chapel: in the first a chapel 3 m long and 4 m wide was cut in the rock above a cistern. Its apse was 2.3 m wide and 1.5 m deep. The roof of the dwelling served as an open balcony in front of the chapel, providing light, and from here also entry to the chapel was gained. Access to the balcony from the chamber below was by means of a ladder from the southern side. The hermitage was approached from the northwest by a path running along a rock shelf. A water channel ran parallel to the path and fed the cistern.

In the second phase the entire cleft was closed by a wall about 11.5 m high which formed a climbing tower giving access to the dwelling cell and to the chapel above. The

which has a red cross painted on its white-washed surface; and fragments of a concrete altar plate. We also found an elongated small bronze leaf which presumably decorated a wooden cross. The window panes in the upper chapel were circular and were fixed into square frames made of concrete.

[3] Idem, *Vita Johannes Hesychastes*, ed. E. Schwartz (Leipzig, 1939), pp. 201–222.

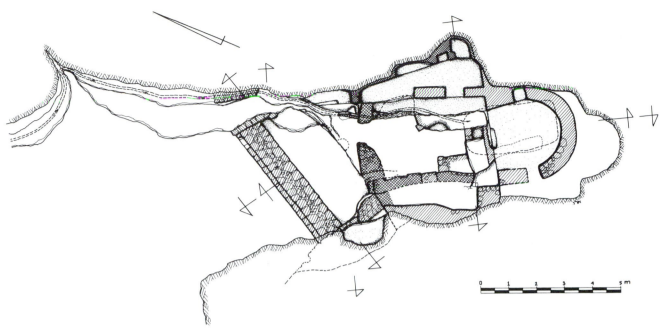

Mar Saba: plan of Hermitage no. 29 attributed to Johannes Hesychastes

Mar Saba: general view of Hermitage no. 29

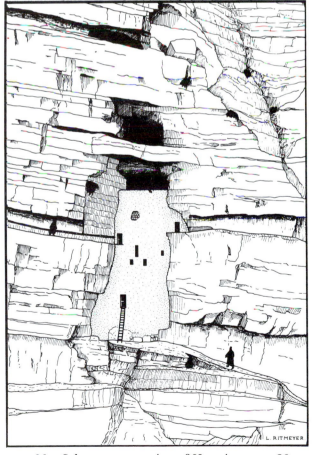

Mar Saba: reconstruction of Hermitage no. 29

239

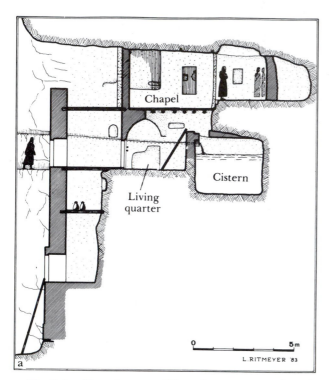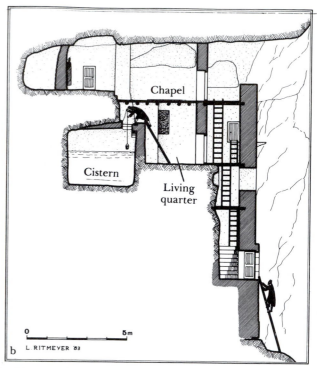

Mar Saba: Hermitage no. 29 — a) reconstructed section, looking north; b) reconstructed section, looking south

chapel now had a prayer room 4 m long and 3.9 m wide, two steps lower than the hoof-shaped apse, which was 2.2 m wide and 2.5 m deep. The apse was hewn to cover the entire area of the previous rock-cut chapel. At its northern side there was a small square niche; at its southern side a door led to the rear and upper areas of the natural cleft. The walls and the rock ceiling as well as the floor were plastered.

Three saints were painted on the wall of the apse on a single layer of plaster of excellent quality. Their faces were deliberately disfigured, and the shapes of their bodies are vague because they were repeatedly covered with red paint. The figures are identified by Greek inscriptions as Sts. Ananias, Zacharias, and Mishael. Presumably the original intention was to depict Daniel's three companions, Hananiah, Azariah, and Mishael. An inscription on the left of the three figures reads: "(The oratory) of St. Johannes of Colonia." There is no doubt that it was written after the saint's death. Probably, the other inscriptions, which are in a similar script, as well as the

drawings, were renewed at the same time.

The construction of the aedicule of the chapel in Hermitage 45 is exceptional. Local tradition erroneously attributes it to Arcadius, son of Xenophon. That is also the case with the traditions pertaining to the cells of his father and his brother Johannes (nos. 39 and 43, respectively) which are indicated nearby. These monks, contemporaries of St. Euthymius, may have lived in the Laura of St. Chariton near Tekoa, where the tomb of the two brothers was shown to the Russian abbot Daniel in 1106–1107.[4]

Hermitage 34 was used by a single monk. The cave has an open balcony in front of it, on top of a towerlike construction containing a cistern. The cave is divided by two barrier walls into a dwelling chamber (3.5 × 4 m), an oratory, and a rear storage space. This hermitage also had a very elaborate water-supply

[4] B. de Khitrovo (trans.), "Vie et pèlerinage de Daniel, hégoumène russe (1106–1107)," *Itinéraires Russes en Orient* (Geneva, 1889), p. 48. Abbot Daniel was guided on his tour through the monasteries of the desert by a monk from Mar Saba.

240

system that includes an upper tank and two connecting cisterns. The oratory was 5 m long and 4 m wide. The aedicule was built against the eastern wall near the northern corner and comprised three niches on a common base. The central niche was the largest. On the central semidome, two crosses were drawn in black, one above the other. All three niches were constructed with stone chips bound with mud and covered with mud plaster, the surface of which was whitewashed. The walls, the rock ceiling, and the floor were covered with a white lime plaster. On the eastern and western walls there are paintings of saints that have been dated to the eleventh and twelfth centuries; the ones on the ceiling date to the nineteenth century.[5]

"The House of St. Sophia" (no. 23), well preserved and recently reconstructed, exemplifies a small hermitage; it consists of a dwelling cell and an oratory separated by an inner court. Entry was gained through a forecourt that contained an underground cistern. The complex was surrounded by a high wall. The oratory is 2.7 × 2.2 m; in its corners there are some remains of a plain white mosaic floor. According to a Greek inscription from 657 C.E., the bones of St. Sophia, St. Sabas' mother, were transferred here. On the walls, paintings portraying the Crucifixion, Resurrection and the Dormition are preserved. There are two or three layers, the oldest attributed to the eleventh and twelfth centuries, the second to the eighteenth and nineteenth, while the uppermost one — depicting Christ on the cross — is accompanied by a recent English inscription.

Conclusions

On the basis of our observations, it can be assumed that each cell had a prayer niche or an altar containing a cross or an icon.[6] In the

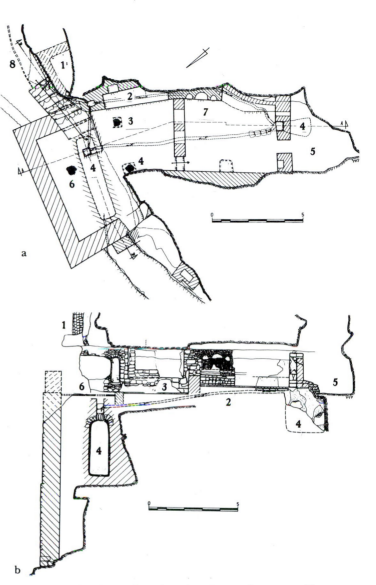

Mar Saba: plan (a) and section (b) of Hermitage no. 45 attributed to Arcadius, son of Xenophon — 1) Upper water reservoir; 2) Water channel; 3) Living quarter; 4) Cistern; 5) Rear area; 6) Verandah; 7) Chapel; 8) Path

more elaborate hermitages a separate room served as an oratory. There is an artist's touch apparent in the chapels, but not in the dwelling chambers. The chapels were embellished with colorful mosaics, frescoes and stucco. All the private chapels described here were an integral part of a hermitage and were used by the monks who dwelt in the nearby chambers. The chapels were not erected to commemorate the monks after their death. However, an elaborate hermitage with a chapel might have been built for the use of a distinguished monk,

[5] Cf. O. Meinardus, "Laurae and Monasteries of the Wilderness of Judaea," *LA* 16 (1965–1966): 350–356, where there is a detailed description of the wall paintings.

[6] An icon of the Virgin Mary holding Christ is mentioned in two of the narratives of Johannes Moschus. See *Pratum Spirituale* (Leimonarion) 45 and 180, ed. Migne; *Patrologia Graeca* 873, cols. 2900, 3052.

Mar Saba: Hermitage no. 23 known as "The House of St. Sophia"

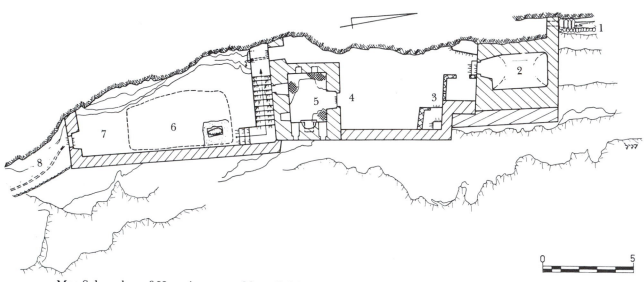

Mar Saba: plan of Hermitage no. 23 — 1) Water channel; 2) Hermit's cell; 3) Service structures;
4) Inner court; 5) Chapel; 6) Cistern; 7) Forecourt; 8) Path

242

either by the authorities of the laura or by his admirers or relatives.

The monks were buried in a communal site in the center of the laura and not in their chapels or dwelling chambers. In fact, a hermitage was never considered to be the property of the monk who lived there.

There is mention in literary sources of separate chapels for various ethnic groups such as Armenians, Syrians, or Iberians. However, everybody was obliged to celebrate on Saturday and Sunday the holy mysteries in the laura's two main churches, the *Theoktistos* and the *Theotokos*. If we interpret the function of the small rectangular niches frequently found in the chapels to the north or south of the prayer niche as being for the preparation of the Bread and Wine, the Eucharistic mass may have been celebrated there. If so, the hermit living in the adjacent dwelling must have had the status of an ordained priest, and special permission from the laura's Superior (*hegoumenos*) to be absent from the communal ceremony. We can assume, however, that the oratory was normally used for daily prayers which did not include the liturgy of the Eucharist.

Inside the walls of Mar Saba Monastery today there are two churches and four chapels. The central church, *Theotokos*, is dedicated to St. Mary, mother of Christ; the second one, *Theoktistos*, constructed inside a cave "made by God," is now dedicated to St. Nicholas. Both are continuations of those instituted by St. Sabas.

The chapel of Sts. Joachim and Ann, the parents of St. Mary, and that of St. John Chrysostom were erected in chambers which were previously monks' dwellings. The chapel of St. John of Damascus (dedicated also to St. John the Baptist) is located in the hermitage where he lived in the first half of the eighth century. It includes his tomb. The chapel of St. George is from a later date, as is that of the Archangels, which was erected about thirty years ago by Archimandrite Seraphim, the present Superior of the monastery. The above-mentioned four chapels serve all the monks of the laura and are not private chapels like those of the hermitages described above. Another chapel, dedicated to St. Simeon Stylites, is located in the nearby Women's Tower.

The Cave-Church at Khirbet ed-Deir

Yizhar Hirschfeld

A special type of church developed alongside the Judean Desert monasteries in the Byzantine period — the cave-church. The Judean Desert, with its numerous canyons and ravines, offered a plethora of natural caves, but few were selected for use as churches. One of them has been uncovered at Khirbet ed-Deir ("Ruin of the Monastery"). This site is located in a small canyon leading into Naḥal ꜤArugot, halfway between Tekoa and En-Gedi (grid ref. 1739/1038), and includes remains of a monastery of the Byzantine period, situated on a spur on the south. The box-canyon, enclosed

by sheer cliffs some 12 m high, is about 100 m long and 20–30 m wide.

The site was discovered during the Palestine Exploration Fund's Survey of Western Palestine in the second half of the 19th century,[1] and was identified by Marcoff and Chitty in the 1920s.[2] In 1982–1983, systematic archaeological excavations were conducted there, during which it became evident that the construction phase of the monastery is to be ascribed to the late fifth or early sixth century C.E., and that it was abandoned in the mid-seventh century C.E., apparently in the wake of the Muslim conquest.[3]

The builders of the monastery fully exploited the peculiar topography of the canyon and the spur above it. It was located on three different levels: in the bed of the canyon, the gardens were laid out; above them, abutting the northern canyon wall, the church complex and refectory were built; and above that, on the spur, the cells for the monks were erected. A paved pathway linked the three levels and their various elements, forming the main artery of life at the site. The church complex included the church proper, built into a cave, a baptistery and a burial crypt. These ele-

Khirbet ed-Deir: general plan of site (1:500). Note garden terraces in river bed

[1] C.R. Conder and H.H. Kitchener, *The Survey of Western Palestine*, III (London, 1883), p. 327.

[2] M. Marcoff and D.J. Chitty, "Notes on Monastic Research in the Judean Wilderness," *PEQ* 61 (1929): 178.

[3] The excavations were conducted within the framework of the Archaeological Survey of Israel, in conjunction with the Staff Officer for Archaeology, Judea and Samaria, and were generously supported by The Dorot Foundation. Youth groups from the the En Gedi Field School and the Geographical Circle of the United Kibbutz Movement took part in the work. The project was directed by the author and Rivka Birger. Erez Cohen served as surveyor, and the photographs were taken by Zev Radovan.

ments are interconnected and together comprise that part of the monastery devoted to worship.

The Cave-Church

A large, natural cave, the opening of which faced the canyon, was utilized for the church. This cave is 26 m wide and 3–13 m deep. Its ceiling rises some 5 m above the floor. This huge space was partitioned into a main prayer hall, a side chapel and three auxiliary chambers. The broad mouth of the cave was largely blocked by a well-built wall, 25 m long and 1–1.6 m thick. At the center of the wall is an aperture 1.2 m wide. In the excavations at the foot of the wall, numerous fragments of greenish glass panes were found — the remains of a window which had apparently been located in the wall's upper part. This window, together with the doorway, enabled daylight to penetrate into the interior.

The inner space of the cave was divided in accord with its function as a place of worship. Perpendicular to the outer wall, an internal partition was built, to set off the hall from the auxiliary chambers to the west. The rock walls of the cave were partly lined with masonry and then plastered over to obtain a uniform surface. The cavity of the apse was evened out by hewing, and a niche for relics was hewn in the eastern part of the cave. The rock floor was entirely paved with a mosaic, and the ceiling was coated with a thick layer of whitish plaster, fragments of which have survived *in situ*.

This construction work yielded a rectangular prayer hall measuring 9 × 11 m. In its eastern part, a *bema* measuring 5 × 7 m was raised. As was common in most churches in Palestine, this *bema* was surrounded by a chancel screen of marble. The 0.4-m-wide stylobate on which the slabs of the chancel screen stood remains *in situ*. The sockets for fixing the slabs are still visible in it. Prior to the excavations, a fragment of a greenish marble chancel screen panel was found on the sur-

Khirbet ed-Deir: aerial photograph, looking north. Note large cave at center right, refectory at left, and living quarters atop spur

Khirbet ed-Deir: the cave-church. To the right, the baptistery; to the left, entrance to burial crypt

Khirbet ed-Deir: general view of interior of cave-church, looking east

Khirbet ed-Deir: the bema in eastern part of cave-church, looking east

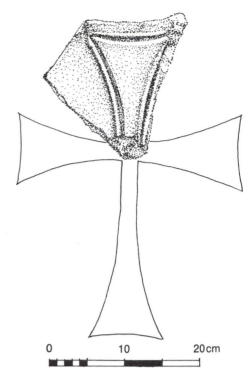

| 0 | 10 | 20cm |

Khirbet ed-Deir: fragment of marble chancel screen

face. On this fragment is depicted part of a "Cross of Golgotha" motif.[4] An identical pattern appears on the chancel screen of the church from the days of Justinian in St. Catherine's Monastery at Mt. Sinai. On the basis of this parallel, it may be possible to reconstruct the original form of one of the chancel screen panels in the cave-church.

The main entrance to the *bema*, 1 m wide, is on the west; a secondary one, only 0.6 m wide, is on the south, toward the reliquary niche. At the center of the *bema*, there are traces of the altar; parts of the table were discovered in one of the auxiliary rooms (see below). The rock-cut apse is square; two niches were hewn in the back wall. That on the right, measuring 0.45 × 0.6 m and 0.4 m deep, was raised 1.2 m above the floor; the left-hand niche measured 1.4 × 1.5 m, but was only 0.2 m deep, and its base was 0.8 m above the floor. These niches seem to have served liturgical needs or to store the vessels used in the liturgy.

The reliquary niche to the south of the *bema* was semicircular in shape, 0.6 m in diameter

and 1.8 m high, and was raised 1 m above the floor. The hewing of this niche was well executed, and traces of marble lining can be discerned. On the basis of its shape and location, it can be assumed that it originally contained a small casket for holy relics.

Two other niches were cut in the rock walls of the prayer hall. One, located in the northwestern corner, was arched and had a wooden shelf, as is evident from the slit running its width. It measured 0.95 × 1.25 m and was 0.8 m deep. The other niche, in the northern, long wall, was aligned with the chancel screen at a height of 1.7 m above the floor; it was oval in shape, measuring 0.3 × 0.6 m, and was 0.8 m deep.

The mosaic pavements. The well-made mosaic pavements of the church are good examples of Byzantine artistry. Their bedding is of a crude mortar, overlaid with a bed of pebbles and another, finer layer of mortar.

The mosaic panel in the forepart of the prayer hall, near the doorway, bears a simple diaper pattern of diagonal rows of florets surrounded by a linear frame in black, red and white. The floor here was made up of me-

[4] I am grateful to Uzi Dahari, who discovered the fragment and turned it over to me.

246

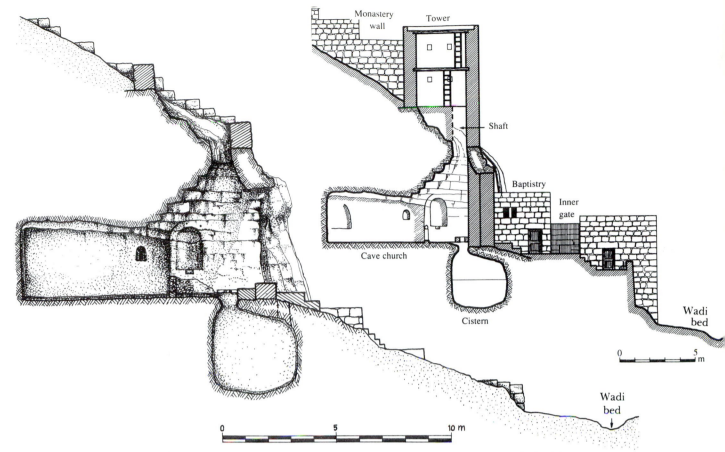

Khirbet ed-Deir: section (E. Cohen) and reconstruction (L. Ritmeyer) of cave-church, looking east

dium-sized tesserae (some 65 per 100 sq cm).

The central part of the prayer hall has a richer and more complex panel. Its border has a fret of alternating round and square medallions, contained between "dog's-tooth" stripes, one facing inward and the other outward (see Pl. XVIIc). The composition of this border is hardly original, there being numerous parallels from the Byzantine period. The unusual feature here is the motifs depicted within the square medallions, including various elements from daily life such as fruit, baskets of fruit, a sickle, and a parasol. The dominant colors in the central mosaic are black, red and various shades of brown and yellow. The central panel contains a pattern made up of crossing oblique lines of florets, each resulting rhomboid containing a cruciform group of four florets. At the eastern end of this panel, toward the altar, there is a Greek inscription within a *tabula ansata*; the frame is 3.3 m long and 0.3 m wide. The three-line inscription is a Greek rendition of the Septuagint of Psalms 105:4–5 (M.T. 106:4–5).

Μνήσθητι ἡμῶν κ(ύρι)ε ἐν τῇ εὐδοκίᾳ τοῦ
  λαοῦ σου,
ἐπίσκεψαι ἡμᾶς ἐν τῷ σωτηρίῳ σου τοῦ ἰδ(ε)ῖν
ἐν [τ]ῇ χρηστότητι τῶν ἐκλεκτῶν σου

Remember me, O Lord, with the favor thou hast to thy people; visit us with thy salvation, that we may behold the good of thine elect.[5]

This inscription is the focal point of the panel, and its designer sought to emphasize it with large letters and by offsetting it with a simple background.

The mosaic panel of the *bema* contains a floral repeat of four-petalled motifs. A zigzag

[5] L. Di Segni and Y. Hirschfeld, "Four Greek Inscriptions from Khirbet ed-Deir," *Orientalia Christiana Periodica* 53 (1987): 368–373 (Inscription no. 1).

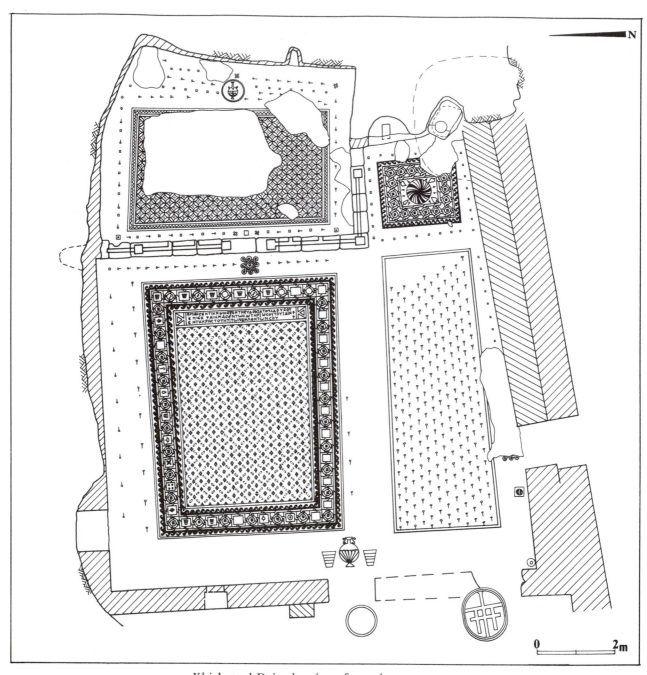

Khirbet ed-Deir: drawing of mosaic pavement

pattern within the border forms two series of triangles, one dark and the other light. In front of the entrance to the *bema* is an isolated element on a plain mosaic background — a fret with an orange-colored ivy leaf at its center (an identical motif appears at the main entrance of the church). The eastern part of the *bema* mosaic features an isolated medallion containing an amphora motif. The artistic design of the amphora is rather plain but handsome.

The richest and most colorful mosaic was located opposite the reliquary niche south of the *bema* — a clear indication of the importance of the niche (see Pl. XVIIb). This is a relatively small, square panel, 2 × 2 m. The

Khirbet ed-Deir: prayer hall of church-cave, looking east

Khirbet ed-Deir: entrance area to church-cave, looking east

Khirbet ed-Deir: inscription in prayer hall, looking east

249

Khirbet ed-Deir: ornamental motif in mosaic pavement
at entrance to the bema

main border contains an intertwined series of medallions with central cruciform motifs made up of florets. The narrow margin consists of a "dog's-tooth" design. In the panel a central medallion displays a solar whorl. The distinct curved rays comprise relatively small tesserae (156 per 100 sq cm), in a wide range of colors, including black, gray, green, red, brown, yellow and beige. This was a very rare feature of the mosaic repertoire of the Byzantine period. In contrast, it is found as an ornament on several stone lintels discovered at ᶜAvdat in the Negev.

Water installations in the floor of the church. In the floor of the church, various water installations were found: in the southeastern corner, at the base of the reliquary niche, there was an opening, 0.4 m in diameter, to a large cistern hewn into the rock beneath the church; nearby was found its stone cover. This cistern has two other openings: one in the adjacent baptistery (see below); and the other within the church, covered by a stone slab 1 m square. A small depression for holding a water jug was located in the southwestern corner of the church. It was 0.25 m in diameter and was made from the bottom of a pottery jar, sunk into the mosaic floor. Nearby was the opening of a drainage

Khirbet ed-Deir: medallion with amphora in
mosaic pavement at eastern edge of the bema

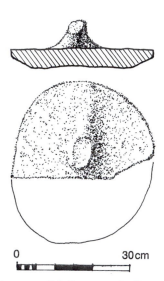

0   30 cm

Khirbet ed-Deir: stone lid discovered adjacent to cistern
opening in cave-church (E. Cohen)

250

Khirbet ed-Deir: opening to drainage channel near cave-church entrance

channel used during the washing of the floor; it had a stone grill, carved in the form of a cross. By this means water was drained toward the gardens in the canyon bed.

Auxiliary chambers west of the prayer hall.
West of the prayer hall three auxiliary rooms were built: a central chamber and two smaller ones branching off from it to the north and the west, respectively. The doorway leading into the central chamber was in the middle of the wall separating it from the prayer hall. In the mosaic pavement, near the doorway, appears an amphora motif flanked by baskets of fruit (see Pl. XVIIa). The design was well worked in red, black, green, blue and yellow. These symbolic motifs are indicative of the ritual use of the auxiliary rooms. The central chamber probably served as the *diaconicon*, the room where the monastery's treasure would have been kept. In an adjacent room, the sacramental vessels used during the Eucharist were probably stored.[6]

[6] I thank Bianca and Gustav Kühnel for discussing this point with me.

Khirbet ed-Deir: auxiliary rooms beneath the collapsed ceiling of the cave, looking east

The central chamber measured 4.5 × 6.8 m. Most of it still lies buried beneath large blocks of rock from the collapsed ceiling. The mosaic pavement to the north of the fallen rocks contained a medallion with a linear double frame in black (56 tesserae per 100 sq cm) (see Pl. XVIId). The pattern of the medallion, 0.8 m in diameter, is unclear because it was only partially unearthed. To the right of the doorway was a small depression for a water jar (similar to that in the southwestern corner of the prayer hall). The mosaic pavement revealed south of the fallen rocks is cruder (30 tesserae per 100 sq cm), and thus it was probably laid down at a later stage in the

251

church's existence. In the forepart of the floor was a fairly large medallion in black, red and white, oval in shape and measuring 1.2 × 1.4 m. Within the frame was a motif, reminiscent of Calvary: a large, central cross flanked by two smaller ones. This motif was oriented slightly askew, pointing to the altar. The eastern edge of the medallion is located along the assumed line of the wall separating the prayer hall from the auxiliary rooms. This would support the assumption that the mosaic pavement was laid after the original wall here had been demolished.

Above the medallion, a hoard of pieces of marble slabs was found — apparently brought here from the area of the *bema*. They were buried beneath the rockfall, and a few of them remain beneath the huge rocks, which were too heavy to move. The fragments recovered enabled a reasonable reconstruction of the original form of the altar table. It was 1.15 m high and measured approximately 0.9 × 1.3 m. The legs of the table were of marble and had originally stood on a stone base, a fragment of which was found. The base is of local limestone, with a smoothed surface; at the

Khirbet ed-Deir: suggested reconstruction of altar table based on fragments found in auxiliary room (E. Cohen)

four corners there were square sockets for the legs, which had been fixed in place with mortar (some of which remains at the bottom of the legs). Along one of the longer sides of the table, a Greek dedicatory inscription was finely carved. The text is as follows:

† Μνήσθητι Κ(ύρι)ε τῶν καρποφορησ(άντων) ᾿Αλαφέου δ[ια]κ(όνου) κ(αὶ) Αἰαν(τος) {or Αἰαν(οῦ)} μονάζ(οντος) {or μοναζ(όντων)}

O Lord, remember the donors, Alaphaeos the deacon and Aias (Aianos) the monk(s).[7]

In addition to the altar table, fragments of a smaller marble table were found, as well as eight triangular marble "tiles" heaped together. Each of the latter was marked on the back with one of the first eight letters of the Greek alphabet. On joining them together in alphabetical order we obtained a square measuring exactly 0.38 sq m. All eight pieces had

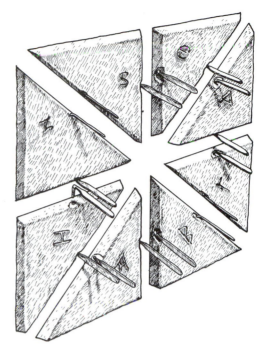

Khirbet ed-Deir: arrangement of bronze nails for affixing the marble "tiles" (E. Cohen)

been sawn from a single block of marble, and their intended arrangement results in a symmetrical pattern of the natural veining. It is assumed that the square had originally been framed in some manner and set on mortar bedding. This is indicated by several bronze

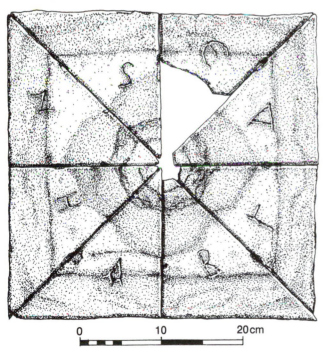

Khirbet ed-Deir: backs of eight marble "tiles" marked with first letters of the Greek alphabet

Khirbet ed-Deir: two of the marble tiles of the plate

[7] Di Segni and Hirschfeld, "Four Greek Inscriptions" (see note 5), p. 386.

nails found at the edges of pieces. This table-top probably ornamented some installation in the area of the *bema*, possibly the stand for sacred books during prayers.

The discovery of the heap of marble pieces is most interesting. It was probably the monks themselves who moved the marble installations from the *bema* for safekeeping to a back room of the church. It is assumed that this took place prior to the abandonment of the monastery, sometime in the seventh century C.E. Soon thereafter, the rock ceiling collapsed, burying the marble pieces for some 1,350 years.

The northern auxiliary room was quite small, somewhat resembling a right-angle triangle in shape. measuring 2.2 × 4.5 m. Its floor was paved with a plain, white mosaic. In the eastern wall, toward the prayer hall, there was a niche measuring 0.6 × 0.8 m and 0.5 m deep. Its location would support the assumption that this room had served some liturgical purpose.

The western auxiliary room was "L"-shaped, measuring 4.2 × 5.5 m. Its mosaic pavement bore a simple pattern of rows of florets within a linear frame, in red, black and white (42 tesserae per 100 sq cm).

The ceiling of the cave. The cave ceiling above the prayer hall has apparently been preserved in its original state, almost without change. It rises some 4 m high above the floor here. Toward the west, its height reaches as much as 6.5 m, while toward the east it descends, being located only 2–3 m above the floor in the area of the *bema*.

The builders of the church constructed a 5-m-high "internal stairway" leading from the church to the tower on the cliff above by hewing, in the eastern part of the cave ceiling, an opening measuring 0.6 × 0.8 m. It is reasonable to assume that a wooden or rope ladder of some sort was used for ascent and descent.

Collapse of the cave ceiling within the church. During the excavation, two phases of collapse could be discerned, caused by the natural disintegration of the cave ceiling. The first collapse occurred while the church was still in use. Not all the stones were discarded; some were used for constructing a megalithic wall the length of the prayer hall. Some of the blocks of this wall were as much as 1.5 m long. The present height of the wall is 2.2 m. Though the stones were not dressed, they were carefully laid in courses, giving the wall a uniform appearance on the face toward the prayer hall.

It can be assumed that, as a result of this collapse, the outer wall of the church also fell, at least in part. Furthermore, part of the wall separating the prayer hall from the auxiliary rooms also partially collapsed. It is probably to this phase that the renewal of the mosaic pavement in the central auxiliary room should be ascribed.

The second collapse of the ceiling took place not long after the monks had abandoned the site. This is indicated by the direct damage to the mosaic pavements in the church. The rockfall from this second episode consisted of particularly large boulders, the largest of them being 2.5 m high and measuring about 6 × 8 m. During the clearance of the rubble, traces of "campfires" were discovered on the mosaic pavements — probably associated with Bedouin shepherds who sojourned at the site soon after its abandonment. Over the years, debris and organic material accumulated, attaining a height of some 2.8 m above the floor of the church.

The baptistery. The chamber used for baptizing was located to the east of the cave-church. A single cistern served both the church and the baptistery; it has two openings, one in each room. The cistern, hewn into the bedrock, measured 3 × 3.5 m and is at least 4 m deep. (At present it is silted up.)

The baptistery was built adjacent to the cliff face. Its external dimensions were 3.5 × 9 m, with walls 0.7 m thick. The entrance to this chamber was through an opening in the shorter wall facing the church. From its threshold, three steps descended to the level of the chamber; this floor was a rather crude, white mosaic pavement (25 tesserae per 100 sq cm). It contained rows of well-spaced flowers, within a black and red frame. The flowers were oriented to the east.

In the southwestern corner of the floor, there was a small depression 30 cm in diameter and 10 cm deep. This was apparently a sump for the last remnants of water used in washing the floor. Nearby was a depression in which a pitcher had been placed. This depression, 25 cm in diameter, was made from the bottom of a pottery storage jar, sunk into the mosaic floor (like the two depressions in the floor of the church).

The baptistery was roofed over with wooden beams, resting apparently on the rear rock wall. A round wall niche was hewn into the rock; its base was about a meter above the floor, and it is approximately 1.2 m in diameter and 2 m high.

The baptismal font was constructed between the stairs descending into the room and the cistern. The walls of the font, 0.3 m thick, are built of small fieldstones joined with a cement. On its inner surfaces, the font was plastered with hydraulic plaster containing crushed pottery. The interior of the font measured 0.7 × 1.09 m, and it was only 0.6 m deep. From the literary sources, we know that Saracen tribes living in the Judean Desert in the Byzantine period were baptized by monks.[8]

The crypt west of the church. Beyond the western wall of the church, a small chamber was revealed which had served for the burial of some personage at the monastery. Opposite this crypt, a mosaic pavement was uncovered with two crosses and an inscription, the contents of which relate to resurrection. The inscription and crosses face the crypt.

The interior of the crypt, somewhat expanded by hewing, measured 2 × 2.8 m and it was 1.6 m high. Within the burial chamber was a rock bench 0.7 m wide, about 2 m long and 0.5 m above the floor.

    [8] D.J. Chitty, *The Desert a City. An Introduction to the Study of Egyptian and Palestinian Monasticism under the Christian Empire* (Oxford, 1966), pp. 83–84.

Khirbet ed-Deir: the baptistery east of cave-church, from cliff top, looking south

The opening of the crypt was carefully made: the threshold stone, 0.9 m long, was preserved *in situ*. It has a hewn margin indicating that a door had closed the opening. One of the stone doorjambs was discovered among the rubble nearby; it measured 0.6 m long and 0.5 m wide and also had a cut margin. A cross was incised on its outer surface.

The mosaic pavement in front of the crypt is located within a sort of vestibule between the wall of the church and those of the rooms to the west. This small room was 1.9 m wide and some 3 m long. The threshold of its entrance faced the paved path south of the church. On the basis of the available data, it was not possible to determine whether the entrance here had been left open or had a door.

The pavement was of crude mosaics (25 tesserae per 100 sq cm) and included two crosses and an inscription. The two crosses differ from one another. One has an attached ring (0.4 cm in diameter) — a form known as *crux ansata* and rather rare in Israel but common in Egypt on Coptic tombstones of the fifth century C.E. and later. The other is of

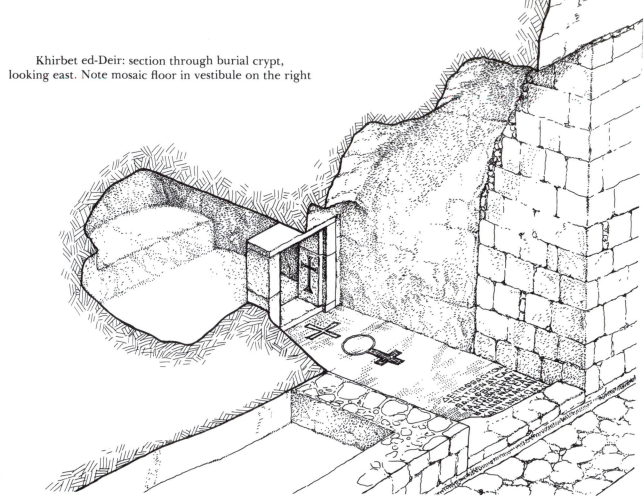

Khirbet ed-Deir: section through burial crypt, looking east. Note mosaic floor in vestibule on the right

Khirbet ed-Deir: cross incised on jamb of burial crypt

simple form, with equal arms — of a type well known on many monastic sites in the Judean Desert.[9] The nine-line inscription is preserved in its entirety. The text was derived from the New Testament (1 Corinthians 15:52–53) with changes in order:

Δεῖ τὸ φθαρτὸν
τοῦτο ἐνδύσασ-
θαι ἀφθαρσίαν
καὶ τὸ θνητὸν
τοῦτο ἐνδύσασ-
θαι ἀθανασίαν.
σαλπίσει γὰρ
καὶ οἱ νεκροὶ
ἀναστήσονται

[9] Several crosses of this sort are noted at various monastic sites surveyed in Y. Hirschfeld, *Archaeological Survey of Israel, Map of Herodium 108 / 2 17–11* (Jerusalem, 1985), pp. 55, 72–74.

256

Khirbet ed-Deir: vestibule of burial crypt, looking north
with inscription and two crosses in mosaic pavement

Literary Evidence of "Churches Built by God"

The cave-church at Khirbet ed-Deir is typical of the monastic movement in the Judean Desert. These churches were built within caves adjacent to, or within which well-known monks had lived. Not just any cave could become a place of worship; a requisite was some unusual event or miracle, or some act of purification, "preparing" the site for a church. The stories of several of the caves which were transformed into churches in the Judean Desert have been recorded. The earliest of these concerned the salvation of Chariton, who arrived in the Holy Land as a pilgrim early in the fourth century C.E. He was taken captive by bandits, who had hidden their treasures within a cave at a place known as "Pharan" (Wadi Farah).[12] The story of salvation involves a miracle serving to explain how the "bandits' cave" (ληστῶν σπήλαιον) became a "Church of the Lord" (ἐκκλησῖα ϑεοῦ). Around this church, which was dedicated by Macarius, bishop of Jerusalem (314–333 C.E.), Chariton founded the first laura in the Judean Desert.

The second cave which eventually came to serve as a church was selected by St. Euthymius, who had arrived at the Laura of Pharan in 405 C.E. Five years later, he went forth with his companion, Theoctistus, into the wastes of the desert. When they came to a particular canyon — Naḥal Og (Wadi Mukalik) — they discovered a large cave on the northern bank. Cyril of Scythopolis relates, in his *Life of Euthymius*, the following details: "This cave was initially the dwelling of animals, but when it had been cleansed with sacred song and the unceasing prayer of the saints, it attained the sanctity of a Church of the Lord."[13] Around this cave-church, a communal monastery was founded which came to be known as the Monastery of Theoctistus.

The most famous cave-church is surely that established by Sabas within the Great Laura which he founded in the Kidron Valley. The

This perishable nature must put on the imperishable, and this mortal nature must put on immortality. For the trumpet will sound, and the dead will be raised.[10]

This inscription, dealing with resurrection, indicates that this was a burial place. Was the founder of the monastery interred here? The situation here closely resembles that in many other monasteries, where the hermit's cell of the founder came to serve as his venerated crypt. In the monasteries of Euthymius, Theodosius and others, their burials are located at the center of the monastery, "radiating" sanctity.[11]

[10] Di Segni and Hirschfeld, "Four Greek Inscriptions" (see note 5), pp. 377–383 (Inscription no. 3).

[11] See B. Flussin, *Miracle et histoire dans l'oeuvre de Cyrille de Scythopolis* (Paris, 1983), pp. 191–192.

[12] G. Garitte, "La vie prémétaphrastique de S. Chariton," *Bulletin de l'Institut Historique Belge de Rome* 21/9–13 (1941): 22–26.

[13] Cyril of Scythopolis, *Vita Euthimii* 8, ed. E. Schwartz (Leipzig, 1939), p. 15.

KH. ED-DEIR: THE CHURCH   L. RITMEYER. 1983

Khirbet ed-Deir: reconstruction of cave-church

biography of Sabas by Cyril of Scythopolis relates the miraculous deed which led to the discovery of the cave. One night, Sabas was wandering alone in a canyon when all of sudden a column of fire lit up the location of a cave. On the morrow, Sabas ascended and, in the words of Cyril,

> found a large and wondrous cave formed in the shape of a Church of the Lord: on the eastern side there was a niche built by God, and on the northern side he [Sabas] found a large chamber arranged as a diaconicon. On the southern side, in contrast, [he found] a broad entrance, receiving sufficient light from the rays of the sun. He ornamented this cave with divine assistance and decreed that prayers would be held there on Saturdays and Sundays.[14]

Cyril calls this church a "church built by God" (θεοκτιστος ἐκκλησία). To this day, it serves the monks of the Mar Saba Monastery.

The description of Sabas' cave-church is astonishingly reminiscent of the one uncovered at Khirbet ed-Deir. The discovery of the latter, with its mosaic pavement and other features, exemplifies in an impressive visual manner this unique type of church which developed among the monks of the Judean Desert in the Byzantine period.

[14] Idem, *Vita Sabae* 18, ed. E. Schwartz (Leipzig, 1939), p. 102.

258

CHURCHES IN THE SHEPHELAH
AND IN
THE NEGEV DESERT

A Byzantine Church at Maresha (Beit Govrin)

Amos Kloner

The Byzantine church with its mosaic floor to be discussed here is located southwest of Tel Maresha, beyond its surrounding ring of Hellenistic caves and approximately 300 m from the mound itself. In the Byzantine period, Tel Maresha itself ("The Acropolis") was not inhabited, the central settlement being located at Beit Govrin (Eleutheropolis). The latter was an important Christian center, and the church described below belonged to one of the many monastic complexes in its vicinity.

The site was discovered during a survey in 1981 which noted surface finds of tesserae and architectural fragments. Over a decade the nearby burial caves had been robbed, and renewed looting in the area made it imperative to commence rescue excavations; they were carried out in the summer of 1985.[1]

The church was practically square and its central entrance and apse had the same east-northeast alignment (30° from the east); for

the purpose of simplification here we will refer to the structure as having an eastern axis. The northern and southern walls of the structure were 0.9 m thick and were preserved to a height of 0.5–1.2 m. The northern wall retained traces of plaster.

The southern wall was almost totally destroyed, its stones being robbed to floor level. A decline in topography in the area of the apse required the construction of a terrace, upon which the eastern wall was built. The removal of stones and erosion of the terrace left only the foundations of the apse area in this eastern end of the building visible. It seems that an appendix was added to the eastern wall, in which the apse was built, possibly including a stepped structure (see below).

The church was a basilica measuring (internal measurements) 9.6 m (east–west) × 9.9 m (north–south); two rows of columns on stylobates 0.6 m in width divided the church into a nave 4.65 m wide and two aisles which measured 2–2.1 m in width. Each row consisted of three free-standing pillars and two pilasters, one at its eastern and the other at its western end. These columns and the surrounding walls supported the wooden beams which carried the roof of the building. The columns were placed upon bases which had square plinths (0.61–0.62 sq m) and a round drum. Our excavations uncovered two bases on the northern stylobate and one on the southern one *in situ*, and a number of column drums and two capitals. One of the capitals was decorated on one level, while the other had two levels of schematically carved leaves and square corners similar to a Corinthian design. The height of the capitals is less than the diameter of their base. We found fragments of

[1] The excavation of the church was carried out in July and August 1985 on behalf of the Israel Department of Antiquities and Museums under the direction of A. Kloner, the District Archaeologist, assisted by H. Stark. In addition, O. Abt, D. Arbeli, Y. Hyman, D. Keren, A. Richter and many others assisted. The plan of the building was prepared by G. Solar, and the mosaic floor was drawn on a scale of 1:10 by T. Krinkin-Fabian. The photographs were taken by A. Kloner and H. Stark. In October 1985, the mosaic floor was removed from the nave to the Israel Museum by the Conservation Section of the Museum under the supervision of Ruth Yekutiel. Volunteers from various youth groups from abroad touring the country within the framework of "Dig for a Day," directed by B. Alpert and I. Stern, took part in the work, and Y. Zoran organized youths from Kiryat Gat and moshavim in the Lachish area to also participate in the digging.

◁ Maresha: drawing of mosaic floor in nave at scale of 1:10 (T. Krinkin-Fabian)

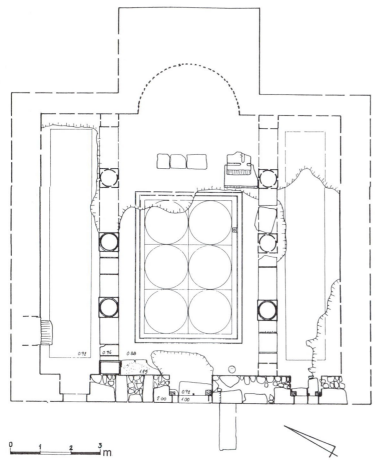

Maresha: plan of church (G. Solar)

plaster which originally covered the column drums.

Three entrances were located in the church's long western wall. The middle entrance opened onto the nave and was 1.2 m wide; the two side entrances led to the aisles and were each 0.8 m in width.

The floors of the nave and aisles were paved with mosaics. In the aisles they took the form of long and narrow panels measuring 1.4 × 7.6 m. Within these panels, on a white background, the pattern consisted of rows based on squares and schematic flowers. In the center of the southern aisle, the design comprised a deer, which was well preserved except for its head, tail and the ends of its feet.

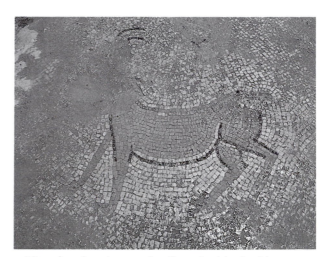

Maresha: deer in mosaic of south aisle, looking east

The floor of the nave was designed like a carpet measuring 5 × 3.6 m. The dominant colors were red, yellow, white and black, but the tones gray, pink and orange are also featured. The central panel was surrounded by a double frame, the outer part of which consisted of a ropelike decoration, while the inner one was a wavy line.

The main part of the carpet was made up of six squares laid out in pairs. Each square measured 1.4 sq m and contained a circle filled with various complicated geometric patterns. The area between the corners of the square and the circle was covered with either triangular or square checkers, shell patterns, parallel

Maresha: western part of church, looking north.

262

zigzag lines, or schematic flora. The density of tesserae in these medallions was 100–110 per sq dm (10 × 10 cm).

West of the carpet, between it and the three main entrances, a Greek inscription was laid out in two lines. The inscription, damaged in the destruction of the building, has been read and reconstructed by Leah Di Segni as follows:

> By the intercessions of the holy angel Michael Your House stands.
> The Lord is the shepherd of Fl(aviu)s Im(erius who built this?) and he will lack nothing.

A layer 0.1–0.15 m thick of burnt beams and charcoal on the mosaic floor, and numerous clay roofing tiles evidenced the destruction of the building. The debris also included some fifty large iron nails; the remains of a limestone chancel screen whose design motif was leaves diagonally-placed; and a small piece of limestone incised with a cross and the letters AW and XP in the corners. The pottery found on the floor and in the destruction layer was purely Byzantine, dating to the fifth–sixth centuries C.E. It seems, therefore, that the destruction of the church could not date later than the beginning of the seventh century C.E.

Along the eastern edge of the mosaic in the nave were a number of square, well-cut stone blocks, perhaps remains of the stepped structure leading to the *presbyterium* in front of the apse which measured 2.9 m (east–west) by 4.7 m (north–south). On the plan of the building shown above, two of the steps are located next to the eastern extremity of the southern row. The debris of the apse, destroyed to a level below that of the nave, included large blocks of tesserae. Further to the north, on a lower level than the stair remains, three stones were found and may belong to the base of the pre-apse, although this is not yet clear. The semicircular line of the apse and the stepped structure which supported it are still hypothetical.

No evidence of any auxiliary chambers flanking the apse was found. In the southeast-

Maresha: church nave and entrances during excavations

ern corner of its appendix, the construction supports the theory that the apse was an eastward extension without any attached room. The foundations of this corner were on a much lower level than that of the floor. As mentioned above, the eastern part of the church on either side of the apse was heavily eroded to beneath floor level, and therefore no evidence remains of rooms. There are three possibilities: 1) that a room did exist on either side of the apse (one of which was the *prothesis* and the other the *diaconicon*); 2) that the church was triapsidal; and 3) that the church had only one apse. The third possibility is the most feasible.

A stone was found incorporated in the floor of the nave in the inner frame of the mosaic and opposite the southeastern medallion. It was 0.17 sq m in size and a hole 0.105 m in diameter was drilled into its center. On the stone and the surrounding mosaic there were prominent signs of burning, perhaps caused by burning oil which was poured into the hole. Remains of a metal grate or screen which originally covered the hole were found fastened to it. From this stone for a few centimeters to the east, a section of the floor dropped in level, suggesting the presence of a cavity or fill material beneath the floor in this area. A probe conducted after the mosaic floor's removal at the end of 1987[2] revealed a burial 0.9 m below it, dug in the soil and covered with five soft limestone slabs. The grave pit measured 2.1 m. in length (east–west), and it contained earth mixed with small, broken bones. The burial clearly preceded the completion of the church, and the stone implanted in the floor was designed to facilitate the pouring of oil, other liquids or incense onto the tomb.

Additions and Repairs to the Structure

The eastern appendix and the inherent topographic problems suggest the possibility that the church was incorporated into an already existing structure. Only further excavation of the remaining parts of the complex will clarify this supposition. Signs of renovation to the building are evident in the northwestern part of the church where two stone benches were

[2] The excavation of the burial below the floor was completed in October 1987 by a group of volunteer students from Beer-Sheba headed by D. Gaspar.

found on the floor. One bench, rectangular in shape (0.78 m long and 0.4 m high), was located in the northwestern section of the aisle. Its function is unknown but it was definitely purposely placed in this spot. The second bench (1.4 m × 0.5 m and 0.37 m high) was situated adjacent to the western wall, between the pilaster and the central entrance to the nave. It was plastered on its top, and within the cement fragments of a red painted fresco and a sherd of a roofing tile were found. The latter probably belong to the initial construction phase of the church, and thus indicate that this bench dates to a later period during which renovations were carried out.

More evidence of changes in the structure was found in the northern wall, 0.95 m from its northwestern corner, where a blocked entrance 0.9 m wide was revealed.

In addition to the benches and the blocked doorway, the careful and tasteful introduction of somewhat larger white stones into the mosaic floor on the western side also bears witness to renovations made to the church.

A Byzantine Church Complex at Ḥorvat Beit Loya

Joseph Patrich and Yoram Tsafrir

Ḥorvat Beit Loya (Arabic: Khirbet Lehi) is a characteristic ruin of the Maresha region (ancient Eleutheropolis) in the southern Judean Shephela (foothills). It is situated 400 m above sea level, at the top of a hill approximately 5.5 km southeast of Beit Govrin and 8 km east of Tel Lachish. In 1961, a burial cave was discovered at the eastern foot of the hill, containing a series of carvings and inscriptions including the "Yershalem" inscription[1] — all dating from the end of the Iron Age. No traces of a settlement from that period have as yet been uncovered at the site.

The remains of buildings have been found at the site together with some hewn subterranean installations, including columbaria, olive presses, water cisterns, quarries, a stable and hideaways.[2] Some of the underground remains were studied and measured by Yigal Tepper and Amos Kloner. The pottery sherds discovered by Yehuda Dagan, in the course of his more comprehensive research on the Ju-

dean Shephela, indicate that the hill on which Ḥorvat Beit Loya is situated had been populated from the Hellenistic until the Mamluk period. On its western slope, beyond the Byzantine residential area, a complex of Byzantine structures has been excavated, consisting of a basilican church and related buildings, an oil and winepress and a burial cave. The church, its annexes and forecourt were enclosed within a wall. The complex apparently functioned as a monastery, whose church also served the neighboring village. The church was furbished with very intricate mosaic pavements.

The History of the Church

The church was probably built ca. 500 C.E. and survived until the eighth century C.E. Sometime during this century, the mosaics — featuring both human and animal figures — were defaced by iconoclasts, perhaps following the edict of Caliph Yazid II in 721 C.E. The damaged parts were immediately repaired with the original tesserae. It is clear that special care was taken to reproduce the mosaic; thus, the defaced images are still identifiable in most cases. This leads to the conjecture that the Christians themselves perpetrated the damage, compelled to do so by the Muslim ruler. Later, perhaps during the same century, the church was abandoned, and the stones of its walls were plundered. Another structure — perhaps a small chapel — was erected to the east, incorporating some of the church's masonry.

Sometime later, the entire site, by then abandoned and vandalized, was converted into a Muslim cemetery. Necklaces of semiprecious stones, two bronze rings, two brace-

---

[1] J. Naveh, "Old Hebrew Inscriptions in a Burial Cave," *IEJ* 13 (1963): 74–92.

[2] The excavations were carried out in December 1983 and in May 1986 under the direction of the authors and on behalf of the Institute of Archaeology of The Hebrew University of Jerusalem in collaboration with the Free Man Institute of Salt Lake City, Utah. The expedition comprised Edna Dalal and Nitsan Preis, area supervisors and registrars, Eliezer Stern, Edna Leitner and Jodie Magnes, all of the Hebrew University. The measurements were taken by David Huli, Benny Arubas and Leen Ritmeyer, with Abraham Hai and Ilan Sztulman as the photographers. Members of Moshav Amaẓia, as well as Hanan Cohen of Moshav Lachish and Shmuel Graciani, were extremely helpful with various administrative aspects. Much support was also given by Amos Kloner, the district archaeologist, and Yehuda Dagan, and the team for the protection of antiquity sites headed by Uzi Dahari and Gideon Avni. Dr. Joseph Ginat was also most helpful, as were the Israel Defense Forces.

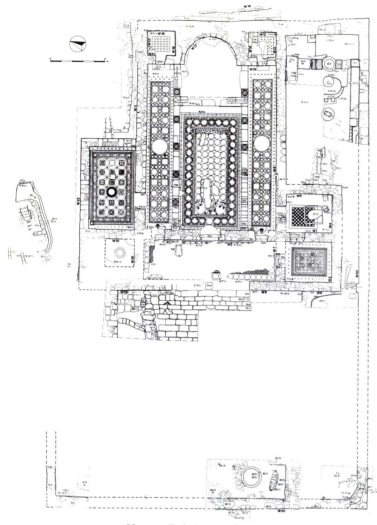

Ḥorvat Beit Loya: plan of church

Ḥorvat Beit Loya: general view of monoapsidal basilica

lets — one of iron and the other of copper tubes with decorated ends — and a number of glass vessels were discovered in the tombs. Digging of graves damaged the mosaic floor in several places; the majority of the tombs, however, were found above the pavement of the then abandoned church. The high mortality rate, as evidenced by the numerous burials, some arranged in three or more tiers, may have resulted from an epidemic. The pottery finds are uniform throughout the layers, suggesting that the cemetery was used for a relatively short period.

The Church Complex

The church was a monoapsidal basilica, 20.4 m long and 13.9 m wide. It measured 18.6 × 12.1 m internally (approximately 60 by 39 Byzantine feet). To the west, in front of the church, there was a 3.6-m-wide exonarthex to which access was gained through the atrium via a 7.2-m-wide staircase with a balustrade. The external dimensions of the atrium were approximately 30.5 × 20 m; the entrance — as yet unexcavated — was located at its southern end. The atrium was paved with limestone slabs, and was surrounded by several chambers. At the top of the staircase, the stone base of a pillar (possibly wooden) supporting the narthex's roof had been integrated into the floor. There were three entrances in the church's facade: a central 1.7-m-wide doorway leading to the nave, and two side openings flanking it, each of which led onto an aisle.

Two rows of five columns separated the nave from the aisles. Each was arranged on a 0.6-m-wide stylobate of stone blocks, raised slightly above the mosaic floor. The columns were surmounted by low-relief capitals of the pseudo-Corinthian and the pseudo-Ionian order. The columns were 1.85 m high, with a lower diameter of 0.43 m and an upper diameter of 0.37 m. The total height of column and capital was approximately 2.75 m. The columns supported a system of wooden beams, instead of a stone arcade.

The nave was 5.7 m wide, and the aisles

2.5 m wide each. An internal apse, less than a semicircle in plan, was situated on the eastern side of the nave, with a chancel projecting approximately 2.5 m into the nave and raised two steps higher than floor level. Although small remnants of the marble revetment of the steps have survived *in situ*, nothing remains of the *synthronon* seats in the apse, or of the chancel floor. Four identically molded convex-faced stones originated from the spring course of the apse's dome. Fragments of the chancel-screen's posts and panels, some of limestone and others of marble, were revealed in different places. Among the finds were the base and pieces of a marble column that had belonged to the *ciborium* raised above the altar. At the eastern end of the aisles there were two rectangular rooms (*pastophoria*), measuring 2.4 × 2.25 m, whose floors were raised two steps higher than the aisles. A large fragment of glass, over 20 cm long, originated from the windows set in the walls. Fragments of glazed wall mosaics were also discovered in several places among the debris.

Adjoining the basilica on its northern side was a chapel, measuring 7.5 × 4.2 m internally. A 1.4-m-wide entrance led into the chapel from the northern aisle. The base of a square column (0.5 sq m) has survived in the chapel's eastern part; perhaps an altar or a table for gifts was set upon it. A baptistery (*baptisterium*), measuring 4.1 × 3.5 m internally, adjoined the southern side of the church; a 1.6-m-wide opening led to it from the southern aisle. Another opening, 0.9 m wide, in the western wall connected the baptistery to an anteroom (see below). The font had undergone changes in the course of time. Initially, it stood on the mosaic floor in the center of the room, but later a hole was dug into the pavement, in which a different font, perhaps of metal, was installed. A marble railing, built around the later font, was anchored to the mosaic floor. The railing had two openings: one in the north, with a Greek inscription worked into the mosaic floor; and the exit to the south. The font was drained by means of a lead pipe, a section of which survived *in situ*. Another opening in the floor provided access to a valve used to regulate the flow of water in the drainpipe.

To the north of the narthex there was a room, measuring 2.7 × 2.5 m internally, whose western and northern walls were over 2 m thick, suggesting that it had supported the church's bell tower. The room had only one doorway — on the south side. The baptistery's anteroom measured 4.1 × 3.6 m internally. It had two openings: a 1-m-wide doorway offering access to the narthex, and the aforementioned leading to the baptistery. The exonarthex, together with these two rooms, extending the chapel and baptistery westward, formed the complex's facade which was 24 m wide.

The walls were 0.9–1 m thick. The internal walls were generally not built on foundations but laid directly on the ground. Most of the walls have been plundered down to their lowest course, and in some cases, even that is missing.

Fragments of clay roof tiles and iron nails from the wooden beams supporting the ceiling and roof were found scattered throughout the church.

The mosaic floor and inscriptions. The church and all of its various adjuncts — the narthex and its wings, the chapel and the baptistery — had magnificent mosaic pavements, covering a total area of approximately 220 sq m. The mosaics of the basilica and the narthex included human and animal representations. These were destroyed by iconoclasts during the eighth century C.E., but were repaired shortly thereafter by the random resetting of the original stones. The figures' outlines were obscured, at times rendering them unrecognizable, but usually permitting identification of the defaced image. Four Greek inscriptions were incorporated into the mosaics: two are dedicatory inscriptions and two are quotations, one from Proverbs and the other from Psalms. At the church's entrance, the edge of a *tabula ansata* has been preserved, but its inscription has not survived.

Only the margins of the narthex's mosaic

floor are preserved. It was bordered by a band of intertwining grapevines forming medallions, into which the figures of various animals were worked (populated scrolls). The animals include a deer, a collared hunting dog chasing a rabbit, a dugged lioness and various swamp fowl. At the center of the western border, behind the wooden post which supported the narthex ceiling, a cross or a tree was apparently depicted, flanked by lambs representing the *Agnus Dei* — "the Lamb of God" (John 1:29). Of this group of images, only the lamb to the south of the surmised cross has survived intact; the other lamb is recognizable only from the outlines of its back and neck. At the corners of the narthex, the medallions encompassed baskets of fruit. The basket in the southwest corner has survived in its entirety, while only part of the northeastern basket remains. The medallions along the narthex's eastern border contain human figures alternating with animal representations. Only the upper parts of the figures have survived. One is a person waving his right arm; and to his right, part of the head, back, and tail of a pet monkey can be identified; to the left of the human figure, one can discern the nose and ears of a bear, rearing on its hind legs. The depiction to the left of the bear may be its trainer; to the monkey's right, a youth carries a stick over his shoulder. In the medallion north of this group of images, the upper portion of a female figure bearing a basket of fruit has been preserved.

The density of tesserae in the animal figures is 90–130 per sq dm, and it is even higher in the heads and limbs of human figures, where use was made of *opus vermiculatum*, particularly in the facial features. A variety of colors was used: white, gray, black, ochre, mustard, yellow-beige, burgundy, red-white, pinkish and orange. The mosaic floor has a bottom layer, about 0.1 m thick, made of small stone chips mixed into a gray-white clay. On top of its leveled surface, 1–1.5 cm of white lime plaster was laid, into which the tesserae were embedded while it was still soft. We assume that the pattern's basic lines were first drawn or carved into the bottom layer to facilitate the placing

of the tesserae, as was the case at other sites, but no sign of such a process is evident.

The pavement of the nave inside the basilica was also decorated with grapevines, from which leaves and grape clusters hang. In addition to the iconoclastic defacement of the human images, this section sustained further damage: a deep fissure, due to grave-digging activities during the Muslim period, ruined part of the mosaic. The grapevines growing out of the central amphora, on either side, form two large medallions, each encompassing a peacock. Above the amphora, the vines form twelve rows of five medallions each. Various animals were depicted in medallions. Despite the damage perpetrated, it is still possible to identify a camel, a pheasant, a wildcat, a goat, a duck, a horse or mule, a rabbit and various winged creatures, including a chicken and a peacock.

The central row of medallions was not damaged by the iconoclasts as it included depictions of various implements and fruits, rather than animals. However, in the central medallion of the easternmost row, there is a still intact image of two birds sipping water from a goblet (see Pl. XVIIIa) — a late example of the famous Hellenistic-Roman scene found in Pompei and elsewhere. Additional birds, located between this row's scrolls, were also not destroyed. In the medallions of the central row there are representations of a wine goblet (see Pl. XVIIIb) and flask, dates and almonds arranged on a broad leaf as if on a tray (see Pl. XVIIId), a wicker basket with fruit, a double-wickered basket full of grapes, a metal bowl of fruit and a basket of apples. The next medallion may depict a cage, as is typical of these mosaics, but the image is too severely damaged to verify this. The following medallion in this row was completely destroyed in the grave-digging operations, while in the westernmost medallion of the row, the right side of a double-handled vase, containing grapes or some other fruit (see Pl. XVIIIe), was partially preserved.

Similar mosaic pavements which also suffered iconoclastic defacement were discovered at other sites in the Maresha region, such as Ḥorvat Ḥanoth near Moshav Mata[c] and Ḥorvat Dichrin north of Kibbutz Beit Govrin.

The nave's central mosaic had a border strip of acanthus leaves (see Pl. XVIIIc) containing various animals which were disfigured. In some cases, the tips of limbs and other body parts eluded the vandals. Thus, it is possible to identify at the nave's southern end a spotted body, an elephant, a deer, and probably a goat, a lion, an ox, a hunting dog and a rabbit; in the east, an ox and an antelope are discernable on the one side, and on the other, an inscription framed by a wreath; in the north, there are depictions of a horse, a spotted leopard, a rabbit, a fox or wolf, a snake and a monkey. On the western side, however, the animals are not identifiable. Wreaths of fruit or luxuriant blooms, depicted in the frame's corners, have survived unharmed. At the western end of the nave, a Greek dedicatory inscription is set within a medallion: Ἀζίζος καὶ κυρικὸς εὐχαριστοῦντες ἀνεθήκαμεν τὸν ναόν, "Azizos and Kyrikos, giving thanks, dedicated this shrine." At the eastern end another Greek inscription, framed by a circular wreath, reads: προσφωρὰ Ἀζζίζον, "The offering of Azizos." Both aisles have similar mosaic designs, composed of a geometrical pattern of alternating circles and squares in two sizes. The smaller circles and squares bear various floral patterns, while the larger ones featured animals, which have all been defaced. A large medallion — 1.47 m in diameter, spanning the entire width of this mosaic — is located at the entrance to each aisle.

The large medallion (see Pl. XIXa) in the northern aisle depicts a boat with two sails containing two fishermen. The one on the left, wearing pointed headgear, holds a fish hook from which a fish dangles. The man on the right is grasping a pair of oars. There is a line of fish in the waves beneath the boat. The fishermen and all the fish — except for the one hanging from the hook and another below the boat — have been defaced.

The large medallion (see Pl. XIXb) in the southern aisle portrays two standing fishermen in profile, their faces turned southward. The right-hand figure carries in both hands a wicker basket containing a fish. The figure behind him holds a fishnet in his left hand, steadying it on his left shoulder. One (or perhaps several) fish hang tail-down from his right hand. Although the mens' heads, upper torsos and bare legs have been completely destroyed, the scene itself, in general, is still clear. The fisherman on the right wears a yellow and orange striped cape and a skirt and undergarment of gray and yellow. The left-hand figure wears a checkered dress whose most prominent colors are gray, green and yellow. The hem is raised above the knee, gathered between and around the legs and tied around the waist. One may be tempted to view these fishermen as the Disciples converting people to Christianity on the Sea of Galilee, but such an interpretation is hypothetical.

The density of the tesserae in these scenes is at least 100 per sq dm, and in the white background approximately 80–90 per sq dm. The figures' fingers are made of long, narrow tesserae, 1.5–2 cm in length and 0.5 cm or less in width.

The mosaic arrangements in the two aisles differ from one another. There are twelve

Ḥorvat Beit Loya: Greek dedicatory insciption, "Azizos and Kyrikos"

269

Ḥorvat Beit Loya: northern aisle

have survived intact. They consist of a pattern of squares and lozenges, and a wreath of flowers at its center forming a medallion with a Greek dedicatory inscription: Ἐπαναγία ὑπερ ἀναπαύσεως καὶ μνήμης Ἀετίου τὴν ψήφωσιν ἀνέϑηκα, "Epanagia, I dedicated this mosaic for the rest and memory of Aethios." The central panel is bordered by two strips, one composed of alternating squares and double meanders and the other of a guilloche. A second four-line Greek inscription to the east is framed in a 0.45 sq m square: κ(ύρι)ε Ἰ(ησοῦ)ς Χ(ρίστ)ε ἀναπαυσον θεκλοὺν τὴν δούλης σου, "Lord Jesus Christ, give rest to your servant Theclon [Thecla?]."

The anteroom of the *baptisterium* was also paved with geometrical mosaics. The pattern consisted of alternating rows of squares and diamonds. Both the design and workmanship are less fine than in the chapel mosaic, but the result is no less impressive. The floor of the baptistery has a simple design, composed of alternating diagonal lines of red, black and white squares. Next to the entrance to the font, the Greek inscription reads: Φῶς δικέοις διὰ παντός, "Light to the righteous in all," a quotation based upon the Septuagint of Prov-

pairs of large medallions in the southern aisle, but only eleven in the northern one. In each pair of medallions the animals are similar, facing each other. In the northern aisle they include (from west to east): an ibex, a goat cropping grass, two chicks, an ass or calf, a hen or pheasant(?), a camel or ass, the boat medallion, a rabbit, a bird, a leopard, a duck(?) and a leaping goat. The southern aisle has representations (from west to east) of a gallinule (porphyrio), a deer or ram, two chicks, a rabbit, an ibex, a collared dog, a fish and crab, the fishermen medallion, a duck, a lamb, another duck, an antelope and a bird (perhaps a dove).

The entrance to each aisle from the west bears a representation of a goblet filled with fruit, flanked by birds: porphyrio in the southern aisle and pheasants in the northern one. The chapel has very intricate mosaics (see Pl. XVIIIf) with geometrical patterns, which

Ḥorvat Beit Loya: Greek dedicatory inscription in chapel of Epanagia

270

Ḥorvat Beit Loya: olive press

Ḥorvat Beit Loya: chapel of Epanagia

erbs 13:9 ("The light of the righteous is radiant").

The ground floor of the bell tower has a relatively crude and simple mosaic. A Greek

Ḥorvat Beit Loya: Greek inscription in tower, "The Lord will guard your coming and going (Psalms 121:8)

inscription appears within a circular medallion in its center. It quotes the Septuagint of Psalms 121:8: κ(ύριο)ς φυλάζ(ε)ι τὴν εἴσοδόν σου καὶ τὴν ἔξοδόν σου, "The Lord will guard your going and coming now and forever." The mosaic pavement of the *pastophorium* north of the apse is divided into squares by strips of black tesserae, while the white floor of the southern *pastophorium* features simple floral decorations.

The olive and winepresses. Excavations have partially uncovered an olive press adjoining the south side of the church, east of the *baptisterium*. The lower part of its eastern and southern walls were carved from the rock of the hill rising to the east. The eastern wall continues the church's eastern wall, while the southern one is part of the wall surrounding the entire church complex. This indicates that the olive press was in fact an integral wing of the church complex, although it probably was built some time after the latter had been completed.

Two post-stones, which kept the beam mov-

271

Ḥorvat Beit Loya: winepress, looking south

ing in the correct direction, were found in the eastern part of the press.[3] A heavy stone, into which the beam was fixed with a screw, was also uncovered. The grooves and holes in it held the screw in place and permitted it to turn. Between the post-stones, a stone basin for collecting the oil, 1.23 m in diameter and 0.85 m deep, was sunk into the soft rock. A large stone, 1.9 m in diameter, which had been part of the olive-crushing system, was found in secondary use on the west side of the atrium.

A well-preserved winepress was situated 20 m east of the church. Its layout can be determined from the lines of its mosaic floor, which was made of relatively large tesserae, 16–20 per sq dm. The walls had been dismantled. The treading area measured 7 × 5.5 m, and an anchoring stone, in which a screw was inserted for pressing the waste, was sunk in the center. The square depression in the center of this stone was connected by a clay tube to the settling pit. The juice from the treading floor was led to the settling pit via a drain. The settling pit measured 0.95 × 0.9 m, and was 0.75 m deep. The collection pit was round, measuring 2.25 m in diameter and 1.55 m in depth. Its walls were plastered and it had a mosaic floor. A rounded depression in the floor, 0.65 m in diameter and 0.45 m

deep, collected the last drops of juice. On the edge of the pit, there are stones with small concavities, ensuring the stability of the storage jars. This wine press is typical of the Byzantine period. The close proximity of the agricultural installations to the church complex supports the latter's identification as a rural monastery.

The burial cave and quarries. A Byzantine burial cave was discovered approximately 5 m north of the chapel, outside the wall surrounding the complex. It consisted of a subterranean burial chamber, 3.25 m long, 2.3 m wide and 1.75 m high, with a staircase hewn out of the rock leading down to it. Three burial niches in the walls were covered by stone slabs; above them, four crosses were carved in the rock which was painted red. Twenty-six ornamented oil lamps with high-set handles, typical of the early Muslim period, were discovered intact. The findings also included fragments of glass vessels and one intact bottle. It is reasonable to presume that the cave was in use much earlier than the Muslim period. It was vandalized during the Mamluk period, and the contents of the burial niches were thrown into the center of the chamber. The vandals left behind a hand-made oil canister decorated with geometrical patterns and painted red. A plastered installation, of unknown function, was found above the cave. The proximity of the graves to the church may indicate that the interred were the church founders, some of whose names are recorded in the inscriptions.

Two small quarries were discovered approximately 20 m south of the atrium in a layer of hard *nari* stone covering the soft limestone. Quarried stones remaining in the area correspond in size to those in the church walls. As these quarries appear to be Byzantine, it can be presumed that they supplied building materials for the church. The quarrying techniques can be determined on the basis of the remains: 10-cm-wide rectangular blocks were demarcated by chiselling and then removed from the rock layer by undercutting.

[3] R. Frankel, J. Patrich and Y. Tsafrir, "The Oil Press at Ḥorvat Beit Loya," *CAHL*, pp. 287–300.

The Church of St. Stephen at Ḥorvat Be'er-shem'a

Dan Gazit and Yeshayahu Lender

Excavations were conducted at Be'er-shem'a (map ref. 1070/0737) in the wake of damage to the site caused by agricultural activity.[1] Ḥorvat Be'er-shem'a (Kh. el-Far) is located in the center of the Besor Plain, some 4 km east of Naḥal Besor and about 22 km west of Roman-Byzantine Beer-sheba. The site covers an area of approximately 125 acres. Remains of walls, cisterns, wells and monumental structures were visible on the surface even before excavation. Ceramic and numismatic surface finds from various surveys dated the site to the Late Roman and Byzantine periods.

In the north of the site there is a man-made

Ḥorvat Be'er-shem'a: general view

[1] Excavations were conducted at Be'er-shem'a in November 1989 and in August 1990 on behalf of the Israel Antiquities Authority with the support of the Jewish Agency (first season) and the Merḥavim Regional Council (second season). The work was directed by the authors with the assistance of Y. Kalman. Much support was provided by Kibbutz 'Urim and volunteers from other settlements in the region, particularly Kibbutz Be'eri. N. Sneh was the photographer and V. Shor the surveyor. The Greek inscriptions were read by V. Tzaferis.

square podium (ca. 80 × 80 m, rising to a height of 2 m above the plain). Alt's belief that the podium represented remains of a military camp[2] led him to identify the site with Birsama (perhaps a Greek transliteration of Be'er-she-

[2] A. Alt, *Palästina Jahrbuch* (1931), pp. 82ff.

m'a), the military center of Saltus Gerariticus, one of the imperial holdings in the western Negev.[3] M. Gichon identified the podium as one of the posts of the fortified border line, *Limes Palaestinae*.[4]

The site lies above a shallow aquifer; within the area there are still wells, the water level of which is at approximately 25 m below the surface. The site is about one day's march from Beer-sheba, Gaza and Elusa. Its prosperity must have been due, in part, to its location on important routes and its proximity to water resources.

Excavations were conducted in the southeastern portion of a square (40 × 40 m) structure whose outline was visible on the surface. A church (12.5 × 21 m) with a basilican plan was revealed. It is divided into a nave and two aisles by two rows of five columns. Seven of the column bases were found *in situ*. The nave terminated in an apse, flanked on either side by a side-room (*pastophorium*) measuring 3.5 × 3.5 m. At the center of each of these chambers remains of a marble-faced hexagonal installation (0.5 × 0.5 m) were exposed, apparently containers for the bones of saints (*reliquiaria*). In the center of the 5 × 5 m *bema* were found the remains of a 0.8 × 0.8 m altar constructed of dressed stone faced with marble slabs. In the northeast of the hall, the 1 × 1 m hexagonal base of the pulpit (*ambo*) was discovered, made from dressed stones. Access to the main hall of the church from the narthex is through three entrances, the central one leading to the nave and the other two to the aisles.

Adjacent to the church in the south are three other rooms. The entrance to the middle room (4 × 8 m) is from the nave of the church. Another door leads from the central room to the eastern one (4 × 4 m). The western chamber served as the *baptisterium*; it was 4 m wide but its length is uncertain. A semicircular baptismal font with four steps leading to its base was found in the eastern

part of the room. The basin itself originally had a marble facing both inside and out, which has not been preserved.

The church was built of dressed stones. Its foundations (1.2 m deep) and the lower two courses of its walls were built of hard sandstone (quarried in the nearby *wadi*s). The upper courses of its 0.8-m-thick walls were of the reasonably soft limestone available at the site. The inner faces of the walls were coated with mud plaster containing sherds and then whitewashed. Remains of painted decoration were discernible on the whitewashed surface. The large quantity of iron nails found in the site most probably belong to the ceiling's wooden beams. The debris in the aisles was found to contain numerous mosaic fragments and balustrade posts, indicating the existence of galleries above the aisles.

The aisles and the narthex, which was only partially excavated, were paved with stone slabs. Probes dug in the aisles revealed a floor from an earlier phase. The apse, the two *pastaphoria* flanking it, the *bema*, the nave and the baptistery were paved with colored mosaics which include ten Greek dedicatory inscriptions. From these inscriptions we learn that the church's benefactor was named Stephanos and that the church was dedicated to St. Stephen. Numerous names of men and women, some of Arab origin, are also mentioned. The inscription on the front of the baptismal font contains the names of residents of the village of Heladios. This was apparently a village in the Gerar region. This is the first time that Gerar (known from the Bible) has been encountered in an archaeological context since the discovery of the Madaba mosaic map.

The Mosaics

The mosaic in the baptistery comprises a leaf motif and geometric patterns, including a cross. A bowl of fruit is depicted as well as three inscriptions. The floors of the side-rooms near the apse bear geometric patterns, and in the southern room there is an inscription in a *tabula ansata* which mentions Victor, the church storekeeper, whose image appears

---

[3] M. Avi Yonah, *The Holy Land* (Ann Arbor, 1979), pp. 123–125, 148.

[4] M. Gichon, "The Sites of the Limes in the Negev," *EI* 12 (1975), p. 153.

in the central mosaic (see below). The mosaic in the apse has a wave pattern.

The mosaic carpet of the *bema* surrounds the altar. Its border comprises a guilloche including geometric patterns. The internal band consists of twenty-two medallions, in which there are geometric and floral designs. Many of the tesserae were made of colored glass. A six-line inscription was revealed to the west of the altar and another inscription in a *tabula ansata* was laid at the western end of the *bema*.

In the eastern part of the nave, there is a colorful mosaic within a guilloche border of circles and rhomboids. Two inscriptions of five lines each, and another, to their east, of one line, are incorporated into the carpet.

The central carpet lies in the middle of the nave. To its west, adjacent to the middle entrance to the nave, is a fragmentary five-line inscription in a *tabula ansata*. The central carpet design (5 × 9 m) has a double border with a lotus-flower pattern on either side of a plaited guilloche. The mosaic comprises fifty-five medallions with figures arranged in eleven rows of five medallions (an arrangement known as "populated scrolls"). The medallions are formed from vine shoots sprouting from an amphora. This design is very common in Byzantine art and is especially typical of sixth-century churches and synagogues in the region of Gaza and the northwestern Negev.[5]

Animals, humans, and various objects are portrayed in the medallions. The intervening spaces contain grape clusters, grape leaves and tendrils as well as birds (partridges, hoopoes, doves and quails). Spaces within the medallions are also filled with grape clusters.

Most of the animals, which are depicted in motion, extend beyond the borders of their respective medallions. The human figures, some of which have no parallel in other known mosaics, are also shown in movement. The shaping of the figures was well executed,

and particular care was taken in the depiction of the clothing of the human figures. Noteworthy is the woman breast-feeding — an unusual subject for mosaic art and for the decoration of a church.

The following are details of the figures portrayed in the central carpet (looking east from the entrance to the church). The middle medallion is described first and then the pair flanking it on either side (see Pl. XX–XXI):

First row: an amphora and on either side a lion crossing both medallions.

Second row: a woman breast-feeding a baby is flanked by a goat and a pheasant on either side.

Third row: a basket of fruit with a guinea-hen on either side, a leopardess to the far left and a lioness to the far right.

Fourth row: a man playing a reed flute with two bulls on either side.

Fifth row: a dovecote made of a hanging vessel, and a pair of doves, flanked by a dog chasing a vixen to its right and a bitch chasing a doe rabbit to its left.

Sixth row: a basket with grape clusters with a man leading a loaded donkey (on the left) and and a

Ḥorvat Be'er-shemʿa: woman breast-feeding

5 For example, M. Avi-Yonah, "Une école de mosaïque a Gaza au sixième siecle," in M. Avi-Yonah, *Art in Ancient Palestine. Selected Studies* (Jerusalem, 1981), pp. 389–394.

Ḥorvat Be'er-shem'a: dog chasing vixen

man leading a camel (on the right).

Seventh row: a bird in a cage, flanked on both sides by bears and ducks.

Eighth row: a man leaning on a club, flanked by a panther next to a deer (on the left) and a wolf next to an ibex (on the right).

Ninth row: a puppy and a crane, flanked by a man leading an elephant with a rider (on the left) and a man leading a giraffe (on the right).

Tenth row: a man, above whom is the inscription, "Victor," carries a tray (with a fish?). This name also appears in the above-mentioned inscriptions. This man may be the storekeeper of the church. He is flanked by a horse and mare, and a marten fighting a snake (one medallion has been destroyed).

Eleventh row: a fruit bowl, on either side of which are two peacocks.

The central mosaic is almost perfectly preserved. The high technical and artistic quality and the splendor of the church evidence the wealth of the local community. It should be noted that there are indications of the existence of other churches in the vicinity.

The Finds

Many of the finds were discovered in rooms south of the church's nave, and it seems that they were moved there after the church went out of use. Among the artifacts were numerous fragments of marble carved revetment pillars, chancel-screen panels and offering tables. Also found were fragments of glass lamps, three coins and a piece of a stone reliquary. According to these finds and the style of the mosaics, the church appears to have been in use from about the last third of the sixth century C.E. through to the mid-seventh century C.E.

A Byzantine Church and Its Mosaic Floors at Kissufim

Rudolf Cohen

A mosaic floor was discovered accidentally in the fields of Kibbutz Kissufim in the Negev.[1] The site, marked on old maps as Birket Abu Radi, or Birket el-Wazza, is situated about 1 km northwest of Tell Jemmeh.

Our excavations at the site revealed that the mosaic fragment that had led to the discovery was part of the floor of a basilica 16 × 13 m in size. The eastern part of the church, including the apse, was completely destroyed during construction work at the beginning of this century. Hollows in the mosaic floor indicate that two rows of five columns divided the church into a nave and two aisles. The columns were probably robbed in antiquity, and the walls, which had been built of *kurkar* blocks, had been dismantled down to their foundations. The narthex (11 × 3 m) and the atrium were paved with stone slabs, and in the latter we found remains of a cistern.

Most of the mosaic floor in the nave was destroyed; only a 0.9-m-wide horizontal strip near its entrance survived. A *tabula ansata* measuring 1.6 × 0.2 m in the center of this preserved section included a seven-line Greek dedicatory inscription. The letters, executed in black tesserae, are on the average 0.8–0.9 m high. The text provides the exact date on which the mosaic floor was laid and elaborates by naming contemporaries:

In the time of our most holy and pious Bishop Michael and of Theodoros, most beloved by God, by the grace of God deacon, monk, sacristan, and abbot [of the monastery] of St. Elias, this mosaic was made on the eleventh of the month of Loos in the year 636, the ninth year of the indiction.

The eleventh of the month of Loos 636 corresponds, according to the Gaza era, to 4 August 576 C.E.

The name of the monk Theodoros is followed by several titles: "deacon," an assistant priest for the liturgy; *paramonarios*, sacristan, curator of the cult vessels and costly objects belonging to the church; and *hegoumenos*, abbot of a monastery. This particular mosaic was named after St. Elias, perhaps the prophet Elijah. For the present, it remains unclear whether or not the church was part of a monastery also dedicated to St. Elias. To the right of the inscription, a falcon with a red ribbon around its throat is portrayed against a floral background. The same design probably appeared on the left, but only the plant is preserved.

The intercolumniations were also paved with mosaics. Two scenes and an inscription have survived from the northern intercolumniations. One shows a man leading a camel laden with baskets and amphorae (see Pl. XXIIc). Above him the name "Orbikon" is inscribed in Greek. The second scene shows two richly dressed women wearing diadems, earrings, and bracelets. They somewhat resemble the attendants of Empress Theodora represented in the Church of St. Vitale in Ravenna, Italy. One of the women scatters

[1] The site was first surveyed in 1930 by Yaakov Ory, the regional inspector of the Mandatory Department of Antiquities. He recorded a mosaic fragment decorated with an interlocking pattern. Salvage excavations were carried out at the site by the author in July 1977, on behalf of the Israel Department of Antiquities and Museums, with the assistance of volunteers and members of Kibbutz Kissufim. I. Watkin was the surveyor, and Z. Radovan and N. Sneh the photographers.

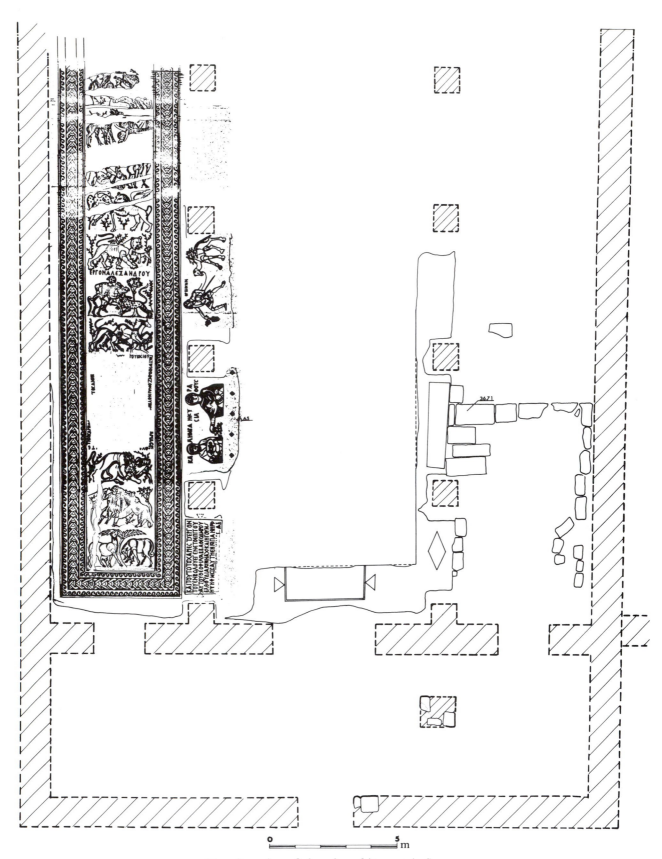

Kissufim: plan of church and its mosaic floors

Kissufim: church mosaics

coins with her right hand. Above her, written in Greek, are the words "The Lady Syltous," or "The Lady of Sylto," perhaps referring to a donor. The second woman is older and has a stern expression. She holds a bowl containing a fowl(?), and above her appears the Greek name "Kalliora," meaning the "good hour" or the "propitious hour." Perhaps this portrayal

Kissufim: Greek inscription at entrance to church

Kissufim: two richly-dressed women in
intercolumniation mosaic

Kissufim: gazelles nibbling at leaves

of the good hour can be compared to female figures on several Antioch mosaic floors, which personify concepts such as pleasure, benefit, and good harvest. The intercolumniations in the southern row of columns were ornamented with circles and squares.

The mosaic floor of the northern aisle is almost completely preserved, except for its badly damaged eastern end. The surviving part extends across the complete width of the aisle and measures 11 m in length and 2.4 m in width. The mosaic is enclosed by a wide border of geometric patterns, and includes an exceptional series of scenes. Due to the destruction of the aisle's eastern end, the exact number cannot be ascertained; only twelve are preserved, some incompletely.

There are three depictions of hunting episodes: a horseman thrusting his spear into a leopard (see Pl. XXIIa); a man bearing a sword and shield fighting with a bear (see Pl. XXIIb); and a hunting dog pursuing a gazelle and a hare. Two scenes show animals attacking other animals: a lion pouncing on a bull (see Pl. XXIId), and a female griffin attacking a swan. Five portrayals are devoted to more peaceful subjects: a lioness and her cub (see Pl. XXIIe); a man milking an animal, probably a goat (here the damage to the floor makes the determination difficult); an elephant; a giraffe and zebras; and gazelles nibbling at leaves. In two other sections impairment prevents identification. Each scene measures about $1.3 \times 0.6–0.8$ m.

Above the rider spearing the leopard is a Greek inscription, ῎ΕΡΓΟΝ ᾽ΑΛΕΧΑΝΔΡΟΥ, "The work of Alexander." This may be the artist's signature; however, in most signed ancient mosaics the name of the artisan is preserved in a separate inscription and not within the body of a picture. The text in question, therefore, probably refers to the deeds of Alexander the Great. Stories about his heroics and exploits were very popular in the Byzantine period. A legend about the life of Alexander that was written in Alexandria in the Hellenistic period continued to be circulated in many versions until the Middle Ages. The assumption that our inscription refers to Alexander the Great is also supported by a Coptic tapestry from the seventh–eighth centuries.[2] The tapestry, which is in the Textile Museum in Washington, D.C., depicts a hunter mounted on a horse; above the former's head is the name of Alexander of Macedonia.

Hunting scenes were popular subjects on mosaic pavements and are found in many churches — such as that at Beit Govrin, Beth-shean, and Mt. Nebo. Their inclusion within churches aroused the opposition of the clerics in the fifth century; for example, St. Nilos vehemently opposed the custom, which he considered pagan. Their appearance on mosaic floors[3] does indeed go back to the fourth–third centuries B.C.E. One of the most famous hunting scenes from that time, from Pella in Macedonia, depicts Alexander the Great hunting a lion. They were also popular in the Roman world, especially from the third–fourth centuries C.E. onward. Numerous examples can be found in Italy, North Africa, at Antioch and in Apamea in Syria.

A tomb was dug in the center of the northern aisle. Its opening, level with the mosaic floor, was covered by a large marble slab of which only fragments have survived. The burial pit at the bottom of the tomb was sealed with marble slabs that we found *in situ* in our excavation. The grave contained five skeletons, laid with their heads to the west, under a small vault. In the mosaic pavement adjacent to the opening of the tomb and surrounding it, there was a Greek inscription. The few preserved pieces of this inscription suffice to indicate that the priest Zonainos was buried there. A woman named Maris also is mentioned, and the text ends with the word "Amen."

Another *tabula ansata* with a Greek inscription was set into the mosaic floor of the western intercolumniation. It measures 1.4 × 0.7 m and the letters, made of black tesserae, are on the average 9 cm high. The inscription reads:

> The superb work in this aisle was done in the time of Father Theodoros, beloved of God, deacon, monk and hegumen [abbot] by the grace of God. This mosaic work (was made) on the tenth of the month of Panemos, in the year 638, the eleventh year of the indiction.

The above-mentioned date corresponds to July 4, 578 C.E. according to the Gaza era. The inscription states that the mosaic was laid in the Ἔνβολος; this incomprehensible word can be read as Ἔμβολος which, in this context, means "aisle." Here it certainly refers to the northern aisle, which was completed as a separate unit two years after the rest of the church had been paved with mosaics.

The mosaics in the Kissufim church are examples of excellent workmanship and striking beauty. The tesserae, partially made of marble, are small and precisely cut, measuring 6 × 6 mm (an average of 140 tesserae to 10 sq dm). The faces of the figures and various other details were executed in even smaller tesserae (5 × 5 mm, an average of 230 tesserae to 10 sq dm). A wide range of colors was employed to emphasize light and shade, principally black, white, and various shades of gray, green, red, yellow, brown, and orange. For the plants lustrous green tesserae, probably malachite and glass, were used. The artist's skill is especially apparent in the naturalistic rendering of human figures and animals. The motifs in the northern aisle are in the main classical, but at the same time clearly faithful to the traditions current in the sixth century; in contrast to the classical period, when hunters were represented nude, all the figures in our mosaic are dressed in accordance with contemporary fashions.

The "Gaza mosaic school," as defined by the late M. Avi-Yonah,[4] was active mainly in the fourth–sixth centuries. To this school should

[2] R. Berliner, "A Coptic Tapestry of Byzantine Style," *Textile Museum Journal* 1 (1962): 3–22; idem, "Horsemen in Tapestry Roundels Found in Egypt," *Textile Museum Journal* 2 (1963), pp. 39–53.

[3] I. Lavin, "The Hunting Mosaics of Antioch and Their Sources," *DOP* 17 (1956), pp. 181–282.

[4] M. Avi-Yonah, "Une école de mosaïque à Gaza au sixième siècle," in *Art in Ancient Palestine. Selected Studies* (Jerusalem, 1981), pp. 389–395.

be attributed the mosaics of the synagogues at Nirim and Gaza and of the churches at Shellal and southern Hazor. All have a similar composition: animals and other motifs arranged symmetrically in medallions formed by vine tendrils that issue from an amphora. As the Kissufim mosaics differ from those of the Gaza school both in design and in subject, they may represent a later stage, previously unknown, in the artistic development of the Gaza school.

The Kissufim church was built during the reign of Justin II (565–578 C.E.) in the midst of a prosperous settlement, which should probably be identified with the town of Orda on the Madaba mosaic map. B. Mazar long ago proposed that Orda should be sought in the vicinity of Tel Jemmeh.[5] In the Byzantine period the region between Gaza and Beersheba was densely populated. This is attested to on the contemporaneous Madaba map, and by the discovery in the area of numerous churches, such as Shellal, Ḥorvat Gerarit (Um Jerar), and Magen.

[5] B. Mazar, "Yurza, The Identification of Tell Jemmeh," *PEQ* (1952), pp. 48–51.

Early Christian Churches at Magen

Vassilios Tzaferis

A salvage dig in 1976 of a mosaic floor discovered about 600 m northwest of Kibbutz Magen initiated four seasons of excavations at the site, during which a large group of early Christian churches was uncovered.[1] The complex comprised four buildings: a large central basilica (Building B), two smaller churches that flank its southern and northern sides (Buildings A and C, respectively), and a baptistery (Building D). Two occupational strata were distinguished; the earliest, phase I, was dated to the late fourth and early fifth centuries C.E. and is represented by Buildings B and C. Phase II was related to the late fifth and sixth centuries and was identified in Buildings A and D.

Building B was built according to a standard basilica plan. It was paved with large, finely dressed local limestone slabs, and includes a spacious atrium in the middle of which is a cistern, a common feature of churches in the Orient. Building B has no narthex, which is one of the indicators of its early date in the fourth century. The narthex does not appear as a permanent element in Christian basilicas before the middle of the fifth century C.E.

Building C, or Church C, was built against the northern wall of Building B and comprised an atrium, a prayer hall, and a room that was used as a baptistery. Although it was contemporary with Building B, it differs from it in both form and character in that it is not a basilica. This church is long and narrow, and it has three rooms that correspond to the conventional divisions of early Christian churches, but it lacks an internal colonnade. The mosaic floor, immediately inside the entrance to the prayer hall, features a large monogrammatic cross flanked by two birds. Above the cross is a Greek inscription that reads: "The holiest dwelling place of the Most High, God is in the midst of her" (Psalms 56:5). The verse is from the Septuagint, and according to Christian theology it refers to the church.

The most important part of Church C, namely the sanctuary, is located to the east of the prayer hall. Among its other uses, this room served as a baptistery. Four narrow steps descended into the baptismal font, which was sunk into the floor in the center of the room. The oblong pool at the bottom of this installation was only 0.4 m wide. The narrow space provided enough room for an adult to stand but not sit. The form of this font is unusual, and perhaps unique in Israel.

Building A, which is located on the southern side of Church B, is undoubtedly the most interesting one in the complex. It contained an atrium, a narthex, and a prayer hall of the basilican type. Unfortunately the apse was destroyed during later building activities. The entire interior was paved with colorful mosaics with geometric, floral and animal designs; there is also a portrait of a man, probably a priest. Interspersed among the decorative designs are inscriptions in Greek. One of them honors St. Kyrikos, to whom the church, dated to the sixth century C.E., was dedicated.

The fourth building, D of the complex, was.

[1] The excavations were undertaken by the Israel Department of Antiquities and Museums and directed by the writer, who was assisted by members of Kibbutz Magen and volunteers from abroad. This description is based on the Hebrew article written by V. Tzaferis and E. Dinur and published in *Qadmoniot* 41 (1978), pp. 26–29. For further details, see V. Tzaferis, *An Early Christian Church Complex at Magen. AASOR* (1986–1987).

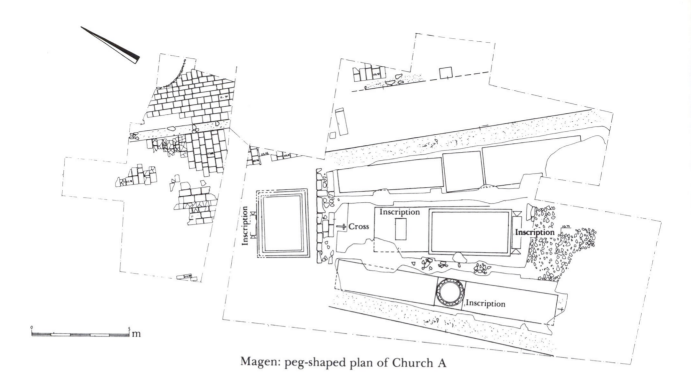

Magen: peg-shaped plan of Church A

Magen: mosaic floor of Church A

284

a baptistery, in the middle of which stands a cruciform baptismal font. Subsequent building activities heavily damaged this chapel.

Although all of the structures include the normal components of early Christian sacred buildings, they display some features exceptional for Byzantine construction, and so provide an insight into the development of early Christian religious architecture. The first point to be made is that each of the churches except Church C (the baptistery) has a north–south orientation, instead of the standard east–west axis. This uncommon orientation does not appear to have been dictated by any peculiar topographical condition; indeed, all of the churches were constructed on a flat, open space. We suggest two possible reasons for this departure: either the architects planned the churches in the winter, when the sun rises slightly to the south, or for some reason Egypt was more important to them than the east.

The second feature of note in the churches is the depiction of crosses on the mosaic pavements in both Building C, dated to the fourth century, and Building A, dated to the sixth century C.E. As we have already mentioned, a large cross was flanked by two birds in Building C next to the threshold in the prayer hall. Its position dominated the church's entrance, so that everyone who entered through that single door was forced to walk on it. Large crosses were also found in the baptistery of the same building, and there was a similar depiction in Church A. Here again the cross was set down directly adjacent to the main, central entrance. About a hundred years lapsed between the building of Church A and Church C.

The setting of crosses in mosaic pavements, and especially in churches where the congregants would be forced to walk on them, is particularly notable in the light of the edict of 427 C.E. issued in Constantinople, which prohibited the display of the cross and other sacred Christian symbols on pavements. This edict was commonly used as a chronological criterion by archaeologists who traditionally dated mosaic pavements with such ornaments to periods prior to its issue. However, the appearance of crosses on mosaic pavements, both ante- and postdating this public proclamation, demonstrates the extent of its observance in the Orient. Thus, we need to exercise extreme caution in using the edict as a guide for dating such archaeological discoveries.

The third architectural peculiarity concerns the design of Church A. Although this building possesses all the components of a basilica and its interior was organized along the same lines as that of an early Christian church, its overall plan with the missing apse is peg-shaped. From the narrow 5-m-wide narthex, the external walls of the church fan out in the direction of the missing apse, which would have spanned the central part of the nave only. This reconstruction gives us a church with an unusual outline — it has two narrow ends and bulging sides — a shape which is astonishingly similar to that of a boat. Perhaps the architects had in mind the regulations stipulated in *Constitutiones Apostolorum*, which state that the church should be like a ship to carry the faithful safely to the port of Jesus. In researching this discovery, a survey of the plans of almost all of the early churches in Israel did not produce a single parallel. Thus, if this boat shape was intentional — and there is no reason to believe otherwise — it is a unique construction in early Christian church architecture.

The identification of the site remains obscure, although conjectures have been offered. Nearby is the tomb of Sheikh Nuran, a sacred pilgrimage site of the local Bedouins. Although we have no way of knowing whether such a sheikh ever existed, we can translate the same *Nuran* (meaning "light" or "lamp" in Arabic) to the Greek *Lichnos*. An ancient settlement in the northwestern Negev bearing this name is noted by Jerome as a place visited by St. Hilarion in the fourth century C.E.

The Cathedral at Ḥaluẓa (Elusa)

Avraham Negev

The cathedral of Ḥaluẓa (Elusa) was located by the author in 1973, in a survey of the ancient site.[1] Although there are several other churches in the vast area of the city, I chose to excavate this compound because the elevated ground at the eastern end of the building (the sanctuary) is less than 40 m from the northern entrance to the Nabatean theater (where excavations were begun in 1973); in view of the interrelationship between the theater in its various forms and the Nabatean temple, I hoped to discover a temple close to or underlying the church.

The Basilica

The church compound is some 100 m in length. For this reason alone its builders could not have found a site within the limits of the city better suited for a structure of such magnitude and splendor. Whatever the time of its construction, many of the older buildings of the town were still standing and in a good state of repair; it was certainly erected a century or two later than the city's period of prosperity in the second and third centuries C.E.[2]

Keeping this in mind we began to excavate the "East Church," our name for it when we commenced our work. I reversed my usual procedure of starting the excavation of a church at its western end and progressing slowly toward the sanctuary. Instead, we began with sections in the sanctuary. Removing the 5,000 cu m of debris with which the compound is covered would have required several seasons of work, so the choice proved to be wise: within a month we understood the church's typological problems. Additional sections at various points in the basilica and the atrium increased our knowledge of the building.

The external measurements of the basilica were 17.7 × 39.45 m, but the chapels that flanked the building on the north and south almost doubled its width. The atrium was 29.6 × 32.8, making this church by far the largest in the Negev, and one of the largest in the Holy Land.

The spacious atrium was surrounded by four colonnades. The eastern portico, 6.21 m wide, was wider than the other three and three steps higher, creating an elevated approach to the three entrances to the basilica, the central one of which was almost 3 m wide. There probably was a well or a fountain in the middle of the atrium, which is indicated by a round depression. We made a probe 2 m in depth in the center of the atrium; it produced clean sand, but we did not reach the bottom of the structure.

[1] The excavations at Ḥaluẓa were carried out under the author's direction in the summer of 1980, on behalf of The Hebrew University of Jerusalem, the Israel Exploration Society, and the Mississippi State University at Starkville. The plans were drawn by D. Chen of Tel Aviv University; the photographer was F. Benci, and the isometric reconstruction was drawn by R.S. Fritzius, both of Starkville, Mississippi. This present study was written in 1981, with the help of the staff at the Cobb Institute of Archaeology, Mississippi State University, to whom I wish to express my gratitude. See also A. Negev, "Survey and Trial Excavations at Ḥaluẓa (Elusa), 1973," *IEJ* 26 (1976): 89–95, Pls. 20–21.

[2] For a discussion of the place of churches within the central Negev city plan, see Negev, ibid.; idem, "House and City Planning in the Ancient Negev, Israel," in G. Golany (ed.),

Housing in Arid Lands (London, 1980), pp. 1–23 and passim; and idem, "The Cathedral of Elusa and the New Typology and Chronology of the Byzantine Churches in the Negev," *LA* 319 (1989): 129–142.

The basilica had ten columns; a pair of pilasters at either end made it eleven intercolumniations long. The nave was 7.27 m wide; the aisles were of unequal width, the southern one being 4.5 m and the northern one 4.35 m.

The sanctuary is T-shaped and two and one-half column spaces long. It was two steps higher than the nave, but only one step higher than the aisles. At the end of the nave and the aisles there were apses, the central one of which was 5.65 m wide, but only 2.47 m deep, forming less than half a circle. The northern apse was 3.58 m wide and 2.25 m deep. The southern one was larger — 3.82 m wide and 2.33 m deep. Most of the space within the central apse is occupied by a seven-stepped structure that is 2.47 m long. It was originally revetted with marble plaques and had a balustrade at the sides of the steps. In all probability this was the stone substructure of the bishop's wooden throne, which would identify the church as the regional cathedral.

The seven-stepped structure in the middle of the apse prescribed the location of the 2 × 2.55-m altar well beyond the chord of the apse. The hexagonal *ambo* is at the northwestern corner of the *bema*, as in all central Negev churches. The *ambo*, altar, *bema*, seven-stepped base, and the ashlar walls of the apses were all covered with Proconessian gray marble that was also used to pave the floor of the basilica.

Hardly anything remained *in situ* in the chancel, but in the debris we found many fragments of screens decorated with crosses and wreaths as well as several chancel posts of the type commonly found in the Negev.

The Martyrs' Cult in the Southern Apse
We observed evidence of a martyrs' cult in the southern apse. Its floor was decorated with an eight-pointed star that was made of variously colored marble, and it had a round inlay of marble, which is now missing. Our proposed reconstruction of the chancel presents an unusual type. One of the chancel screen posts, which we found in the debris at the foot of the step in the southern apse, had three slots instead of the usual two, to support a chancel screen panel. Moreover, the third, perpendicular slot was narrower than the other two, and would have received a thinner slab of marble which may have formed part of a subsidiary chancel that was placed behind the southern apse's main one. It was in the floor of this small space that we found a hole for a small colonnette. The colonnette itself, broken into pieces, lay in the debris. It probably supported a small altar table that was fastened to it with a bronze nail. Half of the table top was also uncovered. It is broken diagonally and half of the hole into which the colonnette was inserted is filled with green copper oxide. The colonnette and table are of marble. In the debris around the southern apse we also found three fragments of a limestone box that was most probably a reliquary.

The location of the sacred relics can be determined with a great measure of certainty: the small one-legged altar table — on which a modest limestone reliquary was placed — stood in the middle of the space enclosed by the screen of the chancel behind that of the southern apse. The positioning of the reliquary on the table would place the holy relics within easy access of the pilgrims who came to honor the saint's memory.

There was no sign of any veneration of saints and martyrs in the northern apse, a feature distinguishing this martyrium from all others in the central Negev. Perhaps, for some reason, only one saint was venerated in this church; however, it is also possible that the Syrian practice of only allocating the southern apse and chapels to the cult of martyrs was followed here.[3] We can only speculate as to the identity of the saint in question; I suggest that he was St. Sergius, a very popular saint of the Negev, frequently mentioned in the Nessana papyri.

Typologically the East Church of Ḥaluẓa belongs to the same class as the South and North Churches at Shivta (Sobota).[4] The lat-

[3] J. Lassus, *Sanctuaires chrétiens de Syrie* (Paris, 1947).
[4] See note 2 above and A. Negev, "Subeita," in *Encyclopedia of Archaeological Excavations in the Holy Land*, IV (Jerusalem, 1979), pp. 1116–1124. The plan of the North Church was drawn under the direction of Dr. Renate Rosenthal.

ter were triapsidal, their chancels were T-shaped, and both side apses were dedicated to the cult of martyrs, although their reliquaries were placed within rounded niches in the apse walls. In fact, the more regularly-planned North Church at Shivta is almost a half-sized replica of the Ḥaluẓa church.

I attempted to show in a previous article[5] that the triapsidal layout of the two churches at Shivta was not their original plan. (This hypothesis gained further validation after a trial excavation I carried out at the site together with S. Margalit.[6]) I suggest that the side apses were added to the original single apse as part of a comprehensive restoration of these buildings, possibly following the severe earthquake that, I believe, shattered the towns of the central Negev at the end of the fifth century C.E.[7] The triapsidal reconstruction in the South and North Churches at Shivta certainly antedates by many years their initial construction as monoapsidal basilicas. The triapsidal layout of the cathedral of Ḥaluẓa was not its original plan either; it too was at first a monoapsidal building, as our excavations have revealed.

The Excavation
We began our excavation of the church at two locations: in a section cut in the longitudinal axis of the sanctuary and by exposing the southeastern part of the building, where our objective was to find its corner. In the first section we discovered the seven-stepped base of the bishop's throne and the wall of the central apse. By carefully cleaning the wall, we learned that there were in fact two successive

apses, built one inside the other, both of which had been faced with gray marble. This was our first indication of there having been two constructional phases in the history of the church.

After finding the southeastern corner of the building, we proceeded toward the southern aisle and came upon a rectangular room adjoining the central apse. A small built-in cupboard was found in its northern wall, while the entrance to it must have been via the southern aisle. This was our first hint that the church we were excavating was a monoapsidal building, reminiscent of the plan of the East Church at Mamshit. This became even more evident when we began to excavate the northeastern corner of the building. There we found another rectangular room, with a similar built-in cupboard in its southern wall.

However, when our excavations in the southern room were resumed, a rounded wall at a distance of one meter from the eastern, rear wall of this small room was revealed. Once the whole length of the curved wall was exposed, we saw that it had been built against the northern and southern walls of the room: it was not bonded to them, suggesting a later date. It became obvious, therefore, that at some stage in the history of the structure, it had undergone a total change of plan.

Wishing to verify these observations we continued our excavation in the northern room, but there instead of the curvature of an apse, we encountered a thick wall parallel to the room's eastern one (1.9 m from it), thus creating a small chamber 1.9 × 2 m. This was entered from a door in its southern side, which was constructed of material in secondary use, including limestone column drums. As we learned later, both the small chamber and its thick wall are of a late date. Cleaning the top of the chamber's thick western wall, we soon came upon the curved wall of the northern apse, which was built against and forms part of it.

In the narrow space behind the southern apse, we reached the floor level at a depth of about 2 m. There we could clearly follow the method by which this apse had been added.

[5] A. Negev, "The Churches of the Central Negev. An Archaeological Survey," *RB* (1974): 400–422, Pls. XVI–XXIII.

[6] A. Negev and S. Margalit, "Shivta, 1985" (Notes and News), *IEJ* 36 (1986): 110–111; S. Margalit, "The North Church of Shivta: The Discovery of the First Church," *PEQ* 119 (1987), pp. 106–121.

[7] For a discussion on this date, see A. Negev, *The Greek Inscription from the Negev*, Stadium Biblicum Franciscanum, Collectio Minor, N. 25 (Jerusalem, 1981), Chap. 2, pp. 47–61; idem, "Nabatéens et Byzantins au Negev," *Le Monde de la Bible* 19 (1981): 37–38; idem, *Tempel, Kirchen und Cisternen, Ausgrabungen in der Wuste Negev* (Stuttgart, 1983).

Ḥaluẓa: general view of sanctuary

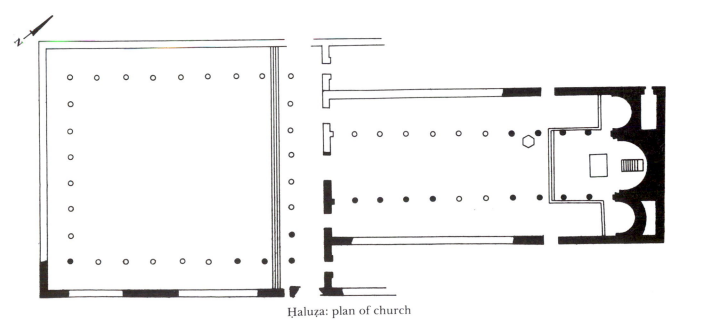

Ḥaluẓa: plan of church

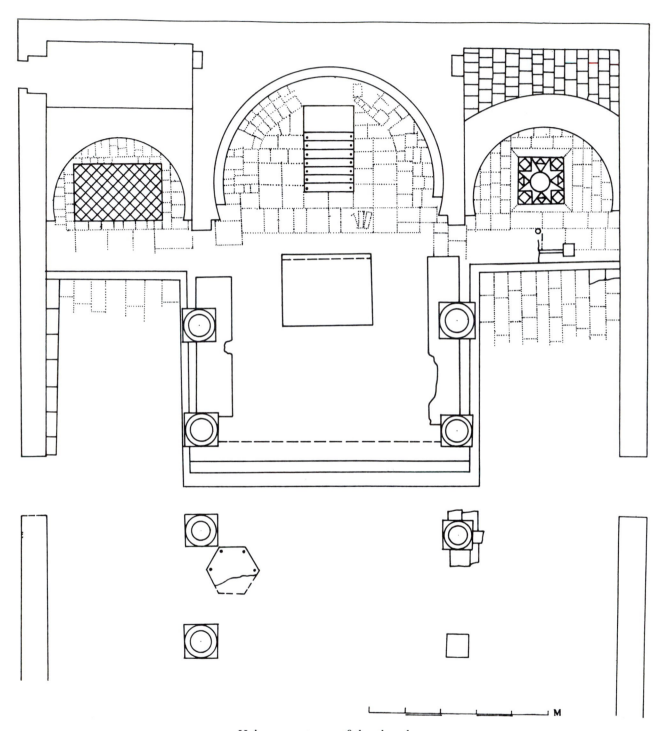

Ḥaluẓa: sanctuary of the church

First the eastern wall of the room had been removed, evidently to be used as building material and to facilitate the construction work. When the construction of the apse was completed, a new rear wall was built. How-ever, because the masons were negligent and did not place the new wall on its original foundations, but a little further in, they covered part of the original flagstone pave-ment of the once rectangular room. As we carefully cleaned the floor that remained, we could distinguish faint traces of the four legs of a small table, probably the table on which the reliquary was originally placed. The situation in the northern room was different. When it was converted into a small storeroom, its pavement was removed, along with every trace of its earlier use.

The Two Phases of the Church

The church was at first a monoapsidal basilica with a rectangular room on either side of the apse. The northern room measured approximately 4.1 × 4.9 m. and the southern one about 4.35 × 4.5 m. The diameter of the apse was 6.44 m and its depth was 4.24 m. It is possible that both side rooms were open to the aisles but separated from them by the T-shaped chancel. In this phase the *bema* was one step smaller than it later became. In the early church at least, one reliquary was placed on a four-legged, small altar table at the back of the eastern part of the southern room. This arrangement resembles that in the East Church at Mamshit.

In the second phase of the church's history, the southern and northern rooms flanking the single apse were blocked and two new apses were built. As no use could be found for the narrow space left between the eastern wall and the new curved wall of the southern apse, it was completely filled in with earth. In the case of the narrow northern room, however, the situation was different. There the original limestone slabs of the floor were removed, and a door was opened in the northern wall. This chamber probably was used as a small storeroom, disconnected from the basilica.

The two new apses were of unequal size (see above). In the second phase, a change was also introduced in the central apse. Its diameter was reduced to 5.65 m by the building of a new curved wall (0.34 m thick) within the original apse. The seven-stepped base of the bishop's throne retained its original form. The *bema*, however, was enlarged one step, which brought its base in line with the side apses. Some alterations were made to the chancel of the southern apse, as described

Ḥaluẓa: chancel screen post with three slots

above. It now was somewhat similar to that in the North and South churches at Shivta in their second phase.

Typology and Dating

Unfortunately no material was found during this season's work at Ḥaluẓa which could date either of the phases. When stripped of its marble revetment and columns in the early Arab period probably not much later than 700 C.E., the building was still in excellent condition. It seems that it was denuded of every movable object. Only the marble Corinthian capitals, the Attic bases, and a couple of broken column shafts, for which the spoilers had no use, were left. On stylistic grounds, the Corinthian capitals can only be given an approximate date in the fourth–fifth centuries. This perforce brings us back to my 1974 chronological analysis.

In my 1974 study I suggested dating the beginnings of church building in the Negev to ca. 350–450 C.E. I based this date on the frail historical evidence of the nascence and growth of the Christian church at Ḥaluẓa and supported it with more solid archaeological evidence from Mamshit. In that study I expressed a hope that further excavations at Ḥaluẓa would lead to a better understanding of the history of church architecture in the Negev, of which this city was the capital. Indeed, on closer examination of what we call "Phase I," we can now subdivide it into two or even three subphases. Obviously the earlier churches at Mamshit, Ḥaluẓa, and, if my reconstruction is correct, the South and North Churches of Shivta can be categorized together, having an almost identical sanctuary type.

Ḥaluẓa was the only *polis* in the whole re-

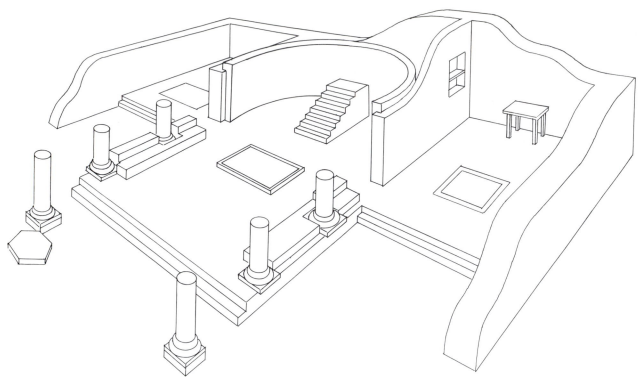

Ḥaluẓa: the sanctuary, phase I

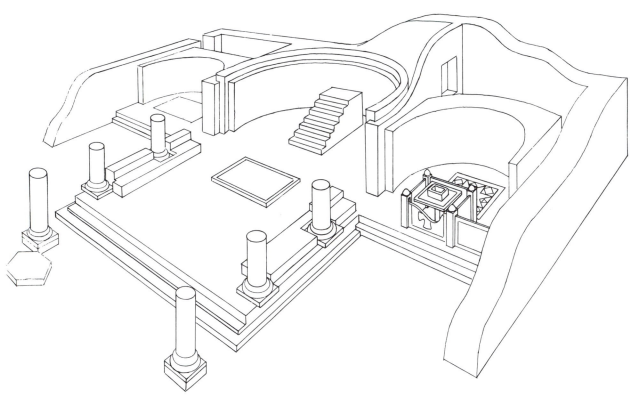

Ḥaluẓa: the sanctuary, phase II

gion of the central Negev, and it served also as the seat of the clerical administration. It must also have been the center of architectural church planning. If this was the case, then the East Church must represent a well-developed type of a monoapsidal basilica, not necessarily the earliest on the site. We have already located four or five other churches in various parts of the immense territory over which the city of Ḥaluẓa spread in the Byzantine period. Only after we investigate all of them can we establish a firmer chronology for the early development of the church in the central Negev. Such investigation has been published elsewhere.[8] Here, I will only mention that the church at Ḥaluẓa was founded in the early fifth century (Phase Ib — 400–450 C.E.) and converted into a triapsidal basilica in Phase II of the architectural development of the Negev churches (around 500 C.E.).

[8] For a detailed discussion, see Negev, "The Cathedral of Elusa" (note 2).

The Early Byzantine Town of Rehovot-in-the-Negev and Its Churches

Yoram Tsafrir

Rehovot-in-the-Negev (Kh. Ruheibeh) was one of the largest settlements in that region during the Nabatean, Roman, and Byzantine periods. In scientific publications it usually appears with its five sister cities: Elusa (Haluẓa), Mampsis (Mamshit), Eboda (Avdat), Sobota (Shivta), and Nessana (Niẓana). These sites are similar in that: 1) they are all situated near roads that traverse the Negev; 2) they have an agricultural periphery of river beds irrigated by rainfall and river floods; 3) they, and smaller settlements in the central and western Negev highlands, are built of local stone; 4) their spacious houses are roofed with stone beams that rest on arches; 5) their churches are decorated with stone carvings; and 6) their buildings have rock-cut cisterns.

Excavations, some of them extensive, have been carried out within the last decades in all six cities, revealing a material culture common to all the central Negev and highland settlements in the Nabatean, Roman, and Byzantine periods. At the same time, however, these studies have thrown light on the individual features of each settlement. Rehovot-in-the-Negev was the last of the six cities to be excavated.[1]

Identification of the Site

Rehovot, as far as area and estimated population are concerned, was the second largest city in the Negev after Haluẓa, yet we do not know its ancient name. Records have been of little help in tracing its history, proving useful only with regard to general background. For example, Edward Robinson, who in 1838 was the first Western scholar to visit the site, was impressed by its ruins and deep well, and conjectured that the Arabic name, Kh. Ruheibeh, could be related to Isaac's well, "Rehovot," in Genesis 26:22.[2] Robinson subsequently rejected the identification, but nevertheless it took hold in scholarly literature as well as in travelers' accounts and even influenced the choice of the modern Hebrew denotation.

In regard to the name of the site during its floruits in the Nabatean and Byzantine periods, the present author has already suggested elsewhere[3] that it should be sought among the settlements listed in the Nessana Papyrus No.

---

[1] Y. Tsafrir, *Excavation at Rehovot in the Negev*, I. *The North Church. Qedem* 25 (Jerusalem, 1988); Y. Tsafrir and K.G. Holum, "Rehovot in the Negev: Preliminary Report, 1986," *IEJ* 38 (1988): 57–58. The excavations were carried out between 1975 and 1979 under the direction of the author on behalf of the Israel Department of Antiquities and Museums, the Institute of Archaeology of The Hebrew University of Jerusalem, and the Israel Exploration Society. In the first two seasons Dr. Renate Rosenthal-Hegginbottom was a codirector. A fifth season (1986) of excavation was carried out on behalf of the Hebrew University and the University of Maryland, under the direction of Prof. Kenneth Holum of Maryland and the author. Preservation and restoration were the work of the late

Zvi Ben-Zvi on behalf of the Conservator of Monuments of the Department of Antiquities. Surveying, plans and architectural restorations were carried out by Giora Solar and Robin Seek. The photographs were taken by Zev Radovan, Claudia Vess and Jan Yosef. Many students, especially those studying archaeology at the Hebrew University, and volunteers from Israel and abroad, participated in the excavations. Sarai Tsafrir and Giora Alkalay acted as administrators of our expedition's camp, which at this remote site required reerection each season. In organization and financing, we were assisted by Midrashat Sede Boqer, kibbutzim in the neighborhood (especially Revivim and Sede Boqer), the Regional Council Ramat Hanegev, and the Israel Defense Forces. We are also indebted to the Dorot Foundation of New York.

[2] E. Robinson, *Biblical Researches in Palestine*, 2nd ed. (London, 1856), pp. 196–197.

[3] Y. Tsafrir, "Rehovot (Kh. Ruheibeh)," *RB* 84 (1977): 423.

79[4] attributed to the early seventh century C.E. This papyrus contains a list of offerings donated to the monastery of St. Sergius at Nessana. Some of the donors are identified by their place of origin, such as Elusa, Sobota, Beer-sheba, Saʿadon (Kh. Saʿadi, a small town located near Reḥovot), and even Thavatha and Phacidia, two villages on the southern coast. A number of places mentioned in the papyrus have not yet been identified: Boteos, Bedorotha, Bertheiba, and Bethomolachon. Presumably, the name of our site, which was the largest of the cities close to Nessana, also appeared in this list. Of special interest are the last two names: Βηρθειβα, Bertheiba, a Greek form of the Semitic באר טוב, באר טובה, "good well," perhaps referring to the well of Reḥovot; and Βετομολαχον, Bethomolachon or Βετομολαχα, Bethomolacha, the place of origin of several donors. Bethomolachon or Bethomolacha can be quite certainly identified with Eboda, which was named after the Nabatean king who founded the town, either Malchu I in the mid-first century B.C.E., or Malchu II in the middle of the first century C.E., or to be more precise, after his dynasty, בית מלכו, the "house of Malchu." Bethomolachon and Bethomolacha are Greek forms of this name.

History of the Town

The earliest remains found both on the surface and in the excavations are Early Roman and painted Nabatean sherds characteristic of the first centuries B.C.E. and C.E.

Reḥovot reached its zenith during the Byzantine period, when all the western and central Negev enjoyed an unprecedented prosperity. Administratively, beginning with Diocletian's reign in the late third century, the area had been part of *Provincia Palaestina*; after the latter's division in ca. 400, it was included in *Palaestina Tertia*. At that time, the road to Sinai from Elusa through Reḥovot and Nessana, once a branch of the famous Nabatean "Incense Road," regained some of its former importance. Now, although no longer serving the international spice trade, it facilitated local trade and especially the passage of pilgrim caravans going down to Mt. Sinai and St. Catherine's Monastery or coming from there to the Holy Land.

The main economic resource of Reḥovot, as throughout the central Negev, was agriculture. The site is surrounded by small valleys and river beds in which fertile loess accumulated.

The largest of the Reḥovot settlements covered an area of about 120 dunam (about 30 acres), and the houses, although spacious, were densely built. An aerial photograph of the town presents considerable regularity in the layout of the streets and blocks of buildings, as if the Roman orthogonal tradition had been continued (unlike other towns in the Negev, particularly Sobota, where no regularity whatsoever is evidenced). Our excavations, however, made it clear that the dispersion of the buildings was not as it seems in the photograph, and that the streets were neither at right angles nor of uniform width. In fact, in most of the city's area, the town plan typical of Palestine in the Byzantine period seemed to be lacking.[5]

We have no evidence regarding the number of inhabitants in Reḥovot in the Byzantine period, but it can be estimated at approximately 4800 according to a factor of 40 persons per dunam. For the present, the question of the origin of the population remains unanswered; its heterogeneity is reflected by numerous names in inscriptions from the cemetery and from the northern church, which are of Semitic (Nabatean or Arabic) origin although Greek in form. (This is an epigraphic feature well known from other sites and from the Nessana papyri.) The settlers at Reḥovot were probably migrants from the north or from other countries, and local descendants of Nabateans, and other tribal newcomers, bound by the might of the

---

[4] C.J. Kraemer, *Excavations at Nessana*, III, *Non-Literary Papyri* (Princeton, 1958), pp. 227–233.

[5] On Byzantine town planning in Palestine in general, see Y. Tsafrir, *Eretz Israel from the Destruction of the Second Temple to the Muslim Conquest*, II. *Archaeology and Art* (Jerusalem, 1984), pp. 317–332 (Hebrew; English edition in press).

Byzantine state and the vast power of the Christian Church in the fifth and sixth centuries. Their conversion to Christianity, which was part of the process of their becoming sedentary, was a far more effective peace enforcer than imperial troops or local militias.

The social fabric of the Byzantine cities in the Negev was shaken during the Persian-Sassanian conquest of Palestine in 614–628, and after the Arab Conquest in the fourth decade of the seventh century, it totally collapsed. The Arab rulers were unable to protect the local population from the incursions of desert tribes, and probably did not devote much effort to assisting them when drought struck. Once the basic conditions necessary for survival in this inhospitable region no longer existed, the town gradually was abandoned. No decorated or glazed Arab pottery characteristic of the eighth and following centuries has been found on the site, indicating that some time after 700 Reḥovot was already almost completely deserted. Those empty buildings that had not yet fallen into ruin were intermittently occupied by nomads who left behind them temporary installations, remains

Reḥovot-in-the-Negev: general view, looking east. The Central Church is in the center

of hearths and ashes, pottery for domestic use, a few coins, and some Kufic inscriptions.

Four churches were identified in the town. One was discovered in its center; another at its eastern limit; and two more beyond its residential area (one in the south near the well and the main road, and the other in the northwestern section of the town). Only the central and the northern churches were excavated.

The Central Church (Area D)

Excavation of the central church has not yet been completed. Only the eastern part has been uncovered, which includes the apse and the chancel, the rooms flanking the apse, and the eastern end of the nave and aisles. The church was a basilica with a single apse, an earlier type than the triapsidal churches that are found elsewhere in the Negev. Two phases of construction were evidenced, the earliest of which may already have dated to the late fourth century; it probably marked the victory of Christianity over paganism at the site. Only a few remains of the earlier church have been hitherto discovered; thus we do not know its exact plan and dimensions. The later church was more than 20 m long; its internal width was 12 m. Because it was built into a slope that descends eastward, the eastern part of the building had to be erected on a platform, supported, at least in part, on arches. The rooms flanking the apse have lower storys, the ceilings of which were carried on arches. The lower rooms have not yet been cleared, so whether they were an integral part of the church and whether there were similar rooms below the apse and the chancel cannot yet be determined.

The apse had a synthronon that is almost completely preserved. The chancel and the nave were paved with large marble slabs, only a few of which are still in place. Hollows in the center of the chancel pavement indicate the position of the altar and the *ciborium*. This is the first time that clear remains of a *ciborium* have been found, although there are indications of the existence of such a feature at other sites. Another unusual component here

Reḥovot-in-the-Negev: apse and synthronon of The Northern Church

is the partition wall built on both sides of the chancel in place of the usual delicate marble or carved limestone screen. The front of the chancel, however, was adorned by delicate lace-patterned marble screen panels and marble screen posts.

Many architectural fragments were collected in the church: capitals, lintels, and bases — a few of marble and the rest of limestone. Fragments of wood, metal nails, and gray plaster from the roof were also found. Some of the finds from the lateral rooms, especially from the northern room, are of particular interest. These include parts of wall fixtures for holding glass lamps, and a goatskin, complete with its stone stopper, that contained the remains of dates.

Fortunately a large fragment of the dedication inscription of the later church was revealed, incised on the marble floor of the

Reḥovot-in-the-Negev: synthronon of The Northern Church

297

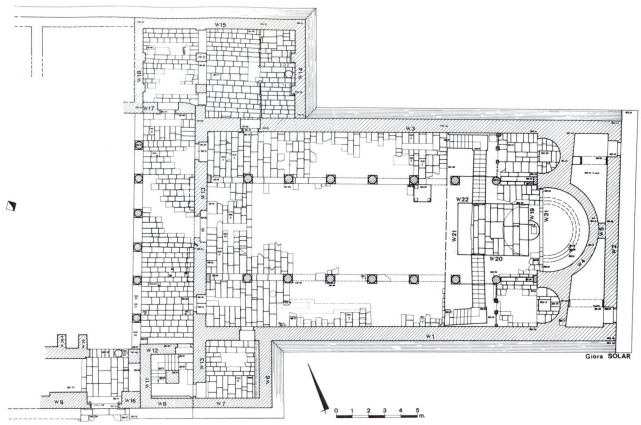

Reḥovot-in-the-Negev: ground plan of The Northern Church

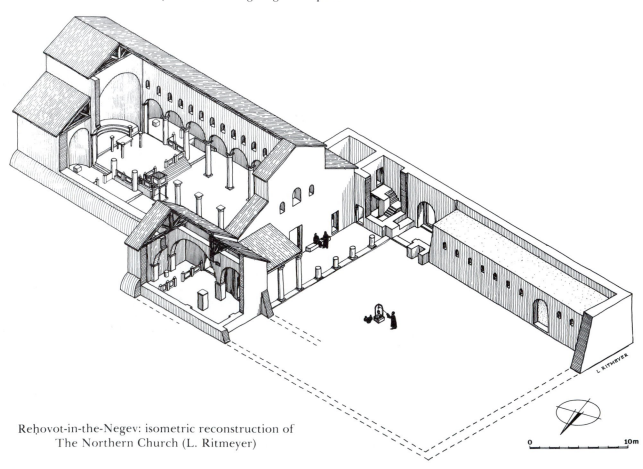

Reḥovot-in-the-Negev: isometric reconstruction of
The Northern Church (L. Ritmeyer)

298

Reḥovot-in-the-Negev: three apses of The Northern Church

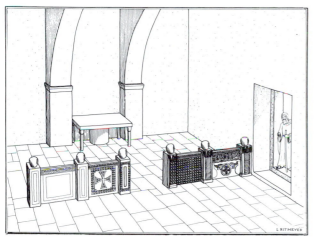

Reḥovot-in-the-Negev: the northern chapel (right)
and reconstruction of its chancel (above)

nave. It provides the date of this church's construction: 445 or 449 of the Arabian era, that is, 550–551 or 554–555 of the common era.

The North Church

The North Church, together with its atrium, formed one of the largest church complexes known in the Negev. It was located in the north-northwestern part of the town, outside the main residential area. It is a triapsidal basilica, particularly similar to the North Church of Sobota. Excavations revealed that

Reḥovot-in-the-Negev: fresco fragment from
The Northern Church

the building had been erected in stages: at first, a rectangle was built with an interior measurement of 24.8 m (80 Byzantine feet) × 13.1 m; then a thick wall was added to the east end of the rectangle. Within the depth of this wall the three apses were constructed. The main part of the rectangle was divided by two rows of columns into a nave and two aisles.

A screen made of marble and limestone separated the hall from the chancel and the apses. Fragments of the main altar were found, and bases of altars were uncovered in the side apses. Behind the side apses there were rooms which did not open onto the church. In the northern part of the church a beautifully decorated chapel was erected. On the south, a staircase tower and a room with fresco and ink inscriptions adjoined the church.

A monastery may have been located in the atrium. The east wing of the latter, which was adorned with a portico, served as an exonarthex of the basilica, while its northern and southern ends (only the southern one was excavated) were occupied by several rooms. The entrance to the church was discovered at

Reḥovot-in-the-Negev: general view of The
Northern Church

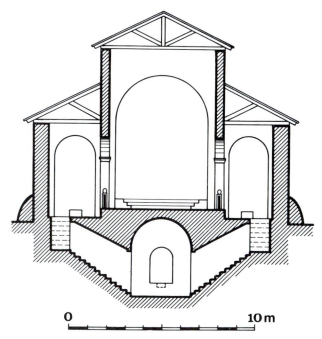

0   10 m

Reḥovot-in-the-Negev: reconstructed section of crypt
and The Northern Church

Reḥovot-in-the-Negev: apse and cavity for reliquary in crypt

the east end of that wing, and a long room there can probably be identified, by comparison with other monasteries, as the *refectorium* (dining hall). It contained a long, narrow table. A large cistern was also found in the atrium.

Both in plan and architectural details, the North Church resembles other churches in the Negev. However, one of its features is unique for this region. A large crypt, measuring about 3.4 × 4.3 m, was built under the chancel. Its lower part was hewn into the rock, while the upper section was built of stone and roofed by a barrel vault. This vault collapsed under the weight of the ruined apse and the fallen columns, and the crypt was filled with earth and many architectural fragments, including marbles and inscriptions. Originally, the crypt was entirely revetted with marble panels, some of which were discovered *in situ*.

Two flights of steps, which are well preserved, led in and out of the crypt from the aisles. This arrangement facilitated movement of processions of worshippers without interfering with the regular services in the church. It was an architectural component characteristic of churches frequented by pilgrims, such as the Justinianic Church of the Nativity in Bethlehem, the Church of Eleona on the Mt. of Olives, and the church of the Monastery of St. Catherine in Sinai, although in the latter, movement was horizontal rather than vertical, in the direction of the "Burning Bush" behind the apse. A crypt similar in arrangement and plan was also discovered at Ḥorvat Berachot in the Hebron region.

The reason for the veneration of the church and its crypt is still unknown, but surely a sacred relic, such as a saint's bones placed in a reliquary, was housed at the spot. No such reliquary was actually found, but the inhabitants may have taken it with them when they abandoned the site. Only the cavity at the base of the apse in the east wall of the crypt remains as mute evidence of its existence.

301

Reḥovot-in-the-Negev: Greek inscription inscribed on abacus of Doric capital, "Of Boethos son of Makedonios"

Two unique small glass plates, measuring 6 cm in diameter, are also of special interest: they were painted in color with images of saints. Fragments of two or more additional plates were found, but some are too small for a proper assessment. The plates' use is unknown; they may have served as inlays in the arms of a cross, or in the frame of large icon, or in a reliquary.

Numerous Greek inscriptions were uncovered during the excavations of the North Church. Some are dedicatory or denote the donors, while others, outside of the hall, engraved on the paving slabs or the walls, provide names and blessing formulae. Most important are the funerary inscriptions inside the church, some found *in situ*. The earliest one dates from the year 383 in the era of *Provincia Arabia*, that is, 488 C.E. Accordingly, we know that the church was erected in the fifth century, probably around 460–470 C.E., and furthermore, archaeological evidence is furnished of the existence of the triapsidal type of basilica in Palestine already in the second half of the fifth century C.E.

Most of the dated burials are from the first half of the sixth century. The latest is noted as being from 555 C.E., but the church certainly continued to exist until the town was abandoned in about 700 C.E. Afterward, Arab tribesmen occupied some parts of the church,

Reḥovot-in-the-Negev: burial and inscription (right end missing) in southern aisle, "Came to rest the blessed Makedonios, on the first day of the month Artemisios, the first year of the indiction, year ..."

with the exception of the hall where the wooden roof and the paving stones had already been plundered. These squatters left behind them the temporary installations mentioned above.

CHURCHES AND MONASTERIES
IN THE SINAI PENINSULA

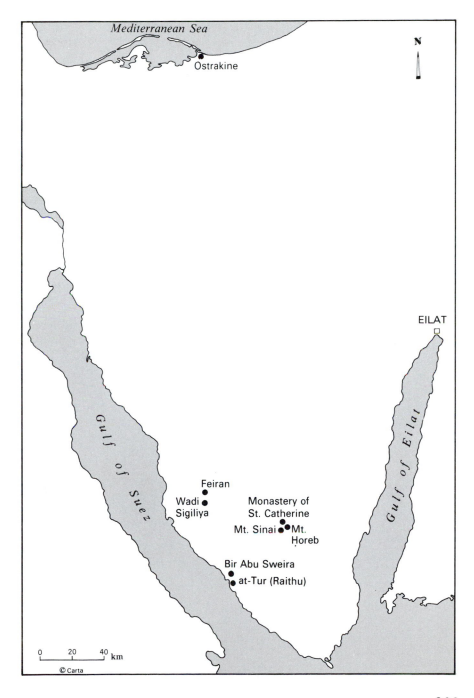

Mediterranean Sea

Ostrakine

N

EILAT

Gulf of Suez

Gulf of Eilat

Feiran

Wadi
Sigiliya

Monastery of
St. Catherine

Mt. Sinai ● Mt.
Horeb

Bir Abu Sweira
at-Tur (Raithu)

0   20   40 km

© Carta

A Christian Settlement at Ostrakine in North Sinai

Eliezer D. Oren

El-Felusyat is situated in North Sinai at the eastern end of the lagoon (Sabkhet el-Bardawil, Lake Sirbonis of the classical sources), about 30 km west of el-Arish and some 3 km from the Mediterranean coast.[1] El-Felusyat is the site of ancient Ostrakine, one of the important stations on the coastal road running from Gaza to Pelusion along the sand bar that enclosed the lagoon. Following the Persian conquest of Egypt in 525 B.C.E., and especially during the Hellenistic–Roman period, the coastal road of North Sinai became the main artery of communication between Egypt and Palestine. Thriving harbor towns and trading stations that originated probably as Greek colonies sprang up along this route — among them Rhinocorura or Rhinocolura (el-Arish), Kasion (Mt. Casius, el-Gals), Gerrha (Tell Maḥmediya), and Pelusion (Tell Farame). These towns owed their prosperity to commercial and industrial activities: international trade and customs collection, shipbuilding, manufacturing textiles and glass, salt curing of fish, growing dates, and quail hunting. The settlements of North Sinai are recorded by historians and geographers, such as Diodoros of Sicily, Strabo, Pliny the Elder, Claudius Ptolemy, Hierocles and others, and in maps and itineraries from the Roman–Byzantine period, such as the *Itinerarium Antonini Augusti*, the *Tabula Peutingeriana*, and the Madaba mosaic map. They flourished until

the beginning of the Arab period, when the importance of the coastal road declined and the Egyptian age-old road, the "Way of Horus," located south of Sabkhet el-Bardawil, again became the principal way for passage.

Ostrakine's location at the junction of the coastal route and the more southern "Way of Horus," and its proximity to the natural outlet from Lake Sirbonis to the Mediterranean (*Ecregma* of the classical sources), endowed it with great importance as a way station and commercial center as well as a garrison for auxiliary military units stationed here as part of Egypt's border guard. It served accordingly as a geographical landmark designating the end of Arabia and beginning of Idumea and Palestine (Pliny V, XIV, 68). The ancient sources detail Ostrakine's exact geographical position between Rhinocorura (24 Roman miles) and Casion (26 Roman miles), or even its distance from more remote Pelusion (65 Roman miles). Josephus, writing about Titus' campaign against the insurgents in Jerusalem in 69 C.E., records that this consul, after leaving Pelusion on the Egyptian end of the coastal road,

> ... advanced a day's march through the desert, encamped near the temple of the Zeus Casius and on the next day at Ostrakine; this station was destitute of water, which was brought from elsewhere for the use of the inhabitants. (*Wars*, IV, V, 661)

In the course of the fourth century C.E. Christianity triumphed in North Sinai owing to the religious politics of the emperors and vigorous missionary activities of the monks. Ostrakine, one of the principal towns in

[1] From December 1976 until April 1977 and again in December 1977 the North Sinai Expedition of Ben-Gurion University of the Negev investigated the remains of settlements in this region under the direction of the author. On earlier investigations at the site, see J. Clédat, "Fouilles à Khirbet el-Flousiyeh, Janvier-Mars 1914," *Annales Service des Antiquités de l'Egypte* 16 (1916): 6–32.

Ostrakine: North Sinai Expedition members cross the "new" lake on their way to excavation site

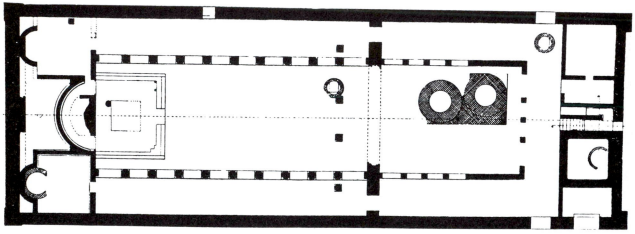

Ostrakine: central church excavated by Clédat

Egypt's *Provincia Augustamnica*, became an episcopal city and the seat of a bishop. Theoctitus attended the Council of Seleucia in 359 and another of its bishops, Abraham (Abramios), participated in the Council of Ephesus in 431. According to Talmudic sources, Ostrakine was a center of the salt industry and of related fish curing.[2] After the Arab conquest,

a settlement with a harbor, called el-Warrada, was established nearby. The harbor was sacked by Frankish pirates in 1249 and subsequently destroyed by an earthquake in 1302.

A detailed survey of the site of el-Felusyat by the North Sinai Expedition of Ben-Gurion University in Beer-sheba concluded that the Roman–Byzantine town of Ostrakine covered an area as large as 2 sq km. Large sections of the town are presently covered by a thick layer of silt and marine deposits resulting from the rise of sea level by about 1 m in the early Arab

[2] According to these sources, the salt, called "Istrakanit," was collected from the saltmarshes near the town. It was considered inferior to that produced in Sedom (Sedomit), as inferred in the Tosefta (Menahot 9:15) which states that "... if no Sedomit could be found, Istrakanit should be brought."

Ostrakine: Clédat's excavation of central church

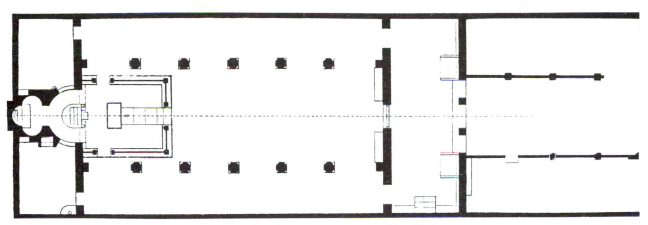

Ostrakine: church on coast excavated by Clédat

period. The group of islands protruding today in the saltmarsh in fact mark the location of major structures erected originally on low sand hillocks. Jean Clédat, the French archaeolgoist who first investigated Ostrakine in 1914, uncovered the remains of well-preserved public buildings such as churches from the Byzantine period and a large fortified structure, perhaps a monastery, whose walls and niches were decorated with many crosses and other Christian symbols. He proposed that the latter was built by the Byzantine emperors to protect the Sinai passes against attacks by the Persians on their way to conquer Egypt. In the large basilican building nearby, under the floor of the main hall, Clédat, excavated burial vaults, most likely of some clergymen. Elsewhere in the church he found about fifty Greek ostraca, many of which are inscribed with the name Ostrakine. About 1.5 km north of the fortress, Clédat exposed another church building with fragmentary remains of a mosaic floor that had as its central motif a cross within a medallion.

Systematic explorations by the North Sinai Expedition uncovered impressive architec-

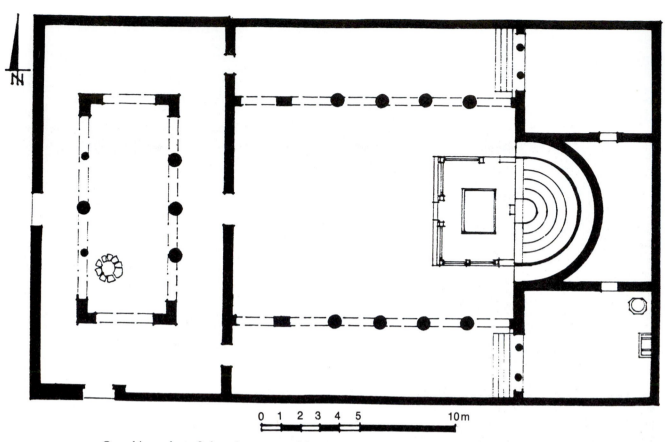

Ostrakine: plan of church excavated by Ben-Gurion University North Sinai Expedition

tural remains of Roman and Byzantine Ostrakine, enabling us now to reconstruct its history and material culture. Thus, for example, the area west of the fortified monastery was occupied by various industrial installations for manufacturing glass and metal objects. Further north, the Expedition recorded the rich remains of the commercial center with its spacious warehouses and shops. About 70 m north of the large basilican church excavated by Clédat, another well-preserved church building was excavated. The building, which measured 33 × 20 m, had a spacious atrium, a central hall with two side aisles and an apse, two small rooms flanking the apse, and another chamber east of the latter. The church walls, preserved to a height of over 1 m, were built of carefully dressed beachrock blocks. The walls were constructed on broad-stepped stone foundations and laid in wide trenches dug into the sand dune. Today, the foundations are partially below

the water table, and the walls are covered with accretions of sand and shells from periodic flooding.

The atrium was entered through one main portal in the west wall and two side entrances. The wood thresholds are still intact, and nearby were recorded the charred remains of the wooden doors alongside their iron pivots and fittings. The atrium was divided by L-shaped piers with a profiled base and by round stone columns aligned with the entrances. A 1-m-deep cistern was located in the southern part of the atrium. The debris of the collapsed walls contained heaps of ceramic roof tiles, which must have fallen onto the stone-tiled floor when the building was destroyed by fire. A thick layer of ashes and charred beams bear witness to the tremendous conflagration that engulfed the building and brought down the walls, the columns, and the tiled roof.

In the last phase of the church's occupation, the atrium underwent extensive changes,

Ostrakine: general view of church excavated by Ben-Gurion University, looking northwest

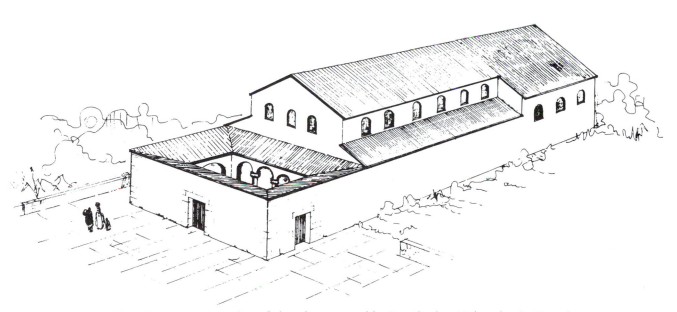

Ostrakine: reconstruction of church excavated by Ben-Gurion University (I. Yagur)

including the addition of partition walls and the installation of cooking and storage facilities; the area of the columns and piers in its northern part was closed off with poorly built stone partitions, and a baked-brick cooking oven with deep compartments was constructed in the enclosed space that was created. Next to the oven a storage vessel that was still full of an edible variety of snails was uncovered. The floor was scattered with numerous store jars, cooking pots and pans, and glass vessels distorted by the heat of the final conflagration.

Two rows of columns divided the hall of the church into a nave and two aisles. The columns stood on square bases and supported Corinthian capitals. Rectangular pilasters were located at either end of each row. It is worth noting that the two easternmost columns, those closest to the apse, were marble, whereas the others were beachrock. The columns carried a series of stone arcades that increased the height of the nave and let light into the church through high clerestory windows. At the east end of the nave was the raised chancel, in which the altar stood on four small round marble columns. The chancel was enclosed by a marble chancel-screen comprising square screen posts with capitals

Ostrakine: decorated marble floor slabs

and panels decorated with crosses and wreaths. The pavement of the hall consisted of well-fitted limestone slabs except for the area near the chancel where thin marble slabs were used. Some of these marble flagstones were carved carefully with various designs — interlocking patterns, rosettes, crosses within medallions, and an amphora with acanthus leaves that support a medallion with a cross in it. The most interesting of the designs is an eagle with spread wings, above which is a cross enclosed in a wreath. In most churches such motifs appear on the mosaic floors; the carving of Christian symbols on the paving stones was perhaps a less expensive alternative. It is possible, however, that these slabs cover the entrance to a crypt or saint's tomb under the floor, but further investigation was prevented by the high groundwater level.

The well-preserved inscribed apse has a three-tiered *synthronon* along the curved wall.

Ostrakine: apse and synthronon

A corridor filled with sea sand and shells was recorded between the latter and the rear wall of the apse. Each of the two rooms flanking the apse measured 6 × 7 m. A series of steps led from the aisles to each room. Two marble columns bearing Corinthian capitals stood on a stylobate between pilasters on the uppermost step. The south room was occupied by a small baptismal basin set on an octagonal slate base, and in the front of the room, two pairs of round columns and a marble basin on hollow bronze feet. A stone reliquary, measuring 20 × 30 cm and surrounded by small round marble columns, stood on a raised step against the back wall of the room. The reliquary contained two bone fragments, apparently belonging to one of the saints connected with the church, and a long bronze needle. It was covered by a beautiful alabaster bowl, perforated in its center, evidently for the custom of sprinkling oil on the saint's bones. At some late date the reliquary was covered first with large stones cemented together and topped by a marble slab with raised edges (an altar?). The floor of the south room was heaped with many copper and bronze objects including chains for suspending candelabra and incense burners.

The north room appears to have been used for storage. A large assemblage of intact pottery vessels was found in a stone storage installation built in the northwest corner. A fine bronze jug whose handle is decorated with an animal figure, and a bronze lamp with a cross on its handle are among the important finds in that room. In the chamber behind the apse, entered from the lateral rooms, were recorded many glass vessels and especially high-footed glass lamps.

Excavations in the nave and the aisles of the main hall yielded grinding and baking installations and a mass of broken roof tiles and charred wooden beams intermixed with hundreds of store jars. Among the many bronze objects were a fine bronze lampstand supporting an oil lamp, scales and a monkey-shaped weight, chains, and three heavy lead pipes over 1 m long. Many of the bronze containers still held remains of sacks and

Ostrakine: reliquary

Ostrakine: bronze oil lamp

ropes. Among the special finds are ivory objects, medallions with crosses, numerous pottery lamps, including one shaped like an open-mouthed fish, examples of decorated pottery vessels, a carved wooden leg from a table or chair, bronze weights, and many coins. Two gold coins were discovered in a gap between the stone slabs of a bench. One is of the Byzantine Emperor Heraclius, minted

Ostrakine: baboon-shaped weight

Ostrakine: baboon-shaped
weight after treatment

Ostrakine: bottle in shape of
woman's head

Ostrakine: ivory
knife handle

Ostrakine: dolphin-shaped oil lamp

Ostrakine: bronze jug

Ostrakine: a) gold coin of Constantine IV (668–685) — obverse; b) reverse of Constantine IV coin; c) gold coin of Heraclius 613–614 C.E.)

in Nicomedia between 613 and 614, and the other is of Constantine IV, minted in Constantinople between 668 and 685.

Architectural considerations coupled with evidence from the rich collection of finds indicate that the church was probably constructed in the fifth century at about the same time when the two other churches of Ostrakine as well as the fortified monastery were built. The decorated floor tiles near the apse may support a date before 427 C.E. for the construction of the church since in this year Emperor Theodosius II banned the decoration of church floors with Christian symbols, especially crosses. The church at Ostrakine, unlike many others in Palestine and Egypt, was not destroyed in the wake of the Persian invasion in 614–628 or during the campaign to Egypt of ʿOmar Ibn el-ʿAs in July 638. In Ostrakine, as in other southern towns, such as Shivta and Niẓana, the Christian community was not suppressed by the Arab conquest and continued its religious practices for several more decades. In fact, the latest coin found in the church, of Constantine IV, shows that the building served as a place of worship for more than thirty years after the Arab conquest. Although many domestic installations for storage, cooking, and baking were built inside it, and the halls and rooms were used to store grain and oil, the furniture, altars, chancel and chancel screen (which bears Christian symbols) were left unharmed. The alterations made in the church may be related to the Umayyad campaigns in the region, and its final destruction by fire may have been perpetrated by Caliph Marwan in 684.

The magnificent churches uncovered by Clédat and by the North Sinai Expedition are illustrative of the considerable size and prosperity of the Christian community at Ostrakine during the Byzantine period. In recent years many Christian tombstones, said to come from the region of Sabkhet el-Bardawil, have appeared on the antiquities market. In the light of the detailed survey in the region, it is now evident that these tombstones originally belonged to Ostrakine's extensive cemetery, which is situated at el-Ḥuweinat, about 2 km southwest of el-Felusyat. In soundings carried out at the site by the North Sinai Expedition, dozens of beachrock cist burials, fragments of tombstones, and various installations were explored. The upper part of each of these tombstones is roughly shaped like a human head, the facial features being accentuated with red paint. Carved on the lower part are crosses and Greek epitaphs, such as "Be of good spirit," "No one is immortal."[3] Spelling and grammatical errors imply that the artisans were rather unfamiliar with the traditional Christian epitaph formulas and knew little Greek. Interestingly enough, in the early fifth century C.E., Jerome wrote in his commentary on Isaiah 19:18 that in Ostrakine, as in other towns on the Sinai coast, such as Rhinocorura and Kasion, the local language was Syriac (Aramaic), not Greek.

[3] Cf. B. Lifshitz, "Ancient Tombstones in Northern Sinai," *Qadmoniot* 13 (1977): 24–26 (Hebrew); A. Ovadiah, "Early Christian Inscribed Tombstones in the D. Pinkus Collection, Israel," *LA* 28 (1978): 127–141.

Ostrakine: inscribed tombstone — "Be well, Heron, no man is immortal, twenty years (old)"

Ostrakine: inscribed tombstone — "Be well, be of good spirit, Zoe, no man is immortal"

In summary, the finds from the churches at Ostrakine and other sites on the shore of the Bardawil Lagoon evidence that in the fifth century C.E. Christianity was already well established there, apparently with the encouragement of the Egyptian Church. The inhabitants were, in fact, "New Christians," who imitated the Christian architecture and funerary customs of the great centers in Palestine and particularly those in Egypt.

Monks and Monasteries in Southern Sinai

Yoram Tsafrir

At the foot of Jebel Musa, "the Mountain of Moses," in the shadow of high peaks, nestles the Monastery of St. Catherine. All who see it are impressed by the strength of its walls, its picturesque buildings, and its greenery. Its isolation within the wild and barren surrounding landscape further enhances its beauty. The monastery's massive walls and the wealth of its treasures bear witness to the days of glory of this ancient monastic center, now watched over by just a few monks.

This article is devoted to those days of glory during which monasticism grew and flourished. They began in the third century C.E., their zenith was under Byzantine rule and their decline in the seventh century at the time of the Arab Conquest. In the middle of that period, in the sixth century C.E., the Monastery of St. Catherine, the masterwork of Sinai monks, was built.

The combination of two factors resulted in southern Sinai becoming a large and important monastic center:

1. The tradition of sanctity: the Christian belief that the mountains of southern Sinai had witnessed the most marvelous of events — the revelation of God to His prophets Moses and Elijah, a prefiguration of the esteemed revelation in the person of Jesus Christ.

2. The natural conditions: barrenness, remoteness and isolation, ensuring refuge for the body in times of religious persecution and for the soul from the temptations of city life, but which also allowed existence, even if meager, from the numerous springs and groves next to the streams.

The history of monasticism in Sinai is not glorified by the sagas of "kings and wars," but rather by a constant and obstinate struggle with the difficult physical conditions and with the hostile tribes of nomads. Due to their remoteness, the role played by the monks of Sinai in general history was definitely a minor one. Their part in the religious wars which raged within the Byzantine Church and divided it, in contrast to that of the monks of Palestine and Egypt, was quite meager.

This situation is also evident in the literary sources in our possession. The monks of Sinai are hardly mentioned in the general descriptions and official chronicles of the period. Our main information comes from the literature of the monks themselves, which usually includes biographies of distinguished individuals and anecdotes about them from the accounts of pilgrims. All the writers were imbued with ardent faith and willingness to hear and pass on stories, even if miraculous and irrational. The contemporary historian who wishes to glean information about Sinai from the many volumes of the Church Fathers must sift the historical kernel from the wealth of traditions and legends.

Prior to presenting the history of the monastic center in Sinai based on this information and archaeological material, we will discuss in more detail the two basic elements mentioned above: the tradition of sanctity and the physical conditions.

Mt. Sinai and Christian Traditions of Sanctity

The path taken by the Children of Israel through the desert and the location of Mt. Sinai are still a riddle. In contrast to the Jewish propensity to obscure the identity of the most holy of mountains, which in fact was realized, there is a natural popular tendency among

Christians to commemorate Mt. Sinai and sanctify it. Hundreds of years after Moses, Elijah the Prophet returned to the "Mountain of God at Horeb" (1 Kings 19:8–9), but those who recorded his life were only able to relate that it was located far away in the desert, a trip of "forty days and forty nights" from Beersheba.

We are not, as noted, concerned with the objective truth but rather with the topography of Mt. Sinai as reflected in later traditions and Christian writings. First of all it must be pointed out that Mt. Sinai and Mt. Ḥoreb are accepted by these traditions as synonymous with the mountain where the Torah was given, or as two mountains very close to each other. Indeed, according to a tradition still current among the monks of Sinai, Mt. Sinai is identical with Jebel Musa, and Horeb is Jebel Sufsafeh, the adjacent peak to the northwest.

In Second Temple times southern Sinai more or less disappeared from the map of the ecumenical or inhabited world. At any rate the common Jewish view transferred those holy sites of Sinai to the desert areas southeast of the Land of Israel and to the mountains of Edom. According to Josephus Flavius, Mt. Sinai stands in Midian, to the east of the Red Sea, and Hor ha-Har, which is "at the edge of the border of the Land of Edom," is near Petra. According to the New Testament (Galatians 4:25), though the passage is difficult textually, Mt. Sinai is in Arabia (Saudi Arabia or Transjordan). In his *Onomasticon* (book of place-names) from the late third– early fourth century C.E. — a work which often adduces Jewish traditions — Eusebius states that Sinai, Horeb and Pharan are situated in the southeastern deserts, whereas places like Hor ha-Har, Kadesh-barnea and Be'erot Bnei-Ya-ʿakan are well known to him, near Petra. In the Aramaic translations of the Pentateuch, Kadesh-barnea is called Reqam-Gea, apparently referring to Petra.

Starting in the third century C.E. and mainly in the fourth century, the tradition of sanctity was restored to the Sinai Desert, following the rise of monasticism, which brought southern Sinai back into civilization. At first the "southwestern orientation" was not accepted by everyone, and Jerome, the important Church Father who lived in Bethlehem in the late fourth– early fifth century, still placed Mt. Sinai somewhere in Arabia, following Eusebius and the New Testament. However, the traditions linking the mountain to the Sinai Peninsula quickly gained strength, and the monastic and pilgrimage centers assured their preservation. Many of the sites connected with the Exodus from Egypt or the divine revelation to Moses and Elijah were marked by the construction of commemorative churches.

We do not know how the tradition came to be revived by the monks. Did they create it by choosing mountains and sites in southern Sinai based on biblical exegesis or even sacred traditions of the local idol-worshippers? While this possibility cannot be rejected, it seems more likely that in addition to the belief that the "Mountain of the Lord" was located in Arabia or Edom, there was a second propensity, linking it to Sinai. On the basis of logical considerations and without any factual confirmation, we may assume that the Jews of Egypt maintained that tradition, for southern Sinai was not geographically inaccessible to them, and that the first monks took the tradition from them, for they too were Egyptian.

Southern Sinai — The Geo-Economic Conditions

In addition to the religious attraction to the mountains of southern Sinai as the visionary scene of the wanderings of the Children of Israel and of divine revelation, there were several geographical advantages making them an ideal place for the development of a monastic center.

Most of southern Sinai is a mass of granitic mountains,[1] the highest of which, Jebel Catherina ("the Mountain of Catherine"), rises to 2,642 m above sea level. Jebel Catherina and the nearby peak to the north, Jebel Musa

---

[1] For the sake of brevity we have termed the crystalline mass "granitic mountains," though large parts of it are composed of metamorphic rock, mainly schist and gneiss.

(2,285 m), are in the middle of a mountain range. The watershed dividing Sinai passes through this locality, and in the vicinity is the crossroads of the most important routes traversing southern Sinai, which influenced the "choice" of the area and its settlement. From here the mountain peaks level off, although not abruptly, until they reach the shores of the Gulf of Suez to the west [Jebel Serbal (2,070 m) and Jebel Um-Shommer (2,586 m) are rather far off to the west], the Gulf of Eilat to the east, and the at-Tiya plateau to the north.

The mass of igneous and metamorphic rocks comprise the main body of the mountain range. On its north is located a strip of Nubian sandstone (an easily-carved stone which features most of the rock inscriptions of Sinai), and further north are limestone mountains. The shores are sandy and relatively narrow.

The tall, rifted granite mountains show a surprising variety of forms. The colors range from shades of red and brown to gray. Their height and steepness make for a rugged landscape, leaving a deep impression on the viewer likely to arouse his religious feelings. The locality was well suited to the spiritual world of the monks, providing a vivid demonstration of the nullity of mankind in contrast to the eternity of the acts of the Creator.

The southern part of the Sinai Peninsula is known for its barrenness. Extensive areas cannot be cultivated, and in the summer even wild vegetation does not grow there. However, it would be an exaggeration to state that the area is entirely a wasteland. Because of the great height of the mountains of southern Sinai the winter is extremely cold, and they are blessed with considerable amounts of rain and snow. On the granite slopes, wherever there is a patch of soil, one can also find perennial vegetation suitable for grazing, and water flows in several streams over a considerable distance.[2] In the valleys of these streams

[2] See in this volume, I. Finkelstein, "Byzantine Remains at Jebel Sufsafeh (Mt. Ḥoreb) in Southern Sinai," pp. 334–340 and U. Dahari, "Remote Monasteries in the Southern Sinai and Their Economic Base," pp. 341–350.

The Monastery of St. Catherine and adjacent gardens, looking south

The Monastery of St. Catherine in the second half of the eighteenth century (Wilson, *Picturesque Palestine*)

and on the adjacent slopes where there is earth, fruit trees and vegetable gardens were planted, many of which belong to the Monastery of St. Catherine. Due to the scarcity of soil, the overall area of these gardens is not great, but since the demands of the monks were extremely modest, the produce sufficed

317

Oasis of Feiran (ancient Pharan) in Wadi Feiran

for many people. In other oases, groves of date palms grow. The largest of these is in the oasis of Feiran (ancient Pharan) in Wadi Feiran, which is 7 km long. This is Byzantine Pharan, a settlement retaining the name of the biblical desert of Paran. From antiquity to the present day, this is the site of the most important settlement in southern Sinai.

Another source of livelihood was livestock. Herders of goats and camels seeking pastures penetrated every corner and ravine, and in many places they left behind inscriptions in the stone. In various periods copper was mined, and the turquoise for which southern Sinai is famous was also extracted. The inhabitants of the area made their living both from mining and from guiding caravans and providing for their needs. We do not know to what extent the mines were operated under Christian rule, but in any case it is unlikely

that the monks engaged in such activity. On the seacoast there were a number of fishing settlements also serving as ports and way stations. At least in their vicinity on the western coast there were monks. One of those towns, Raithu (present-day Bir Abu Sweira near at-Tur), was the third most important center of monasticism after the regions of Jebel Musa and Feiran.[3]

The Local Inhabitants of Southern Sinai
The local inhabitants of southern Sinai were nomads whose way of life was very similar to that of the present-day Bedouin. To a large

[3] The settlement of the monks of Raithu, including chapels, was found in Abu Sweira, an oasis north of at-Tur. As far as we can discern from the sources, the monks of Raithu also lived on the slopes of the mountains to the east, some 20 km or more from the sea. Many ruins and ancient orchards were discovered there which must have belonged to the monastic settlements.

extent their relations with the monks shaped the character of the Christian center in Sinai. The number of nomads did not exceed a few thousands; it seems that the anonymous pilgrim of Placentia (Piacenza) in Italy (ca. 570; see further below) exaggerated in claiming that there were 12,000 Saracens in Sinai.

Some information regarding Sinai and its inhabitants prior to the arrival of the monks can be found in the works of the geographer Ptolemy (mid-second century C.E.), who describes the map of the world.[4] Ptolemy knew that the peninsula was triangular and lay between the Gulfs of Ailana (Eilat) and Heroopolis (Suez). He named the southern point of the triangle after the the nearby village of Pharan. The mountain range between Pharan and Judea is termed the Melana ("black") Range. The name of Sinai itself is not mentioned. The following tribes living in Sinai were recorded: the Pharanites, at the southern end; the Munichiates, to the north; the Saracens, to the northwest; and the Raithenes, to the east, near Arabia.

The Pharanites are doubtless the inhabitants of Pharan and its vicinity, frequently mentioned in other sources. The Raithenes, the term used for orientals in general, might have been preserved in the name Raithu on the western coast. "Saracen" was a general appelation for Arabian tribes until the Middle Ages (it derives, most probably, from "Sharki," easterners in Arabic).

Surprisingly, in the Sinai Peninsula, which belonged to *Arabia Petrea*, the name "Nabateans" is not retained; their origins are frequently reflected in the writings of Ptolemy. From the many Nabatean rock inscriptions throughout Sinai, particularly in the sandstone areas, along the trade routes, and in the most isolated pastures, we learn of their wide dispersion. Nabatean remains at Tel Pharan show that they reached there no later than the first century C.E. From the dated inscriptions it emerges that these tribes preserved their independence and language until at least the end of the third century C.E., i.e., almost two

hundred years after the Nabatean kingdom was annexed by Rome and many decades after the complete collapse of their cultural existence in Edom and in the Negev.

The Nabateans, the original tribes, and other tribes coming from Arabia or Egypt were reliant on animal husbandry, growing dates, and oasis agriculture. The inhabitants of the coast were fishermen, and many of them supplemented their livelihood from transportation, supplying food, and also from plundering the camps of miners and caravans of pilgrims.

A gloomy picture of the state of the inhabitants was painted in the above-mentioned report of the pilgrim of Placentia who traveled to Sinai with a group of pilgrims:

> The families of the Saracens or their wives came out of the desert and sat by the side of the road and cried. They lay their bundles on the ground and asked those who passed by for bread. Their husbands came bearing leather bags of cold water from the interior of the desert. They gave us some and in return they received bread.

Although his reports are generally exaggerated, the foregoing remarks cannot be doubted. Numerous accounts attest to the dreadfully low standard of living of the tribes of Sinai, especially in drought years.

Under the influence of the monks many of the Saracens accepted Christianity, but after the Muslim Conquest they all converted to Islam. Originally, they were idolaters, and, like other desert dwellers, they had worshipped heavenly bodies, particularly the moon and the morning star, Venus. The above-mentioned pilgrim describes a ceremony in honor of the moon which was held some place on Mt. Sinai or Mt. Ḥoreb. In the center was a statue or *bethil* (holy stone) the color of which changed from marble white to black and back again to the astonishment of the Christian pilgrims. The renowned monk Nilus (ca. 400 C.E.) tells about the cult of Venus as the morning star. His son was captured in a

[4] C. Ptolemaeus, *Geographica*, III, 17, 1.

Saracen raid against the monks, and nearly sacrificed to the morning star.

The two cults were very ancient. Worship of the moon was widespread among the Arab tribes. Indeed some scholars link the name of Sinai with that of Sin, the Mesopotamian moon god. That theory is, however, unconvincing, for it cannot be proven that the Mesopotamian cult had spread as far as the remote southwest. The worship of the morning star, sometimes in its western guise as Aphrodite or Venus, was very common among the Nabateans, and it may have been them who brought it to Sinai.

From these stories we can deduce the existence of an ancient tradition of sanctity attached to mountains and sites in southern Sinai. When the monks settled in the area, it is quite likely they were also assisted in locating the holy places by the local traditions of sanctity.

The Beginnings of Monasticism

It is widely held that Christian refugees from religious persecution in the second half of the third century C.E. were the founders of the monastic center in Sinai.

The Christians of Egypt were frequently obliged to abandon their homes and flee from pagan Roman officials. In the seventh decade of the fourth century C.E., a substantial number of Orthodox Christians sought refuge from Arian Christian persecution. In Roman Egypt the phenomenon of *anachoresis* ("withdrawal" into the mountains or deserts) was common, and not necessarily for religious reasons. The debt-ridden peasants often fled, abandoning their settlements for fear of servitude and forced labor. After some time the term "anchorite" came to be applied to monks who withdrew into the desert.

Indeed Christians did take flight in times of persecution, but one ought not exaggerate the need for a refuge as the main factor in the growth of monasticism in Sinai. The letters of Dionysius, the patriarch of Alexandria, which were preserved in Eusebius' *The History of the Church*, indicate that in the reign of the Emperor Decius (ca. 250), the refugees preferred

to hide as near as possible to their homes so that they could return there quickly when the danger had passed. Some of them went as far as "Arabia" (here meaning the eastern desert of Egypt, or perhaps even Sinai itself) and were killed by the Saracens. Very few took up permanant residence in their place of exile; the majority, even after a long period of asceticism, isolation and austerity, preferred to return to their homes.

A notable change occurred at the end of the third century C.E., when the Egyptian monk Antonius (Anthony) established desert monasticism and made it known. Many Egyptian Christians followed his path, and undoubtedly among them were those fleeing religious persecution. One might assume that quite a few reached southern Sinai, combining refuge from external pressure with the realization of an internal spiritual ideal. Several martyrs were indeed linked with southern Sinai, but in general these associations were legendary. Such is the tale regarding Cosmas and Damianus, the Arabian doctors, whose monastery is pointed out by the monks as having been in Tholas (Wadi Tlaḥ near the Monastery of St. Catherine, today Deir Foqara); or a story regarding St. Catherine herself, according to which she once fled to Sinai. A kernel of historical truth apparently lies in the narrative regarding Galaction and Episteme, who came to Sinai from Emessa (Ḥoms) in Syria and established small religious communities near Mt. Sinai. Ten monks dwelt with Galaction, and four nuns with Episteme. We are told that Galaction was captured by the Roman ruler and executed, and his celibate wife Episteme chose to die with him. Their bones were brought back to Sinai and, near the place where they had lived, on the slopes of Jebel ed-Deir (the Mountain of the Monastery), to the northeast of the Monastery of St. Catherine, the monks erected a small chapel, which exists to this day. This story is presented at length by the church scribe Simeon Metaphrastes. It is not clear to what degree the details are exact, and whether we may conclude from it that the representative of Rome had some degree of control over the area of Sinai. However, there is no doubt that it substantiates a flow of monks from distant Syria to Sinai, about which we have much other information.

The bilateral movement of monks between Sinai, on the one hand, and Syria and Palestine, on the other, was of great significance in determining the way of life of the monastic center in Sinai. In Egypt, in the course of the fourth century C.E., life in large monastic communities (*coenobia*) became established, a process in which Palestine and Syria greatly lagged behind. The emphasis was placed on total isolation or the establishment of communities of hermits meeting for prayer and meals only on Saturdays and Sundays (the *laura* monasteries). One can assume that the organization of such cenobitic communities in Sinai, under the influence of Syria and Palestine, was also considerably delayed.

The story of the life of Onophrius, one of the most famous Sinai hermits in the fourth century, shows how Sinai was exploited as a place of refuge for ascetics who did not find complete satisfaction in Egypt. At first Onophrius lived near Thebes of Egypt in a community of a hundred monks, but afterwards he preferred withdrawal, moved to Sinai, and for many years dwelt alone there in a shed, gaining sustenance from the fruit of a nearby date palm. The historian Sulpicius Severus recounts a story from the second half of the fourth century, told by the Italian pilgrim Posthumianus, regarding a hermit whom he had seen on the heights of Mt. Sinai. The man had lived there for about fifty years, naked and alone, avoiding all contact with people ("a person who converses with people will not be spoken to by the angels").

Not many submitted to such extreme solitude and austerity. The majority were disciples of an exemplary individual (called *abba*, "father," in Hebrew and Syriac-Aramaic, and later in Greek), living with him, serving him, learning from him, and trying to imitate his way of life.

The Monks and Their Environment

The development of monastic communities did not depend solely on internal organization and the admittance of new monks, but to a large degree was determined by external factors. First of all the climate forced the monastic communities, except for the most austere hermits, to locate themselves near water sources, either large or small, which are plentiful in the area of Jebel Musa, Sufsafeh and Um-Shommer.

Moreover the hostility of the Saracen tribes forced them to cling together. The Bedouins of those days regarded defenseless monks and pilgrims and their supplies and gifts as easy prey. True the booty was meager, for the monks were not wealthy, but it is known that raids took place, culminating in theft and murder. We have already mentioned the slaughter of the monks recounted by Nilus, when his son was captured and then ransomed for money in a Negev city. Somewhat earlier, around 373 C.E., the most famous incursion took place; it was described by Ammonius, an Egyptian monk who visited Sinai on his way to the Holy Sepulchre in Jerusalem. Incorporated in his account of the massacre by the Saracens of the monks in the area around Mt. Sinai and Raithu (at-Tur) are quite a few imaginary details, such as the bursting forth of fire and smoke from Mt. Sinai, and even the number of victims near Mt. Sinai — forty, apparently corresponding to the forty days which Moses spent on the Mountain of the Lord. (The wounded monk Sabas was said to have perished as he thanked God for the privilege of completing the number forty!)

However, from the collection of legends and miracle tales one can distill a number of authentic details: the names of the monks, of the tribes, and of the monastic settlements around Mt. Sinai (among them apparently also "Horeb"). The realistic origins of Ammonius' story are indicated by the name of the ruined monastery in Wadi Leja, south of the Monastery of St. Catherine — *al-Arba'in*, "the forty." Descriptions of the attacks of the Saracens on the monks and pilgrims are presented in many sources. This situation ultimately led to the construction of the Monastery of St. Catherine and largely determined its character and fate from its beginnings to recent times.

The monks therefore congregated in large centers and built fortified churches and towers for self-defense. Thus, in the course of time the three main centers of monasticism in Sinai arose: in the vicinity of Jebel Musa and the Monastery of St. Catherine, at Pharan, and at Raithu near the coast.

The monks also sought ways of living in peace with the Saracen tribes (for warfare and the bearing of arms were forbidden), and they were largely successful. Careful examination of the sources reveals that attacks were mostly under exceptional circumstances. The raid on Raithu described by Ammonius was carried out by "Barbarians," the tribes of the Blemmians, who came from overseas, "from the direction of the Gulf of Aila" (apparently from the Nubian coast), whereas friendly and commercial relations were maintained with the local tribes, who even fought against the Blemmians. The Saracens attacked Mt. Sinai and its vicinity after the death of their king, "the Guardian of the Desert." Nilus recounts that after the Saracen raid the heads of the community of Pharan complained to Amanes, the new king, about the violation of the agreement between them. Hence one can deduce that in Sinai as well as in other border areas of the Byzantine Empire, the Christian inhabitants gained security by means of payments and tribute. This was no doubt achieved with the assistance of the Byzantine authorities, and in that way they harnessed the Saracen "Guardians of the Desert" to the system of border defense of the empire. Thus the raids were reduced to "localized" skirmishes, or perpetrated by tribes from the outside, with whom no such arrangements had been made. Serious problems arose when governments changed, when an intertribal arrangement collapsed, or when the Byzantines showed signs of weakness.

Occasionally, exemplary monks also gained fame among the Saracen tribes, particularly when they were endowed with unusual powers of healing. In the fourth century C.E. in southern Palestine the monk Hilarion gained renown. According to Jerome, many Saracens flocked to him to be cured, and he spread Christianity among them. Of similar repute, in southern Sinai, was a monk named Moses, of whom Ammonius tells that for seventy-three years he lived in a cave near Raithu, and that he was the most famous monk among the tribes because of his power to cure people of diseases and exorcise demons. On the strength of his personal abilities he managed to convert the idol-worshippers of Pharan to Christianity.

This monk is possibly the hero of the well-known story recounted in the writings of Evagrius, Socrates and other Church historians about the war, probably in 376 C.E., between the Saracens and the Byzantines under the Arian emperor Valens. The king of the Saracens died, and his widow, Muavia or Mavia, led her army against the Byzantines on the borders of Palestine and Egypt and routed them. The queen and her people would not agree to stop waging war until they were promised that the famous monk named Moses, who was also of Saracen origin (Orthodox and not Arian and not favored by the emperor), be named bishop over them. The geographical setting here is not clear (the events apparently took place further north in Sinai), and there is no way of knowing whether reference was to the Moses previously mentioned. At any rate these stories show an increased movement toward conversion among the Saracen tribes in Sinai as in the other border areas of the Byzantine Empire.

Most of the inhabitants of Pharan — who belonged to the non-monastic population — were undoubtedly of Saracen origin. A considerable number accepted the new faith with devotion and fervor, but the majority apparently followed it in an external and superficial fashion, and after the Muslim Conquest they made no bones about converting again and clinging to Islam, the faith of their "compatriots."

Material Property and Spiritual Life

The literature of monasticism is not rich in descriptions of material life, but we have already noted that many facts are provided incidentally in the stories of the monks' way of life. In addition to the monks' literature we have the testimony of contemporary pilgrims and also information gleaned by modern travelers and researchers on their surveys and excavations. The archaeological finds generally confirm what is known from written sources and are substantiated by the present-day monks' cells and gardens, the monasteries and churches, and even their graves.

The identification of archaeological remains as "monastic" is difficult and frequently we are even unable to distinguish between early and late remains. Still, there is a large amount of material the identity of which as "monastic" is certain. An example of an interesting complex of Christian and monastic remains are the discoveries in the Pharan area. The large oasis of Pharan became, as mentioned above, the central civil settlement of the region in the Byzantine period. The community was laical (as noted, a considerable number of inhabitants were converted Saracens), but many monks also lived there. The bishop of the Sinai Peninsula also resided in Pharan, and his diocese included the Monastery of St. Catherine and Raithu. The inhabitants gained their livelihood from the large date plantation, vegetable farming, and animal husbandry. The settlement was concentrated at Tel Maḥarad, a large mound where ancient pottery and Nabatean remains have been found.[5] The mound's acropolis includes a large church, the walls of which are preserved to a great height, and tall buildings with towers some of which apparently were used for defense. (The itinerary of the pilgrim of Placentia mentions a garrison posted to defend the settlement and the monasteries in the vicinity.) Not far to the south rise the mighty cliffs of Jebel Serbal, which some scholars have claimed, although without substantial evidence, to be Mt. Sinai.

Pharan itself, situated on the main caravan

The Monastery of St. Catherine: monks standing outside their cells

route between Jebel Musa and Egypt, was identified in Byzantine times with biblical Rephidim. The rock upon which Moses stood when Aharon and Hur supported his arms during the war against Amalek was associated with the peak of Jebel Taḥuna ("The Mountain of the Mill"), a high steep hill north of Tel Maḥarad. A well-trodden and partially paved path with stairs leads up to it, similar to those used to this day in the area of the Monastery of St. Catherine. Along the path, on the slopes of Jebel Taḥuna, are four churches and chapels, and on its summit is another church

Tel Maḥarad in Wadi Feiran

[5] U. Daharı, "Feiran Oasis and Serbal Mountain in Southern Sinai During the Early Byzantine Period." Master's thesis, The Hebrew University of Jerusalem, 1981 (Hebrew).

323

which was converted into a mosque with two prayer niches (miḥrabs) after the Muslim Conquest. Some of the churches are large while others are quite small chapels (4 × 5 m). Churches built in caves or on tombs may have been erected to commemorate a certain monk. Inscriptions on a rock along the path at the top of the hill portray crosses and record names, apparently of pilgrims, such as Menas, Leontis, Serpis, Kosmas the Priest, and others. Two buildings adjacent to the two churches on the path apparently served as monasteries. A large room (4 × 6 m) in one of the churches may have been a refectory.

There are many tombs in the vicinity of Pharan. Some of them are dug into caves in the walls of the ravines, while others are constructed of stone cluttering the surrounding slopes (the Bedouins call this kind of tomb *nusra*, "guard post"). The tombs may be attributed, although there is no conclusive proof, to the monks. Most of the structures are simple, with a large cell in which the deceased was laid. They are 4–5 m in length, 2–3 m wide and 1–2 m high. However, there are also three- and four-storied structures with four or five cells on each floor. The monks told stories about their teachers who sensed their imminent death and accepted it with serenity, even

The Monastery of St. Catherine: skeleton of St. Stephen (sixth century C.E.). According to tradition, he sat in this position on the path leading to Mt. Sinai in order to verify the purity of pilgrims.

with gratitude. Generally their disciples buried them in the cave where they lived or nearby. Occasionally they were given a more elaborate burial by lay admirers. In time the form of burial common in many Greek Orthodox monasteries was also adopted at the Monastery of St. Catherine: the skeleton was dismembered after decomposition of the corpse in a temporary grave, and the bones were laid in heaps. The source of this custom may lie in the shortage of burial space in rocky regions, though it also certainly had a spiritual message — the negligibility and anonymity of man.

The monks devoted many hours each day to prayer. Among them were ascetes such as Onophrius or the monk Moses who devoted their entire time to prayer and fasting and were engaged in directing their disciples. Their meager subsistence consisted of food

The Monastery of St. Catherine: heaps of skulls

324

brought to them by attendants and gifts from the people in the surrounding area. Most of the monks also worked when necessary. Some wove baskets of palm branches, a craft common among monks, and others cultivated gardens. The flourishing gardens which one finds today around the deserted monasteries in the area of Jebel Musa are only a vestige of the numerous ones which once grew on the slopes, as indicated by the abandoned terraces and tiny fields on the surrounding mountains. Sometimes the monks created the gardens from nothing, scraping soil or carrying it up to the terraced area in baskets. Of Silvanus, one of the most famous monks of the seventh decade of the fourth century C.E., it is told that his disciples "doubled" the size of his garden against his will when he was absent from his cave one day. This monk, born in Palestine, afterwards returned there and established a monastery in Naḥal Gerar in the northwestern Negev. He stood for the rejection of extreme austerity and the value of work. When one of his guests admonished him saying that physical labor is "a need of the flesh" and adversely affects the life of the spirit — that is, there should be uninterrupted prayer at all hours of the day — Silvanus "educated" him by denying him his daily meal, for that too was a "need of the flesh."

The monks also engaged in missionary and educational work among the local inhabitants or in copying prayer books. In a general sense they preferred "deeds" to "studies," spending long hours in prayer and fasting, telling moral tales and praising the Lord and His saints, but little time at theoretical studies. This is the main explanation for the small number of significant theoretical works and intellectual studies which emerged in the monasteries of Sinai. Even the literature for which the monks of Sinai were famous during the second half of the sixth and early seventh centuries C.E. consisted mainly of books of moral edification and stories, some of them quite marvelous, about the monks' lives. The main figures were Johanes Moschus the Jerusalemite, who lived in Sinai for a long time, and Anastasius and Johanes Climachus, both of Sinai. To this day the monks of Sinai read chapters of Johanes Climachus' famous book, *The Ladder of Paradise*, as they eat their common meal in the refectory. The few books possessed by the monks themselves were mainly liturgical and theological works. In every community there were undoubtedly also a few copies of the Bible and the New Testament, such as, for example, the splendid *Codex Sinaiticus*, discovered in the mid-nineteenth century by Tischendorf in the library of the Monastery of St. Catherine. In his opinion this magnificent manuscript was copied in Constantinople in the fourth century and contributed by the Byzantine Emperor to the monastery when it was founded. Tischendorf borrowed the *Codex Sinaiticus* for examination and copying, but, abusing the monks' confidence, did not return it. To justify his act rumors were spread concerning the ignorance and carelessness of the St. Catherine monks, which were strengthened by the reports of other nineteenth-century travelers. Indeed, in earlier generations, there were, along with the spiritual leaders, also many poorly educated and ignorant monks.

Among the thousands of monks who lived in Sinai or wandered there as individuals or in groups, a considerable number did not succeed in maintaining the high standards. Our sources even tell of infamous monks and of penitents. Johanes Climachus mentions the

The Monastery of St. Catherine: manuscript title page of Gospel according to Luke dating to the fifth century C.E.

The fortified Monastery of St. Catherine

"prison," whose location is known to the monks to this day, near his cave in Wadi Tlaḥ. Though most of the inmates were monks who came to him willingly in order to mortify themselves, some undoubtedly were also detained there as punishment. We may assume, however, that it was mainly the spiritual elect who reached the distant Sinai monasteries, as those who adopted the monastic life for less ideological reasons, such as escaping debts, taxes, or military service, or in pursuit of religious and political advantage (as was common in the Byzantine period) stayed closer to home. Nevertheless, one must be wary of attributing to them excessive idealization, for despite their devotion, they were men with regular human weaknesses.

Some leaders of monasticism perceived the danger of unsupervised isolation, and in any event did not view it as a path to be taken by many. Pachomius directed a cenobitic community in Egypt, and Basilius of Capadocia perfected his system and emphasized the im-

portance of structure — hierarchy and supervision. Under conditions of strict discipline and absolute submission, the individual can more easily avoid sin and pride. Naturally this path offered more comfort and security to the individual, while the monastery benefited from the labor of the monks, accrued property, and became an economic force. In Sinai this process took place relatively late, but with the establishment of the fortified monastery of St. Catherine, it was natural that it too should be largely founded on these principles. To this day the monks' way of life is based on a mixture of discipline according to the *regula* of Basilius and the traditional anchorite system of ancient Sinai.

The Monastic Center around Jebel Musa and the Foundation of the St. Catherine Monastery

From the very emergence of Christianity in Sinai a unique status was accorded to Jebel Musa, identified with Mt. Sinai. The name

Jebel Musa was given to it by the Arabs, who also regarded it with veneration. At first it was known as *Tur-Sina*, based on the Syriac-Aramaic *Tur-Sinai*, but in time they simply called it *at-Tur* (a term used to denote venerated mountains), that is, "the mountain." In the surrounding area the early monks pointed out the places connected with the Exodus from Egypt and the Giving of the Law. One of the earliest descriptions, and also the most detailed, generally providing an accurate picture of the topography, is that attributed to the pious pilgrim Egeria, who visited Sinai and Palestine in 381–384 C.E. Egeria came to Mt. Sinai from Pharan via the well-known pass Naqb el-Hawa, where her guides showed her the "Graves of Lust" (see Numbers 11:34), apparently the stone mounds at the foot of the mountain. She climbed to the peak of the "Mountain of the Lord" and to that of Mt. Sinai (the summit of Jebel Musa), where she came upon a church and many monks. Near Mt. Sinai she saw Mt. Horeb (Jebel Sufsafeh), the cave where Elijah hid and the church erected in his memory. At the foot of the mountain she viewed the "Holy Bush" (today the monks still point to a raspberry bush as the "Burning Bush"), and she prayed in the nearby church. At the outlet of Wadi ed-Deir, "The Stream of the Monastery," she was shown the place where the Tablets of the Law were broken and where the golden calf had stood (Jebel Harun, "The Mount of Aharon") in the plain where the Children of Israel had camped (the er-Raha Valley, "The Valley of Repose"). Egeria wrote at length about the many devout monks living on the mountain and at its foot, who had stories about every site mentioned in Scriptures.

There are many other sources which identify Mt. Sinai, sometimes simply called "The Holy Mountain," with Jebel Musa. An exception is Cosmas Indicopleustes ("the traveler to India"), who remarked that Mt. Sinai is located six miles from Pharan; his description is more applicable to Jebel Serbal. It is difficult to explain why Cosmas, who visited Sinai in the mid-sixth century C.E., while the Monastery of St. Catherine was being constructed,

should have expressed such an uncommon opinion, and it seems more likely that an error was simply made (the text itself raises other difficulties). Furthermore, this is the only such identification, and it is a rather late one. Therefore, there is no substance to the claim of modern scholars that at a certain time the monks identified Mt. Sinai with Jebel Serbal.

The church which Egeria saw on the peak of Mt. Sinai could have been the one built by Julianus Sabas, a famous monk of the mid-fourth century C.E. who came from Edessa in northern Syria (today Urfa in Turkey). The church she mentioned in the valley near the site of the Burning Bush was doubtless the earliest kernel of the Monastery of St. Catherine, which local tradition attributes — with no historical basis — to the Empress Helena, Constantine's mother. Two sources tell us of the construction of the fortified monastery by Justinian, the greatest ruler of the Byzantine Empire and its most famous builder. One source is Procopius, Justinian's historian, in his book *On Buildings*, and the other is Eutychius (Ibn-Batriq), the patriarch of Alexandria, whose account is more detailed but, due to the time lapse (the first half of the tenth century), surrounded with legendary details.

Eutychius recounts, and what he says seems reasonable, that the monks of Sinai appealed to Justinian requesting that he defend them from the Saracens. Procopius tells of the marvelous monks of Mt. Sinai, "whose lives are a careful rehearsal of death, whom were gathered in a fortress by Justinian."[6] The emperor placed soldiers at their disposal and built them a church dedicated to Mary, the Mother of God (*Theotokos*). Eutychius reiterates the well-known detail that a church already stood on the site (also dedicated to Mary), in a fortified tower where the monks crowded together in times of danger. Of the defenders of the fortified monastery and its servants, Eutychius relates that some were Egyptians and others were Slavs enslaved by Rome. The descendants of the latter are believed to be the

---

6 Procopius, *Buildings* V 8.

Bedouins waiting outside The Monastery of St. Catherine

famous Jebelieh tribe who live near the monastery and serve it to this day.

Two sources emphasize that the monastery was situated in the lowest part of the valley bed, where there was water and where the "Holy Bush" stood. According to Euthychius, this was an inferior position from the point of view of defense, allowing the Saracens to throw stones into the compound. Procopius, who emphasizes the general value of the fortress as a base for the defense of Palestine, explains the location of the monastery by repeating the familiar claim that no one could spend the night on the mountaintop. Eutychius simply says that the emperor's emissary

erred in choosing the site of the "Burning Bush" and that he gave precedence to proximity to water rather than defense, and that he paid for his mistake with his head. Even if there is a grain of truth in these accounts, and the walls of the monastery were too low to block stones thrown from the outside, they were certainly high and thick enough to prevent a successful attack.

The internal design of the monastery testifies to the perplexities of its architects and proves that it was built primarily to defend the site of the "Burning Bush" and sanctify it. Of greater danger to the walls than the Saracens was the riverbed next to which the monastery was built, for its course is deep and its winter floods are strong. The "Holy Bush" grew in a garden close to the bottom of the riverbed, and so it was necessary to construct the church, which faces the east, in precisely that place. If they had erected the monastery compound with the church in the middle, the walls would have blocked the riverbed and have been destroyed by floodwaters. The builders, therefore, built the wall as far to the south as possible, parallel to the stream, oriented northeast–southwest. Consequently the wall of the compound and the church do not have the same axis; only a narrow passage was left between the compound wall and the northeastern corner of the church. At first, as shown by the American-Egyptian expedition (Alexandria-Michigan-Princeton), the monastery included only the church and the hospice (upon which, in their opinion, the mosque was built during the Middle Ages). That plan confirms our information that the monastery initially served mainly as a refuge in times of danger or as a shelter for pilgrims. Indeed, it is evident that its residential quarters were built later. The exact year of construction is not known, but it would seem that the fortress was completed early in the second half of the sixth century C.E.

Today this building is considered one of the most famous Christian monuments in the world, but we can here only provide a brief description. It is square measuring approximately 80 sq m. It is built of well-hewn granite

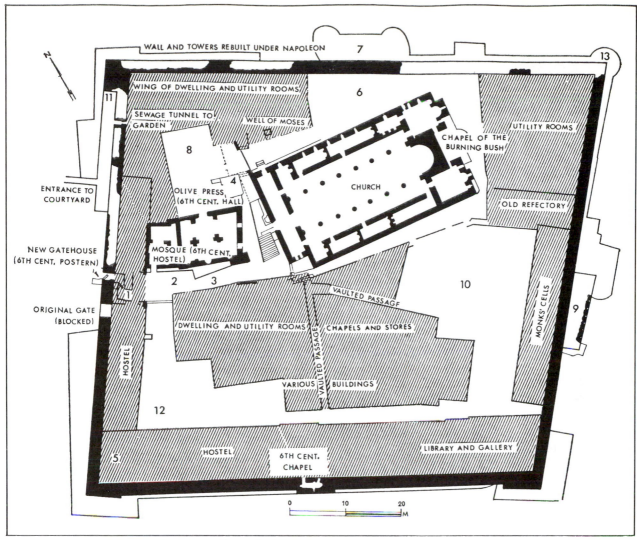

The Monastery of St. Catherine's: plan (Forsyth, *DOP*, Fig. 1). White areas outside walls are post-Byzantine towers and sloping revetments. Legend — 1) Entrance under hostel; 2) Inner square; 3) Vaulted passage; 4) Moslem minaret; 5) West corner, supported by arches at lower level; above, archbishop's residence; 6) Open square and garden; 7) Tower reconstructed under Napoleon; on top, St. George's Chapel; 8) Paved square, above lower olive press; 9) Lavatory wing; above it, later tower; 10) Monks' courtyard, below it, bakery; 11) Northwestern corner, site of 'Archbishop's Gate'; 12) Open square with well of St. Stephen; 13) Round Napoleon-period tower

stones and fortified with watchtowers and machicolations (for pouring boiling oil on attackers).[7] Crosses and figures are carved on many of the stones in the wall. Above the original gate, which has been blocked with stones (apparently in the first centuries after the Muslim Conquest), there is a Greek inscription: "This is the gate of the Lord, the righteous shall enter through it." The inscription mentions the name of the ruler Justinian,

[7] For a detailed description of the walls, see Y. Tsafrir, "St. Catherine's Monastery in Sinai: Drawings by I. Dunayevski," *IEJ* 28 (1978): 218–229.

and it seems that it was carved at the time of construction.

The plan of the church building is outstanding, though renovations and changes have been made which effected its original style and architectural layout: the granite pillars were painted in bright, glossy colors; the chancel was sealed off by a screen (*iconostasis*); and a greenish gilded ceiling was added. Nevertheless, the spaciousness of the building is still evident, as is the somewhat heavy style of the columns and various forms of capitals. The capitals are coarsely worked and without

Church of St. Catherine: the sanctuary. The tomb of St. Catherine is beyond the altar (Forsyth and Weitzmann, Pl. LXXXIV)

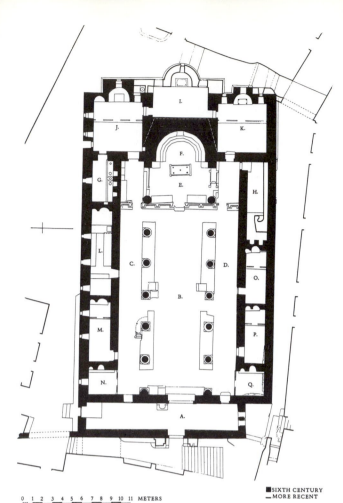

Church of St. Catherine: plan; sixth-century elements are shown in black. Legend — A. Narthex; B. Nave; C. North aisle; D. South aisle; E. Sanctuary; F. Apse; G. Sacristy; H. Storeroom. Chapels in church: — I. Burning Bush (medieval); J. St. James the Less; K. Forty Martyrs (Holy Fathers); L. St. Antipas; M. SS. Constantine and Helen; N. St. Marina; O. SS. Anne and Joachim; P. St. Simeon Stylites; Q. SS. Cosmas and Damian.
(Forsyth and Weitzmann, Fig. B)

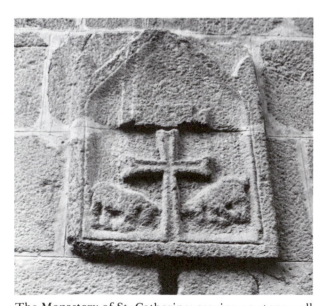

The Monastery of St. Catherine: carving on stone wall

doubt were made locally. In marked contrast, the wooden elements — such as the doors and beams — are carved with a high level of artistic skill (see Pl. XXIVb), apparently by a craftsman who came from afar. Thanks to the dry climate the wood is well preserved. According to an inscription found on one of the roof beams, the builder was Stephanos of Aila (Eilat), the tomb of whose daughter, Nonna, was discovered at the beginning of the century in Beer-sheba.

In the opinion of the American scholar G.H. Forsyth, who explored the church, the plan of the church derives from the Syrian-

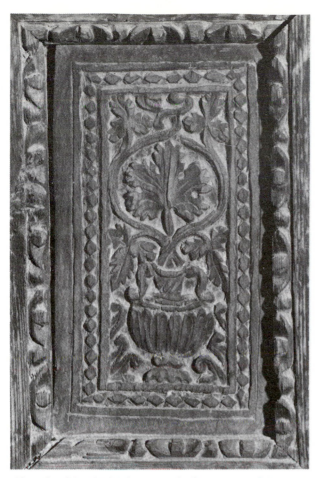

Church of St. Catherine: panel of nave portal (Forsyth and Weitzmann, Pl. XLVIIIc)

perhaps Constantinople. On the mosaic above the apse Moses is portrayed in two scenes: in one he kneels before the bush, and in the other he holds the Tablets of the Covenant. The main motif in the apse depicts the Transfiguration (see Pl. XXIII). In the center Jesus is shown with Elijah and Moses on either side. His disciples kneel in awe at his feet. This scene, combining Jesus, Moses, and Elijah in a single picture, is a personification of the

Palestinian tradition of commemorative churches (*martyria*). The pilgrims walked through the aisles of the church and the chapels at the sides of the apse and went out into the open area behind the latter, where there was a small garden with the "Burning Bush." After the bush withered in the Middle Ages, the low "Chapel of the Bush" was built on the site where the monks hold a liturgical service every Saturday. (According to tradition, the Chapel of the Bush is considered the most ancient part of the church.) The roof of the apse is covered to this day with lead sheets installed in the eighteenth century, and it is assumed that the entire roof of the Justinian church was covered with such sheets, which were replaced from time to time.

The mosaic, laid down not long after the church's erection, is one of the most ancient and beautiful church mosaics in the East. It too is the work of artist from an urban center,

Church of St. Catherine: nave seen through portal from narthex. The arcades, walls, carvings on ceiling beams and portal all date to sixth century (Forsyth and Weitzmann, Pl. XLIII)

Christian outlook, according to which God revealed Himself twice in that place, to Moses and to Elijah, thus announcing the third and redeeming revelation in the form of Jesus.

These figures and the images of many other saints are the subjects of hundreds of ancient icons (see Pl. XXIVc) preserved in the rooms of the monastery. This is a rare collection both in its value and beauty, for it survived the destruction of the iconoclasts in Byzantium in the eighth and ninth centuries. According to Byzantine sources, the church was dedicated to Mary, the Mother of Jesus, and only in the Middle Ages did the monastery gain renown as the Monastery of St. Catherine. The first written source on the deeds of Catherine is from the eighth or ninth century C.E. The story was transmitted orally over the centuries, resulting in the development of numerous versions of the details of the events. Catherine was the daughter of a noble family in Alexandria, who became a Christian. Following her example, the family of the king, Maximianus or Maxentius, in the early fourth century, and the best of his sages, also converted to Christianity. She died after being tortured and her body disappeared and was brought by angels to the highest peak in Sinai, Jebel Catherina, near Jebel Musa. A monk who dreamed about a treasure hidden on the peak discovered her body. At the foot of the mountain, a church was built in her memory, and in time her bones were brought down and buried in a golden box in the chancel of that church. There are conflicting traditions regarding this matter: some sources date the event early and others place it in the middle of the medieval period. Since then the church and monastery have been dedicated to St. Catherine. The great reverence in which she was held in medieval Europe was one of the reasons for the fame of the monastery and the frequency of pilgrimages made to it from the West.

Conclusion

Initially the monastery served as a place of refuge in times of need for the many hermits, most of whom preferred to live outside its walls, but in the course of time it became the center of monasticism in Sinai. Frequently the Bishop of Pharan and of all Sinai resided there. The thousands of pilgrims to Mt. Sinai from all over the Byzantine Empire found refuge within the walls of the monastery. They came as individuals or as members of small or very large groups. Anastasius (early seventh century C.E.) tells of a group of 800 Armenian pilgrims. There was bilateral movement between Sinai and neighboring areas. Many people dwelt in Sinai for a certain time and then became famous elsewhere, such as Silvanus and Johanes Moschus, who settled in Palestine, Gregorius, who was appointed patriarch of Antioch in the late sixth century, and others. Examination of the origins of the monks of Sinai shows that this was an almost cosmopolitan society, including Egyptians, Palestinians, Syrians, Cappadocians, Armenians, Georgians, etc. A considerable number were pilgrims from the West. Praise of the hospice of the monastery reached the ears of Pope Gregory the Great (ca. 600), and he contributed to its maintenance.

The monastery formed particularly close ties with Egypt, from which the easiest of the access routes to Sinai led, and with southern Palestine and Jerusalem (southern Palestine and southern Sinai were included in one province, *Palaestina Tertia*, under the Patriarchate of Jerusalem). Two roads linked southern Palestine with Sinai: one, from Niẓana (Nessana), passing through the Desert of at-Tia in the north, and the other through Eilat in the northeast. The latter route, which the pilgrim of Placentia calls the Arabia Road, had eight stations. In various places along the way, especially in the famous stations near ʿEn Ḥudra, rock inscriptions left by pilgrims, including some from Transjordan, have been found.[8] A papyrus from Nessana tells of the close relations with the monastery: a group of agents traveled to the holy mountain, took part in the prayers, and offered gifts, but their main purpose was to receive a large sum from a man named *Abba* (Father) Martyrios,

[8] A. Negev, *The Inscriptions of Wadi Haggag, Sinai. Qedem* 6 (Jerusalem, 1977).

perhaps the head of the monastery or the *Economos*.

In the tempestuous period of the struggle with the Monophysites and the establishment of the Coptic Church in Egypt, southern Sinai was a quiet enclave of Orthodoxy. We hear very little of Monophysites coming to Sinai, such as Theodosius of Jerusalem who "rebelled" against the Patriarch Juvenalis after the Council of Chalcedon (451 C.E.). Theodorus, the Bishop of Pharan, was also accused of deviating from Orthodoxy, but in general the monks of Sinai did not intervene in religious controversies.

The monastery experienced difficult times after the Arab Conquest. The monks lost their sovereignty and became subjects tolerated by the grace of the new rulers. While there were later periods when hundreds of monks lived in Sinai, there were also frequent occasions when the monastery was about to be closed due to the small number of monks and pilgrims. In the fifteenth and sixteenth centuries, it was even abandoned several times. Its gate was blocked, and the famous wooden elevators were installed. Smaller monasteries in southern Sinai were abandoned completely. It was only natural that the few residents of the monastery became the protectors of its valuable treasures, and physical labor largely passed into the hands of the Bedouin of the Jebelieh tribe. The few monks sent there from far away did not always fulfill the expectations of westerners in regard to their education and knowledge of the history of the region. The monastery was in a delapidated state, and more than one traveler summarized his visit by expressing disappointment at the impoverished present state as compared to the splendid past still evidenced by its walls, the artistic treasures and the numerous huts of hermits in the vicinity. Intensive building activity in the late nineteenth, but mostly in the twentieth, century changed considerably the face of the complex, and enabled the accommodation of a large number of tourists. But even in the most difficult periods the monks continued to hold their prayers and services on Mt. Sinai and at the site where, according to ancient Byzantine tradition, the Burning Bush was located.

The uniqueness of early monasticism in Sinai lies in the ardent belief in the sanctity of "The Mountain of the Lord" and in the mystical tendency to truly identify with the surrounding mountains and landscape. There is no better expression of this than the story told by Anastasius, in the seventh century, about the priest who brought an offering to the peak of Mt. Sinai, and for half on hour the mountains answered his call "Holy, Holy, Holy!" But only those whose ears were open could hear it.[9]

[9] I wish to thank my many friends and colleagues for their advice and counsel during the writing of this article, especially those at The Hebrew University of Jerusalem, The Israel Nature Reserves Authority, Israel Defense Forces and the civil administration in Sinai, as well as the monks of the Monastery of St. Catherine and Abbot Damianos. The churches of Pharan were surveyed in August 1969 with the help of Nadav Baor. See Y. Tsafrir, "St. Catherine's Monastery," in Z. Meshel (ed.), *Southern Sinai, Views and Travels* (Jerusalem, 1971), pp. 68–89, 224–235 (Hebrew); G.H. Forsyth and K. Weitzmann with I. Ševčenko and F. Anderegg, *The Monastery of St. Catherine at Mount Sinai*, I. *Plates* (Ann Arbor, 1973); K. Weitzmann, *The Monastery of St. Catherine at Mount Sinai, the Icons*. I. *From the Sixth to Tenth Century* (Princeton, 1976); P. Mayerson, "The Ammonius Narrative: Bedouin and Blemmyes Attacks in Sinai," in G. Rendsburg (ed.), *The Bible World (C.H. Gordon Volume)* (New York, 1980), pp. 133–148; I. Finkelstein, "Byzantine Monastic Remains in Southern Sinai," *DOP* 39 (1985): 41–75.

Byzantine Remains at Jebel Sufsafeh (Mt. Ḥoreb) in Southern Sinai

Israel Finkelstein

The 1970s witnessed increased research on monasticism in Sinai.[1] In this paper, we present the results of a thorough survey of the important center of monastic activity at Jebel Sufsafeh[2]. Our work sheds light on life in small monastic communities in the rugged mountainous region near the Monastery of St. Catherine.

The Mountain

Jebel Sufsafeh, traditionally associated with the biblical Mt. Ḥoreb, rises south of the St. Catherine Monastery in a broad ridge, running northwest from the peak of Jebel Musa (Mt. Sinai of the Byzantine tradition). Its extremely steep slopes rise from about 500 m above the surrounding terrain to a height of 2,168 m above sea level. It is composed of red granite, which forms a landscape of stretches of rock and rounded peaks. The climate, like that of other mountain peaks in southern Sinai, is comfortable in summer but quite harsh in wintertime. At night, and sometimes during the day, the temperatures drop below freezing. Compared to other regions of the Sinai Peninsula, this area is blessed with considerable precipitation (65 mm per year, on the average), some of it falling as snow. As the red granite of the region is almost impermeable, the available water flows as runoff to the low-lying areas. At the junction-points between ridges where eroded soil has accumulated, small depressions (*farsh*, as the Bedouin call them) have formed, permitting the cultivation of small groves and some furrows of vegetables.

The special nature of the granite mountains — isolated valleys and soaring peaks, cliffs and rock caves — attracted those seeking an anchorite way of life in the vicinity of small monastic centers. Furthermore, the sanctity of Mt. Horeb and its proximity to Mt. Sinai and the Monastery of the Bush affected the activities of the local monks. The summit of Mt. Sinai itself was sacred, and dwelling there was forbidden, so the monastics, wishing to live as close as possible, settled in the nearby valleys, on the ridge of Jebel Sufsafeh.

Historical Sources

Few historical sources give direct accounts of the Mt. Horeb monks. However, since this site is located near Mt. Sinai and the Monastery of the Bush — a center of activity for the monks in the region — there are several allusions to them.

A place named Horeb is mentioned in a narrative ascribed to the monk Ammonius. According to this story, the Saracens slaughtered forty monks in Sinai, apparently in the year 373 C.E.: "In Gethrabi they killed everyone they found, and in Horeb, too, they did the same to the men of Codar, and to all whom they met in the vicinity of the Holy Mount."[3]

The detailed descriptions by Egeria, a pil-

---

[1] On monasticism in Sinai, see in this volume, Yoram Tsafrir, "Monks and Monasteries in Southern Sinai," pp. 315–333.

[2] This paper is a translation of a Hebrew manuscript completed in 1980. The study, carried out during the years 1976–1977, was headed by the author and Avner Goren, Staff Officer for Archaeology in Sinai. We were assisted by the Tzukei David Field School of the Israel Nature Protection Society and the Archaeological Institute of Tel Aviv University. Benjamin Sass and Judith Dekel participated in part of the survey and Ora Faran prepared the plans. For a more extensive report on the results of the work, see I. Finkelstein, "Byzantine Monastic Remains in the Southern Sinai," *DOP* 39 (1985): 39–75.

[3] *Ammonius* (ed. S. Combefis) (Paris, 1960), pp. 91–93.

Jebel Sufsafeh (Mt. Ḥoreb): view from er-Raḥa Plain, looking south

grim who visited Sinai toward the end of the fourth century C.E., reveal that there were, already then, many hermits on the mountain, and that a number of churches linked to sacred traditions had been established. We should note that Egeria also describes agricultural activity on the mountain.

As we were coming out of the church the presbyters of the place gave us "blessings," some fruits which grow on the mountain itself. For although Sinai, the Holy Mount, is too stony even for bushes to grow on it, there is little soil round the foot of the mountains, the central one and those around it, and in this the holy monks are always busy planting shrubs and setting out orchards or vegetable-beds round their cells. It may look as if they gather fruit which is growing in the

Jebel Sufsafeh: Farsh el-Qasr Valley

mountain soil, but in fact everting is the result of their own hard work.[4]

[4] *Egeria* 3:6 [trans. J. Wilkinson, *Egeria's Travels* (London, 1971), p. 94].

335

The Pilgrim from Placentia, Piacenza the Holy, erroneously known as Antoninus, visited Sinai, apparently in the seventh decade of the sixth century C.E., at the height of the monastic movement there. His account tells of construction of the fortified monastery by order of Emperor Justinian, issued several years earlier, and of the monks at Mt. Ḥoreb and Mt. Sinai: "Mt. Sinai is rocky, with very little soil, and all around are cells for the servants of God, as on Horeb. But they say Horeb is good soil."[5]

Finally, the historian Procopius, a contemporary of Justinian, describes the erection of the fortified monastery and the Mother of God Church in Sinai. He says of the Sinai monks: "On this Mt. Sinai live monks whose life is a kind of careful rehearsal of death, and they enjoy without fear the solitude which is very precious to them."[6]

The Remains

The main body of remains is located in fifteen monastic complexes in the small valleys of the ridge. Interspersed among them are chapels, small monasteries, water systems, dams for preventing soil erosion and fences demarcating the various agricultural plots. Also found were cells for seclusion, step paths and an extraordinary network of prayer niches. Several of the ancient chapels were rebuilt during the Middle Ages and remained in use until the modern period. The majority of these remains, however, are not mentioned in modern research literature, and are not known today even to the monks of Sinai.

Because of the limited area of cultivated plots, as well as drainage problems, most of the small monasteries in the center of the monastic complexes were erected on bedrock at the edges of the valleys, or on artificially raised and flattened surfaces. The harshness of the winter climate was also a factor in the choice of the building sites: for the most part, a southern exposure, facing the sun, was chosen. The structures served small groups of monks, thus accounting for their relatively small size: they covered only 100–200 sq m. There were a number of rooms in each building, one of which served as a chapel. Many of them were almost totally destroyed, and only in a few cases was it possible to reconstruct a plan, or even to locate the apse.

In the valley named Farsh el-Qasr, on the southern side of the mountain, the chapel is not located inside the residence building, but adjacent to it. The round apse survived to a height of 3 m. The inside of the building is filled with debris; there may have been two stories. The structure was erected on a sloping rock surface and reinforced by revetments.

An impressive structure survived in the Valley of el-Lozeh, named for the two almond (Arabic: *Loz*) trees growing there. On the slope adjoining the cliff closing off the valley, the ruins of a monastery can be seen, one room of which served as a chapel. The apse protrudes in a semicircle, facing northeast, as dictated by the ground contours. At the top of the slope only the foundations remain, while at the bottom, the structure is far better preserved, the annex on the southwest rising to a height of some 5 m.

Jebel Sufsafeh: ruins of monastry in Valley of el-Lozeh

[5] *Itinerarium of Antoninus*, 38 [trans. J. Wilkinson, *Jerusalem Pilgrims Before the Crusades* (Warminster, 1977), p. 87].
[6] Procopius, *Buildings*, 5:8 (trans. H.B. Dewing, Loeb Classical Library, Vol. VII, p. 355).

In the middle of the valleys, cultivated plots were bordered by stone fences, apparently serving to keep sheep out. The plots are not large — 62–250 sq m — but much effort was invested in their preparation. In an attempt to prevent soil erosion, the lower ends of the valleys exits were blocked off by dams built from relatively large, unhewn boulders with spaces between them to allow for drainage of the plots. There is no doubt that in some of the valleys, soil had been brought from elsewhere and piled behind the dams. While the fieldwork for this study was in progress, we witnessed, near the St. Catherine Monastery, the creation of plots by this method. A hermit, living in the Church of al-Magafah, traditional site of Galaction and Epistemi, on the slopes of Jebel ed-Deir, brought soil for his garden on the back of a donkey.

The economic potential of plots as small as these can perhaps be understood from a study by A. Perevolotsky of the Bedouin orchards in the Sinai heights.[7] An average Bedouin grove is about 312 sq m in area and has about fifty trees, along with vegetable furrows. This is sufficient to supply half the needs of a Bedouin family for a year.

The water systems of the monastic complexes are among the most interesting of all the remains studied. The monks, who required water both for drinking and irrigation, learned to exploit the natural qualities of the region which is, as mentioned above, blessed with relatively abundant rainfall and a strong flow of runoff. The monks stored the water in reservoirs. They utilized deep gorges shielded from the sun's rays by their sheer walls. They constructed dams and plastered their walls and the rock crevices. The dams, partly crescent-shaped to withstand the water pressure, comprised two parallel stone walls with a fill between them. Some of the dams were equipped with devices for releasing surplus water. The size of the reservoirs was usually a function of that of the complex. Their aver-

Jebel Sufsafeh: dam of Complex 230

age area was 25–50 sq m, but some covered 200 sq m. Today, they are all silted up, but judging from the height of their outer walls and the traces of plaster remaining on the inner walls, their original depth can be estimated at as much as 4 m or more.

During the rainy season the reservoirs were filled with water flowing in the gullies themselves or in aqueducts that ran along the foot of the slopes directing the runoff from the rock surfaces. In the latter case the water flowed through channels — between the rock walls on one side and rows of stones set alongside them on the other side. Only few of the channels were plastered. These aqueducts were between 250 and 300 m long. When the need arose, retaining walls were built. The largest aqueduct studied was fed by water from one of the central wadis of the ridge. A large dam crossing the gully channeled the floodwaters into a well-built, plastered ditch, running the length of the rock wall. At one point, the channel runs on top of a retaining wall 40 m long and 4 m high. Finally, the water reached a large reservoir at the head of one of the monastic complexes.

In all the monastic complexes, Byzantine pottery of two types was found. One consisted of rather coarse locally-made vessels. The second type was made up of numerous examples of imported pottery, such as African Red Slip Ware.

During the Middle Ages, seven chapels were erected on the mountain; they remain in existence to this day, and they contained

[7] A. Perevolotsky, "Orchard Agriculture in the High Mountain Region of Southern Sinai," *Human Ecology* 9 (1981): 331–357.

337

Jebel Sufsafeh: structure constructed in natural rock-cover on southern slope of Mt. Ḥoreb

glazed Islamic pottery. Except for the latter, the pottery found at all the other sites is entirely Byzantine.

Cells of anchorite monks who lived beside the smaller communities were discovered in the vicinity of the monastic complexes. Others were situated in some rather spectacular localities, such as rock outcrops and high peaks. There is no better manifestation of the monastic lifestyle in the mountains than these rock shelters, which must have offered even a single person only a bare subsistence. Caves and natural niches were utilized; their openings were closed off by simple walls. An especially interesting structure was discovered on the southern slope of Jebel Sufsafeh. It was constructed in the natural rock-cover, in a spot overlooking a panoramic landscape. The cliffs, both above and below it, are almost vertical. Over the rock step in front of it, an aqueduct and a path extend in the direction of the nearby complex. A wall closing off part of the rock shelter created a sort of courtyard, which offered access, through a lobby, to the main room, whose rear wall and ceiling are solid rock. The room measures about 2 × 2.5 m and is approximately 2 m high. This part of the structure was found completely intact. On the rock wall of both the courtyard and the cell are a number of white-painted crosses.

The most surprising find of our survey was a group of fourteen extraordinary stone structures built along the ridge, mostly adjacent to the pathway which crosses it from northwest to southeast ascending to Jebel Musa. They average 2 × 2.5 m in size.[8] A number of them have survived to their original height of 0.75–1 m. All face east and are open on the west. Their eastern sides comprised a semicircular or square apse. These structures apparently served as prayer niches for pilgrims seeking to offer prayers in places held sacred by tradition. It is proper, in this context, to recall Egeria's description, when she came to offer prayer at various sacred spots which had been pointed out to her by the monks of the mountain:

> Now we were outside the church door (at the summit), and at once I asked them if they would point out to us all the different places. The holy men willingly agreed.... They showed us all the other places we wanted to see, and also the ones they knew about themselves.... Thus the holy men were kind enough to show us everything, and there too we made the offering and prayed very earnestly, and the passage we read was from the book of Kingdoms.[9]

Jebel Sufsafeh: prayer niche

[8] I. Finkelstein, "Byzantine Prayer Niches in Southern Sinai," *IEJ* 31 (1981): 81–91.

[9] *Egeria* 3:7–8 (see note 4).

The above-mentioned path most probably led from Sheikh Haroun ("Aaron"), the traditional site of the Golden Calf at the foot of the mountain, to an ancient stairway ascending to the summit of Jebel Musa. This peak is visible from several of the prayer niches, and in some cases, the view is spectacular.

Another nine apses were discovered at various places on the Sinai heights. The most interesting of these is located at the top of Naqeb el-Hawa, which was the early route taken by the pilgrims on their way from Egypt to the St. Catherine Monastery. The apse was erected at the exact point where the pilgrims could first catch sight of Jebel Sufsafeh. Egeria recounts the story thus:

> In the meanwhile we were walking along between the mountains and came to a spot where they opened out to form an endless valley — a huge plain, and very beautiful — across which we could see Sinai, the Holy Mount of God.... When we arrived there our guides, the holy men who were with us, said, "It is usual for the people who come here to say a prayer when first they catch sight of the Mount of God," and we did as they suggested.[10]

The dating of the apses to the Byzantine period, although based on circumstantial evidence, is quite certain. They were definitely built during the only period of extensive activity on the mountain, i.e., the Byzantine period. Furthermore, in the Middle Ages, when the currently existing chapels were constructed, the recognized pilgrim route, as known from the sources, was located in a different area. It should be recalled that a number of the apses are directly connected to the Byzantine monastic complexes; a sherd of a Byzantine vessel was found near one of them.

On Jebel Sufsafeh and its slopes, we investigated a dense network of pathways connecting the wadis on either side of it and the monastic complexes situated between its peaks. They were laid out in complete accordance with

Jebel Musa: path leading to summit and gate

the topography, i.e., they conformed to the rock formations and the flow-course of the runoff. We could discern, along the length of the pathways, sections of stone slab paving, step-paths made from large unhewn stones, revetments and channels. A number of previously-unknown tracks were also located. Of special interest is that called by the Bedouins *Sikket Shaharij*, "The Reservoir Path," after the cistern on the mountain peak. This path, southwest of the ascent still used today, extends along a series of paved sections and stairways to the summit of Jebel Musa. It follows a steep narrow dike, where the above-described apse pathway ends.

[10] *Ibid.*, 1.

Summary and Conclusions

Due to their proximity to Mt. Sinai and the Monastery of the Bush, the isolated valleys and lofty peaks of Jebel Sufsafeh served as an important focal point for monastic activity. Indeed, no other Sinai mountain can boast of such a large number of Byzantine remains. Thanks to the finds of our study, we can better understand the special character of monastic settlement in the region.

The need to survive, the way of life and the deep faith of the recluses served as catalysts in the undertaking of extensive building activity upon the mountain. It appears, however, that if not for the special physical conditions of the region — the extraordinary topography and climate — the monastic phenomenon would not have reached the proportions that it did. Due to the mountains' height, this area receives more precipitation than the other Sinai regions and more water is retained because of the almost impermeable red granite. The monks' profound knowledge of the nature of the area was evident in all aspects of their activity: in the water systems, the hermits' cells, the paths, and especially in the sophisticated use of the valleys for construction and agriculture. A rough calculation, based on the number of monastic complexes, the size of the buildings and agricultural areas, leads us to cautiously estimate that the mountain supported more than a hundred monks in the sixth century C.E., assuming that all the buildings were in use at the same time.

It is difficult to differentiate between the settlement stages on the mountain. The local pottery collected at the site cannot be precisely identified chronologically, while the imported vessels, found in most of the monastic complexes, confirm only what we know from the sources, i.e. that there was considerable activity here from the fourth to sixth centuries C.E. Egeria's descriptions are evidence that the mountain was bustling already at the end of the fourth century C.E., although the apex of the monastic movement was probably achieved in the sixth century, with the construction, at Justinian's command, of the monastery of Mt. Sinai (St. Catherine's). We may, therefore, reasonably assume that many of the structures studied were erected in that period.

Remote Monasteries in Southern Sinai and Their Economic Base

Uzi Dahari

Due to the scarcity of food and water sources in the Sinai Desert, its inhabitants banded into groups and led a pastoral, nomadic way of life throughout most prehistoric and historic periods. Consequently, the population was dispersed. In contrast, monks living in the region were not nomadic. They invested great effort in developing the land. The monastics settled mainly in mountain valleys, each monk living off a small plot of land. Their unique lifestyle in the desert is, therefore, an interesting and important topic of research.

During the years 1978–1979, the author conducted excavations in seven typical monasteries in southern Sinai.[1]

The Wadi Sigiliya Sites

A paved road connects the Wadi Sigiliya sites to the oasis at Feiran (Tell Maḥarad, the acropolis of the Byzantine city of Pharan). It runs along Wadi al-Aleiat, crosses the divide between it and Wadi Rim, and continues from the latter to the heights of Jebel Serbal and to the watershed between Wadi Rim and Shaʿab Abu Silm. Here there is a two-room building,

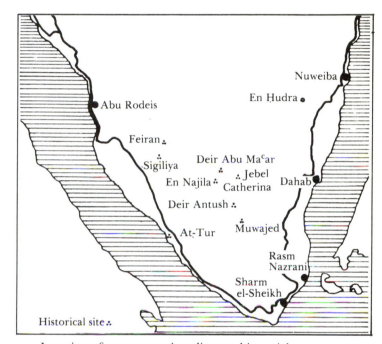

Location of monastery sites discussed in article

which served as a rest and observation station, next to a prayer apse facing east. From the watershed the road winds down through Shaʿab Abu Silm to Wadi Sigiliya, where it forks. One path leads westward to Deir Sigiliya while the other crosses the wadi and climbs the slopes of Jebel Sigiliya (see Pl. XXIVa) to three other sites: al-Karm ("The Vineyard"), "The Church" and "The Palm Grove."[2]

Explorers from the British Palestine Exploration Fund visited Wadi Sigiliya in the late nineteenth century,[3] but spent only one day

---

[1] The author conducted the excavations while working as a guide at the Nature Protection Society's Tzukei David Field School in the vicinity of the Monastery of Saint Catherine. He was assisted by Avner Goren, Staff Officer for Archaeology for the Sinai Peninsula. Volunteers participated in the seven excavation seasons, each of which extended for two weeks. None of the sites were accessible by motor vehicle. This necessitated long hikes, with equipment and food transported by means of donkey, camel, helicopter or on foot. The author's thanks are extended to all those who assisted in overcoming the complicated logistics involved. For a preliminary report, see U. Dahari and A. Goren, "Sinai Monasticism in the Byzantine Period in the Light of Archaeological Excavations," in A. Lachish and Z. Meshel (eds.), *South Sinai Researches 1967–1982* (Tel Aviv 1982), pp. 36–47 (Hebrew).

[2] U. Dahari, *Ḥadashot Arkheologiyot* 69–71 (1979): 80–81 (Hebrew).

[3] C.H. Wilson and H.S. Palmer, *Ordnance Survey of the Sinai Peninsula*, I (Southampton, 1869), pp. 215–216; and E.H. Palmer, *The Desert of the Exodus*, I (London, 1871), pp. 223–226.

Wadi Sigiliya

Wadi Sigiliya: hermit's cell at *al-Karm*

there, returning without plans, photographs, or descriptions of the archaeological remains.

Measurements were taken of two of the sites in the Wadi Sigiliya complex: Deir Sigiliya and The Palm Grove, but they were not excavated. Excavations were carried out, however, at *al-Karm* and "The Church."

The *al-Karm* site (Grid ref. 1655 5644 UTM). In an enchanting spot in the valley, about 1,200 m above sea level, there is a small monastery, surrounded by steep slopes on the north, south and east, and bordered by the Red Sea on the west. The remains indicate that four or five monks lived there.

The site has a small fresh-water spring, and five date-palm trees. Four hermit cells were discerned. The monastery is surrounded by small fertile agricultural plots, each of which

is bounded by revetments and has a small cistern connected to the nearby spring by a canal. A winepress — one of the five discovered in the mountains of southern Sinai — was uncovered in the middle of the tilled area. It has a treading floor, a sedimentation pit, and a collection pit for the newly extracted wine. The winepress is built of unhewn boulders covered with two layers of thick plaster. A staircase, uncovered near the winepress, leads to an underground room with a barrel vault. The numerous storage vessels found in the room suggest that it served as a wine cellar.

One hermit's cell was hewn out of the rock underneath an overhang. Steps lead up to its narrow entrance. The cell is divided lengthwise by a low partition separating the cooking area from the sleeping area.

A. Khirbet ed-Deir, auxiliary chambers' entrance: amphora flanked by two baskets of fruit

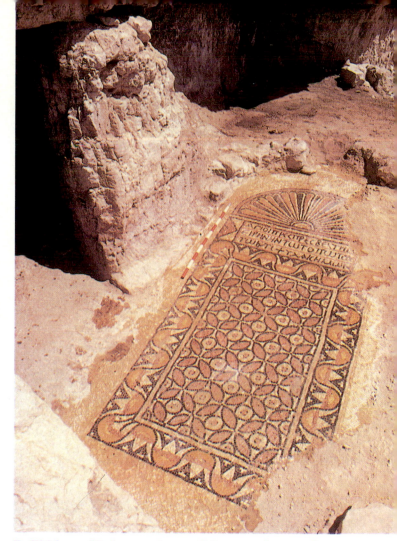

C. Khirbet ed-Deir: mosaic panel in central part of prayer hall

B. Khirbet ed-Deir: mosaic panel opposite reliquary niche

D. Khirbet ed-Deir, central auxiliary chamber: medallion in mosaic floor

PL. XVII

A. Ḥorvat Beit Loya: two birds sipping water from goblet

D. Ḥorvat Beit Loya: dates and almonds arranged on broad leaf

B. Ḥorvat Beit Loya: wine goblet

E. Ḥorvat Beit Loya: double-handled vase

C. Ḥorvat Beit Loya: border strip of acanthus leaves

F. Ḥorvat Beit Loya: intricate chapel mosaic

Ḥorvat Beit Loya: A. Boat with sails, north aisle (above); B. Standing fisherman, south aisle (below)

Horvat Be'er-shemʿa: details of mosaic (see List of Plates)